HENRY
MAURICE
GOLDMAN

HENRY MAURICE GOLDMAN

DENTAL EDUCATOR and PIONEER

A man whose vision for graduate
education in dentistry remarkably
advanced the dental profession

ROBERT ALLYN GOLDMAN

This book is dedicated to all my sons
with love and affection:

Anthony Robert Goldman
Nicholas Allyn Goldman
Timothy Brett Goldman
Christopher Scott Goldman

and

fond memory and love for my daughter
Stephanie Beth Goldman
(September 4, 1972-September 6, 2002)

APPENDIX NOTE

The appendix to the book is of particular interest in that there are four sections in particular which are of historic significance. The first section is a lengthy factual depiction of the birth of Periodontics as a specialty in the cities of Philadelphia and Boston. Drs. Milton B. Asbell and D. Walter Cohen revisit the events which laid the groundwork for the specialty programs at The University of Pennsylvania in Philadelphia, and, The Beth Israel Hospital and Boston University in Boston. This is a copy of the original article penned by the two authors. Dr. D. Walter Cohen is an acclaimed, erudite former Dean of The University of Pennsylvania who only needs introduction to the newcomers of the profession, now three generations distant from Henry M. Goldman. Dr. Cohen has been the mainstay of the dental profession for so many years as a formidable leader as well as a friend to so many. Though his reputation has spanned over so many years, his scientific contributions and friendship to so many should never be undervalued. In addition, he has imparted so much of his kindness and moral support in seeing this project to fruition. His loyalty to his mentor, his sustained dedication to scientific progress, and profound humility are a lesson to all.

The second portion of the appendix is a very significant timeline of the founding of the Departments of Periodontology and Periodontal Prosthesis at The University of Pennsylvania, and, its relationship with the development of specialization in Boston through Henry M. Goldman. Dr. Arnold Weisgold, former Chair of Periodontal Prosthesis at The University of Pennsylvania School of Dental Medicine, has been a most significant teacher, lecturer and practitioner over many years.

He kept a very detailed diary of the timeline and was kind enough to share it as a ready historical reference. This is a very thoughtful contribution from a most generous, engaging and genuine individual.

The third section of the appendix is really a wonderful gift of Ernestine Gianelly, the widow of Dr. Anthony Gianelly, the brilliant, academically insightful and devoted former Chairman of the Department of Orthodontics at The Boston University School of Graduate Dentistry. Before his passing he wrote a comprehensive primer on basic orthodontic principles which is reprinted here. For those dentists interested, this is a gift bequeathed as a memory to a man whose devotion to his specialty and colleagues was unmatched. This is a very special supplement that reflects both the excellence of his teaching and masterful sense of scientific presentation. His unique people sense and feeling for his residents and colleagues all over the world has additionally earned him such a posthumous love and respect from so many that his memory remains sacrosanct. This contribution rightfully extolls the virtues of Anthony Gianelly's lifetime commitment to both teaching and learning.

The fourth section is as well another timeline of Boston University's grand entrance into the world of dental education commencing with the inaugural year of 1958 with the Department of Stomatology at Boston University Medical Center. The timeline is a linear reference for those with a sense of historical interest, and even for those who casually want to view how intrinsically wide-ranging and expansive the school has become.

And finally, a list and photo display are presented to depict Henry M. Goldman's prestigious pioneer status as one of the early Presidents of both The Academies of Periodontology and Oral Maxillofacial Pathology. In addition, he was the youngest among the group of founders of the American Academy of Oral Pathology (aka today The American Academy of Oral Maxillofacial Pathology). The drawing caricature of this illustrious group of Oral Pathologists can be found in the photo section.

This Appendix is a wonderful supplement to the story of Henry M. Goldman's formidable undertaking. As a creative thinker he surrounded himself with like minds whose spirit and vigor acquitted Boston University with both luster and cachet.

PROLOGUE

This book is about a dental educator and scientific investigator who made a formal shift in graduate education. He had a very interesting life before succumbing to Parkinson's disease. Readers will come away recognizing that he was so very much more than the title suggests.

What should be the audience for this story? Anyone with a dental-medical position, be it in private practice, laboratory research, or in a hospital based appointment will find this story interesting at many levels. The issues for which he worked his whole life have impacted all people, whether in dentistry or medicine does not make a difference. Specialization became his life's work to improve dental health.

Also, for any lay person who would like to learn about dental issues affecting them, this story will be a window through which poorly understood issues can be viewed. Most people have no idea to what extent dentists are trained and practice, but the subject of this book created an environment for their development.

Several problems in the dental profession were identified early on after WWII which became the basis for graduate education. However, two things must be identified beforehand. Firstly, with increasing advantage to deliver enhanced therapies through technology, people have been provided greater opportunity to keep their teeth through extended geriatric living. Who in the dental profession will provide the necessary treatment to accomplish this has become a source of controversy. Does the patient deserve the most highly trained specialist or simply a general practitioner with significantly less education and training? With expensive dental care becoming increasingly more expensive and insurance companies setting coverages that do not closely meet patient's needs through their extended survival rates, the need for more specialists are more needed than ever. However, the cost of dental education has had a severely limiting effect on the numbers that will be available to meet the requirements of a swelling world population. So, the circular problem presents such a quandary that a definitive answer may never be found. Occam's razor encourages the most simple and practical solution. The answer is that costs in education must come down so specialty training and education programs can increase with increasing population numbers. Additionally, the general practitioner in the interim continues to attempt treatment procedures far beyond her/his basic training. But, the general practitioner is "caught between a rock and a hard place". Most graduates are so buried in debt that there is an urgency to make money. And, the days of going further into debt as a solo practitioner are gone. The exception would be in a more rural area where immediate need would more easily reconcile the debt. However, an urban-suburban practice where principle investment with overhead costs would be untenable for an individual without a supplementary source of aid. Years of experience in general practice, however, does not instill wisdom even with the limitations of continuing education. The years of experience merely provides more time to experiment and compound mistakes (with the additional mental strain of patient management problems). There are too few programs in specialization where affordable graduate training becomes cost effective and justifiable. Specialization needs are sorely increasing as people are simply living longer. This is especially true in the field of Periodontics where natural dentitions are falling victim to out-of-control placement of implants. Diagnostic insights only come from specially trained teachers in graduate programs. This is not a Yogi Berra problem solved by simply proceeding when approaching the fork in the road?

Secondly, readers do not need to have a dental/medical education in order to appreciate what can be accomplished when motivation meets extreme determination. Be it manufacturing, entertainment, teaching children, space exploration, biomedical and cancer research, or any enterprise demanding more than just a low level interest, this is a story of a person seriously underappreciated for his accomplishments and the gift he left behind. The wow factor is not just the institution he founded but really the inspiration of his achievements. He was truly the artful multitasker. His pursuits were centered on eliminating problems which seemingly are further compounded today with the emergence of low-level clinics where cost-effective does not conflate with quality. The story will bring Henry into focus as he arose from poverty to meet these challenges head on.

Finally, it is very appropriate in these times for people to learn something about the least understood profession. Teeth are too casually considered by most people. The story presented in the forthcoming pages uncovers how much he provided for the world through so many of the dental educators he so meaningfully touched with his wisdom. His "uber effect" is not sufficiently understood until now.

Robert Allyn Goldman

FOREWORD

As a dental practitioner for 50 years, I was very fortunate to have practiced with Dr. Henry M. Goldman who was the most significant person in my career. I was quite blessed to have studied and practiced as well with other teachers and practitioners. However, it was Dr. Goldman who allowed me to study periodontics in a four year part time program so that I could continue in general practice in order to support my family. This allowed me to specialize whereby any other arrangement it would have been financially impossible.

The most serendipitous day of my dental career was Dr. Goldman asking me to join his practice. This exceptional opportunity opened a lifetime relationship with this remarkable and brilliant man on a daily basis. This enduring connection afforded me the time to truly understand and appreciate his intelligence and objectives as a practitioner with tireless, unselfish efforts to improve dental education.

So many dentists have been historically recognized for their contributions to the dental profession, but it was Dr. Goldman who laid the groundwork and set the stage for their good fortune. He did so through his singular vision for a graduate school in the dental specialties. Foreseeing its architectural requirements, he was personally responsible for funding the school and then staffing it with primarily volunteer clinicians and lecturers. Later he pioneered the development for the pre-doctoral program to advance the education and training of potential specialists for the graduate programs. The graduate school became the model for many other programs throughout the world. Many dentists ventured to Boston to benefit from diverse courses at the school made possible with his wisdom, untiring strength, remarkable intelligence and unfaltering determination.

Historical precedence impacts all walks of life as in President Woodrow Wilson's struggle to create world peace through his prescience for a League of Nations. This was his particular lifetime dream he so faithfully pursued until his dying days. With a very similar unwavering persistence, Dr. Goldman rose to the top of the dental profession where he explored new directions never previously ventured. The Boston University School of Graduate Dentistry stood as a landmark for change in dental education and a major turning point directed through his extraordinary intelligence and steadfast courage.

Any dentist who was fortunate to be a witness to the level of excellence in dental education at the Boston University School of Graduate Dentistry should always remember that it was this man's vision and stalwart character who worked his lifetime so conscientiously to enhance the dental profession. His boundless pursuit established a unique thinking and everlasting evidenced based scientific principles which define the profession today. I consider myself so very grateful to have been a direct eye witness to this great man, Dr. Henry M. Goldman.

Alan M. Shuman, D.M.D.

A TALE OF TWO CITIES
BY D. WALTER COHEN, D.D.S.

I graduated from the University of Pennsylvania, School of Dental Medicine in 1950. In June of that year I went to Boston to begin a fifteen month research fellowship in Pathology and Periodontics with Dr. Henry M. Goldman at the Beth Israel Hospital. The program was quite intense, but the original faculty at the hospital provided a great learning environment from which I took away a great deal. I was able to participate in forty autopsies while serving in the Departments of Pathology and Dental Medicine. I was also fortunate to spend one day a week in Dr. Goldman's office.

Dr. Jack Bloom preceded me in the program and Dr. Gerry Kramer was completing the program on a part time basis. Dr. Goldman was also teaching a one week course in Periodontics at that time which I was able to attend as well.

In the spring of 1951 Dr. Frank Beube of Columbia University brought his faculty to Boston for the first meeting of the Columbia-Beth Israel Study Club at which I had the good fortune of meeting Drs. Lewis Fox, Saul Schluger, Melvin Morris, Leonard and Isador Hirschfeld, Herbert Bartlestone and Robert Gottsegen. Over the next three to four years this group continued to meet twice a year.

When I completed the program, Dr. Goldman gave me the opportunity to join him in his practice and to take a position at the hospital. Unfortunately, I was obligated to return to Philadelphia to join my father in private practice. I did this on a half time basis so that I could take a teaching position at The University of Pennsylvania School of Dental Medicine the other half time.

In 1952 the Dean of the Dental School, Dr. Lester Burkett asked Dr. Goldman to give a one week course at UPenn. The course consisted of lectures and clinical demonstrations at which I assisted. Later in 1954, Dr. Burket asked Dr. Goldman to inaugurate a two year graduate program in Periodontology, one year at UPenn and the second year at The Beth Israel Hospital in Boston. Dr. Goldman was appointed Professor and Chairman of Periodontology in the Graduate School of Medicine. I became responsible for the teaching of the first year. The program effectively started in 1955 and continued until 1963 when Boston University School of Graduate Dentistry was charted and opened with Dr. Goldman as the founder and Dean. He had been appointed the Chairman of Stomatology at The Boston University School of Medicine prior to the new school opening.

Meanwhile at UPenn a new two year program began in the Division of Advanced Dental Education where I took over as director. This program has endured into its now sixtieth year with over a thousand students having matriculated over that period of time.

One of the conditions of my original acceptance by Dr. Goldman was agreement to devote a significant portion of my time to dental education. From 1951 until 1962 I spent half my time in teaching until I was appointed full time as Professor and Chair of the Department of Periodontics. Dr. Goldman continued his annual course at UPenn until he had to forego his routine because of his responsibilities with the Boston University School of Graduate Dentistry.

In 1978 at the centennial celebration of The University of Pennsylvania School of Dental Medicine distinguished individuals were honored. Dr. Goldman was awarded an honorary doctorate with a citation noting him as "The Father of Modern Periodontics".

I became Dean of the dental school in 1972 and served until 1983. During these years I had many interactions with Dr. Goldman one of which was serving as co-author of "Periodontics" published by C.V. Mosby. Dr. Goldman authored the first edition in 1940 when he was 29 years old. This second edition became a classic in the field and was followed by several editions. Another book was later published,

"Periodontal Therapy", and Drs. Saul Schluger and Lewis Fox joined Dr. Goldman and me in this publication.

Dr. Goldman became the founding editor of The Journal of The American Society of Periodontics which merged with The Journal of Periodontology in 1968 as a result of the merger of the American Society of Periodontists with the American Academy of Periodontology. Dr. Goldman endured an illustrious career and was noted for his many contributions to the field of Periodontics. He was honored by several universities both at home and abroad for his many efforts in dental education. With the first and only graduate school in dentistry, Boston University named the school in his name in 1977.

From a personal point of view, Dr. Goldman changed my life. He was my mentor in addition to affecting the lives of tens of thousands of students around the world. Everybody at UPenn was grateful for his untiring work. The 1960's, 1970's and 1980's were truly the golden era for students who were graced with his teaching excellence. In addition, this period was also the beneficiary of many other great teachers such as Morton Amsterdam, Leonard Abrams, Arnold Weisgold, Louis Rose and many others. Many of Dr. Goldman's former students went on to senior positions. Several became deans, such as Charles Jerge, David Beaudreau, Harry Bohannon, Peter Robinson, Michael Fritz and Ian Davies. Along with Robert Genco, they all followed in the giant footsteps of Dr. Goldman.

Dr. Goldman asked me to succeed him as Dean at Boston University when he retired, but my Deanship at UPenn did not allow this.

After his retirement, he continued in teaching after Dr. Spencer Frankl took over as Dean at Boston University. We continued to update "Periodontal Therapy" and then went on to publish "Periodontal Medicine" with Dr. Robert Genco and Louis Rose. Eventually, Dr. Genco went on to become senior author of "Periodontics".

When I was inaugurated as president of the Medical College of Pennsylvania, Drs. Goldman and Schluger were both present. Unfortunately, Dr. Goldman passed away soon thereafter in 1991 from Parkinson's Disease. He had a rich and fulfilling life and was an iconic legend in the field of dental medicine.

Henry was a devoted husband to his wife, Dorothy, and father to his two boys, Richard and Gerald. Dorothy often accompanied Dr. Goldman on his academic journeys throughout the world and served as the perfect hostess. Henry and Dorothy were a wonderful team in all that was necessary to get Boston University up and going as a full time operation. When I lived in Boston, Dorothy was like a caring sister to my wife, Betty Ann. It was always a pleasure and a treat to be received in the Goldman home.

ACKNOWLEDGEMENTS

The Boston University School of Graduate Dentistry just passed a most momentous period in its history, its semi-centennial. It was the work of one man, Henry Maurice Goldman, framer and custodian of new age concepts in dental education. He brushed aside the mechanical age and ushered in the biosciences as the foundation of dental medicine. His forte was his open-mindedness to individuals wanting opportunity and a desire to excel. The thrust of his success was wrested from his early academic experiences which he channeled the rest of his life. My decision to frame this as the lead thought throughout the book was important in order to emphasize how non-opportunistic and truly wholesome were his ambitions.

This book is the story of a man known by very few. But, he is an icon for certain. I wrote the story because he should be remembered for what he accomplished. I have a theory that I have carried within my thinking for all of my adult life. After watching great people excel in so many walks of life, I came to the conclusion that they are endowed with a touch of nobility. However, this is unfortunately not always the case. And, this is how I have atoned in my mind for the solipsistic personality types who are, to the contrary, ignoble. They seem to be the "dark for the light", or, the "dullness for the luster" in drawing the preeminence from the history makers. So, I came up with my own "third generation theory". This states very simply that on the third generation out, other than family, a little known person is forgotten. Only the person who may transcend history for a specific global event or contribution may continue to have generational significance. That being said, I often wondered why certain people behave the way they do, thinking in their small world that somehow their persona is going to be etched permanently in history. That's where my theory comes into play in this story. Along Henry Goldman's long journey, he confronted some of the most self-centered egotists. How he dealt with this situation was quite germane. The decade when this graduate school in dental specialization reached its zenith, it was layered with so many personality agendas that it took a strong personality resolve to keep harmony and balance. A great many of the faculty (both junior and senior) believed they were inviolable in defiance of my "third generation theory".

Well, this is the story of a great man who achieved as high as possible in his field. The accomplishments he brought to society will forever affect people. And, yet, when I ask third generation dentists today, they do not know who he is. This confirms my theory, somewhat disturbingly, but a fact of life. So, for all the egoistic personalities who spend a lifetime desperately chasing immortality, and, simply not living and working for a purpose, it is unfortunate. Nevertheless, there are many books written about this human condition.

In this story, I shall paint the picture of a truly devoted man with convictions so clear that he sustained his focus with undeterred balance throughout his professional life. And, during this life, he was almost taken down by one of these solipsistic individuals whose dishonorable behavior deceived a great deal of people in trying to purloin his ethos. By the end of the story, I hope readers will understand the depth of Henry Goldman's dedication and success. He changed how society continues to view the importance of oral health. He saw a serious void in health care only to rise above the political fray to challenge the system with indefatigable resolve.

In writing this book I came to the realization that the lay public is quite uninformed about the dental profession. Even in the present times of such a rapid pulse in communications, it is overwhelming to me how unenlightened patients are about their dental health and what separates a general practitioner from a specialist. For, after all, Henry Goldman's raison d'etre was graduate education in dentistry for specialization in the American Dental Association recognized specialties. This pathway to training conflated a public need with an educational opportunity. General dentistry was greatly insufficient for sustaining the public need. And there lies the heart of why Henry fought so hard for dental specialization. At its foundation was the need to transform a profession wherein patients were conditioned to believe a general practitioner "could do it all"! Well, he/she cannot despite this incantation. It was in the public interest to change this mindset and, in so doing, contribute to the greater good: improved dental health for a population living longer.

Henry Goldman was a Stomatologist, a very recondite reference in the United States. As an offshoot of European Medicine, Stomatology was established in Eastern Europe as the specialty dealing with oral diseases. In that section of the world (and in certain Western European countries up to very recently when significant change in educational curriculum was altered), all dental specialists have a medical education. In the United States, this specialty was marginalized for various reasons, politics being the most significant. Simply put, Stomatology is really dental medicine insofar as the mouth's (Stoma: opening) manifest connection with organ system health and disease. This country was much slower in understanding this relationship. As a result, being a dental cripple fomented many premature deaths because of the ravages of oral disease. President George Washington is ubiquitously cited as the classic example for his incurable travails with tooth loss, ill-fitting false teeth, and probably ill health. How this may have compromised his immune health has never been investigated. However, from what we know today, it can be assumed there was at least a causal relationship.

This country would eventually emerge from primitive dental care, but it took many years to forge a change in grassroots dental education. This country not only caught up, but, by today's standards, has leapfrogged the rest of the world in boldly furthering clinical standards of practice and research methodology. This is where Boston University can be acknowledged for leading the way in this transition. Not everything however has become "Sunshine, Lollipops and Rainbows" as Leslie Gore sung in her 1963 album. Many great advances sprung from Henry's untiring hard work, but I shall address many of the great battles he fought which still endure today. Even though the country could have benefitted by his living another lifetime, sometimes the immovable object can't be moved successfully by the irresistible force.

In the 19th to the earliest part of the 20th centuries, the man who commanded the center of attention by every dental school in the country was Greene Vardiman Black, aka G.V. Black. His contributions to Operative Dentistry are historically significant, but it took many years to override the machine-driven reputation cemented in the teaching curricula to realize a new world philosophy in American dental education. And, this is where my story will begin.

Therefore, the story in this book is twofold: what Henry did to bring the profession into modern times in a way that permanently reshaped the profession, and, all the dissonance he faced during that process. It was really beyond what one man could do, but Henry's defiance made him persist. His DNA was very different because he would not quit until his contributions were permanent. His philosophy of teaching and life consumed his life. In one sense, he was one-dimensional. But, I came to realize that this is what made him great. His creativity and compelling mission nudged everything else aside. This was the reality that sparked my interest in his story.

When I sat back to organize this book into a reader friendly framework, I decided to break it up into three sections. I did this in order to offer a sense of order for the average reader. Section 1 goes into his upbringing, education and early academic connections which set the stage for the major event in his professional life. Section 2 delves into the major events in his professional life which defined his role as the real father of modern dental education. And, finally, Section 3 probes very deeply into topical aspects of the dental profession which stirred up his greatest interest. It probes his critical thinking into very significant and relevant issues. It also opens a window into his most intimate thoughts and emotions. These three sections should demonstrate not only Henry's unique perspectives but also highlight how his once-in-a-lifetime achievements serve as a benchmark for all that is evolving today. He was a guidepost for change.

Finally, I want this book to be a source for all people in order to give insight into the dental profession. Some of the very tricky conflicts in which he found himself give clear insight into what constitutes ethical practice and what defines a dentist's training. I want all people to understand that Henry Goldman had a mission to upgrade the standards of his profession at all levels of teaching, research and practice. He wanted to make people think that in a world where generation to generation contributions are forgotten, with the incomprehensible blind spot that endlessly compels a reinventing-the-wheel thinking, maybe the march forward in science will use past thinking as a meaningful stepping stone. In his thinking, this would serve to improve the quality of education by maintaining more effective continuity.

As many as seven to eight years ago, my son, Anthony, and I were discussing the school. He prodded me to write about Henry and Boston University. I understood the story should be told, but it took me a while to absorb and ponder on our long discussions. Finally, I discussed the matter with Dr. D. Walter Cohen, Henry's first student who was an ardent and most faithful supporter, and certainly a prodigious over-achiever like his mentor. Well, over the years two things glaringly stood out in my mind. I learned an incredible amount about the magnitude of the project as I read into all of Henry's challenges and seemingly end-less days. Secondly, I found how truly remarkable the original faculty of Boston University was. It was a mix of people so very pristine and uncertain at the beginning who blossomed into very complex person-alities. But, they all possessed one common trait, an urge to succeed. And, for the most part, they projected honest scholarly images which found respect among their residents. I tried to delineate their individ-ual differences with deference to Henry because his choices ultimately brought worldwide distinction to the dental school as well as the uni-versity at large.

I learned one more thing as my work progressed. I always knew Henry was prominent worldwide, but I uncovered the most important fact of all: everybody who thought they knew him did not, and, all the people who realized his scholastic contributions did not know half of them. Reading the book should make people walk away with a feeling for how he, and only he, could have managed the collection of pressures and bureaucratic entanglements necessary to successfully build his graduate school which he carried to its maturity before his death. The gift that his memory rightfully deserves is the continued reverential reminder when the school was renamed The Henry M. Goldman School of Dental Medicine at Boston University.

During my four to five years of work I talked to a very large number of people. I think they shall all be interested to realize how much he had to overcome. My discussions with them convinced me that Henry's great achievement has either been too casually forgotten, not forgotten (but not properly remembered), or remembered without sufficient recognition due to alliances which have tried to overlook him as they look to the future with their own ambitions. Finally, I endlessly deliberated how one man could be at the helm to effectuate such an overwhelmingly complex undertaking. I concluded that his greatest inspiration and support came from deep within his family. With all the Sunday mornings I spent with Henry and my father, Edward, Henry's older brother by four years, I came to realize the nobility of his character. As a professional, his insights were preternatural. His wizardry went beyond what anyone perceived, even me. The most frustrating fact I uncovered was all the old guard traditions in education that remain resistant even today. Old conventions die hard! He was somewhat of a pugilist in his youth so he could take some rough body blows. He may have been down at times, but he was never out for the count. And, he always stood up and proudly continued on like nothing ever happened. As a great problem solver, he valued the presence of any challenge. However, he never cowed with a defeatist attitude.

I have to confess that there were times I did not think this project would come to fruition. But it has and I would be remiss if I did not celebrate the people who aided me along the way. There is not enough space to remember everyone, but to some a few words for their very willing contributions:

Firstly, I have to acknowledge all the middle management people in government service at The National Archives, The Social Security Administration, The Smithsonian, The National Personnel Records Center, and The Massachusetts Archives. In the hundreds of phone calls, emails and faxes. I learned there are many hard working, caring people who extend a willing hand if their efforts are rightfully respected.

Also, I have to recognize all the nice people at The Gotlieb Archives at Boston University, The Boston Public Library, The Medical Library at Boston University, and The Van Pelt Library at The University of Pennsylvania.

Thank you to all that I could not mention. But, along the way there have been numerous secretaries, administrators and teachers who provided me with very useful and needed information.

Drs.Victor Dietz, Robert Ferris, Howard Kay, James Kohner, Richard Lazzarra and Howard Rubenstein were all extremely understanding and supportive.

To Dr. Robert Eskow, my deep appreciation for both his many opinions and exchange of ideas, and a person who has been on the frontline over so many years to support Oral Medicine in its many years to become an ADA recognized specialty.

Thank you to Ernestine Gianelly, Dr. Anthony Gianelly's (Chairman of the Department of Orthodontics of the original faculty at the Boston University School of Graduate Dentistry) wife, who gave me permission to reproduce for this book his wonderful primer on "Basic Orthodontic Principles" which he wrote just before his passing. And, of course, to Dr. Victor Dietz again for being the go-between.

I'd like to thank the present Dean, Dr. Jeffrey Hutter. And, a very special appreciation for tolerating my numerous calls with such understanding and kindness to Dr. Hutter's secretary, Lisa Case.

I want to thank Dr. Arnold Weisgold for his aid in the production of the University of Pennsylvania-Beth Israel Hospital timeline and his information about The University of Pennsylvania School of Dental Medicine's Periodontal Prosthesis Program. Recently retired as Chairman of that department, he is both assuredly outstanding in his field as well as a most straightforward and modest man.

Thank you to Mr. Dennis Vandenberg, a West Palm Beach attorney with whom I have had the pleasure in knowing as a person and working with him on liability cases. I want to recognize him for his kindness and honesty in all our conversations over many years. Mr. Vandenberg was one of a host of attorneys who worked on the Dr. David J. Acer versus Kimberly Bergalis AIDS case. It was the impact of this legal case which ushered in the regulatory changes in dental practice administered through the Occupational Safety and Health Administration (OSHA).

I'd also like to acknowledge all the wonderful professors I had as an honors History major at The University of Pennsylvania who prepared me well for this undertaking. Who knows where life's circuitous path may meander? The lesson is to be ready and well prepared.

A very kind thank you to: Hyman "Smokie" Smuckler, a wonderfully bright, accomplished man with whom many conversations over the years have been instructive as they have been additionally edifying.

To the only surviving chairman of the original faculty, former chairman of Oral Surgery, Donald Booth. He gave a lot of his time on the phone with me for which I am very thankful

A very special acknowledgement to Drs. A. Stephen Polins, Edward Hannigan, Ralph Pollack and Steven Richmond. Their perspicacious observations were revelatory and quite important to me. Steve has always been a wonderful colleague and dear friend. And Ed was a classmate and one of the brightest colleagues I have had the opportunity to know. Ralph was an engineer turned Periodontist, a classmate and dear friend. And finally, another classmate, Steve Richmond, his friendship and genuine insights have always been unwavering.

To Dr. Jack Krauser, Periodontist/Implantologist, is a very good friend and colleague with whom I spent countless hours discussing everything possible concerning topics covered in this book. Jack's perceptions and critical analysis reflect his deep analytical thinking. His opinions were admirably candid and razor-sharp.

To Dr. Melvyn Harris, an Oral Maxillofacial Surgeon in Boston, Massachusetts for many years and transition Chairman of The Department of Oral Maxillofacial Surgery at The Boston University School of Graduate Dentistry between Drs. Kurt Thoma and Donald Booth, he has been a kind friend and colleague my whole life. Mel also served Dr. Henry M. Goldman in reading biopsy specimens for the school over many years. I can't thank him more for all his great advice and friendship.

To Dr. Murray Awrach with whom I was a Fellow in Pathology at Boston University Hospital, I would like to thank him for the fraternal experiences we shared which gave us both greater insight into health and disease under the mentorship of Dr. Karoly Balogh, Chief of Pathology at Boston University Medical Center. We certainly developed a lifelong friendship as well as a greater understanding into Henry Goldman's "method to his madness" in putting both of us in that lion's den. By our intellectual growth under Balogh, it was really a reflection of Henry Goldman's genius in formatting such an educational experience for us both.

To Dr. Gerald M. Bowers, retired Chairman of the Department of Periodontology at the Naval Graduate Dental School from 1969-1974 and Director of the Postdoctoral Program in Periodontics at the Baltimore College of Dental Surgery from 1974-1996, was an exceptional teacher, friend, adviser, and dedicated man. As permanent Secretary of the American Board of Periodontology for many years my special appreciation for all his advice and insights. He is one of the most pure educators I have had the good fortune to know. Our many conversations over many years meant a great deal. I found them very helpful in the writing of this book.

To Drs. D. Walter Cohen, Anthony Gargiulo and Alan Shuman, you are all inspirational. Walter, being Henry's first student and acceding to the highest level of prominence in the dental profession as a former Dean of The University School of Pennsylvania School of Dental Medicine and Chancellor of the Medical College of Philadelphia, was thoroughly honorable in supporting all my efforts to complete this book. Walter is responsible to a very significant degree for all the educational changes in dental education since Henry's passing. He is truly a remarkable man. In addition, a very special thank you for all the wonderful photographs from halcyon days that seem more special every time I review them. Dr. Anthony Gargiulo energized me with his thoughtful advice for so many important matters that I can't thank him enough. He is one of the great dental educators in his own right.

His counsel and friendship has been so solid and steadfast over many years. And, Alan, as Henry's partner over his entire professional life, has always been there when I needed a very good and loyal friend. Our discussions on every subject have always been memorable and with mutual esteem.

Thank you to all.

CONTENTS

Projections

"Beauty is truth, truth beauty,-that is all
Ye know on earth, and all ye need to know."[1]

---

[1] *"Ode on a Grecian Urn" by John Keats, in www.poetryfoundation.org/poem/173742*

CHAPTER 1

Growing Up; the Education Years: Escape from Poverty; Why Dentistry; the War Years: Influences, Thoughts and Projections

Henry Maurice Goldman was born on Saturday, December 9, 1911 in South Boston, Massachusetts and died Tuesday, July 23, 1991 at The Massachusetts General Hospital in Boston, Massachusetts. South Boston in 1911 was a highly undeveloped, very poor, ethnically mixed area consisting of Jewish and Irish families. The mothers and fathers both held jobs, primarily in factory jobs. He was born to Rebecca (Levy) and Joseph Goldman. Rebecca worked as a tailor and Joseph as a side laster at Bancroft-Walker Shoe Company, a nearby shoe manufacturing company on Wormwood Street in Dorchester, Massachusetts. (184) It was a fifteen to twenty minute walk from Seneca Street where Henry grew up. The family also lived on Oneida Street right next to Seneca. He was four years younger than his older brother, Edward (who was born Isadore and, in his thirties before marrying, legally changed his name to Edward). No one ever knew Edward was Isadore because he never discussed it and was uncovered somewhat after his death on Thursday, November 22, 1990. Whether by coincidence or synchronicity Henry grew up, lived, and went to school within a mile to two miles from where The Boston University School of Graduate Dentistry was established. In between he moved around all over the world, be it as a student, Army Captain, or educator. (184,214)

Soon after the boys were born, Rebecca divorced Joseph and was the only parent they knew for their entire young lives. She only re-married until many, many years later in 1938 to Eli Borovoy. He was of Russian descent and actually fought in the Russian army against the Bolsheviks in 1917. When things did not look like he was going to sur-vive, he somehow made a secretive departure for the United States.[2] He was a very handy repair man and was able to make a living as a tailor also and a part time handyman. Later in life both Henry and Edward adopted him like their own because he was such a likeable, friendly man with a very quiet reserve. He was also a voracious reader and could discuss most historical topics of any dimension with reasonable authority. He was self-educated, but his range of reading made him quite conversant on most subjects. Interesting how opposites attract, Rebecca was not formally educated and virtually never read anything. No one knew if she could actually read. She was the boss of the family when the boys were growing up and even later when she remarried. Eli was very submissive and never questioned Rebecca on anything. He spent most of his time chauffeuring her around as she never took it upon herself to get a driving license. She was very authoritarian and cracked the proverbial whip to keep both boys in check. If they got into fights on the neighborhood streets, they knew to be ready for a whipping when they got home.

She was a driven disciplinarian because she was going to see to it that both boys would get a good education as their father, Joseph, was a hard drinker who spent more than he made. Henry really never knew him, but Edward was always intimately involved with him, never letting his mother know that he took care of his father throughout his entire life. For some reason that he never divulged, Edward followed his father into the shoe business. He started off as an elevator boy at the famous John Irving Shoe Company in Boston, Massachusetts. He picked up a lot of knowledge from his father to be able to reasonably handle his job at John Irving. In fact, he became expert in the entire manufacturing process of both ladies' and men's shoes. He developed

---

[2] Eli Borovoy came to the United States after WWI; he fought in Russian Revolution, 1917; www.Massachusetts States Archives.

a tremendous facility for designing ladies shoes. As an elevator boy through most of life, he took a white collar job with John Irving after graduating from Harvard Business School. After a long learning process, he became President of John Irving Shoe Company until he went out on his own and became a successful manufacturer of high styled lady's shoes in Wakefield, Massachusetts under name of Copley Shoe Company until the plant burned down on a crisp, frozen, very windy Monday night, February 7, 1972. His shoes were marketed under the name of "Styled by Mr. Easton" all over the world. He was as successful in his business as Henry became in the dental profession. The business connections Edward made were quite significant as he was the force in fund raising when Henry engineered the founding and building of The Boston University School of Graduate Dentistry many years later.[3]

It seemed that Henry grew up in the protective guidance of his older brother as they were without a father figure their entire young adult lives. However, they could both thank their lucky stars that their mother was extremely overbearing. Her authority over them was uncharacteristically zealous because most of their friends were living the life on the streets playing handball or stick ball while they were inside reading or doing homework. She was also extremely rigid in pestering them about cleanliness, organization, and proper dress. Neither could return home with any of the dirt or grime from the streets on any portion of their clothes. Should they return even the slightest bit wet or dirty, a very high price was paid with endless cleaning around the house. And, "the house" was a small broken-down step-up, very small brownstone with extremely cramped quarters. It taught them both what a Spartan life was all about.

"Southie" (184) as it came to be known was not a dangerous crime area. It was simply an ethnically rough area where the boys both learned how to box their way to and from school. Frequently encountering neighborhood thugs (both Jewish and Irish gangs), they learned early on how to mix it up for their own physical survival. They also learned how to sneak home so they wouldn't have to answer with twice the penalties if caught

---

[3] All personal communications; he was my father.

dirtied or bloodied. Boozing drunken factory workers were a frequent sight, particularly on Friday nights when revelry started early. Henry was a far better fighter than his older brother, who was smaller and not as daring. He learned the art of boxing to some proficiency so that when he later got to Brown University he performed in some intercollegiate events. He possessed big palms with stout and stubby fingers which made for a boxer's dream advantage. When hit with the thrust of that kind of a hand, it was felt with authority. Edward could protect himself, but he never took any interest in physical competition like Henry. A lot of professional boxers came out of that area of Boston. The great ones who achieved international stature, however, came out of the North End of Boston. This was virtually all Italian and heavily controlled by local gangs attached to The New England Mafia. As tough an upbringing that the boys experienced, it was never mob controlled gangs to be feared in "Southie". It was just the routine fisticuffs and brawling neighborhood miscreants. This was bad enough when they were answering to a martinet at home demanding studying and early bedtime.

For some reason, neither boy grew up with the typical flat, homespun, ignorant sounding Boston accent. It was an admixture of an Irish Gallic-Yiddish (Jewish) manner of speech that made eloquence sound foreign to the ghetto. If "The King's English", as Edward (Isadore) noted with a wry but robust laugh, were spoken, get ready to have your nose rearranged on your face. Maybe that's how they perfected their boxing skills. During their lives, they escaped the nickname of blockhead because of the very noticeable Boston accent.

Walking to and from grade school in the area, their mother made them take handkerchiefs to put underneath their pants if they sat on a curb. This is no exaggeration. And, it resulted in a fair amount of bullying until a few of the teasing locals got tired of going home sufficiently bloodied. The Goldman boys developed a reasonable reputation for energized fisticuffs. For them it was simply getting by the neighborhood ruffians. At least those were the stories they told and were confirmed by some of their childhood friends many years later.[4]

---

[4] Author was always in their midst growing up, listening to all their tales.

Because of their very impoverished neighborhood and their mother's fixation on getting them educated, they had no religious upbringing. This was interesting because their grandfather on their mother's side, Jacob Levy, was readily fluent in Hebrew and Yiddish. Through him, Edward became reasonably proficient in reading Hebrew and speaking Yiddish. Henry grew up almost unable to even understand or read anything in either language. According to the state records, Jacob was twenty-eight when he married Fannie Renari, age 22. (186) His father's name was Issac Levy and mother Bertha. Her father's name was Joseph Renari and mother Louise. In addition to Rebecca, she had an older brother, Maximum Levy, who grew up to be a famous Harvard Chemist. He was a rather laconic man who worked on naphthalene, the chemical foundation of the rubber industry. He lived with a woman, but he never married nor had children. She also had a very younger brother, Robert Levy. He was so much younger that of his two children he had with his wife, Muriel, the youngest, Mark Levy was a contemporary of Eddie's and Henry's children. Robert and Muriel also had an older daughter, Eleanor who married a man, Bruce Lunder, who was also in the shoe business. He was in a coma for many years from a horrible car accident before he finally succumbed. He was extremely likeable, bright and financially successful. (186)

Jacob manufactured cigars near the North End off Rose Wharf. He married in 1880 and died in 1960. His wife had died at the age of 49, and he remained single the rest of his life, dying on the surgical table having prostate surgery. It is unknown where he learned such proficiency in Hebrew and Yiddish, unless it was from his father Issac, but Jacob was born just before the Civil War. The archival investigators could not answer to this. Their mother had a reasonable understanding, but even she could not speak either with any fluency. So, Edward probably picked up the language gift from his grandfather, Jacob. It is interesting that Henry really never picked up any words his entire life. Even later when he married, his future wife, Dorothy Alter, had a father who was also quite fluent. He was a butcher in Brookline, Massachusetts. Dorothy had a younger brother, a very pleasant, alert, conversant, nice person. But, neither spoke Yiddish or Hebrew as well. [5]

It was to Henry's advantage to have such an authority figure like Rebecca because he was imbued early on with the importance of education. When it was time for high school, Eddie went to Boston English High School. (153) Henry, on the other hand, went to The Boston Latin School. (154) It was during this time that they moved away to 217 Harvard Street in Dorchester, Massachusetts. The walk to school was not usually severe except during some of the harsh winters because of narrow roads and snow accumulating during a period when snow plows did not exist.

To this day, The Boston Latin is considered the top public school in the country. (154) The school was founded on an 18th century based Latin-school curriculum. It was compulsory to take four years of Latin. Founded in 1635, it was modeled after Boston Grammar School in Lincolnshire, England. In addition, the school was (and still is) noted for "Declamation". Students were required to give an oration in their English course three times during the school year. If a student qualified, the school held a "Public Declamation" contest every year. Henry took some very difficult and challenging courses. The school also challenged Henry's abilities with highly sophisticated extracurricular programs: The Boston Latin Theatre Company, the Junior Classic League and two publications, *The Register*, the school's magazine as well as *The Argo*, the school newspaper founded by George Santayana.[6] Suffice it to say, it was a preparation which laid the foundation for the thinking and dedication to hard work for which he was noted throughout his professional life. English High School of Boston where Eddie attended was a very good public school, but it did not reach the same level or expectation from its student body. It really did not make any difference for Eddie as he was a very self-disciplined, ambitious person. And, if he did not conform, his

---

[5] Jacob Levy, Robert Goldman, apartment on Winthrop Road, Brookline, Mass., growing up; teaching and conversations over many years.
[6] See Website:www.bls.org; George Santayana was one of many famous people to graduate the Boston Latin School.

mother would see to it that her standards were more demanding than either school. In both cases, it was a huge leap in the scholastic format from the elementary and junior high school (The Quincy School) they both attended. Henry was 13 years old when he entered high school so that his age may have contributed to some degree to his shyness, lack of confidence in Declamation, and somewhat uneasiness with the very advanced Classics that the school demanded. Without a father at home to instill guidance, it is fair to surmise that the internalizing emotionally must have been a challenge. The Boston Latin School's reputation preceded itself so that the intensity it set for its students' developmental level more than likely redounded to this as an early psychological test.

Upon graduation from The Boston Latin School, Henry entered Brown University in Providence, Rhode Island in the fall of 1929. (157) To say that it was uneventful would only be true in the sense that it was a sanctuary for those students seemingly insulated from the nightmare that was the 1929 Stock Market Crash. On "Black Monday", the market lost about 13% its value. And, this was followed by "Black Tuesday" the next day when the market followed up with about another 12% loss. The 1920's, aka "The Roaring Twenties" were noted as a period of excess, high crime, and bootlegging (of all drinking spirits). The serious consequence of the financial collapse was the feeling of loss, emptiness and hopelessness which led to so many committing suicide by jumping out of windows. The mass numbers lining up on bleak, frozen winter mornings in bread lines just to get a meager breakfast with coffee did not know from one day to the next if they would survive. The contrast between the downtrodden and the well-off was stark. Even the money made by underworld criminals through intimidation and murder was so outrageous that it made many capitulate with the loss of all their possessions through blunt execution or violent submission. These were the times for decisions.[7]

Perhaps the intimidation of a stringent mother's imperious demands

---

[7]   www.UnitedStatesDepartmentofCommerce   and   www. GovernmentAccountabilityOffice; these are their statistics reviewing many areas on both sites dealing with the social-economics facts.

were productive in an oblique sense. The alternative that faced some of the neighborhood kids who were lost without anyone to give them a sense of direction was gut-wrenching. Even though the absence of a father's presence may have had a deleterious effect, having a mother sullen and devoid of humor for the sake of just getting through the difficult days turned out to be an advantage. For Henry, poverty was a counterbalancing influence so going to college was somewhat of a protected escape. From his entry into college in 1929 to the time the United States was forced into WWII in the "Pacific Theater" (with the Japanese attack on Pearl Harbor on December 7, 1942) and in Europe with gradual soft peddling in1941 to a direct involvement by 1942, Henry's professional development was tempered like a red-hot piece of glass being shaped into its final dimensions. It was a unique period for him, and fortuitous as well. The world was ablaze in contrasts that were demoralizing and devastating for most and he was going to a quiet college town sanctuary to study. In most times, it would have been encouraged with well-deserved admonitions, but there really was nothing thrilling about 1929. So, off he went, worthy but wondering about so many, many things. Even his mother could not give him a ringing endorsement for what he had accomplished as she was too worried about an empty house and what the future would bring. The United States has witnessed a great deal of misfortune in its comparatively young history, but this very unpleasant year was as harsh as any other of its gruesome downsides. (90)

From 1929-1931 he spent two years without any significant eventuality in mind. He was far too young (not yet 17 until December 9th of his freshman year) to truly have a feel for what he was going to study let alone make a career judgment. His friends, however, were likewise of poor families. Almost like in group therapy, they came from families who believed that going into a profession would be a very predictable escape from the nothing that was their expected worth owing to the financial collapse of the world around them. His small group of immediate friends had mostly decided on medicine because it was a known profession. Making a "reasonable living" was expected. Dentistry was not a profession understood by most of Henry's high school friends because medicine was far more familiar to the average person.

By the time he matriculated at Brown though, things changed quite ironically. He came to meet a few individuals who were going to dental school immediately after two years. There was absolutely no other reason for his choice to go into dentistry other than circumstantial friendships. They were all poor and Henry saw professional school as a turn to employment. This was the thinking of his friends' families. Henry's mother was simply working to survive and could make any reasonable argument to justify her thinking. But, Henry's friends had fathers who also seemed to push their sons in this direction. There were others going to medical school, but his closest ones decided on dental school. It sounds strange, but this is how such decisions were made. His brother, Eddie, who went to Tufts College would have gone to medical school because that is where his friends registered, but he was squeamish and couldn't stand the sight of blood. So, Eddie went to Harvard Business School. It all sounds fanciful, but the mere disastrous economic realities of the 1920's and 1930's makes the argument quite reasonable. So, with a reality suddenly taking shape, and Henry being used to academic focus, he suddenly had his eyes on Harvard Dental School. The two years he spent in Providence, Rhode Island would turn out to be the most uneventful years of his young life. He took courses in the sciences for the most part because they appealed to him, not because he had to satisfy a future that would incline in that direction. He did some collegiate boxing, but only briefly to satisfy a given internal drive. It was not uncommon in those days to go to professional school after two years because college was considered a luxury for people of penurious home lives. Thus, he was off to dental school without any expectation of what his future would bare. His mother was satisfied knowing that a profession would be respectable and remunerative. And, most of all, he would not have to grovel like so many. Just as well, the two years at Brown kept him off the streets and with the benefit to sort out his possibilities. To her this was a fortuitous blessing. Mothers, of any stripe, worry. Fathers, hardened by life's experiences, are casual. Henry never experienced the latter.[8]

It is essential to realize that with all that he experienced later as a great educator and leader, the subversive threats he endured lacked the countervailing "punch" needed to fully override the after-effects. He inherited his mother's very moody, often surly and unnaturally withdrawn personality. Just like her, there was a heart larger than the planet, but his introverted countenance imprisoned his warmth inside an exterior steel curtain. Unless and until he felt comfortable, he was generally quiet and mysteriously withdrawn. If the public were to judge him by this measure of habitual demeanor, it probably would have had him entrusted to some psychiatric watch list, or maybe to a lifetime of therapy. The behavior was so sheer and over-the-top that it is a wonder how he got as far as he did. He took his mother's persona and nursed it to a fare-thee-well. Ironically, Eddie was just the opposite. He was not the social butterfly or, to the extreme, the life of the party. But, he was an open, happy, confident man. He was social, talkative, extremely conversant on a multitude of subjects, and, for the most part, extremely entertaining. These were two sons emerging from the same rather bleak upbringing with diametrically opposite personality types. They were antipodes of significant concern. Eddie was decisive, never lost the effect of the moment, and reacted to threat or difficulty with very effective, immediate, resourceful decision making.

It is unfortunate that Henry did not possess this personality type because it would have served him well at a time when he was most in need. However, all this being said, he was such a kind, gentle man who found so many ways to indulge others with favors and help when they were most in need. He was so selfless in all his life's work. It was always for others. He possessed some sensorial awareness of others that he worked tirelessly to "make good on" his goals so others would benefit. There is no doubt that his personality belied a wonderful spirit buried so deeply within his body that most people never got to appreciate the real man. Years later he took up golf. He was neither good nor bad. But,

---

[8] Family communications over many years.

he was ecstatic when he strung three or four pars in sequence. It was like a burst of ebullience and enthusiasm that others never witnessed. His joking and striking candor leapt from his soul with such thrust that it seemed like Boyle's law of gas pressure was being resoundingly show-cased. Then, very typically, in good time the good-time-felling would return to its cell of confinement. That was his nature. Too bad. It was his reality. But, it did not diminish his accomplishments.

In the fall of 1931, Henry entered his first year at Harvard University School of Dental Medicine. He took up residence in a Dorchester, Massachusetts lower middle class neighborhood at 94 Esmond Street.[9] Interesting enough, it was quite near where he lived while attending The Boston Latin School. And, it reflected the modest living style in which he would naturally default for the rest of his life. There is no doubt how it represented the essential being that he was.

He was an excellent student and very early on got involved in a number of activities that really set the stage for the rest of his professional life. He was a member of "The Phillips Brooks Association" which was named for Bishop Phillips Brooks, a clergyman, who grew out of a rather intemperate beginning and emerged as one of the great, humble and self-deprecating men of the cloth in Massachusetts. (172)

The association was named and dedicated to him in 1900 and serves as a social, religious and philanthropic venue for the support, care and personal needs of the indigent around Metropolitan Boston. Phillips Brooks was the Rector of Boston's Trinity Church (the oldest Episcopal Church in Boston, dating to colonial times). Briefly, he came from a known Boston family: a descendant of the eminent Reverend John Cotton and Samuel Phillips, Jr., the founder of Phillips Academy in Andover, Massachusetts (aka Andover Academy, one of the long established, esteemed, private boys' preparatory schools in The United States). Phillips Brooks went to The Boston Latin School and graduated from Harvard in 1855. Upon graduation, he taught at The Boston Latin School until he was fired for dishonorable behavior. This had a

---

[9] See photos for view of house where Henry lived; white house to the lest of brick apartment building on right side.

profound effect on his life. (153) He turned to religion and in 1859 he graduated from the Virginia Theological Seminary. He became rector of the Church of the Advent in Philadelphia and in 1860, after being ordained as a priest, he became rector of the Church of the Holy Trinity in Philadelphia. Upon his return to Boston as rector at Trinity Church, his modesty, simplicity and community outreach emboldened him to his mission. He was low on formality and high on service to people. He became Bishop of Massachusetts in 1891 and after only fifteen months died. However, the man crossed all religious barriers and became an endeared unifying leader to all people. His funeral at Harvard was that of a fallen man of greatness who inspired the average man with his zeal and obvious dedication social need. The Phillips Brooks Association, dedicated to this wonderfully charged man in 1900, became a center for all university related individuals with societal philanthropy of any measure in mind. This was certainly Henry's intention when he became a member of the Harvard Dental School association committee from 1933-1935. (172)

It was clearly in Henry's mind that the association had a mission which was hand in glove with his outlook on life. He was always giving to others, never asking anything in return. So very quietly it was understandable why he would get active in dental clinics and social affiliate organizations which would be an aid to the surrounding less fortunate neighborhoods. Later as Dean and Founder of The Boston University School of Graduate Dentistry, the Department of Dental Public Health was established with a mission that resounded with the spirit and dedication of his dental school contributions. But, it was not limited to this extended hand to people in need, the aid he quietly gave to residents out of his own pocket is legendary. Very few knew of this because he was so silent about his generosity. (173)

Harvard Dental School long endured a reputation for graduating researchers only, and usually with limited clinical training and skills. Therefore, in Boston, if you wanted strictly clinical practice, Tufts University School of Dental Medicine should be the optimal choice. (205) This was casual blather borne of jealousy and continued through many generations. Maybe it sounds like good banter or resolves some psychological deficit. In any case, it is hardly the case. As the often heard thought, it is not where a person goes to school, it is what he/she does with the knowledge acquired. This is very true in all phases of education so that myth should be put to sleep. Harvard's lofty image and reputation was grown, not out of adventitious good fortune, but through merit and meaningful dedication to the purity of education.

Probably, the most significant, life changing influence came when he was a student. Dr. Paul E. Boyle, a graduate of Harvard Dental School in 1923, was an instructor in Oral Pathology and had a profound influence on Henry's career. In addition, Dr. Kurt Thoma was the Charles Brackett Professor of Oral Pathology. But, he was also an Oral Surgeon who founded the residency program at The Massachusetts General Hospital. They both caught Henry's attention and interest because of their outstanding teaching and depth of knowledge in the field of Oral Pathology. As a student, Henry was very closely aligned with Paul Boyle, who eventually went on to become Dean of (Case) Western Reserve University School of Dental Medicine.(160) So, as Paul Boyle became an instructor in 1932, he spent a great deal of time with Henry. The irony is that Henry ascended so quickly up the academic ladder that he became one of the seven founding members of The American Board of Oral Pathology (along with his two mentors, Paul Boyle and Kurt Thoma).(138) When Henry graduated dental school in 1935, he became a research fellow for two years under the guidance of Kurt Thoma. This led to his becoming an instructor of Oral Pathology after his fellowship ended in 1937. This lasted until he entered The United States Army as a Captain and Chief of The Dental Division of The Armed Forces Institute of Pathology. During the war he was called to The White House to treat President Franklin Delano Roosevelt for an abscess of a lower incisor tooth. This notably remained very quiet in his memory bank during the rest of his life. This information came from the very eminent educator and Dean of The University of Pennsylvania School of Dental Medicine, D. Walter Cohen who studied under Henry's tutelage in Periodontology. At the end of his service, he was given a special commendation by President Harry S. Truman. (34, 66, 214,133,180)

But, it was under Kurt Thoma that Henry had studied the disease patterns of bone destruction around teeth and became interested in the causes of tooth loss, hence the term periodontology. Henry's interest in Periodontology was piqued as an Oral Pathologist studying under Kurt Thoma. (66) Thus, the reason for dentistry as a life's work and Periodontology as a career specialist evolved around circumstances which, as best as can be related, were simply happenstance. He was around friends or teachers who tweaked his fascination and attention and thus he made life changing decisions based upon these profound relationships. He did not have the benefit of a father's guidance so all these people became his surrogate support group, and particularly Kurt Thoma. It was with Kurt Thoma that he published the fifth edition of *"Oral Pathology"* in 1960. It remains one of the most comprehensive books of its kind. Only Kurt Thoma and Henry Goldman of that generation balanced careers in two separate (but intimately related) specialties. (138,140,143,)

On June 7, 1936, Henry married Dorothy Alter, a graduate of Simmons College in Boston. They were married on Eddie's wife (Helen Ruth Rubenstein Goldman, also a graduate of Simmons College) birthday. Dorothy gave birth to two sons, Richard and Gerald, but neither went into the dental profession. (186)

Henry went on to serve as President of both the Academy of Periodontology and the American Academy of Oral Pathology. (see appendix:#'s 5 and 6) Eddie bought him his first dental practice on Bay State Road in Boston, Massachusetts after the war. Eddie was very quietly the hidden force behind all the money Henry had to raise to fund The Boston University School of Graduate Dentistry. With similitude Eddie was as selfless and humble as his brother Henry. There was amazingly no jealousy between them their entire lives. Though very different in personality, they fastidiously supported each other inextricably. It was a most unusual relationship. They were always there for each other, never a slight edge to be redeemed.

Henry published many textbooks in Periodontolgy, either as lead author or contributor. In addition, he went on to publish another textbook with the esteemed Oral Pathologist, Robert Gorlin. (63) He also wrote many articles in Periodontology and edited several major journals (116,138,143) He was a treasure trove of knowledge and a most inexhaustible, energetic force behind dental education.

Throughout all of his acclaim, the bond between the brothers remained sacrosanct. Like all families, there were ups and downs. But, they never relented to pettiness, jealousy or fractious competition. Their mutual trust evolved from their upbringing which was meticulously controlled by their mother. The will to succeed and move on came from the steel curtain she metaphorically wrapped around both of them. Henry's detailed, tenacious manner grew out of her influence and was thoroughly cemented by his education at The Boston Latin School. In today's terms, his epigenetic influences were not going to permit failure. He had too many inspirational guides along the way. Interesting enough, he became an inspirational leader and teacher, but he never imposed the demands he put on himself on others. As Henry James noted in his *Portrait of a Lady* (79) when he wrote of his main character, Isabel Archer, "...he put wind in her sails..."[10] Henry Goldman energized his students, put wind in their sails, and he allowed them to flourish by their own instincts. This Jamesian life philosophy seemed like a mantra very akin to Henry Goldman's. As James expressed:

> *It is my belief that it is the obligation of every individual to fulfill his or her fullest potential. Integrity and reliability are important. Each task should be assumed with full responsibility towards its completion. Judgment should be made on the basis of values and not whim and fancy.*[11]

Sigmund Freud would have defined this as a reflex conditioned

---

[10] James, Henry: *"Portrait of a Lady", Copyright 1961-Reprint Edition, Houghton Mifflin.*
[11] Ibid; 144.

behavior (44). Henry's life was refined by all the phases of his life. But, he never detoured whimsically and was always faithful to his beliefs and words. He was indeed so very fortunate to have a brother to support him in time of need, but there is no doubt he was a one-time man who was responsible for all the great lessons he provided along the way.

CHAPTER 2

The Paradigm Shift: The Early Professional Years

The early years at The Boston University School of Graduate Dentistry were a daily grind for everyone concerned including residents, professors, and all the administrators. Everything was fresh and unfamiliar. There were mutual concerns because this particular school was a departure from the norm. Most dental schools were in the business of training future general practitioners. Boston University, on the other hand, became the very first institution to take already educated general practitioners and train them in the dental specialties: Prosthodontics, Orthodontics, Endodontics, Oral Pathology, Oral Surgery and Periodontics. These were the very primary fields for specialization, but they were reinforced by the growing disciplines of Oral Medicine, Oral Diagnosis, Oral Biology, Radiology and Implantology. (137)

It was an uncertain, capricious time because the school was a living, breathing experiment. Most of all, the residents were professionals who had sacrificed existing practices in a great number of cases to return to training in hopes of an improved personal future. Others were just out of the armed services, some right out of dental school, and a fair number who were in government services like the federal prison system, in public health, or in state or federal administrative positions. So, to a large degree, it was figuratively a step back to take a leap forward. Nevertheless, it was so fragile in those early years because there was no precedence for anyone concerned. And, most of all, there were families who were risking everything to venture through these completely unchartered waters.

Henry, the newly established Dean, was "a new kid on the block" in a very old and established colonial city with educational institutions predating the birth of the country. The challenges were granular and overwhelming. What he did to get this academic engine going was to gather established clinical practitioners within the Greater Boston area to lead each specialty area. For the most part, these were people with absolutely no pure academic training let alone any formal training in graduate education. No one would question this approach because there was no precedence. It was really a glorified group apprenticeship for everyone involved. And, if this was not enough of a departure from tradition, these individuals would not have to give up their lucrative private practices. Sufficient money was lacking to inveigle these practitioners into an academic setting that could not compete with private sector earning power. Therefore, adjustments were necessary to attract quality faculty. Existing institutions survived on this basis because salaries of full time academicians could not match the earnings of practicing dentists. Faculties were therefore expanded through part time clinical appointments without compensation for private practitioners. This tradition offered students exposure to real time clinical training. The actual academic teaching was delegated to full time, paid academicians. It was arguably a rather paltry compensation, even for those days.

When Boston University opened its doors formally in 1963, (173) the challenges were everywhere: financial, administrative and bureaucratic. As much as these considerations were pervasive, it was imperative to address them with diligence. The school had to be viewed as a worthy partner in the overall spectrum of dental education. If this failed, the school would have never endured. To commit to full time training would be as difficult an experiment for the numbers of neophyte residents as for the school with its unseasoned faculty. The accurate way to describe the times would be a period of nervous expectations filled with the excitement and anticipation of a new challenge. Henry was stalwart, never revealing any weakness in his armor. He stayed the course with exemplary leadership qualities necessary to en-sure calm and orderly progress. Faculty may have appeared confident and self-assured, but nervous energy thrashed inside the exterior calm. Like the seemingly unruffled duck with churning webbed feet escaping danger, the general atmosphere kept its composure despite obvious ambivalence. And anyone in denial was either living in an altered sense of reality or struggling to adjust. It was a potpourri settling in.

The original faculty was an odd assemblage of people. The one commonality shared by all was limitless "egos". If you asked each one of them (which, of course, never happened) who was "the best", you would get a different answer for each person. Well, this was somewhat encouraging for a newly established school on the rise because success would be rooted in a sense of confidence. However, to an independent observer, this would be very problematic. This was a faculty with such over-inflated personalities that Dean Goldman had to perform Kabuki dances around this circle of mysteries to keep a lid on the school. At times he even had to be fatherly and remonstrate with tough love to keep a sense of order. On the other hand, such a group of prideful edu-cators had one very important trait which contributed immeasurably to the school's rising reputation. They were perfection driven and would not tolerate mediocrity. Therefore, residents matriculated with this immediate perception, and they were trained with this mindset. Time would inevitably reflect "a cloning affect" which grew in time, at times positive and at times very questionable. Residents had to develop into their own sense of self, but this faculty seemed to corner the market on mind control. To a large degree this was beneficial when the end result was fostered by clinical excellence. However, when it was tinged by a personal Buddhist-like trance, it was almost like some residents developed a hypnotic identity to their mentors. As the years past and the school stabilized, the differences were quite evident.

For Henry, there was no time for side issues. It was necessary to develop a properly clear and broad curriculum for each specialty with specific attention addressing the guidelines of the American Dental Association's prerequisites for dental specialties. (137) In the late 1950's when these issues were being addressed, they were relatively specific, but not nearly as stringent and compelling as they are today. Today's ADA site visits engender months of preparation by full time faculty members in each department. In the 1960's there was far less rigidity to the preparation and the methodical review. All things being equal, the times for certification may have been less demanding, but relative demands bred relative worry!

The identification process generated continuous worry and sleepless nights until the visit was over. The expectation that the school has successfully measured up to the scrutiny and satisfaction of independent outside educators selected by the ADA was significant for all schools across the country. Measuring up to very high academic standards determined by probing educational committees was as much a concern then as it is now. That is a fact without question. When Henry began his odyssey toward the establishment of a post-doctoral training center for the dental specialties, it was also unchartered sailing for the ADA as well. So, perhaps, it is fair to say that the demands were not as strident as a site visit today. But, it would be naïve to think that the Dean and faculty were not aware of the pressures for detail and preparedness in the development of each department. Over time, the faculty revealed its true colors. The level of competence was noticeably steady and strikingly keen. It might have seemed that Henry's good fortune stemmed from sheer luck, but this was not the case. He had developed networking connections in all academic dental fields around the country which may have appeared chancy. But, au contraire, each chairperson arrived with creditable history and solid training. The only void was the steadying effect necessary to settle the atmosphere. That came with time, and it did with remarkable notice.

What was never contemplated during these years was the overwhelming effect that this institution would have. It was not just national, it was worldwide. Even if the school is not the same today, it spun a web of interstitial connections so vital for its growth: entailing businesses tied to technology, research and research development, methodologies for teaching, the business of dentistry, medical science applications, the coordinated training of dental-medical clinicians and science investigators, and full time educators. A very cogent argument can be made that this evolved out of the sheer brilliance and capabilities of the original department chairpersons Henry Goldman carefully selected. They were all master clinicians who developed into masters of the art of teaching. And, if research was the Achilles heel early on, somehow they were able to hurdle this obstacle with aplomb and conviction.

Henry foisted his influence on the sails of a very undersized boat rocking and banging through the turbulent waters present in the center of American medicine and dentistry in the United States right after WWII. For a small group of self-appointed clinicians who understood that tooth loss had overwhelming and devastating medical and social consequences, it became apparent that attention had to be paid to the diagnosis and treatment of diseases which ravaged the soft and hard tissues around teeth. Consideration had to be directed to the patient's overall physical health and well-being. Such thinking was at the centerpiece and thought process in the birth of the field of Periodontics. This was the impetus which conflated with the idea of a center for the teaching of the dental specialties. But, unbeknownst to dentists in those days, Henry was going to shift dental education into an area heavily weighted in the basic sciences. He was a highly trained Oral Pathologist, a research investigator into oral diseases which would later give definition and exposure to the disciplines of Oral Medicine, Oral Biology and Oral Diagnosis. Because of his broad based foundation in the dental and medical sciences he certainly had the knowledge and where-with-all to undertake the establishment of such a complete center for the education and training of dental specialists. And, to make this endeavor successful, the faculty had to reflect his sensibilities and perceptions. Even if they were not sufficiently well-versed and definitively trained in the biologic underpinnings of dentistry, they still possessed a high degree of mastery in the art of clinical practice. Henry's ulterior motivation was to effect biology as the basis of therapeutics in dentistry. For the fledging dentist of today, so ensconced in technology, and the pre-and post WWII practitioner, tethered to the mechanical art of restorative procedure, it is necessary to stand back and contemplate how dramatic an undertaking this would be. If nothing else, it reflected a quixotic undertaking. It is really difficult to appreciate how bold a move this was. Perhaps it is as equally important to realize the likes of avant-garde notables like Horace Hayden, Chapin Harris, Gillette Hayden, G.V. Black, and many other custodians of so many changes to the dental field in transforming it to a respected profession. But, Henry's contribution was Da Vinci, Plato (the Greek Lyceum) and Constantine in scope. He created and molded an institution for the ages. And, this is what separated him from all the greats in dentistry, before and to this day.

It is easy to understand what an undertaking this would be. In many ways, one would have to be somewhat naïve not to imagine that there would not be trying times. The school was a pipedream at best. Initially the faculty was a supportive and coordinated group of clinicians. But, the full timers were high stakes gamblers. As Dr. Donald Booth, Oral Surgeon extraordinaire, so amusingly and unhesitatingly admitted, Henry's reliability was quite suspect.[12] Truly, Don Booth was leaving private practice for an unproven position at the behest of a man who was laconic and never convincing. Yes, it is comedic as it is presented today looking back in wonderment. But, it was not then. Henry was everything but a communicator so Don Booth was like the riverboat gambler, giving up the known for the unknown. Henry's word was solid, but, in those days, the whole business of dentistry did not make the prospect of throwing tradition aside very attractive. And, this generally was the picture. Such change was gutsy, laughable today but certainly almost very troglodytic then![13]

The newness and challenges were inspirational. The resourcefulness

---

[12] Dr. Donald Booth, Robert Goldman, phone conversations, 2014; in very interesting and, at times, very jocular reminiscences of the early years when taking the job was like gambling at a Las Vegas casino! Don Booth was a very easy person to discuss such unpredictable times.
[13] Ibid.

and good feeling spilled over to all involved. The work was highly co-ordinated and universally supported. Everyone involved contributed in a very detailed, coordinated effort because they all respected the deep meaning of this daring enterprise. But, would it translate practically into a living, a fulfilling life, and a success story?

Henry was very introspective and quiet mannered, yet purposive and methodical. He was neither gregarious nor engaging, but he was a man of incredible determination and indefatigable energy. His leadership and direction for a newly chosen group of academic trailblazers was never in question. And, he was a most friendly man, albeit very shy. This encompassed good and bad in a very open-ended way. It was very different for the full timers and the part timers. The latter had the financial security of their practices if everything else failed in their teaching commitments. But, for men like Don Booth, Morris Ruben and Spencer Frankl who came on fulltime at the beginning, it cannot be over-emphasized the magnitude of the financial gambit. Henry was not a salesman type, and, he did not convey confidence by his words. His heart and spirit were genuine, but they were glancing and often did not hit the mark.

To Henry the sum was always greater than the parts. But, in this instance, the parts were crucial. The susurrations of rivaling academicians were accepted realities. He shrugged this off as trivial and too much time wasting to ever consider. To his mind it was blather, wasteful talk. His world could not be bothered by such claptrap. But, wherein the school was concerned, Henry took a very strident resolve to be in control. He was not naïve, but he believed in his heart that one word from him was all it would take to purify the atmosphere. Discordance in reaction to casual talk and pettiness had no play in Henry's handbook.

The initial specialty areas for which the school would become known were the aforementioned six, but there was latitude for very special post-doctoral programs which combined either a masters or doctorate degree in combination with training in one or two of the clinical specialty training programs. This was the ultimate aim of someone who wanted both clinical and research training. All the programs were arduous, and they required a deep personal financial commitment. In the beginning, the time for certification in a clinical specialty was two years, except for Oral Surgery. This was always three years (and continues to be such). However, over the years Periodontics expanded to three as well when implant training became mandated into the training curriculum. The other four continue to remain two years. With time for research training and time for a masters or doctorate degree, a candidate could add in another year to eight years. Thus, Henry was able to formulate and institute a very comprehensive center in all the dental specialties.

It was not very long before Boston University's reputation grew worldwide. Dentists started to enroll with hopes of exposure to interdisciplinary relationships to gain insight into comprehensive clinical care of complex dental needs. In many situations, it was not so easy or matter-of-fact. These were men and women who were well settled in their practices with growing families. So, the uprooting and resettling were difficult, demanding and emotionally draining. They came from all different countries, but the majority arrived from France, Italy, Colombia and Argentina. Even Americans dusted themselves off and moved their families from the various states to acquire the marvelous training they expected from such a respected teaching institution as Boston University. The number of candidates who matriculated right out of dental school was a very small percentage of the total. In fact, there were numerous instances of residents who came after military dental service commitments. Even at the most basic level of specialty training, it was a deeply thought out resolve each made. It took a very special person with a profound sense of discipline and sacrifice. This same individual with far greater training and clinical insight would become more competent and secure in the diagnosis and management of advanced and demanding cases. "The eyes would never see what the mind was not made to know"[14]became an understood principle

---

[14] Rochefoucauld, Francois de La: Maxims, Copyright 1959, Translation, Penguin Classics..

of the training programs. The general practitioners who committed to this took this huge step backward to project forward fell into a financial black hole. In most circumstances it was a universal family sacrifice. Therefore, this new genre of professional person learned to grapple with all kinds of change in life patterns and circumstances. As the school grew and matured over time its graduates set a standard energized and indulged by a school with ascending outside community respect and a growing international reputation.

At the time the first residents matriculated at Boston University, the physical plant was a makeshift operation.[15] There was an obvious absence of a main building, and a hodgepodge of old, rundown buildings characteristic of the poor side of town. It had yet to fully take its rightful place as an integral part of Boston University. Like most medical centers within the lower forty eight of The United States, their locations were for the most part sections of indigent, and, to some extent, blighted areas. In the case of Boston University Medical Center, it did not carry the cachet of the more established institutions, Harvard and Tufts. And, Boston University was in the throes of change at the time that its graduate dental school came into being. So to say that its status quo was in flux was a vast understatement.

When the first graduate residents descended upon the school, everything was frankly in a total state of confusion. The feelings were at best uncertain. These were people, as stated, who were taking a very big risk to give up staid, settled lives in a retreat to academia with the hope of not only far greater future reward, but also to satisfy a desire for a greater professional challenge. To these individuals, specialization would render far greater personal and family benefits.

There is the philosophy that there is only one time to make a first impression. When these residents were suddenly thrust into a totally new, disorganized, disjointed environment, most felt extremely insecure, nervous, and very doubtful that this would work out. Maslow's pyramid of human needs was totally subverted. (197,202) The basics were so poorly provided that it is a wonder that anyone stayed, survived

---

[15] Author's personal experience.

and flourished. These people turned out to be the robust, courageous pioneers who blazed the trail for the school that today entertains an international reputation of excellence in both pre-doctoral and post-doctoral dental education.

Probably the one feeling which ran rapid through each resident's soul in the mid-to late-1960's was fear (with a capital "F").[16] In a quiet moment most will admit to this. In many cases, there were children, wives and husbands at home who were literally abandoned for the sake of long, arduous days and evenings spent in lectures, seminars, and libraries researching and coordinating literature. No one outside of dentistry could imagine such an unremitting sterile and toilsome existence. And, the fact is that as overstated as this may seem, it is definitely not. The intensity of the daily academic responsibilities was simply off the charts. It is incomprehensible how literally "fried" some of these residents felt merely days into this sudden descent into this academic maelstrom. By the time the clinical commitment to patients was integrated into the schedule, the pressure was bordering a nuclear meltdown. Extreme sounding. Yes. And, as will be shown later, in many cases this took on a very tragic reflection.[17]

The specialties were very much guided by the Chairmen of the basic specialties. Periodontics was by far the most intense training specialty mainly due to the oppressive time commitment (seemingly 24/7; definitely 7; and, if not 24 in body, definitely in mind). The other specialties were rigorous, but not as prodigious. For the most part, the Chairmen at that time were not totally full time academicians with backgrounds in basic education. They had private practices and were some of the most highly touted and respected practitioners in and around the city of Boston at that time. All of a sudden they were endowed with a power and command totally out of their prior life

---

[16] Wise, Jeff: *Extreme Fear: The Science of Your Mind in Danger,* Copyright 2011, Palgrave Macmillan Trade.

[17] Amen, Daniel G.: *Change Your Brain, Change Your Life: The Breakthrough Program for Conquering Anxiety, Depression, Obsessiveness, Anger and Impulsiveness,* Copyright 1998, Times Books of Random House.

experiences. They all learned on the go. To assume that it was all roses and lollipops would be naïve. In many ways, they were more buoyant and unsure than their residents. But, in the end, the commitment meted out very positive results because everyone concerned worked hard and in tandem with the schedule demands.

When Henry M. Goldman began this immense undertaking, his supporting cast was few. At the time, the late 1950's (1958 to be specific as The Department of Stomatology at Boston University Medical School) to early 1960's (the school began in its inchoate, truncated design in 1963 as a coordinated Boston University-Beth Israel Hospital effort), there were many dental institutions around the United States which were pre-doctoral teaching institutions with postdoctoral specialty department. (Appendix #'s 3 &4) But, there did not exist a school which was completely committed to graduate training. In this sense, this came to be a transformative undertaking. For this alone, Henry is to be respected in the annals of dental education as one of a kind. His mission reached out globally and upgraded the level of research and clinical education worldwide.

The supporting cast which aided in this development was essential for laying the groundwork of each department. The personality of each Chairman would be reflected in the climate established. To this end, the choices were carefully thought through, both for competence and compatibility. They were in the direct line to expect the unexpected, and yet able to deal with all eventualities. Naïve and yet motivated with a sense of idealism, they were confronted with administrative details which were very time consuming as everything was new and time sensitive. Organizational skills for the tasks at hand had relatively no precedence. Because these individuals were prideful and bold, they were thorough, deliberate and energetic. They were not going to be adversely exposed. Even if at times they skated through unruffled on the surface, underneath there was always concern for order and readiness. They were kicking furtively under the water like the seemingly untroubled duck. These were people who knew all too well that "the devil was in the details". (173)

The academic demands were far greater than any resident could ever have imagined. Unlike other residency programs, there was a very heavy emphasis on the pure academic aspects of the basic sciences and literature review. For example, in Periodontics there was a complete and thorough review of everything from histology and anatomy to pathology and physiology. The literature reviews were so comprehensive that the time consumed in preparation was as much at night and on weekends as the time spent during the day in class or with patients. The majority of residents got by and succeeded, but there were some who fell by the wayside and quit (not being able to sustain the stamina and the mental fortitude). This was an unnecessary reality conflicting with level-headed teaching and learning trends. The academic demands were exhausting and laborious through the entire length of the residency. It was certainly like an academic boot camp to the extent that it was physically and emotionally trying. Henry was aware of the format but never of the scope and commitment. The certification process was two years for any of the specialties (except for Oral Surgery which was three). (173) For those committed to a master's program, it was at least three years (and less if the research, animal experimentation, and writing could get done during the clinical training period). If the resident was also in a doctoral program, the comprehensive training could last as long as seven to eight years. But, the length of time was hardly the issue. It was the emotional drain. Residents commuted from outlying suburbs in the early morning and pretty much did not return home 'til ten to eleven o'clock in the night. So, to say it was only a two year commitment hardly reveals the reality. In the Periodontics Residency Program the size of the group varied from eight to twelve. There were enough individuals that they were able to relegate responsibilities in a group effort for any of the preparatory academic demands.

There were the intangibles which wore the residents down. Yes, they spent an inordinate amount of time in lectures and seminars. But, these were interspersed with patient treatment, library work to review the literature on innumerable subjects, attendance at special colloquia and professional meetings, and research projects for advanced degrees (which, in and of themselves, required the tireless, persevering efforts to coordinate animal procurement, laboratory availability, protocol preparation, and library literature review). It is amazing that emotional stability remained because the mental pressure was the all imposing variable.[18]

If one were to observe from the outside, this pressure cooker environment could not be perceived. The other residency programs were just not perceptibly as threatening. Perhaps this is an ugly truth that is hard to digest. But, it related to leadership that was not as truculent and demanding. Each specialty reflected the essence of its Chairman, and Periodontics was willfully inured to unrealistic scheduling. The constant grind of producing perfunctory duties over and above the essential daily responsibilities wore the residents down. For example, the coordination and printing out of hundreds of pages of reviewed literature on one subject to be dispersed to over a dozen residents (for review and comprehensive discussion) was an ever present albatross whirling around an already congested day. This alone could have sufficed for a full schedule. To say that this tedium reached critical mass early on is a gross understatement. The older residents no doubt handled the daily demands as an understood ordeal (simply a means to an end) while the younger ones were much more unaccepting. But, it was "a do-or-be damned" situation. No doubt, Henry was never privy to this uncommon oppressive atmosphere (that is, until years later when unrelated circumstance brought this out into the open). At the end of the day so to speak, getting through such duress was directly related to the emotional maturity of each resident. It took a long view to get by each day (with the unexpected lurking all the time). Let's just say this was a most unpleasant reality kept under guard at a most unusual period in the school's history. In another time and place this behavior would never have been tolerated.

Perhaps the origin evolved from Dentistry's very early formalized educational conditioning. The one thing the dental profession always possessed that no other profession did was its "boot camp" mentality (a

---

[18] Author's personal knowledge.

hapless quality not lost over time). Henry often referred to this process state of affairs as "acquiring a union card" because he felt the standards were plagued by perfunctory training that did not contribute to the development of the mind. He thought it was more of a military mentality that lost itself in a discipline-style learning which never advanced into more appropriate cutting edge scientific discovery. Establishing a learning environment rather than an atmosphere of regimentation was Henry's essential goal. He acknowledged that graduate education should be a time for thought and self-actualization. Ironically, right under his eye, the Periodontics residency program accomplished that goal, but with a gravely onerous environment.

Over the years small mentoring programs existed throughout the United States within large medical centers, at Veterans Administration Hospitals, and at all military installations of the Army, Navy and Air Force. However, Boston University's School of Graduate Dentistry was to be a major separation from the traditional way of doing the business of training dental specialists. In fact, it got very complex because many residents were able to modify their training by integrating research and clinical training in multiple disciplines. This led to full specialization in two to three of the American Dental Association's fully accredited specialties as well as an advanced degree at either the Masters or Doctoral levels. Of course, this was not a general behavior because the vast majority of individuals were there for clinical training in as limited a time as possible in order to quickly return to a conventional lifestyle. For the selected few whose training was multi-disciplined the years were extended to a point whereby completion at times was uncertain. And, the format of each specialty was certainly not "one size fits all" in scope or academic commitment. Henry made this available in a very flexible schedule for those who wanted this a la carte training. This was a wonderful adjunct to a conventional training process that other programs could not provide.

The days seemed like a merciless grind along with many, many sleepless nights. It can't be overstated that the residency programs in those days were generally very demanding, but the mentoring was very special. Commonly most of the programs of specialty programs could not handle the numbers like Boston University. Boston University, as noted previously, had far greater numbers, averaging sometimes ten to twelve in some years to a low point of six to eight in its heyday. The numbers allowed for interaction between the specialties as they were grouped in close proximity. During this period there were a great number of very high profiled Chairpersons around the country. Even Tufts University was likewise known under the leadership of Dr. Irving Glickman. He was a character with great academic and clinical skills, but with the force of personality that was boisterous and markedly cruel at times.(205) But, in general, most of the great educators of the day were coming into their own at the time Boston University was setting standards of excellence equal to anywhere else in the world.

Henry did not really concern himself with the day-to-day functioning of the school. His mindset was an almost myopic concentration on the building of the school's image and integration into Boston University Medical Center. (173) There did not exist a pure office for the administration of very basic daily responsibilities. In fact, there was more of a pooling of secretaries and various full time professors who were able to do Henry's bidding as necessary. It was essentially "make shift". No matter how perfunctory a need or question which related to course scheduling, seminar or speaker assembly, or even library hours and needs, there was always someone to provide help. In today's world this would fall into the office of an administrative dean for academic affairs. But, in its infancy, Boston University was run on the fly. Seemingly unconventional, it worked very well. And, with all the pressing items on his mind, he was always available and attendant to anyone's needs. So, where would henry find support?

Unlike long enduring medical schools and centers, full time positions were very sparse. They existed, but they were few in number. As in professional baseball where some teams are blessed when an owner can sign an all-purpose utility infielder/outfielder, Henry was very, very fortunate to find a man without whom the school most likely would not have developed as uniquely and magnificently as it did. This man,

Morris Ruben, was truly a renaissance man. His probative mind was seemingly limitless, his imagination and scope of knowledge all-pervasive, his communicative skills matchless, and he was invested with a sense of inspirational selflessness. He was a gentle soul with a quiet humility. His eloquence and profoundly descriptive lecturing style was uniquely overwhelming. In a short period of time he could relate such constructive information from so many basic science fields that it had a drowning effect. However, there was absolutely no sense of charlatanism, it was pure and beautiful in its astonishing brilliance. Other faculty members were no match for his teaching powers and relevance. Many people possess knowledge which is wide in scope but very shallow. His was seemingly and bona fide limitless both in scope and depth. He carried the school because of his inexhaustible commitment to education and the kindliness with which he related to people. As the history of Henry's venture unfolds, it will appear how devotional and resourceful a man he was. And, this is where Henry found solace because this man filled a void that would have a lasting and profound effect.

The composition of the faculty was configured to lend clinical know-how to graduate residents who thirsted for the type of training which would translate to everyday practice. These residents were not new to the dental profession, but they were neophytes insofar as their expertise in their various specialized fields. On this basis, the Chairs of the various departments were the types of private practitioners who fancied themselves as intrinsically pedagogic and vectors of categorically sourced scientific information. Most realized their limitations and the reality of what they could bring in terms of their clinical skills, but there were a few who were uniquely positioned in a new academic milieu where they very quickly became merchants of excellence in teaching. For the most part, they were certainly effective, but they were also quite theatrical. They were imaginative and creative but in a most scientific manner of exceptionally high standards. These appointees were significant because the mantle of training to which the post-doctoral residents aspired was fully maintained and managed with the necessary commitment to serve both the year-to-year responsibilities and orderly function of the school. In this sense, these leaders in their respective fields were emboldened to the training of quality specialists. At times their teaching styles and behavior created an atmosphere of conflict throughout the city of Boston and its competing universities and professional societies. However, this was the result of their rather rapid rise to national acclaim that created friction and jealousy. This was not their fault. It was common to a city which was represented by three highly touted dental schools with very imposing personalities which came into conflict from time to time. Was this inevitable? Most certainly. Reputations and domineering personalities are certain to engender a kerfuffle in any walk of life. And, such was the case in Boston, like any other major city of the world where education was of the highest standards. Perhaps Boston was slightly a more sensitive environment because Boston University was a school of specialization?

There was an underlying singular virtue about the entire faculty for which there was no denial. It beaconed as the cream of the crop in the dental profession. Over time, however, perhaps their financial success in dental practice empowered them to believe too deeply in their own press clippings, so to speak. Although this may seem hyperbolic on its face, this is exactly how it was in Boston beginning in the 1960's.[19]

When Henry opened the school in 1963, it turned the city on its head. Harvard and Tufts were the only games in town since the inception of their respective beginnings. Perhaps from a psychological viewpoint a new school with a faculty drawing from the same pool of professionals emerging on the scene with worldwide presence was too overwhelming for a small large city? International educators would become part of the mix, but, for the most part, the everyday faculty was sourced from the metropolitan area. Henry already had a regional reputation as well as rapidly evolving internationally. This provided him with leverage in attracting teachers with great clinical reputations in all the specialties. But, for Harvard and Tufts, this was a competing

---

[19] Allison, Robert: *A Short History of Boston (Short Histories),* Copyright 2004, Commonwealth Editions, Paperback.

institution for which there was most definitely an undercurrent of resentment and jealousy. Maybe the faculty elicited a sense of "noblesse oblige" which may not have encouraged warmth and harmony. Who really knew at that time! A small dental community where respect was gained and academic acceptance very slowly forthcoming.[20]

As the years passed, the divisions and gossip within this milieu deepened and widened into a chasm of academic warfare. It was certainly fortuitous for the school to embody such great teaching, but it was very unfortunate to be tarnished by constant gossiping because of a faculty that was not threatening but appeared to be covetous of power and position. They were all perfectionists with emblematic clinical teaching skills so they obviously threatened the status quo. And, Henry knew this. The balancing act, however, was consequently very difficult for Henry because he was a graduate of Harvard Dental School and his new venture demanded a soft landing into the arena of Boston education, not an entry with all guns blazing. He had a very keen awareness of this inherent pitfall, but he felt he could override it in time to make it work for the sake of the school's success and the international reputation it was garnering.

To some degree this would happen, and the school blossomed to take a seat among the best schools in the world, but this did not happen without the most complex, convoluted transition in a fashion of disbelief never told. Its history revels in a great story because the field of dentistry has been greatly affected by what happened, and most particularly by Henry's imprimatur on the profession throughout his great struggle and success with Boston University's evolutionary development. The challenges were constant and numerous, but never insurmountable. And, he proved that though individuals would feel entitled, he would never allow them to falsify their allegiance to the school. In his view, the sum would always be greater than the sum of its parts because the institution was more important in its totality than the individuals who comprised its faculty, including himself He also had a fatalistic attitude that hard work would always prevail and

---

[20] Ibid.

that institutions outlive egos. To this end, he proffered the school's future would be predicated on his nurturing the best in his faculty while quietly remediating their failings and idiosyncratic professional deportment when required.[21]

---

[21] Author's communications over the years with Henry.

CHAPTER 3

Captain of the Ship

Henry Maurice Goldman was a very quiet, introspective man whose every moment seemed to express purpose and preconceived design. He was always deep in thought, and yet he had so many things going on at the same time that his movement was instinctive and purposive. Always self-propelled as if rushing to get it all out for fear that something would be forgotten, his day was like the proverbial "Grand Central Station at the rush hour". Seemingly like a pure thoroughbred exploding to the finish line, the ordinary person could hardly keep pace with his moving from point to point let alone with his thought process. He was the vintage multitasker before it became vogue. He put the expression "ask a busy person to do something extra" to shame. If an objective observer were to stand back and watch him, it would look like a video in fast mode. But, he was organized, never forgot a detail (nor did he ever refer to a personal appointment book), and was always on time with his daily projects and meetings. It's no wonder that he accomplished what very few, if any, could.

Walking into his office was unique unto itself. For a man at the literal top of his profession, one would automatically think that he would station himself in a beautifully appointed executive office. But, he grew up extremely poor, and he carried forth throughout the rest of his life with that memory affixed to all his pursuits. His office contained a very large convertible table sprawled out at the far side against a large window. It resembled what one would expect to find in the office of an architect or a mechanical engineer not that of a Dean and founder of a new graduate school for post-doctoral resident training in the dental specialties. Across that table there was a sense of organized piles of papers, magazines, x-rays, color slides, books, and instruments which all related to some issue or ongoing project. Even his secretary would not dare to go anywhere near this mammoth "table of treasure". It certainly dwarfed his own personal desk which was off on the other side of the room with nothing on it save a telephone, a couple of pencils and maybe a sheet of paper on which there was always some sort of doodle drawn during a meeting or phone conversation. The room atmosphere was always bright and alive because it was situated on the sunny side of the building and the windows were quite resplendent with light and glare. In the winter this allowed for warmth and comfort, especially in Boston when there could be the deception of azure colored skies but single digit temperatures driven by blustery circular winds spinning through the buildings relentlessly. He would always be standing or going back and forth between one end of the large table to the other reading or shuffling papers. Always mumbling to himself, there was never a wasted thought. There was never any background music simply because his stale upbringing never allowed this accoutrement. Music was a luxury he could not afford. Besides, the tonal qualities would have upset his concentration. This office ritual was only interrupted by an occasional verbal yell to his secretary in the ante-chamber (despite the fact that he had an early model intercom), or, if someone walked in who had a specific appointment. He would never stop what he was doing to summon up any formal greeting because this was not his style. To a stranger this lack of any semblance of comity or simple politeness would be taken as plain outright rudeness. However, he was hardly a rude man. He was simply almost the troglodyte, unpolished and skittishly shy. If it was a very important meeting, or even a quick, passing communication, it didn't make any difference. He would proceed on with his sense of purpose and talk with his head down in the direction of some place on the table to which he would slowly saunter with a new paper or book. One would think that whatever was said by any visitor would be half heard or not at all, but instead he was keen to every detail spoken. And, he would hasten the conversation to a directed end swiftly and efficiently. He would never mince any casual or trivial ideas because every moment to him was ever so vital. He was expeditious in all conversation. When he came to what he considered an end, he would just walk away like the person was not even in the room. People generally got used to this very rough-edged style. He was Henry Goldman and he did not answer to anyone. As this reputation grew over time, it did not matter one whit because he never cared what others thought. He only cared what was important for the nurturing and care of his baby: The Boston University School of Graduate Dentistry. This was simply his modus operandi. However this almost rude behavior was discerned, there was not a scintilla of doubt that this man was one of the most caring, beneficent men anyone could encounter.

Outside of the academic atmosphere which was his life, he was ill-mannered and devoid of social graces. Even non-professional acquaintances could discern this. Thus, his ongoing personal relationships were very limited. His wife and sons were his life, and he really had only one friend over his lifetime besides his older brother, Edward. What would be confused for meanness or his silent retreat into himself was really a personality defect nurtured from youth through desperate poverty which compelled his unrelenting devotion to an academic work commitment. There was never time for complete relaxation or enjoyment. Underneath his austere and faceless appearance was an extremely soft, gentle and kindly man. The problem was how terribly misunderstood he was. Almost childlike, he would demand constant stroking and approbation. He was horribly lacking in self-esteem, and the person who saw this could deceive him with superficial niceties and kindness for their own advantage. Because of such naivete, many people in fact took advantage of him.

How could a man who was so quick on his feet and replete with incisive knowledge in his field be so duped by what would be considered obvious to most people? He could not size up a personality effectively. His choices seemed arbitrary and hasty. Once he made up his mind, he would never immediately redress the consequences of a mistake or miscalculation. He walked them back or with awkward demands, but rarely with explosive anger. He did not talk about it and never addressed untoward professional behavior. This would cost him at a later time when his reputation and all that he had accomplished came into question. His inability to distinguish between those sycophants around him (who pretended to greater position and power) and the people who singularly contributed and worked tirelessly was his most astonishing weakness. He was so easily deceived by the kind of personality missing in his own. It was almost as if he was aware and reached out to overcome his own deficiencies through the people who knew opportunistically when to smile and be sycophantish. The person who could persevere and bring a smile got ahead with aplomb and material gain. No doubt, his Achilles heel was his inability to carefully judge character. There were very good and able people around him, but there were opportunists as well.

The very few who coveted his influence and recognition were abundant. But, stirring up conflict without conscience left him chagrined and led eventually to deep and significant consequence. Short term such a misguided, rash affront could linger without blowback. But, it only served to embolden him to those whose ambitions and deception was willful and blatant enough to jolt his inner spirit. He might have been overly unsophisticated, but the cloying types did catch his attention. Somehow he would send an alert to the distant recesses of his memory bank without ever calling attention to his awareness. He would quickly move on because treacly behavior bothered him. It was a time waster, and very pointless in his thinking. His way of giving notice would be to shake his head, smile sardonically and move on to another matter or point of conversation. The subject would change with bold certainty.

Without doubt it was serendipity that Henry developed a love for the game of golf. Or, like most for most people, it was his love-hate relationship with the sport that diverted his attention and offered a bit of sanity to his frenetic schedule. He tuned into the golf game like the violin to a symphony orchestra. On vacation or during the summer at home, this game was his outlet from the tremendous pressures which consumed his daily work life. He was not a good golfer, but hitting a spectacular shot grabbed his fancy for many days (sometimes weeks) later. But, he was a joy to be with on a golf course. The man chasing this little white ball around was humorous, entertaining and talkative. To joke with him was a pleasure. It seemed to allow his inner soul to relax. If he hit a bad shot or whiffed at a ball with a poor lie, it was not out of the realm of possibility to hear "an expletive deleted", though not common. He was a very refined man, but, even Henry Goldman let his guard down occasionally on a golf course. He would even chase that ignominious "white thing" like a possessed dog after a bone at times. Very amusing and celebrated with many laughs. Like all golfers, he fell victim to "the masochistic, bedeviled possession syndrome" characteristic of most amateur golfers. He was mesmerized by the magnetic draw on him. It was antithetical that this overly disciplined man could be disposed to complete mindless banter when on a golf course.

Probably one of the most interesting, but not surprising, aspects of his personality was his rather narrow intellectual curiosity. In spite of his very disciplined exposure to classical learning at the premier public high school in the country, the Boston Latin School, Boston, Massachusetts, he essentially never read a book nor consistently read a newspaper of conceptual depth. He was really a very one dimensional man. From an analytical point of view, most likely his narrow life focus most likely stemmed from his total commitment to his school and the immense demands they made on his psyche. His social skills were also inadequate for the lofty position he was assuming. His very retiring, quiet countenance in public reflected his very deficient conversational skills. Yet, when spoken to, he was quite gracious and engaging with a rather pleasant smile. If he heard something with which he disagreed he would blurt out with a very one-sided statement and retreat to silence. He definitely was never the life of any conversation. People accepted him for the unblemished, accomplished reputation he deservedly earned. None of this is to discredit his persona, it was just a fact that his social hesitancy was quite noticeable as well as his quite limited circle of friends. Yet, he commanded tremendous respect and drew the interest and concerns of people with his very patient, warming demeanor. More than likely a psychologist would revert to his barren, grueling upbringing to find an answer for such comportment.

The people who were selected as the first faculty were far more extroverted. With their natural ease tempered by need a lot of what went into creating an immediate image was derived from their very established temperaments. The way the world was and how people interacted the public perception would have been a hard dose of reality if the school's image were to be founded on Henry's personality alone. Thankfully, the chairmen were, for the most part, socially engaging. They made up for what could have been an initial struggle to garner attention veiled by gravitas. For established institutions reputations were established and vouchsafed. Boston University in the late 1950's, early 1960's was a complete unknown within the city and greater metropolitan community. It was essential to alert the other schools to its substantive value with a sense of ease and its low key modus operandi. It was essential to encourage support, respect and acceptance. In this regard, Henry's supporting cast blended its academic merit with the kind of social draw which immediately gave the school standing it the Boston community. Men like Schilder, Frankl, Mori, Chaikin, Talkov, Baraban, Margolis, Booth and Harris expressed charisma with a sense of congeniality that was extremely sustaining for the school. They were hardly of the same disposition, but they allowed Henry to lead under cover without having to force a sense of exuberance that would have been forced and not natural. Henry's scope may have been narrow, but, fortified with the leadership qualities his faculty furnished, he was able to implement his plans without perfunctory interruptions. Henry talented at finding the right people for the right needs. This allowed him to get things done effectively, and with authority. In spite of his lack of charisma, however, his talent to make a dream materialize captured the world's attention. And, this gave him cachet, something that did not require romancing and bluster.

Nothing in his professional life was totally out of his control. Yet, if anyone wanted to understand what a pleasure it was to be in this man's presence, it was to walk eighteen holes with him. He played very often with his older brother, particularly late on Friday afternoons. Edward never possessed any athletic penchant like Henry so his game was a personal expose, an amusing but fitful exercise in self-abuse. Golf could always spotlight a person's true inner self as it teased insufferably even the most stable people. But, the two of them enjoyed one another's company and it gave them time to banter back and forth. It was also a time for airing out issues or problems. And, yes, the laughs and personality quips went back and forth like resonating echoes of friendly put downs. This was at times the theater of the absurd to witness. But, to the point, it revealed a man who was just the nicest man that anyone would want to be around. It truly brought out the very real persona when he was away from tension and stress. It was unfortunate that no one ever witnessed this side of his personality. Those were times he was so relaxed that he could attempt a really funny joke, something he could never contemplate nor dare when lecturing to a professional group of his peers. This side of a most humble, happy and engaging man was the true soul gushing forth. His self-appointed mission in dental education elicited his serious, purposive side. And, he never lowered his guard in pursuit of this goal.

If Henry were alive in today's technological world, he would most likely dismiss all the fanfare over its gadgetry as a misguided sidestepping of learning "the fundamentals". He always felt that there had to be a greater purpose for dental education rather than the repetitive teaching of its mechanical basis. For over many centuries dentistry was practiced as an art, not a science. The fluff surrounding the computer-telephone-app industry with a new application or an advance de jour updated constantly can be likened to Henry's pet peeve with dental education's emphasis on the fundamental mechanics of restoring teeth rather than on the biologic reasons for tooth loss. Even today this very unrelenting riff still predominates. Why? Well, Henry constantly reasoned that the profession couldn't get out of its own way, accept the challenge to reverse its old guard teaching methods, and put its emphasis where it always should have been: the biology of oral health and disease.[22] He would not accept a stare down with the relics within The American Dental Association so he just avoided confrontation. He would do it his own way because he understood that mechanical dentistry had to take a back seat to the core principles inherent in the relationship between oral and systemic disease. He certainly felt the importance of advancing new technologies in the application of new dental materials. But, he felt it went to the extreme. It frustrated him to no end to see the profession stuck "on dumb" (as he often voiced).

Henry remonstrated the mouth as a gateway entity of biologic consequence to the rest of the body. Teeth were immersed in a factory of physiologic activity reflective of and consequent to regulatory organ balance and harmony throughout the human body. Today this serves as the basis of nutrition and diet. Henry understood this focus without flare. Pre-doctoral education, in his view, was stuck on fustian teaching method and concentrated on old-guard educational design. It was this deficiency inherent in dental education that served as the basis for all his ideas which ultimately materialized in The Boston University School of Graduate Dentistry. Rather than go toe-to-toe with people who could not fathom necessary change and their essence steeped in the art of politics, he decided to lead by example. Like Thomas Jonathan (Stonewall) Jackson at Marye's Heights at The Battle of Fredericksburg,[23] Henry stood like a stone wall and dug in for the long run. (25) Henry was principled and stalwart in his vision for change and would never relent. He was never defiant, but always steadfast.

The science of Periodontology, as the world knows it today, became the very basis for the manner in which Henry redirected dental education in order to advance research in the causes and treatment of tooth loss. Oral Medicine and Oral Pathology were disciplines which broadened the basis for relating the oral manifestations of systemic

---

[22] Author's personal conversations.

[23] Catton, Bruce: *The American Heritage New History of the Civil War,* Edited and with an Introduction by James McPherson, Copyright 2005, Harper-Reprint Edition.

disease to future clinicians. In Henry's mind the kind of teaching and research expertise necessary to carry the profession to a new mindset was extremely dependent on both a new age teacher and student. There is no doubt that his purposive emphasis on this paradigm shift in dental education reflected his personality and background. He referred to dental school many, many times as a place to put in time and get the necessary "union card" so as to be able to comport to necessary national and statewide standards of dental practice. He could not bear to see this self-propagating drumbeat continue. And this is where the rubber met the road. His style and personality would occasionally come into conflict with the faculty which effectuated the necessary changes. In many regards the school as it exists today succeeded because it survived faculty who did not always agree. But, they followed his lead with similar passion. Henry was a very determined, prescient scientist, but he could be stubborn and inflexible. He simply did not see the benefit of engaging people in open discussion to air out differences in order to modify procedures for overall consensus regarding course structure. Therefore, the ideals, dominant in his thinking, sometimes came into cross purpose and conflict with longstanding maxims and standards.

It should not be assumed that this faculty was a disparate, hell-bent group with rogue attitudes. Not in the least. Henry certainly had his weaknesses and at times he was staggered by the aggressive, overpowering personality types who marched to their own drumbeat He had a long view that did not connect with renegade behavior. He had an uncanny feeling that he should let them carry on in their own style. Because Henry was on surface personable and kindly in a laconic, quiet manner, he could easily be taken for feckless and spineless. To the contrary, he saw and understood everything. Unless of major consequence, he preferred to let everything take its course. He understood the egos of all his faculty members, He simply felt that they should be able to be personally accountable for their own conduct in their day-to-day responsibilities. He gave them all free reign to express their own sense of leadership. Many people who might have felt him curiously absent at times confused this quality with what they construed as the proper standard for oversight and management. They simply did not know Henry. He was always aware of and attentive to all details.

In the very early years, Henry was into everything that advanced the expansion of the school. He was peripatetic, tireless and certainly boundless in energy. He walked with a fretful, furtive gait. This is exactly the manner he walked through every day. He never lost a beat. He was quick, to the point, never wordy, and generally steps ahead of everyone in thought and planning. Perhaps he was not eloquent, but he was always ready for action. Everything he said and did was measured to the precise direction and outcome he had already preplanned. It seemed at times that he was overly charged and frenetic. He was not. He had purpose for everything and never relied on anyone when consequence was factored into any decision. He would never rely on anyone for anything he could do himself, His office was his bully pulpit where he enunciated his outline for the day, made pressing phone calls, and then proceeded all over the medical center to engage in meetings along the bureaucratic chain of command to rigorously articulate the needs of his residency programs for full integration. He complied very fastidiously on all regulatory laws and guidelines. This alone was a herculean task in addition to all the administrative obligations necessary to get through a day.

When he walked down a corridor, he was treated with incredible respect and admiration. Sometimes when people saw him appear with a clinic gown on, they quickly withdrew behind a wall, cubicle or a mountain of boxes stacked in an open corridor. He carried a sense of authority and awe that either mystified or generated an awkward circumstance to avoid. It was simply a case of misunderstanding Henry's demeanor. He just lacked that "je ne sais quoi", the intangible the French would describe as the unknown which could entreat people to his side. Not smiling and looking austere, of course, did not help. He was merely lost in own thoughts. He was so desultory and predictable that he was easily comforted by a quick salutation as he raced around. His manner was at times a contradiction in terms. On the one hand he needed to increase his appeal, and on the other he was dismissive of the simple social graces as unnecessary and superfluous. And yet these would have gone a long way to grease the connections to people and make the "realpolitik" around the school flow with ease and harmony. He simply generated a disquiet that people simply did not understand. His stripes were leopard like, and they were never going to change. The misfortune is that the people who could not perceive his inside soul as a measure of his true caring were guided by their own unfortunate narrow mindedness. Henry's conduct was certainly a throwback to his upbringing in abject poverty where there was no time for small talk and comfort relationships. Rather than embrace his inability to adapt, for whatever psychological inability, he made his lack of social skills become his own menacing hurdle he could never overcome. When he graduated to the frenetic world of business, he did not transition with the necessary skill sets which would have filled out and balanced his core excellence and reputation in his field. It required a learned behavior which he could not cultivate because his insights were blocked by his own penchant for denial. And, this masked the very qualities of giving, kindness and selflessness which were really his essence.

Henry had an incredible vision. He was, in the very pure sense, a renaissance educator. He was far and away ahead of his time. Discarding the accepted repetition of the same curriculum and technique courses, he articulated a whole new level of educational design which would prepare future dentists for changing population health needs. He anticipated that new technologies would revolutionize research and clinical practice. The secret was to judiciously rid the profession of its stolid, change resistant character. He alone possessed the conviction and determination to hurdle any hindrance which stood to defy him. He was certainly aware of the politics, but, to a certain degree he was alone in pursuit of his dream.

Early on before computers and ultra-speed communication he was compelled to maximize what was then standard. He had a trait very uncommon in most people, even today. He could multi-task at very significant levels of need and speed. He would never forget so that he was able to be one step ahead of everyone. This was his mantra. People knew it and consciously felt off-guard and unsure around him. Not everyone, but certainly most colleagues were very different in their demeanor when in his presence. There was a quietude, almost a genuine call to attention when he spoke. Some of the most esteemed educators of the day were humbled by his very presence.

In private, he was a force. In public, he was not. The strange irony was that his breadth of knowledge was broad and deep. It was almost as if his mind was a storage depot for facts and very meaningful scientific concepts. But, in a public forum, he stumbled and groped for the proper words. The stuttering problem he had as a youth he carried late into his adult professional years before he was able to get professional help. He was strangely inarticulate and treaded water at times in awkward efforts to search deeply for the proper trove of scientific information he certainly possessed. At times, he was overwhelmingly boring, but, at the same time his reputed knowledge bank was never, never called into question. He was the real deal. His colleagues did not have his background training nor his experience. Nevertheless, this incongruity haunted him his entire professional life. In fact, his arch rival of the day, Dr. Irving Glickman of Tufts University School of Dental Medicine, was his antipodes, his Yin to his Yang, the man whose brash, aggressive, loud, boisterous articulations stood in stark contrast to Henry's. Irving was undeniably bright and fortified with uncanny dimensions of knowledge, but he could not rival Henry's depth and scope. Irving's forte was his ability to turn a word. To Henry's opposite, he was unrefined, impatient, extremely domineering, and without compassion. At professional meetings, their differences were glaring. Their reputations were set in stone and a bitter rivalry built that probably would never have gained ground if they did not represent institutions in such close proximity (Tufts and Boston University Medical Centers being within a few miles of one another). In fact, this combating duo reached international fame for many years as the story will reveal. Like everything in life, people like to rubberneck at the site of an auto accident, watch a boxer get his face mercilessly bloodied, a football running back get stilled by a haunting stop in his tracks by a building substituting as a lineman, or a helpless, unaware hockey defenseman get his poor innocent body get nailed to the side boards by an oncoming projectile in the guise of a salivating opponent ready to convert his manhood into a pile of protoplasm draped bloody on the ice from a sudden slam with the horrific momentum of his huge frame. For some reason, people enjoy the combat, and the Glickman-Goldman rivalry became blown up by the covetous Boston dental following that encouraged a continuum of public encounters. In fact, meetings were framed around their verbal sparring knowing perfectly well that attendance would increase. There was never any contest because "Glickie"[24] most always got the best of Henry. He was voided somewhere along the line with a sense of public decency. The result was his trolling for moments when he could obscenely make anyone his victim of very loud, insulting verbiage and demeaning aspersions. Irving Glickman was a character and never took any prisoners. He was known to pillory his colleagues from the audience who presented legitimate questions at one of his presentations. He waited for the right victim and then he verbally jumped at the right moment to verbally assault an innocent questioning attendee with the satisfaction of a satisfied predator. This went on for years, and it gave the dental community around the world something to enjoy around professional cocktail circuits. Henry was never hurt in substance because he rose above the fray and never fell to "Glickie's" puerile behavior. He kept silent and only responded by short, authoritative comments. He was always the gentleman, leaving the dental public to their amusement. This misbegotten warring rivalry finally ended in a locker room at a golf club where they finally brought together in a handshake. Many stories of their rapprochement have been offered up, but this is where and how all prior ill-feelings were put to rest. It was set-to molded by a tempest in a teacup which evolved and endured at the pleasure of a charged up professional group that enjoyed the sight of grown men victimized by their thirst for displeasure and

---

[24] Dr. Irving Glickman had an infamous reputation. Somehow he acquired the moniker: "Glickie".Whether he was approached with a glad-handed greeting with the moniker is doubtful, but this was his very customary reference.

social excitement. And, certainly, "Glickie" had the will and the way. In retrospect, "Glickie" was a talented man who let his physical deficits encumber his inability to restrain the release of his personal disdain for his own self-image to the detriment of others with his sharp, serpentine tongue and quick, undisciplined verbal skills. History has buried this uniquely awkward period, but it served to support Henry as a no-nonsense, serious educator.

Henry never passed himself off as an ambassador for change per se. It was his idea to refine the base and advance the existing qualities inherent in dental education. In his mind he so earnestly wanted to supplant the old guard thinking for the sake of conceptual theories relating to the biology of disease. This was in his bailiwick from his years at Harvard and the AFIP. (173, 133,180) He cultivated a sense that dental training was very much antiquated. He was very practical in his understanding that restorative training would always be required training. But, his exposure to the biologic sciences opened his eyes. He clearly saw himself as a trailblazer. Dentistry, in Henry's thinking, would never progress as a profession unless he could make dentistry see and understand what he had come to see during his years in Washington during WWII. (189) There was no getting around the fact concerning the known relationship of oral with systemic health. This reality had to be accepted as the basis of change in dental education. This settled in Henry's mind as a sine qua non for a transformation which would capture his concentration for the rest of his life. Wherever he was, whether in his school office or in treating patients, his every manner was directed toward this goal. All that can be said is that he dedicated the rest of his life to this proposition. And, he had both the will and the way to embolden enough people to make his dream a reality. If nothing else is gleaned from his life, it is without question the courage and continued conviction he sustained to make it all happen. His feat was the kind of persistence very few can muster to make the improbable probable and the impossible possible.

There was no wasteful energy expended. His communications to patients, students, faculty and even friends were precise and poignant.

Every thought, motion and interaction seemed on surface quite desultory. However, his actions were measured and with prescribed purpose. He understood what it would take to make everything happen. The multidimensional demands, the attention to detail, the ability to bring the right people together, and the persuasive argument that would have to be made for financial and political support would either allow his plan to material or fall apart like a frayed dream without memory. Henry had the capabilities to incorporate his insights to make the right people come together with the same will to see his project through. The dream became a reality which became a story that can be seen like a holographic tale. It was an Odyssey like he did not contemplate, but it succeeded because his untiring focus and his devotion to the people who gave him the opportunity to learn and then pass the knowledge on.

Each of the original faculty departmental chairmen was a separate story. As a group they knew exactly for whom they worked, they knew their mission, and they all had long leashes to exercise their independence. But only to a point because they all deeply respected Henry Goldman. In spite of Henry's seemingly insouciant exterior, he cared and cared very dearly. He had the cunning of his mother and the drive of a fatherless upbringing. Nobody was going to deter him from his certain mission, and this was to create the finest institution of dental learning in the world. He carefully insulated himself with an aloofness that gave him the edge in every relationship. To some this was misinterpreted as a callous and calculating leader. On the one hand this was irksome because he could be, in a figurative sense, unreachable. But, conversely, this played to his advantage because it always kept his faculty on its toes. Was this behavior an act? Or, was it real? There is no final answer. But, a careful study of this man shows unqualifiedly that this was most likely his true nature. He simply did not care about what others thought. And, as long as he succeeded in achieving results, he totally ignored anything contrarian to his designs. The drawback was the undercurrent of criticism constantly afloat at Boston University School of Graduate Dentistry. Ultimately, the atmosphere deteriorated to some degree of intolerable, ill-spirited gossiping and side talking.

But, this was probably no different in life with other large undertakings. Camps of alignment and rallying around divided leadership is an inevitable manifestation of human nature. Newness brings excitement, but it also incites the unexpected and the competitive juices. There is no doubt this played a large role during the ten years that events played out: the planning, the building, the growing and the growing pains, the great successes that evolved, and finally the transition to Henry's retirement and passing. History records the good and bad, the successes and failures, and ultimately sustainability. What Henry engineered was so transformational that it has grown, perhaps with the new growth that seasons bring as different people will come along to cultivate their own ideas and ambitions. This is the nature of human nature. But, at the core are the workings of Henry's model creation that has sustained the test of time, and will continue to grow and sustain.

CHAPTER 4

Boston's Academic Environment

At the time Henry Goldman sought funding for his new school, there were already two schools, The Harvard School of Dental Medicine and Tufts University School of Dental Medicine. They were well entrenched and had ongoing, lofty reputations. Harvard was a very small institution with about a dozen students per each of the four years. Its curriculum was heavily weighted toward research investigation, though providing a modicum of clinical training. Tufts had about a hundred and fifty per class and was expanding. Very simply, Tufts had the reputation as a clinical institution which prepared the future everyday private practitioner. Some graduates went on to serve in the military, some did a year residency at some hospital across the nation, and some went on to specialize. But, the preponderance went on to assume a position as general practitioners within their newly established offices or as an associate with an existing older practitioner. Most went to big city areas or to metropolitan suburban locales where the quality of lifestyle was wealth appropriate for the aspirations of a young unmarried person or existing family. Very, very few went to either limited settled or almost totally unsettled, remote areas of the country. Conversely, some graduates sought out post-doctoral programs for research training in specific areas of study. But, of course, a few went on in the more conventional routes of private practice whether as a general practitioner or clinically trained specialist from a known established program. That being said, what was Henry's motivation? Was it a purposeful self-centered calculation? Was it a move away from the establishment? Or, was there a unique anticipation for adjustment to the way dentistry was changing, and this was the direction he felt it should proceed? And, if so, how could he pull this off in a city with old, established thinking and tethered instinctively to its colonial roots?

Henry had a unique style, very laconic and deliberate. He believed strongly in the old adage of not believing what he heard and only half (if that) of what he saw.[25] There was a comfortable skepticism in his outlook. As he gathered himself, composing his mission, and breaking out his plans for a new school with a very different purpose, he was able to depend on two very crucial ingredients: the business acumen of his older brother, and, the intimate social contacts of philanthropic people in the Boston metropolitan community upon whom his brother could entreat financial support. This was genuinely critical because Boston had to be convinced there was a need to fulfill. Thinking could be re-directed, but resources were fundamental to this imposing effort. But, Henry had the right idea, convincingly on target. He was not going to reinvent the wheel, he was going to carry dentistry into a recrudescence. Advancing the specialties clearly to integrate scientific method into clinical training. To him the ongoing model of educating the community dentist was old-guard, doctrinaire, and certainly inflexibly tied to outdated science. The changes needed would perhaps make a lot of people look in askance, probably bewilderment. But, he would never feel compelled to look over his shoulders. His would never feel shy in his peremptory endeavor. His approach was to alter the tide of the academic communities settled comfortably into professional complacency. To be successful he knew inscrutably this was doable, yet demanding. So, his thought was to sidestep the establishment and to make an end-around run past this with a new, enlightened approach.

His background training in Oral/General Pathology and Oral/Internal Medicine during WWII made him acutely sensitive to the drawbacks in dental education. If Dentistry was to assume a much more responsible and integrated role in the treatment of "the whole

---

[25] Author's personal communications.

patient", then the profession could not remain complacent, seemingly embalmed in a permanent state of academic torpor. The profession was still wallowing in the hangover of the old "barber surgeon" reputation without any societal respect other than its position as a refuge of last resort for the treatment of pain. Essentially, nothing more, nothing but. Henry was not a philosophical man in any respect, but he knew with great foresight that this conundrum was both a vacuum to be filled, and, the effort was going to be weighty, prodigious and perhaps insufferable. In order to take a position within the academic medical community, the profession had to be retooled from the inside out. Just resurfacing its image would not work. And so he aimed to reformat the curriculum in a way that the biomedical sciences would become the inherent training platform for dentistry. This concept was the forerunner of evidence-based scientific inquiry and practice as it is known today. Henry was never the kind of man who could or would use promotional terminology as the basis of a thought process or developmental technology. His education in the arts was minimalist so that his creativity and inspiration for conceptual thought was extremely self-limited. Yet, his ideas and motivations were both inspirational and purposive. The frosting on the cake conveyed very little in his mind if the cake was baked without sugar. One way or the other he was going to get from point A to point B with as little notice and disturbance as possible. His personality was right for the times in which he lived, and would have amped up the tempo of change in any other historical period.

The Boston community exuded a very confident air which appeared self-serving and often bled extreme arrogance. Presumably like most eastern seaboard cities, New York especially. But Boston was very different because of its pint sized physical dimension. Everything Boston could boast New York had in numbers. It made Bostonians very defensive and overbearing in their demand for recognition. The advantage of size, however, was not necessarily a virtue because it was fortuitous to be a big fish in a small pond rather than the converse. Size, however, allowed for someone to run and hide when publically embarrassed or exposed. Not in Boston.

The social and political milieu into which Henry competed was a contradiction of enormous proportion. New York could outdo Boston every single day of the week by exercising its imposing and splashy bounty of magnificent buildings, parks, theaters, hotels, community developments and certainly its population diversity. And, of course, crime in the guise of mafia families gave the city a sinful flare that was a magnet for books, movies and very public trials. Yet, Boston's little enigmas were vastly more significant because the city was so small that it was like a kettle of fish in which the really bad people were not marginalized. They were ever present affecting sound business could not avoid the large net thrown over everyone by organized crime. In what other city could the President of the Massachusetts Senate be connected directly to a true crime impresario by virtue of being his brother. But, actually being more corrupt by virtue of his legislative manipulations in stashing money in his pocket, he grew his power base, and compelled business, finance and political favors to pass through him. His brother's sins were a travesty and covered many years as he ripped through the lives of families with his mayhem and murder. But, the President of the Massachusetts Senate, William Bulger, aka "The Corrupt Midget", as Howie Carr[26] (the great journalist of The Boston Herald and hall of fame radio talk show great) made reference for so many years, delivered a slow death to business for many years. He held so many prominent people captive by virtue of his control and position of power. Anything that happened in Boston had his signature all over it. It was into this mix that Henry would find himself when the planning, construction and legal arrangements were evolving and secured. The building of a brand new institution of such size was not a small enough entity not to be touched by a Billy Bulger imprint. The actual location of the school was near to the center of South Boston (aka "Southie") which he and his brother ("Whitey") completely controlled in every conceivable life force known to man. New York had its "Five Families" with its grandiosity spreading its celebrity over its vast

---

[26] Carr, Howie: *THE BROTHERS BULGER: How They Terrorized And Corrupted Boston For A Quarter Century,* Copyright 2006, Warner Books.

boroughs for many, many years. But, Boston, a little city, had "a little man" headlining The Boston Globe front page for so many years that his presence drew significant meaning from his legislative power and influence. His tentacles extended everywhere that his greed manifested by his devastating influence peddling into construction contracts with kickbacks and favored company status to his special insiders. This went on for years and does not even begin to cover his rapacious assault on the city's business community. His clarion call was his eloquent public presentations to the legislative body and many public news conferences and speeches. He could turn a word with a snarky, sinister expression with his highly articulate, vocal manner. It was mesmerizing because he had style in a very jocular way. The force of his bellow belied his diminutive size. However, in time not even this could alter the fact that he was every bit how Howie Carr depicted him, a public crook. Even for people who read newspapers and viewed him from a distance, it was obvious that he had his grip on most of all business in a most voracious, insatiable style. His very classy appearance belied his very declasse being. Nevertheless, if business had to be done, his presence always hovered to be recognized because he had such an onerous effect on bankers, business moguls, and, yes, even trades people. Even the future of Boston University had to be aware of his stamp of approval. The city was fortunate to see him disappear even if it meant being President of the University of Massachusetts for a while (which should speak for his influence if he could wrest that job from genuinely talented candidates with all his ignoble behavior for so long)[27].

In spite of its seedy political underbelly, the city became known as a mecca of great universities, cultural attractions, and its great colonial history. Certainly the city of Philadelphia in many ways mirrored many of the same characteristics, but, like New York, with a magnitude far greater than Boston. Just to walk from one side of Boston would not take more than a half to three quarters of an hour at a normal pace. Maybe this does not seem pertinent, but in this space the Museum of Fine Arts, the Boston Science Museum, the great pre-Broadway Theaters (The

---

[27] Ibid.

Colonial and The Shubert), the Boston Commons, Faneuil Hall, and Bunker (Breeds) Hill stood very prominently amidst its great communities, universities and numbers of cultural attractions. All these in a comparatively small territorial swathe of the city.

In Henry's day there was definitely a holier-than-thou flare that predominated. A psychologist might offer the "small city syndrome" like "the Napoleon complex" for the diminutive people set. And, to a certain degree, there is a measure of truth because of the arrogance which sprouted from the likes of Harvard and M.I.T., the theaters along with Boston Globe theater critics which mercilessly determined which pre-Broadway shows survived them and could financially go on to open in New York, or its plethora of avant-garde literary greats (Harvard's George Santayana, Henry Thoreau, William Dean Howells, and many others), its lineage of aristocratic Governors (William Bradford, Leverett A. Saltonstall, and Henry Cabot Lodge, Jr.), and many other models of Boston colonial history. Its smallness never bred mediocrity, but it certainly illuminated its complexities and strange ironies with a focus that its newspapers and television-radio media feasted on.[28]

As a messenger for educational change, Henry was in the right city. But, he immediately fell into its business-cultural maelstrom that made its politics not only impossible to avert but a reality that was necessary to negotiate and embrace. Henry had a prolonged learning curve because of a blend of naivete and inexperience. His wakeup call was his exposure to the corruption side of construction and labor union political alliances. His brother gave him a quick review of relevant expectations. Adjusting to this got his hackles and dander up, and he never relented with the negative feeling of disgust he contained for the adverse favoritism and "brotherhood" connections which affected the speed of getting the school up and ready. Gradually, he accepted the reality. Once he did, his tone was appreciably decreased and his sense of purpose more focused. Between regulations, lawyers, architects, builders and commercial developers, Henry suddenly found himself

---

[28] Allison, Robert: *A Short History of Boston (Short Histories)*, Copyright 2004, Commonwealth Editions, Paperback.

in a world that was both an anathema as well as an inspiration all in one confusing feeling. However, as a city that was known for its lofty educational standards, this was the right time and place for Henry's unexpected innovation.

The Boston dental educational system abounded in this ethos. Certainly traditional and overwhelmingly inbred, it was not going to be resilient enough to bend in the name of change. Tufts was certainly the more mainstream of the two existing schools. Harvard possessed a sense of self in lock step with the rest of the university. It could be more appropriately described as "noblesse oblige", the king of the mountain self-image within a sense of community. Its reputation was more manicured by being a part of the overall excellence of all the other departments within the university system so that it never had to stand alone on its own financially or educationally. It was very small with an emphasis on laboratory and clinical research. Tufts, by contrast, was very large and its curriculum was weighted almost totally directed toward clinical technique training. The manifest differences between the two schools were major.

Without imposing on either institution, it was natural for a man like Henry Goldman to step into this environment and carve out his own niche. Maybe the country was ready for him to take the recognized dental specialties and put them under one roof? And, to develop and upgrade some of the less traditional sciences which supported and rounded out the training programs. For example, Oral Biology, a grass-roots science, provided residents remedial insight into molecular based biosciences. In general, this exhausted their patience because most did not easily sashay up to tendentious theories which diverted their focus away from more time devoted to clinical training.

The idea was revolutionary as a concept if it could be financially effectuated. Anything new, however, did not occur without its naysayers, particularly in a city like Boston which was so "big" and yet so "small". The prevailing feeling was that things were operating without issue so why upset the natural flow. But, Henry's perception was that it was the right time. The conventional wisdom did not run in synch with his, but he was singularly of one mind and purpose. In a sense, he was a gentle giant because he walked softly and carried a very large, imposing stick. His reputation was out front, and he possessed an understated will to carry out his mission.

Business and professions with an organized, defined purpose enjoyed the good fortune to precede the days of onerous regulatory commissions and bureaucratic layers in the banking system. In this sense, a new idea in America's oldest, most staid city experienced less resistance, particularly when the most connected in financial circles were part of Henry's social milieu. This was an undisputed asset.

Just an aside, organized dentistry in the 1950's was universally in its infancy. Some found it comical to reference the period as its "Stone Age". It was a mechanical art, hardly a sophisticated science. It was respected as a profession only because it no longer produced "The Barber Surgeon" with a tightfisted control over the trembling, victimized patient.[29] The dentist, at least, was no longer a rogue, spiritless pain generating automaton. In this regard, there was a level of compassion, an educated warmth and sensitivity that this professional was bringing to comfort a patient still very much daunted by the unknown, the fear and consequences of what may happen, and certainly the profession's vast historical reputation. This was not an indicator of a permanent, irrevocable character trait, but it was certainly a marker of mischaracterization which beset Henry to overcome old ideas and an almost permanently stained shroud hovering around dentistry with an imposing lock. For it was not this way. Dentistry was no longer a barber craft. It was scientific in outreach, yet still saddled with befuddling popular thoughts harkening to halcyon days of various treatments without anesthesia. And, to boot, in remote areas of the country this stilted sentiment lingers even today. What really made Henry's mind grind was how he could distill the virtues of the profession in such a way as to affix up-to-date methodology. In the reality of such business,

---

[29] Ring, Malvin E.: *Dentistry: An Illustrated History*, Copyright 1992, Harry N. Abrams.

a thespian performance seemed out of place, but was in fact necessary to be quietly assertive in face of a very comfortable status quo.

Henry was prescient because his exposure during WWII to Oral Pathology imbued him with a keen sense and awareness of oral disease being manifestly tied to the systemic health and welfare of the total person. Up to this point in time the mouth was never considered in its potential to reflect any general infection and biologic disturbance in the body. In the 1950's the immune system to a dentist might as well have been the latest turbo charge system for sports cars. What the dentist would come to know is that it was the body's turbo charge system which regulated health and disease in a multifaceted series of connected biological functions. The vitality and quality of life were never even fringe issues considered in the everyday practice of the general dentist. The new thinking seemed time appropriate and fit for Boston. It would be a reformation no different than the Puritans who exported their Calvinist theology to escape the traditions of the Church of England. The city's historical ties were to people like Paul Revere, a dentist-silversmith, such that a watershed period was inescapable. And, although Dentistry was still struggling to emerge as a more sophisticated profession, Henry knew this was the milieu into which he could exercise his thoughts and really throttle change. This was his home, where he was educated, and despite the indisputable "reformation" which augured resistance, he felt comfortable in his quest.[30]

What was this milieu? The personality type of the general dentist was that of an outwardly engaging, socially active, and a person of genuine ethical and moral rectitude. He was generally the pillar of society, the focus of a community's established leadership, and usually trustworthy, dependable, and always convivial. As a representative of a local scientific group of medical personnel serving a community, he was often the person to whom everyone could turn when there was an issue of dental significance. This included not only the lay residents but also the medical internists and specialists. He was also typically

---

[30] Allison, Robert: *A Short History of Boston (Short Histories)*, Copyright 2004, Commonwealth Editions, Paperback.

fully engaged with the local hospital, police and fire departments and other community businesses. And, his presence as a member of the local business associations kept him in touch and an active presence in order to secure their trust and long term respect. On the one hand, he was the source of the local public trust for treating dental problems of every conceivable kind. On the other hand, these circumstances quite often demanded answers far beyond his (female dentists during this period were virtually non-existent) training and capabilities. And, the specialties at that time were limited solely to the local Oral Surgeon to whom the local generalist could refer problems he could not resolve. This obviously led to extractions and often partial or complete tooth loss. Over time this was the road to dental jaw dysfunctional maladies of all dimensions. The coveted local elite of the community shared equally with the blue collar factory worker or others of very pedestrian financial net worth in this oral-facial conundrum. It was this generational pitfall in dental education that Henry viewed as a lingering, yet self-perpetuating deficiency. In general, the everyday practitioner was the caretaker for dental problems which could not be comprehensively addressed. Dentistry at this time was just embarking on the scientific method. The idea that a dental school curriculum would invest a lengthy period of its time to investigate the internal function and behavior of cells was cutting edge. But, this is where change was beginning to stir. From this point to 1963 when Boston University joined the national mix of dental schools, the trade format transformed into the science of dentistry. As a profession it never looked back. Henry would now take it to a new dimension. But, this also meant shaking the indomitable oak that the "dental tree" was and genetically imposing a new makeup so it would seed future generations with advanced qualities. Dentistry was very set in its ways and Henry had to see the challenges to be so inveterate as to be "genetically elemental".

The other issue which stood out very glaringly in the 1950's was the total absence of continuing dental education. He understood very well that graduate school idea would advance research and clinical training. But, it would be necessary to bring the fruit of its labors along "the information highway" to the community dentist. And, so the idea that there could be a forum for the exchange of ideas as the presentation of research and clinical advances would of necessity require central planning and defined arrangements. This was the birth of continuing education in the specialties. The general practitioner was wallowing in education stagnation. As the person to whom the community relied, he was really going in reverse from the day of graduation.

Tooth loss in those days was an expected circumstance, and, although the local dental practitioner was virtually "an extractionist" or "driller, filler and biller" (two very ignominious euphemisms engendered by adventitious social circumstances), the net effect on society was egregious. Aging people looked and functioned with inadequacy and pain, and, young people visibly aged faster as their dentitions deteriorated. Because people lost proper dental-oral function, diets became altered and circumstances contributed to alterations of physical health. Dietary restrictions compromised nutrition and most likely eventuated in a shorter life expectancy. If the general dental practitioner could serve the community with greater impact, dental educational standards had to improve. For Henry, this meant restructuring and fashioning a new approach. The mechanical approach to problem solving the matrix of dental disease was obviously not working and very antiquated. Like trying to get a square peg into a round hole, dental schools were comfortably lost in outdated thinking and teaching. But, in his mind, continuing education would and had to be an extended arm of the institution. His idea was formative in his bringing diet/nutrition ideas to a changing population. With dentistry as mired in its primal past, the practicing dentist could not be left out of the equation.

Where did this leave Henry Goldman? For this man words were wasted on him. He was "a doer". Not much for bluster, he would whittle down in a sentence or two what others would say in legions of words. And, in the 1950's the Boston dental community was a small, but very vocal group. Most professional people in those days would not have committed to the fight Henry would confront. After all, why did Boston have need of change in a profession which was doing very well as it existed "thank you very much"! As pointed out, in the arts and sciences, it was a city full of itself. The image cast to the rest of the country was that of a center where ideas evolved and material change was embraced.

The educational institutions were viewed with similar sensibilities because they were authoritative, innovative and vanguards of change. They were modeled on the concept of great organizations uniquely skilled to produce a unique set of results because of their always advancing set of standards. This was the inherent image cast upon a public who took notice over and over, from one generation to the next. Believing their own press clippings, leadership across the board did not allow for openness when considering other areas of the country for their possible creativity and impact. Boston, no doubt, was an educational hub in medicine and dentistry, but in dentistry was closed to change. And, it would reject criticism. To some degree this was understandable in that the wounds of WWII were still raw and the watershed 1950s were subject to social forces in the established northeast cities which threatened institutional thinking. Organized dentistry was very comfortable and the traditions were emotionally acceptable. Henry did not have the patience to reason conceptually the idea and need for a paradigm shift. It was not his style, and he certainly did not have the desire for a public forum. He would proceed at his own pace and with no thought of relenting in the face of tremendous institutional obstacles.

The Boston dental community in the 1950s was pretty much standard as it reflected the rest of the country in the way dentistry was practiced. Yes, it was a center in reputation and opportunity. But, what it did not have was a man of Henry's breadth in training and education. The field of "Periodontia" (143) was beginning to take hold as early as the first part of the twentieth century. It was part of a change in thinking that the saving of teeth was a dynamic without which the treatment of teeth at a rudimentary mechanical level was of diminishing value. Even the likes of Horace Hayden understood this as early as the very early 19th century. (69,100) No matter how well teeth could be restored, they would not survive in a biologically diseased support foundation. In that respect, some of the early pioneers of this new field were the earliest proponents and teachers of the "art of scaling" teeth to preserve them in health and function. They learned that inflammation of supporting tissues around teeth would ultimately determine their survival, but the precise answers would not come for many years. Viewpoints were rudimentary at an anecdotal level. However, this was only one piece of the puzzle. And, this is where Henry Goldman stepped into the picture and would make his mark. Although there were substantive ideas beginning to embolden as a result of articles and early textbook publications on the role of supporting structures of teeth, Henry understood that this shift was not the entire picture. Boston at this time was most influential in propagating the importance of a healthy periodontium (the supporting apparatus of teeth) because Tufts had one of the early pioneer leaders in the field of "Periodontia". As mentioned, he was Dr. Irving Glickman. (205) His leadership and superior direction was extremely important because his character allowed him to invoke and disseminate an importance to the field that Henry could not. Irving as noted was arrogant, brash, opinionated and universally disparaged as condescending. He had a reputation for being tyrannical and deplorably mean to residents under his tutelage. But, he was brilliant, highly motivated and forcibly efficient. His eloquence, even though incomparable for the times, was directed with a venal and often toxic layering of his thoughts. He was highly charged with an abrasive, contentious manner of expression, taking an obvious visible and cynical pride in the public embarrassment of his peers. He more than possessed ability along with an insatiable hubris. Some of his public displays of rowdy behavior were very upsetting. But, he was more than able to expound and absolutely articulate on resounding scientific concepts, rhapsodically effusing on cutting edge research models and clinical methodologies. Irving could acquit himself in this public arena far better than Henry. And, this was the milieu into which Henry would fashion a new academic model the country had not expected or understood. However, as stated, Henry had been treated for childhood stuttering so he did rise up to contend Irving in public. And, even if he did, he probably would have come out the loser. It would have been extremely difficult to contend with an individual who had little care what people thought of him. Most lecturers would have taken Henry's approach because no one in dentistry could debate the likes of this man with the likes of his verbal terror. He lavished in his admonishments as they fed his hunger for public theatrics. But, the world of dentistry was unaware (except for a very few) Henry's verbal skills limited his public presence. Over the years he improved immensely, but he would never be able to handle the likes of an Irving Glickman. The case could also be made why he also demurred to a great extent while he was Dean, not overly noticeable but wherever he could.

To embolden the point, Boston was not unlike any other city in the United States at that time vis a vis dental practice. The characteristic trait of a general practitioner was that of a business entrepreneur, doffing his metaphorical hat to the patients who grew his financial success. And, success was certainly measured by a display of opulence through material gain. It was simple display of their pleasure with a newly acquired lifestyle. Their offices were the domain of a tapestry of exhibited art work, floral arrangements, unique collections of acquired valuables from international travel, and expensive, usually gaudy interior decorating and design throughout. The individual operatories were usually replete with framed certificates and the latest in ergonomically sound dental equipment. This was the image the average general practitioner had cast, an important reflection of his place in society. What was missing, however, was the formulation of a training background for which patients would seek counsel and expect authentic, reliable answers. But, only Henry truly understood this clash of unreasonable expectation with a reasonable education deficit. At that time, patients most likely expected too much of "their" dentist who do it all!

Henry always loved to refer to dental school as a four year conscription to acquire a "union card" membership in the profession.[31] For some reason, he would always laugh quietly when making this reference. He possessed a quiet sense of humor, and, the jocular manner in which he related this compelled him to distill a serious undertone. Realizing

---

[31] Author's personal communication.

the very inertia, the snail-like advances in dental education, he often vocalized a need to rise above it all to breathe change with the effort he knew so well would be necessary. He spoke of this very often. There is no doubt he spirited a unique level of commitment to pursue this with a tenacious attitude and vigor day-in and day-out. His energy and attention to detail went way beyond ego or hubris. Only a very special personality could rise above all the complexities and pressures with the heavy lifting the project would require. This point alone was one of the greatest failings for the profession to understand. While so many great dental educators went on to well-deserved positions in education, there was very little appreciation for what it would take for one man to effect the building of an institution which ultimately lifted the school's prestige within its city and international. This was a feat which is vastly underappreciated. Additionally, he gave so much credibility to those who trained there and eventually expended this lineage to see their own reputations grow robustly.

Henry was deeply bothered by the status of dental education. It was languishing, not progressing. He realized that the practitioners who intrinsically felt compelled to advance their skills and interpretive insights were a minority. Financial success was an aphrodisiac hard to relent. He would shake his head as a measure of his sensibilities and awareness. His perspicacity lingered deep in his soul. He curried favor with a lot of educators in order to reinforce his instincts. His drive and will was his sustenance to persevere.

The typical dental school in the 1950s was still languishing in the cage-like domain as depicted mercilessly of "the butcher" image pain-fully yanking teeth from the gyrating, convulsed victim (beautifully sketched on a famous black and white print). And, the profession has been tirelessly struggling to shed this visual ever since. But, its chosen manner of revising its public reputation has irrefutably conflicted with all the political fanfare surrounding such attempts. Henry stepped away from the sanctimony which made the profession a regressive entity and articulated a whole new dimension for dental education. It would be progressive and cleansing. It would transfuse because it would be a projection of vitality completely out of the box. Rather than an inward assault on a stolid, self-perpetuating system, he would upgrade the existing academic setting by a colloquium of specially trained dentists whose development would be totally centered on "the biology" of disease in every link to the very granular level of evidenced based sciences which affected the mouth in health and disease. To understand Henry's state of mind when it came to dental education, it is necessary to separate him from the state of the profession and the grandiose nature of professional practices which controlled Boston dentistry in the 1950's. This paradigm shift, from "the dental mechanic" to a veritable scientist intellectually groomed with a new sense and feel for probative investigation, was both colossal and resounding for the day. But, Henry was not imbued with self-righteous bombast and self-promotion. He was a very simple, almost self-effacing man with broad shoulders and singular purpose. Totally different than any living dentist of the day, only a man of such self-reliance and sense of resolve could mount and sustain such an unremitting, tireless effort. He was a lone wolf, a war horse type of incredible spirit and moral purpose.

The Boston academic environment for the professions was very different than that of the core university. The essential teaching centered around students with an extremely broad based interest in a myriad of subject matter relating to the arts and basic sciences. The kaleidoscopic nature of cultural diversity drew from an elaborate pantheon of instructors and professors. Their interests were quite varied and often crossed over into combination disciplines. The professions were not comparable in this regard. Most often the faculties were composed of much more linear and one dimensional individuals. The contrast was remarkable because their backgrounds were rarely diverse, and most often tunneled. The individual with training in the arts was a rarity. Usually lost in their scientific worlds, these were people most often confined and limited by their daily commitments. Anything else that would expand their intellectual curiosity was not out of possibility, but it was the exception not the rule. This is not to lay disparagement, it was simply the factual differences between the reality and the dream of every professional school. And, dentistry was the most extreme example of this one dimensional stereotype. (Mind you, there are exceptions to every rule).

Henry cultivated a unique individual for his faculty. All, with the sole exclusion of one person, were full time practitioners in the various specialties. They were all men at this time because women were uniquely absent from the profession. Women gradually entered the dental profession in the latter portion of the mid-1960s. The academic environment was really a composition of successful practicing specialists devoid of formal academic training in education. Their proclivities were groomed by heuristic training with mentors, not by a depth of scientific inquiry fostered over time in training and laboratory-clinical investigation. The 1960s were very different times for teacher training. Advances in methodology were based on anecdotal theories and workable successes in clinical settings. However, the body of practitioners Henry gathered under one umbrella was really "the crème de la crème" for the day. They may not have fulfilled the image of the masterful academics in the various specialties as judged by today's standards, but they were certainly the marquee players of the day. And this subset of standard-bearers were significant for their clinical reputations as well as for their braggadocio and bravado. Suddenly, Henry had a mélange of unique characters who vitalized his newly created institution in many more ways than anticipated. In its sudden appearance on the Boston scene there was something for which to take notice, but over time not always for the right reasons. And, for whatever reason, rivalries developed and entrenched deeply in its fabric. Human nature, being what it was, made for interesting times.

CHAPTER 5

Henry and His Cast of Characters

Several reasons why The Boston University School of Graduate Dentistry emerged with its immediate pre-eminence were the times, the relative innocence of the day, and the leadership qualities of its first faculty. In education, there was still plenty of room for the creative spirit with which Henry sought a paradigm shift toward graduate education in Dentistry. The faculty embraced this spirit with the full thrust of a Sherman tank in the heart of a military attack. Because Henry beamed with relentless energy, his mantra was "don't let me hear it can't be done because I'll show you it can be done"![32] He said this with a wry laugh, but the serious intention was rightfully understood because he always said what he meant, and, meant what he said. He would never ask of someone what he could not do himself. However, be it due to the adventitious presence of so many talented men or the careful scrutiny and planning to ferret out such talented men, Henry did not have to look very far to gather in his embrace a faculty so deep in quality and quantity. They were rising stars with a genuine willingness to assert their sense of pride for the sake of excellence in dental education. Never before, and never after has there been such a gathering of eagles. Henry's challenge was to keep a sense of order and respect for the kind of institutional harmony necessary to foster a reputation for cooperation with its neighboring long term established schools, Tufts

---

[32] Conversations with Henry concerning the ability to get things done with hard work, but never ever giving up!

and Harvard, as it reached out internationally to extend its will to grow its own presence. It was a delicate balance. But, it was done with a flurry of ambitious people who engendered "a wow factor" because of their talents and depth of character. In this regard, Henry was very fortunate. In every instance, this center for specialization flourished with immediacy due to the charisma and social qualities which made these leaders so invaluable and necessary for the success of The Boston University School of Graduate Dentistry. (173)

To the extent that a school of specialization was necessary is very controversial. At the time when Henry started to crystallize this concept specialization in dentistry was in its infancy. And, most dentists merely limited their practices either due to apprenticeships or because they felt comfortable providing one service all the time. A myriad of reasons accounted for this very limited circumstance in the years after WWII. Henry's exposure to Oral Pathology during the war altered his thinking about dental practice. His mentor was Dr. Kurt Thoma, a very well respected and recognized Oral Pathologist and Oral Surgeon with whom he wrote a textbook in Oral Pathology long after his student and graduate level affiliation.[33] This experience made Henry recognize that there was a scientific basis to oral and dental disease. Today dental scientists refer to this as evidence based disease. But, in what can be referred to as the incubation period for change in dental education, Henry recognized that dental education for the specialties had to render a scientific basis in its programming to be creditable. He recognized that teaching techniques had to be supported by animal research at all levels of the integrated disciplines: biochemistry, patho-physiology, genetics, nuclear medicine, electron microscopic applications, etc. Unlike in Europe where clinical research was fairly routine, the United States was limited to animal studies. Nevertheless, Henry understood that opening a school for specialization required a faculty widely versed, amenable to change, and comfortable with this vision.

The difference between what Henry had in mind and what existed

---

[33] Goldman, Henry M. and Thoma, Kurt H.: *Oral Pathology, Fifth Edition,* Copyright 1960, C.V. Mosby Company.

at the time was putting all of these disciplines under one roof and solely relegated to the training of specialists. There was less bureaucracy in the 1950's and fewer cumbersome state and federal regulatory controls. What Henry created in his mind in those post war years would be almost insurmountable today. It could happen, but with much government interference. In 1963 when Henry's dream materialized in its brick and mortar form, many of the federal regulatory agencies and laws did not exist; e.g. HIPPA, OSHA, etc. (174,192) In fact, office surgery was being performed without protocols which governed the use of masks and gloves. This merely demonstrates how much less the scope was for the physical requirements. But, on the other hand, from today's perspective, it should not minimize how difficult an undertaking was Henry's mission. The relative degree of commitment was certainly immense for the day.

Henry was the type of person who would surveil every detail, and would never forget nor overlook a thing as well. He was very organized and thorough. Yet, he could see the large picture and prioritize the important matters. The faculty which ultimately took fold was very much a reflection of his own criteria for leadership, collegiality, and dependability. It did not bother him that there were disparate personality types. It was important that in spite of their differences, they all understood the common good. As it turned out, the group that came on board as full time turned out to be intellectually superior and mutually cohesive. And, they all came to respect Henry's qualities of leadership with the utmost respect. There was never a feeling of self-centeredness despite the sudden sense of authority which came with new positions of leadership. Reflecting upon those early days, it was truly serendipitous how dedicated each became to the welfare and growing respect for the school around the city of Boston. Tufts and Harvard were long established institutions, but, to re-emphasize, Tufts grew very quickly into a teaching center due to the presence of Dr. Irving Glickman. Dr. Glickman was a local Periodontist who ballyhooed intellectually his own sense of self-worth while competing with anyone he could engage. The rising stars of Boston University's new faculty buffered Henry from

Glickman's overwhelming personality. To get along in a very competitive and contentious academic environment like Boston this would turn out to be fortuitous for Henry's long term viability.

Reflecting on this period in the modern historical record, what Henry accomplished was both singular in nature and truly monumental. Greatness cannot simply be defined by the construction of buildings or the expansion of academic centers through the cooperative efforts of politicians and fund raising. This is not to minimize such vigorous feats. But, most are the product of happenstance or synchronicity. Sometimes Deans happen to be present when there are changes within an academic environment that have either been in progress or just seem to be timely during their presence. On the other hand, Henry's was a dream enhanced by his perspicacity. His timing was perfect because he sensed that a colloquium format in graduate education could simulate the classical Greek model. Just as Socrates could peripatetically apply his teaching skills, it took his acolyte, Plato, to establish a center for intellectual exchange among metaphysical philosophers, the Lyceum.[34] To this end, Henry's greatness was his inner sense that the time was appropriate for a center where dental specialists could interrelate during their training. This idea set Henry apart from every other educator before and after him. Boston University represented a unique learning center which spawned the many leaders and teachers worldwide of today. So many of the leaders in dental education today are the progeny in some form from this center. This was a byproduct of the school's success. Certainly not a manifest destiny, but his perceptions and timing resulted in the kind of academic excellence that has been a template for teaching all over the world. His faculty grew a tradition of teaching and learning for today's academicians. Each individual had to grow into a style which was comfortable. Whatever may be said, it was most difficult at the outset because of all the uncertainties and the makeshift physical plant which was so extemporaneous it was fortunate to the faculty faithful to its commitment. The area was highly unattractive,

---

[34] C.D.C. REEVE, Translator and Introduction: PLATO: REPUBLIC, Copyright 2004, Hackett Publishing.

the buildings so old and downtrodden that it was perhaps humorously like an abattoir which couldn't attract flies. But, somehow each faculty member stayed the course, particularly in view of the fact that Henry had nothing to sell but an idea. In some way, it can be wondered what anyone was thinking?

The shining star and Henry's greatest academic find was Dr. Morris P. Ruben. All members of the faculty were justifiably noteworthy. However, Morris Ruben contributed to the needs of the school in ways no other faculty member could. He had a basic science background that allowed him to converse sensibly and authentically at the biological grassroots in the fields of Periodontology and Oral Biology. He was the most au courant and indefatigable. He could lecture and teach with fluency in subject matter no one else could. He was like a wind-up doll. He got into the interstitial depths of subject matter with a memory bank that was unlike anyone else. He was like a mystic with a high caliber mouthpiece. He was a lucky find because Henry did not realize at the time that Morris was endowed with such abilities. In fact, at times Morris was so incredibly blessed by such a surfeit of basic science knowledge that he could lecture effusively for hours without interruption. All residents would mock him for his uncanny style, but gradually they recognized him for his matchless insights and recall of facts.

Morris Ruben could never be compared with the rest of the faculty because he was unique across all academic circles around the country. He soon developed a national reputation for his wonderful skill in relating very dry science with noteworthy and balanced detail. He possessed profound sensitivity and was most approachable. No question was ever too simple or complicated for him to answer. He never admonished anyone in public, He was a gentleman, made his effortless, gracious nature abound. He covered subject matter with incredible clarity and fluidity. If interrupted by a question, he could pause for a very insightful and useful answer and then continue without losing a beat. He had a wonderful background in laboratory, nuclear, and electron microscopic sciences which were relevant to the clinical specialty training programs. His multi-dimensional qualities made him a fortunate find. It is very difficult to imagine what Henry would have done had Morris not come his way. Anyone who matriculated through the various programs knows exactly this statement of fact. What this man lacked in clinical acumen he more than made up in bare bones scientific knowledge. His gift was giving of his abilities for so many years to so many residents.

Henry was very grateful for Morris Ruben, at many levels. Morris was very retiring by nature, respectful, always conciliatory, socially a true and pleasant gentleman. He was a moderately built man, average height and stocky, but certainly not corpulent. Balding, fair skinned and very poor eyes so that his glasses close up appeared of very high magnification. He was not a fancy dresser by any means. He appeared very average, like a typical Midwestern high school teacher. This exterior appearance quickly evaporated from one's mind the minute he started to lecture. He was in a league of his own.

No one else on the faculty could be as autonomous because he was simply irreplaceable. His capacious knowledge base ran so broad with his recall of evidence based research protocols he could lecture without notes. He was never doctrinaire, and reasoned with the ability to understand and accept opposing views and opinions. Extremely open-minded and enlightened, he was the educator among great teachers. His lectures at seven thirty on a cold winter's morning could be soporific, but he managed to hold everyone's attention. Everyone knew how far better they were for this experience.

His docile and quiet personality masked his profound insights and very significant ability to cover subject matter in a most orderly manner. He was never overwhelming and had a pleasant sense of humor. Because he was so grounded, his appeal was universal. He took very controversial and sensitive subject matter and presented it with a venerable style that became his mantra. In fact, he often contrasted to other faculty members whose sophistry often covered for subject matter deficiency. Morris never offered opinions he could not support, but he was always careful to never diminish another for sake of his own ego.

What was his role at the school? He was like the utility infielder on a professional baseball team. He could "play" any position, and do it with an inspiring facility to capture everyone's steadfast attention. By the time most residents got to this level of training, they had been exposed to what seemed like an endless procession of teachers, lectures and other assorted representatives of the scientific community. But, no one ever impressed like Morris Ruben. Residents would shake their heads because of his undaunted ability to make them feel arcane subject matter was important to learn. He possessed a calm personal style that made everybody around him feel good about themselves. He was never demagogic, and his pleasing manner infectious. There were people who were put off by him, and insulted by his way-out presentations. To them he was a bore, dabbling in the abstruse, featuring data of impractical value, and skirting the important clinical material for which they squirmed in their seats anxiously awaiting without satisfaction. But, these were the younger residents who hadn't matured enough to witness the legions of historical related material they could enjoy, possibly utilize when it came time for board certification, or simply round out their graduate education. As a side, some were so sanctimonious that their counter-intuitive judgments made them seem "certifiably bored" From a practical point of view, he would never appeal to anyone with a very jejune approach to what was really a very sophisticated training program. The truth of the matter is that Morris was the only one capable of relating such cogent information, let alone in such a well-outlined fashion. But, it took a very sentient, appreciative person to engage his unique sagacity.

Like everyone on the faculty, Morris shared an unswerving, genuine sense of awe for Henry's creativity and bold leadership. He understood Henry's background like no one else. Most people considered Henry a clinical Periodontist who had authored some of the early literature and a number of textbooks. But, Morris knew better. He understood that Henry was a formidable Oral Pathologist with an extensive background in General Pathology. There was absolutely no one on the faculty who matched Henry's extensive training and background. Morris was keenly aware of this so his respect for Henry was quite profound. He may not have come close to Morris's elegant use of language, but there was not a whit of technical science information missing in Henry's toolbox.

Morris also understood very well that nobody but Henry Goldman had the ability to make an idea come into being as a brick and mortar entity as expeditiously as Henry did. He was sensitive enough to accept such a development with a narrow minded, passing happenstance. The stakes were far too high and being present early on, he experienced the evolution of the whole process as it materialized. It had Henry's imprimatur all over, from the adoption of old, rundown brownstone buildings in a dilapidated Boston neighborhood to the building that exists today. Morris, save for the other older, transitional early faculty members, was the only one around all the time to be witness to the progressive material changes. In this sense, he gleaned a sense of the future about which others might have been somewhat refractory, especially expecting more of a glamorous endpoint hasten. At that point, there was barely anything but the semblance of a skeevy neighborhood which hardly portended a bright future. Morris, however, was committed to a person, not an idea. He got it loud and clear. His intuition exceeded most everyone else. He had the talent to find a home in any other dental institution where his presence would have been coveted. He did not need the quick fix, the immediacy of established, ongoing success. He understood Henry and had an indelible faith in him.

When Morris started teaching, his concentration was limited to the basic sciences related to basic scientific investigation studies. Through his understanding and ability to develop animal experiments for topical issues and study, he integrated them into the graduate master's degree program. And, this eventually evolved into a full-fledged program in Oral Biology. He became most proficient in the fields of Oral Medicine and Oral Biology. It would be interesting to speculate where Boston University might have been without Morris Ruben? Certainly, no one is completely indispensable, but the twists and turns would certainly have been less predictable and finite. Morris gave Henry the certainty and confidence so he could divert his attention to other issues requiring his undivided attention. He had no idea if Morris would work out, but he readily began to count his blessings as he came to realize how invaluable he was.

Across the landscape of the country the 1960's were very interesting. Coming out of the very peaceful 1950's, political events really pulled the plug on the trusting, serene nature that was pervasive and seemingly endless. In the year that the school opened, John Fitzgerald Kennedy was assassinated in Dallas on Thursday, November 22, 1963.[35] It seemed to be a watershed moment for this country which retrospectively was certainly a cultural blow of major proportions. Both Henry and Morris were staunch Democrats so that this diverted their attention from the media maelstrom which ensued for a very long time. Henry's poise was undeterred, but he appeared loquacious at times. On the other hand, Morris who was usually quite talkative suddenly became stoic. It was unexpected, yet understandable. The history shows that everything worked out, but the political events stole everyone's attention.

Both Henry and Morris came from most humble circumstances. They dressed always in very plain clothes, no frills or eye-catching suits. In this regard, they markedly contrasted to the surrounding faculty. They set a tone which matched the overall serious nature of the times. It was not planned at all, it was just an interesting take on the way they were. Mindful of their purpose, their personalities seemingly fit the times.

The 1960's were explosive. The times belonged to the Beatles, the TV and Media explosion, industrial and commercial growth, the break out bigtime of sports entertainment, elaborate Broadway shows, the cavalcade of American Bandstand Rock Stars with Dick Clark, [36] the surge in muscle cars manufacturing, the advent of international jet air travel in new full bodied aircraft with head catching appurtenances, the spike in community suburban development (Levittown, Long Island, New York, the suburban neighborhood prototype), and, of course,

---

[35] Holland, Brent: *JFK ASSASSINATION: From the Oval Office to Dealey Plaza*, Copyright 2014, JFK Lancer Productions & Publications, Inc.
[36] Brunson, A.R. *Dick Clark's American Bandstand*, Copyright 1997, Harper Perennial.

The Nuclear Age (and the concomitant institutional research it engendered) which could no longer hold even the most linear personalities unexcited. Even Henry and Morris were forced to come out of their shells and realize the emergence of "a new day" and an altered "frame of reference". The side benefit of growing industrial complex would be federal money for research and development (aka "R&D"). This augured favorably for new advanced degree programs.

Theirs was a very unique relationship. Although both were seemingly indefatigable and extremely regimented, Morris was more relaxed. He did not carry the weight of the world on his shoulders as Henry did. Henry's intellectual reach was very limited, whereas Morris was uniquely expansive. He was most conversant on most subject matter, from Opera to Shakespeare. He was very well read, and very enthusiastic about Symphony and Art. Henry was never formally educated in the social sciences, nor ever exposed to the arts even informally. Therefore, unless his professional position compelled him to make his presence compulsory at any culture related event, he would never voluntarily make an appearance. He was very one dimensional. But, this difference between them was a reflection of their backgrounds. Morris's family was a traditional one in a small, rustic community in Ohio. The family was lower middle class, but his parents supported the idea of general education. They wanted more than the farming communities could provide. Unlike Henry who fortuitously found an educational wizard in the likes of a Kurt Thoma, his educational pursuits were both quite limited and random. Eventually he found a newspaper job at an entry level position. But, Morris had a very high IQ with a natural ability to write. At a local newspaper in Warren, Ohio he honed his skills in investigative journalism, but somehow he was dissatisfied with his lot in life. Eventually, he headed east and found dentistry as a means to a greater sense of independence and perhaps a decent weekly paycheck. But, it was evident that Morris spoke in a very articulate manner and was able to use his newspaper background to script material related to dental research and clinical methodology. This made him immediately an expedient teaching source. For Henry, Morris was heaven sent!

Henry was not fluid in front of a podium so Morris could imme-diately fill so many needs. The relationship was quite symbiotic, and there was a subliminal sense of compatibility that was never questioned nor contested by anyone. Henry indulged him with independence to function at his own speed and mindset He never had invade Morris's private or professional space. It was as if Henry prayed to a parallel di-mension and poof there was the person whose jack of all trades could fill the large need that Henry might have had to fill with three or four people. Here was an all in one special sent from who knows where. There were prolonged periods they never conversed. But, Henry knew he never had to look over his shoulder to check on any missteps. How many Deans would, could, should have prayed for such a dream talent and would be left in a trance of pipe dreaming. An argument could be made that Morris made Boston University in its early days. Case closed. Years later as times changed there was no longer the need for a general utility type. But, for day, it was Manna from a parallel universe. Morris Ruben understood his role perfectly well, and with a profound sense of understanding and commitment. And, because of some concatenation of epigenetics and a DNA proclivity, it ne'er once altered his balanced ego. This may make a few Deans shake their heads in disbelief! It was a glorious relationship most Deans would crave. There was only one Morris Ruben. Over time, in the city of Boston he was almost revered for his incredible cerebral depth and communication skills.

No one knew the pertinent dental-medical literature as Morris Ruben. Some of the facts he could recall were jaw dropping. Morris staggered classes with his unique performances. To witness some of his everyday presentations either left one dazed by his brilliance or in bewilderment as to the kind of exams were in the offing.

The general feeling at that time was no one could be so robust with categorical stores of knowledge readily surfacing in the most spontaneous situations. This ability contrasted with every other faculty member, who, by the way, were all immensely stalwart at the podium. Morris possessed an intellectual depth to match his factual informa-tional base that made his effectiveness contrast conspicuously. This is the role into which Morris was so appropriately slotted. By the time residents found themselves into the clinical portion of their training, they were edgy and frothing out of so much time sitting while listening to Morris Ruben's waxing refrains. To some degree they were all frustrated by the amount of lecture and library time, but, in the end, it served as a meaningful basis that only Morris could provide. Gradually, the very small world of Periodontists got wind of his masterful ability to communicate convoluted scientific theories. Most universities have Morris Ruben types, but it was his authentic journalist background that set him apart.

In social settings Morris demurred from shyness, but he was always a gentleman. He preferred being alone as he was very uneasy with small talk. He easily managed a casual smile and a pleasant greeting. Yet, he was a man of deep feeling and responded vigorously to a meaningful question with a very opinionated and impassioned by the back-and-forth. Never relinquishing his newspaper background, he would shine and exude very visceral feelings when the dialogue hit a nerve and boosted his interest. As Thomas Jefferson expressed in his editing of "The Declaration of Independence" about "the felicity of expression", Morris possessed this eye-catching ability.[37] When Henry became editor of The Journal of Periodontology, he editorialized most of the articles.

So, with all that said, it is very hard to overestimate Morris Ruben's net worth at a time when Henry was in serious need for such a person with his readily available skills. Nothing about his presence went unnoticed. He was certainly not a background figurine. His presence was frothy and lively because he was "the jack-of-all trades", but the master of oh so many! He personified a unique greatness that has to be etched in the memory of the school. So many of the more glamor types have been immortalized, but this is the person whose face would and should be on the BUSGD Mount Rushmore. He brought the kind of support that went way beyond the financial, the brick and mortar, and the marketing. Henry was loath to ever express his inner feelings,

---

[37] Meacham, Jon: *Thomas Jefferson, The Art of Power,* Copyright 2013, Random House Trade Paperbacks.

but how he must have inwardly sighed a sense of relief. And, the other faculty, though would never ever come forth were keenly aware of the enormous void he filled. There is no doubt he was the eight hundred pound gorilla in the room!

Beyond Morris Ruben came the legendary cast of characters who came as unknowns and departed as demigods, inspirations destined for dental immortality!

What emerged in the selection process was a Chairman for each specialty with a full time academic appointment to Boston University. Most were able to retain a full time clinical practice. The manner in which each arranged the time differential between school and practice was left to each. It was a tidy construct rooted in the trust that the primary responsibility was to the school. But frankly there was no other way. The resources were not available for all full time chairmen. For the most part, each department chairman hired numbers of unpaid part time clinicians to fill the need for clinical training. Each department had its own defined budget so this ability to draw from the outside standardized the teaching schedules for each department. It also gave each resident exposure to the differences in the way clinicians ran their individual offices and how they managed practical daily issues. This was always a "teaching moment". Residents developed close relationships which endured for years. Because the salaries for a Chairman were far below what each could generate in private practice, it worked for the times. This standard no longer exists in the way Chairpersons are hired. Today they are full time with all the benefits negotiated in a contractual agreement.

These Chairmen really had nothing to lose. If, for whatever reason, the plan failed, they could all fall back on their established practices. On the other hand, it was the opportunity of a lifetime for those that took on the responsibility. A new graduate school provided all kinds of possibilities. The men who finally acceded to their respective positions were people who acquitted themselves with the highest clinical expertise and very high academic insight. They differed only in personality, but they worked cohesively in integrating the school into Boston's dental educational environment. Being already established in private practice was one thing, but now they had to integrate into an academic environment. This presented a whole new "kettle of fish". The rivalries in academia could be punishing.

It is not surprising that this new venture performed so well. Wherein Morris Ruben provided the substance, these men gave the school pizzazz. They were all unique, measured by their individual personality styles. And, that is an understatement. Always well dressed in a manner equal to the latest styles of dress, typically coiffed from an up-scaled salon, always well-shaven with a redolent scent of a known fragrance, and eye-catching, well-polished leather shoes of noted quality like Bostonian or Johnston & Murphy. Their public personae were always memorable. Boy did they ever contrast to the very pedestrian appearance of Henry and Morris. Henry and Morris carried on without fanfare, but these men almost slobbered in their festooned manner of dress. It was show time! It was merciful that their peacock imagery was only superseded by their intellectual distinction.

Supporting their very clean, impressive look were oratorically well organized presentations. Their lectures were usually performances of often theatrical genius. Some who tired of their thespian styles thought some were a bit schmaltzy. But, they were fundamentally expert clinicians.

They were driven and detailed to the extreme. They all developed a dedicated, loyal following over time because dentists understood, perceived and respected their love of patient care. They taught with a sense of earnest and caring purpose. Often controversial, but never boring, they might appear bumptious to some extent, but it was not borne out of self-centeredness. Their very high standards of practice and teaching were noticeable. To most observers they had it all. Their reputations became so widespread that they were always sought out for speaking engagements and teaching clinics at conferences and continuing education programs. They very quickly put Boston University on the map. There was a quickly developing cachet for which the school was becoming known. This resulted in its appeal worldwide drawing residents-in-training from countries around the world. Boston soon became a Pantheon of teaching excellence because of Tufts, Harvard, and now the new "school on the block", Boston University. For a period between 1963 and 1977, the city's well-deserved reputation for a place to be for dental education was well earned. Boston University's faculty significantly contributed to this exclusivity due to its imposing personalities.

What kind of individuals were they? They were avant-garde, highly intellectual, quite conversant on many subjects, relentlessly enthusiastic, and energetic (almost to a fault). On a personal level, they were mostly affable and talkative. For people without any basic credentials in basic education they excelled in all phases of teaching.

Because it was a graduate program in dentistry motivation for residents was not a factor. They readily understood why they were there. Some had come right out of dental school, but most had either been in general practice or were in one of the military services. Foreign dentists were attracted for other reasons. But, as the faculty's reputation expanded into many other countries, their numbers significantly increased. Word of mouth and the connections made by this faculty resulted in worldwide exposure. Henry was already a recognized educator so the faculty followed his lead. Egos played into their behavior on the world scene, no doubt. The drive to sell themselves was ever present because honoraria, once the forbidden fruit, grew in size and frequency. Nevertheless, as they grew in stature so did the school as well. It was certainly a symbiosis par excellence!

Before this period in dental education the advancement of ideas in research was very limited. Most were anecdotal or based on animal studies which were hard to project to the clinical level. However, during this period, continuing education programs started on a very restricted scope. It grew through the 1970's, but really exploded through the 1980's and 1990's to where today it is commonplace and replete with subject matter ranging in tandem with the technology explosion. Schools had found a cash cow to support its financial needs as well as their fund raising programs. The Boston University faculty that came into being early on markedly drew from this as opportunity to expand their own reputations, but always in behalf of the school and its growing range of teaching. They were sufficiently charismatic to quickly find their niche and become impactful. Their lecturing and clinical course teaching fees grew with such significance that their supplemental income made them extremely well off. This was the unique opportunity that Henry provided. In addition to offering this faculty to serve as agents for the school's mission, he also provided a stage for them to "sell" their skills and "grow" their own professional recognition. In any walk of business this is what the free market offers. Yes, it was fortuitous for these men being at the right place at the right time. But (a "Big But") credit Henry for the direction he provided and for the courage of his convictions.

The clinicians who framed these pioneering years were: Donald Booth, Anthony A. Gianelly, Herbert I. Margolis, Bernard S. Chaikin, Gerald M. Kramer, Herbert Schilder, Spencer Frankl, and Donald Mori. Others followed as the discourse will show. These were Chairmen of the following departments: Oral Surgery, Orthodontics, Periodontology, Endodontics, Pediatric Dentistry, and Prosthodontics. Henry was the original chairman of Oral Pathology. Dental Public health, though a recognized specialty did not have a permanent chairman at the outset. Oral Biology (which at Boston University was inclusive of Oral Medicine and Oral Diagnosis) and Oral Diagnosis (at that time Oral Diagnosis incorporated Oral Radiology) were informally part of the Boston University program layout. Implantology was not a clinical factor in those days as there was no formal department. It loosely fell to Periodontolgy and Prosthodontics to parcel out any teaching clinical learning cases. But, a didactic format had not yet been programmed into the teaching schedule. In addition, the early cases were blade implants as root forms were not yet being marketed in the United States. Oral Medicine was a factor in teaching because of Henry's emphasis. As a result, both he and Morris Ruben provided all the lectures. Gradually Dr. Melvyn Harris, an Oral Surgeon in clinical practice, came on the scene contributing both in Oral Surgery and Oral Pathology (particularly reading the biopsies out of the school's biopsy service). And, he became the pro tempore Chairman of Oral Surgery for a very short time between Dr. Kurt Thoma and Dr. Donald Booth. Of the original faculty, these are the only surviving linkage to the past, with Don Booth the only full time original faculty member living (in retirement). But, Dr. Harris's contributions were extensive, eventually becoming one of the most eloquent lecturers on the teaching staff. This composed the original faculty who made the school's worldwide reputation noteworthy and memorable. They were all defined by excellence in teaching, superb clinical skills, thoughtful and provocative scientific inquiry and formidable international leadership. Many of the noted academicians and clinical investigators of today evolved from this primary teaching tree.

Each one of these chairpersons rounded up the support of many local practicing specialists practicing within the outlying areas. They contributed their time gratuitously to the teaching support of all the specialties. This is a continued arrangement which still exists. But for the absence of this necessary disposition throughout all dental schools in the country there would be a severe teaching shortage. In so many ways this both enhanced and detracted from the entire teaching process as a noticeable pedigree developed in terms of the thinking, mode of practice, and allegiances which became attached to this group of leaders. In many ways, it was an intensive indoctrination to a way of professional practice ideology. Loyalties were enhanced because of the charisma and uniquely overpowering influence these men cast under their own umbrella of viewing, interpreting and solidifying the thinking of the day. It was certainly not pure brainwashing, but it was most definitely crafted like followers of a specific line of belief and philosophy of practice. This became an umbrella under which Boston University defined its reputation as the influence of this faculty grew and matured its belief system over time. As the number of residents from around the world matriculated through, the breadth of the school's influence became expansive and solidified.

The Department of Periodontology gathered the most attention at the outset because Henry, being the school's founder, was a practicing Periodontist. Despite the fact that he made his primary contributions in Oral Pathology, Periodontics defined his place in dentistry within the school's community of teaching specialists as well as within the city of Boston and the other two dental institutions. In truth, he was really the quintessential Stomatologist, which was a very rare specialist combining Oral Pathology, Oral Medicine and Periodontics as clinical disciplines. Stomatology embraced the management of oral diseases as they are influenced by and relate to overall systemic health. Henry was the only Stomatologist in the country at that time. Even Morris Ruben whose real expertise was in the field of Oral Biology was known as a Periodontist because of his affiliation with Henry and the American Academy of Periodontology, and, as a Diplomate of The American Board of Periodontology. Both Henry and Morris were involved in the dental-medical sciences way beyond for what they were publicly known and recognized. It was all so seemingly esoteric because few in Dentistry were and are so credentialed.

The first Chairman of The Department of Periodontology was Bernard "Chick" S. Chaikin.[38] In 1963 he was already 62 years old. For all intents and purposes, he was already advanced in age by standards of the day. However, he lived to 94 and so retrospectively he still had a third of his life remaining when he assumed the Chairmanship. He was a very charming, kindly man on the exterior, but inwardly, he was a driven, perfection centered man in seemingly perpetual motion. He was bright, extremely talented, multifaceted, and very opinionated. He had so many hobbies, the most favored being his penchant for his marvelous silver creations. Like Paul Revere, "Chick" Chaikin was a wonderful craftsman of so many objects of art from silver. In a day when this was a well- known area of creativity for many Boston artists, his works were splendid and impressive. Like his imposing works of silver art reflected a love and dedication likewise was his professional life. As a Periodontist he was detailed and creative. But, he was also very demanding and could be very critical and intolerant of mediocrity or a difference of opinion. He was so quick in the way

---

[38] Bernard S. Chaikin, aka *"Chick"*: "Chick" was his moniker: Author played golf many times with he and his son, Richard (former staff at BUSGD).

he gathered facts and then translated them to patient management. He was loath to tolerate others with slow or a more pensive reaction time with less zip for rapid interpretation. It was difficult to keep up with him and he was frequently annoyed with either slow reaction time or indifference. However, in spite of this trait, he was sharp, method driven, and sincere with others. He was not a nurturing type to slow walk residents. His nature was more suited to refine, to round out the sharp corners and rough edges of a resident who already was well beyond the fundamentals. Like Henry, he was not one to command the attention of an audience because his lecturing skills were not the focus of his concern. But, both could be very effective in a small group or a one-on-one teaching opportunity. "Chick" Chaikin was cheery and very contrite, but he could get very impassioned with criticism or outright remonstration if he detected lack of concern or laziness. He was quick to remediate these situations with immediacy. He was also considerably older that the other faculty when he took over the chairmanship of Periodontology (except for Herbert Margolis, Chairman of the Orthodontics Department). But, Henry's choice of Dr. Bernard Chaikin was rooted in his respect for his clinical excellence over a very long time in the early days. He was a pioneer and gave the Department immediate cachet and bearing. He came to Boston University with professional history and credibility.

Bernard Chaikin, aka "Chick", was the epitome of a gentleman's gentleman. He was an incredibly well-rounded individual demonstrating the same remarkable enthusiasm for everything he did in life. Whether it was teaching, practicing, playing golf (the game he hated to love and loved to hate because it was so elusive), or turning out masterpieces of silver creations, he was precise and demanding of excellence. He was at Boston University for five years. In bringing "Chic" Chaikin over to Boston University, Henry was presenting an established Periodontist of reputed leadership qualities in both clinical teaching and practice. He was a very important addition to complement the academic-research skills of Morris Ruben. His only drawback was his fitful quickness. But, he was very exacting and he did not mince words. It could make people around him a bit uneasy because he did not waste his energies on marginal, inconsequential issues. Keeping his attention demanded alacrity and precision. But, he was an extremely outgoing and very socially charming.

Under Chaikin's leadership, the Department of Periodontology achieved credibility because of his stellar local reputation and impeccable recognition nationally among the elite teaching institutions. He was a known quantity. He was established in clinical practice and teaching, tethering his established and affirmed qualities at a time most needed for Boston University. Maybe it can be said that his brief tenure was timely and mutually beneficial. He was an honest and trustworthy man.

Harvard had Dr. Paul Goldhaber, Dean and, like Henry, a recognized Periodontist. (172) Tufts had (as noted) a chairman in Dr. Irving Glickman who was very mercurial, unrestrained, and always a controversial personality. Chaikin was a fastidious, highly refined type and stood as a polar opposite. Irving Glickman was an entertaining, wordy but eloquent public speaker. A buffoon, stooped and corpulent as he stood, he veiled his position as an educator with his very harsh public displays. He garnered an international reputation through some very enlightening research in Temporomandibular Dysfunction and Diabetes research. Both were compelling and very significant for the times.. As noted, for years the country took delight in the ponderous Glickman versus Goldman rivalry. It was so truculent and consequential for a very long time, but its energy was sustained for a very long time because of "Glickie",[39] not Henry. It gave the world of dentistry something to throw around. Therefore, Chaikin, in his role to lead Boston University through these early years was the perfect choice, particularly for a contrasting high-class and refined demeanor.

Boston was so small that gossip was like a nanoparticle ricocheting from one school to the other with seemingly the speed within a sub-atomic particle collider. There was a certainty principle in those days that "stories" would travel so unbridled that resentments grew faster

---

[39] Irving "Glickie" Glickman: Former Chairman of Periodontology, Tufts University School of Dental Medicine: "Glickie" was his moniker.

than the truth could untangle the myths between Tufts and Boston University. For whatever reason, Chaikin was able stabilize this atmosphere with a very passive aggressive manner. He was effectively self-confident in a way that he never had to address any of the ridiculous riff which persisted for many years. Henry Goldman and Bernard Chaikin were socially and personally intertwined so there was an unquestioned trust which enabled a very sobering stability against the thrust of merciless commentary which burst from the Tufts' academic inner sanctum. It was most contrarian and laughable in its measurable untruths. The early days became a breeding ground for intrinsic differences over therapy and, over time, vitiated any relationship between the schools except at the most public level. As unfortunate as this was, Chaikin was so stalwart that he was able to keep complete restraint so that this hollow misfortune never interfered with his ability to keep focused on the reality that was Boston University. And, it was hollow and really empty.

The cachet that colorized Bernard Chaikin's nature was his inherent style of dress which contrasted to his very down-to-earth, pleasant, forthright personality. Often in a suit and bow tie with Benjamin Franklin type spectacles, the formality of his appearance betrayed his gregarious smile and unexpected relaxed manner, quite engaging and infectious. He was a very cheery, uplifting man without the quixotic thoughts of greatness that usually inspired most academicians of the day. Like anyone in a lofty teaching position that was measured daily, and especially in Boston, he certainly understood and placed his imprint on establishing an emphasis on clinical training without losing sight of the research literature. The residents who matriculated through the years of his chairmanship became aware of his unqualified academic relevance. He contributed to a noted textbook in "Periodontia" with Drs. Louis Fox[40] of the University of Connecticut and D. Walter Cohen so that his facility with the academic literature and clinical relevance

---

[40] Fox, Lewis: Former Dean of the University of Connecticut, School of Dental Medicine, Farmington, Connecticut; close friend and colleague of Henry M. Goldman.

rendered substantive quality to his chairmanship. (56) He was a perfect blend of authenticity and the conservative personality style that Boston University so needed at the time. He also blended with Morris Ruben because neither was contentious nor personally combative. And, yet they were able to bestow a sense of sobriety and collegial support at all times. The roles that Morris and Bernard played could be casually overlooked in the overall very meaningful historical perspective of the school. Though the rest of the faculty engineered and refined the art of global attention, these two men gave the school substance during a time of its greatest need, its early beginnings. The old saying that it's not how one starts, but how one finishes is true in sports and gambling. But, certainly not in education. And, Bernard "Chick" Chaikin made the school relevant early on.

Five years after assuming the position of Chairman of The Department of Periodontology, Bernard Chaikin stepped down and the mantle of leadership was assumed by Dr. Gerald Kramer.[41] 1968 was a transformative year in many ways, but, most of all for the personality change. To say that Gerald Kramer was different and directed The Department of Periodontology according to his own belief system with a total restructuring would be simplistic and severely understated. He came with a Sherman tank and drove it through the department blowing through the doors like they were "Paper Mache". Wherein Bernard Chaikin was reserved and traditional, Gerald Kramer was driven and iconoclastic.

Personality aside, most people who went through the residency program while he was chairman would almost universally agree that he was one of the finest clinicians of his day. He had a lot of pizzazz and moxie. In many ways he was a unique character actor, and the school was his stage. He was also one of the great, entertaining lecturers among his peers. He took both the art and science of his profession

---

[41] Kramer, Gerald M.: Former Professor and Chairman of Periodontology, BUSGD: 1968-1980; Graduated from Tufts University, School of Dental Medicine with a Doctor of Dental Medicine before training under Henry M. Goldman in Periodontology.

very seriously. His professional life was a thespian exhibition amidst a musical composition in the likeness of a Johann Sebastian Bach sonata for violin. There is no doubt that he acquitted himself with remarkable assiduity. He was always over-prepared, never with nonchalance. A very intriguing leader of his day, his intellect far exceeded the limits of his profession. He was a provocative thinker and a leader with the highest expectations to make Boston University the center of the "dental universe". He exuded extreme self-confidence and possessed the awareness of an Impala surreptitiously exploiting its unmatched speed through the Serengeti to overwhelm and besiege its prey. Gerry was a game changer, the man who put Boston University on the map with an unfaltering certitude and conviction. Likewise, he was such a beacon of controversy that it is hard to imagine why anyone would want to go through life with the burden of controversy he carried.

He was handed a wonderful opportunity to lead under one of the great educators of the day, and, he did his best to make life as emotionally trying as he could. He knew it, and with remarkable audacity, he acted like a man with a tormented soul. He was seemingly a conflicted man to spend his entire tenure trying to overshadow the image of the Dean, pillory others in life's path, and never question the purpose. It seems he had hatred deep in his spirit and just was in turmoil shrouded by a sanctimonious smile. Although many have suggested Buddha extolled commentary on the subject of hate and jealousy, it is unclear as to the original source for the following. In fact, some credit George Santayana as well as others. Nevertheless, it is poignant for this discussion from his "Reason in Common Sense":

> *Holding onto anger is like drinking poison and expecting the other person to die.*[42]

Yes, he was a man for his time, and his time only.

What did he do that was so dramatic? How did he do it? What was

---

[42] Santayana, George : *The Life of Reason, Volume 1*, Copyright 1998, Prometheus Books as a "Great Books in Philosophy Series. (History)

so provocative about his character? And, why characterize him with prosaic abstractions? Simply put, he "blew the doors down", "chased the bulls out of the ring", and put his stamp on a teaching method that demanded perfection, made science an art form, and tethered scientific advances intimately with his passion for clinical excellence. William Shakespeare would have had a field day with him. He was a walking art form with a memorable style. Gerry Kramer was not mediocre, he stood above the crowd. He was a performer, and that was a good thing because he was daring and challenging. He was definitely a perfectionist who rightfully believed in iatrogenic periodontal disease (that is, for lay people, gum disease caused by poor dental work). To say he was disturbed by this was an understatement. So, he lionized those who lined up behind his message. And, for most intents and purposes, he was spot on. If perfection was his goal, then the challenge to accepted method and thought was his vehicle. He would never accept an idea or an approach that had not been distilled by evidence mediated research and thoroughly supported with clinical results demonstrating unmitigated consistency. He sincerely believed in himself and his teaching methods. He bucked headwinds. Other practice and teaching philosophies were contrarian to him, even an anathema at times. He preferred a one thought, one approach system in tandem and guided by his particular thinking. He most certainly demanded more of himself than others, and, though his protégés would like to deify him with Delphic imagery, it is impossible. He was a Don Quixote type dreaming of his own greatness. And, this was his downfall. He wasted so much time being something he was not when all he had to do was to what he was. He was talented, but burned inside with some unrequited, unfulfilled dream. The origin is uncertain. What is certain is that in his time he was a man who inspired excellence but somewhere he thought he could create the world's most beautiful diamond with elemental carbon squeezed in his own hand. He beatified Periodontics like no one else. Something was not properly configured in his mind. It was that exaggerated. And, it did not have to be so dramatic. He came to the top of the mountain and somehow went off a cliff.

What was disturbing was his cherry picking, his favoritism in his selection of residents, and the manner in which he displayed such an obvious cloying nature to gather these individuals as a theistic like following. This was quite disturbing to Henry who had personally selected him as the Chair in Periodontics based on merit and ability to be so engaging. To Henry at the time, he demonstrated a very sharp intellectual, confident and well-spoken manner that was most appealing. Like all his other Chairmen, he gave Gerry complete independence to develop the program in periodontics, always with the best interests of the school in mind. The most significant attribute Henry possessed was his laisser-faire attitude. He was not an interloper. He believed in allowing sensible people to lead by example, with their own discretion, and always with consideration for the best interest of the school first and foremost.

Gerry had all the ingredients necessary to instill interest in the growing specialty and usher in a new horizon for the forthcoming practitioner of the future, a student guided by the research literature, personal research investigation, and the clinical modalities of patient treatment planning and therapy. There was no doubt that he had all the vigor, determination, and most of all, the desire to actualize this mission. However, he had something deep in his soul which compelled him to be irksome, contentious, and haughty. There was never a question of his abilities, there was always a question about the way he did things, the way his exterior fooled while his interior managed to be disruptive. The old saw: it's what a person is inside, and, how the person manifests the inner self, was Gerry's very striking personality issue over time. Competence was never an issue, it was all about the mystery to the man that confounded Henry with all the blowback from every direction which increasingly surmounted acceptability. He had a gift and a channel for its expression that he couldn't intuitively control in harmony with established behavior (consensus building).

When Henry replaced Bernard Chaikin with Gerald Kramer in 1968, the relaxed environment became gradually and chillingly tense. Most of the older residents who had been in service or practice before returning to specialization accepted the demanding commitment without fanfare because they knew it would make them the best that they could be. But, there were predominantly younger residents right out of dental school who were not so accepting of the challenges laid out. Some were drastically consumed with fear, some were just overwhelmed and couldn't survive the daily brood, and some fretted but took the torrent of work in journeyman style. In any event, the work load was immense, the days were extraordinarily long, and the commitment to schedule unimaginable.

Gerry Kramer took an eight hour day, a five day work week, and a sense of daily order and turned it upside down, twisted the entire concept of regularity and habituation, and made the week seven days plus, weaving hours into productive ones that didn't exist, and made grown men and women worrisome, personal time deprived, marriage-family challenged, and discombobulated through-and-through. It was unlike any residency program before, during, or after his time. To say it was an effort would be an understatement. For those that were not concerned with other life responsibilities this lifestyle change had little bearing. But, for the most part, it was disturbingly draining and head shaking for the majority. Basically, culture shock!

To most there was little to no interaction with Henry, but he was completely aware of the elevated tension. Any resident who might be less self-assured and more of a mild, simpatico mentality was suddenly stunned by the serpentine, very emotionally threatening mental and emotional assault that came their way. The upending experience was onerous and bestowed relentlessly by both Kramer and his hand-picked associates in a style so disarming and threatening to only these vulnerable, uninitiated souls and not the specifically "chosen", pre-selected devotees. Many suffered, some into quiet submission and some by public rebuke that took away their sense of decency and spirit. This continuum so bothered Henry that he took Kramer's behavior quite seriously because he was notoriously developing a mixed reputation within the academy for public unfaltering infelicity with a very incorrigible frequency. Taken in mind, Henry watched quietly from a distance.

Lectures were served up in gratuitous, untimely scheduling to be followed by successive library commitments, and lectures and meetings that went late into the night. And, weekends followed the same time indulgence in orderly fashion. All in all, it was a daily travail which transitioned into a farrago of commitments. The blend of fatigue, worry and assorted potpourri demands from their families resulted from the long days and the exhausting weeks. Those that did not own up to this reality either were abnormal, devoid of humanity, or empowered by an over-inflated ego that was unconcerned about normal relationships. None of the other residency programs at Boston University were even closely confronted with such adversity. They were normal: hard work with intervals of rest and personal time. The Department of Periodontology became noteworthy during this time for its zany schedule. The reason for Henry's uncertainty was Kramer's circumspect, smooth manner of couched deceit and disdain and that never publicly surfaced. Thus, the other chairmen never saw the real persona in all its explicit display. It bothered Henry deeply for many, many years, but it was so very overwhelming because the man was building a cult following. Because Henry was rarely seen around the school, most probably thought that complete allegiance to Gerry was expected and that his control was inviolable.

Gerry Kramer was an admirable clinician with a dedication to principles that made his contribution to teaching highly relevant and consequential. He was a captivating lecturer with a great command of the English language. He would romance his subject matter into a mystical quality that would at times make some guffaw and others to lapse into a somnolent state. To the extreme, he could wander into scientific images that were not real and way out of his field of training and expertise. To the innocent, it was like a Buddhist intercession. Their thinking capitulated to thoughts he tortuously presented. It was certainly entertaining, but the man on the street could define it with more embellishment. His attempt to be principled was so blemished with sophistry that it was hard for his residents to perceive this. He could take things he read and saw and reprocess the information with insidious scientific distortion. He possessed a certainty-uncertainty fashioned by his own brilliance and at times petulant, snarky reaction to ideas and statements he found baseless or, in his mind, profoundly without merit. For the naïve and uninformed it was a sideshow. Unfortunately, this would, at times, bring him into a contentious engagement with others that made such scenarios unappealing and pretentious. At times he was intolerant and impetuous, but he was always consistent. With all his talent one would have to ask why? It was just so platitudinous and unworthy of his position.

As a clinician, he would perform in surgery like he was Pablo Picasso. He was at his best when putting on a public performance. And, his acting was first rate. He loved to display elaborate techniques, elevating them to a state of elegance. He was like a virtuoso on stage. However, his imagery and his ability to convey it to his residents was incomparable. He made them drool like they thirsted for every pearl of wisdom being selectively dispensed, methodically precise and reasoned to capture their devotion. It was right out of Hollywood, and one of a kind. It was incredible how it was staged. He possessed an ability to make teaching fascinating, even if he made great leaps of faith in reasoning. He lapsed into principles of pathology which were far flung and inaccurate. He captivated the attention of his audience with his romantic speech and style. He conspicuously vexed his colleagues with intricately unconventional presentations as if to deliberately tantalize both the literati and cognoscenti of the profession. He shamelessly seemed to fancy his own ability to anger some, demagogue others, and occasionally overtly remonstrate against ideas and belief systems he just wanted to cavil for personal enjoyment. One thing is for sure, he was a very interesting man with not too many dull moments in his professional life. But, again, why? An intellectual death wish? Who knows?

Henry was very taciturn when it came to Gerry Kramer's rather intemperate decisions as he made plans to reorder and reshuffle the department priorities. Continuing education was a growing part of the school's future. Like Harvard and Tufts, Boston University was able to muster the resources and quality faculty to make very significant inroads into this rapidly expanding teaching experience for domestic as well as foreign practitioners. It was a significant revenue enhancement for all the schools. For each department the chairman concentrated its energies where it was most practical. Gerry Kramer used his very silky, smooth, engaging personality to aggregate a loyal following in European and South American countries as the school's reputation grew. Henry was very aware how "Kramerized" the department had and continued to become. No question, it was not timely for him to address this with so many more significant issues at hand.

Kramer was a tall man for his day, about six feet two inches. He was not physically fit as it was not the madness of today with daily workouts and specially designed diets. However, he wore styled, custom made suits like Louis of Boston which gave him a noticeably svelte appearance. He customarily wore fashionable silk shirts with attention grabbing paisley floral ties. He most often wore Bostonian shoes, rich in appearance and elegantly shaped. His hair was dark brown at some point, now being overtaken by white shocks, and sat up high and thick as it combed completely back in a very smooth appearance. It was a Fernando Lamas (a 1940's, 1950's Hollywood smoothie) throwback appearance. His outside presence matched his inside mindset, very carefully arranged. In spite of his surface charm and controlled demeanor, he was very unsettled.

Before not too long his personal stamp was deeply ingrained. For the school this was arguably very fortunate as the image of the other departments also made their presence resoundingly known as well. At this stage in the school's development, it was very inopportune for Henry to think about a change in leadership. Overall more residents matriculated from around the world for the specialization programs. As these practitioners returned home, they developed their own following and the school profited from the feeder system which developed as a result. It was a golden age for the field of Periodontics, and, he spearheaded this mission with a driven quest to grow his reputation. Bernard Chaikin's day had transformed into the dawning of showmanship and personal advancement. The role was that of a far greater activist leadership. Gerry Kramer was in his glory. His cult of personality was time appropriate. It can be argued that perhaps a more tempered personality may have fulfilled the school's needs. But, the school was a new kind of institution and it demanded a more aggressive, engaging management. Though Henry never verbalized this, intuitively he felt it, and it argues sensibly why keeping Kramer through these times was the fitting decision.

Kramer enjoyed lecturing to large groups. In small seminars he could be of any mind-set. He could humiliate, encourage, belittle or simply glance over in a manner to challenge someone's presence or intelligence. When he lectured, he went on for hours, making points that were often adorned with hyperbole. Some of the statements he made were so wrong in fact that it was just self-serving as they did not add to anyone's experience. However, at times it was entertaining.

Euphemisms are conveniently inoffensive for the sake of being agreeable and simply to get a point across or the truth exposed. Well, describing Kramer's "Monday night seminars" for the periodontal residents cannot be described euphemistically. It effectively began as a seminar like a forum for an exchange of ideas regarding treatment planning philosophies based on literature review and personal opinions. In that sense, it originated from a sense of value to stimulate thinking and to give a presenting resident the opportunity to defend a course of therapy. However, it evolved into "a dog and pony show" courtesy of Kramer and his henchmen and their self-serving "one trick pony" manner of exposing their own self-serving penchants. However, while euphemisms can divert reality and serve hypocrisy, this reality showmanship was hurtful. Many were "dressed down" and humiliated in front of their fellow residents. It was like "Monday night at the movies" to watch Kramer or one of his intimate group serve up their tactless, abusive pillory at the expense of a nervous, degraded and shamed resident. They were bullies and took delight in hectoring the indefensible souls fumbling for a morsel of their own dignity. In today's world this would be litigious froth for righteous retaliation. Of all the poignant missteps in Kramer's time this stands out as all that was exemplary of how he and his conceited minions thwarted the very core of Henry's principles of graduate dental education. Unbeknown to every other Chairman, to the world outside as well, this group of sophist understudies for true educators were promoting a charade as if to deride and trample with unprincipled behavior. Henry was very much aware, particularly in view of the failure to letup and tone it all down. He did not feel it timely to react, but, under advisement, he planned for a major retrenchment. Of all the unfortunate exhibitions of misguided leadership and decision making, this rather selfish and vain behavior was horribly officious and disrespectful. The major misfortune was the other Chairmen were in the dark, and Henry's silence allowed it to continue far too long. Abusive conduct should not have been condoned under the veil of euphemistic showmanship, but no one was really aware of its prevailing nature. This is how "Kramerized" the department had become. It was nothing shy of brazen and bold. And they got away with it. Worse yet, the attitudes became infectious. The fair-faired became endowed clones. Institutional politics at Boston University were no different than any other school.

However, Gerry Kramer was the consummate politician amidst his other formidable talents. He thought he could entice a cat off a fish truck. As if a time warp had interceded, he appeared to emerge from a "Boss Tweed" Tammany Hall photo op. He had a very gracious, easy manner always manifesting a generic smile, shaking hands with a swift extension of his fingers such that his palm would never be palpable. It was oh so oleaginous. Retracting rather quickly, he would hasten into conversation only if there was purpose to linger. Otherwise, he glided away as his smile fell into a deep, concentrated thought as he walked with long strides away to some more pressing obligation. He was always on the move as his brain programmed all the thoughts being inwardly categorized for immediate discharge. He was a man on a mission, never a wasted moment to exploit dawdling. And, to the extent that he engineered a fluid, sophisticated residency program, it can never be denied that he was a master over-achiever. It remains a mystery that a man of his potential would waste so much energy on the frivolous. He was so busy maneuvering around others that it seemed like he never took the time to consider where it was all leading.

Wherein Morris Ruben was the consummate resource of information and Bernard Chaikin the prevailing clinician of his day, Gerry Kramer proceeded to change the entire training program and, in his mind, elevate the academic standards. His chairmanship was stamped with his own personal imprint. Other training programs had two to four residents at a time, but Boston University expanded to as many as twelve and higher. Academic master's and doctorate programs paralleled the clinical teaching residencies and were made individually available. Of course, this was done under Henry's authority, but Gerry engineered the oversight (along with Morris Ruben's input). The research projects were topical, bringing attention to challenging clinical issues (like healing bone defects in a diabetic state).

To reiterate, his years were pocked with great duress. Any personal life that any resident had in mind was quickly expunged. The program was a full professional life commitment for the two years. When Implantology was later approved for academic recognition, the residency program expanded to three years.

When Henry brought in Gerry Kramer, he had no idea that there would be such astonishing recognition for the school in so short a time. Whether from a positive or a negative perspective, a great deal of judgment was predicated on how Gerry was viewed. Locally or internationally, he was a one-way tour de force. He did not compromise his style or thinking. Whether insulting, demeaning or defiant, he managed to appear articulate and reasoned. Most of his residents became brain washed, non-self, group followers. Not all, but the greater number were like Jim Jones's followers in Jonestown, Guyana in 1978. (167, 168.) This sounds like hyperbole, but it was truly amazing how a great number became obsessed with Kramer's aura.

His ability to collectivize his residents' thinking was done with an intellectual cudgel approach. There was no doubt about this. He created his own fiefdom through progressive conversion which eventually rooted his following all over the world. Appropriate or inappropriate was anyone's value judgment, but there was this that brought him into conflict with Henry. While Gerry engineered, inspired and effectuated the greatness of the residency program, he also negated a lot of this accomplishment with his force of character and wayward persistence. The result was that he grew to be tiresome. The turmoil it created at the time has been washed away with time, but, at the time, it drove a stake right through the school's esprit de corps.

Why take so much time now to share the impact of his time as Chairman? Because his tacit defiance and belligerence was so deceptive and confusing. Most on the faculty stayed away from getting involved because he was a hot coal, a seething cauldron ready to flame over. His buoyancy fooled a few other of the faculty, but the perceptive ones knew what he was all about. They kept their distance with fitting diversionary tactics. They were intelligently risk averse, and he was a magnet for nothing but ill-fated trouble both at school and within the Boston dental community.

It is very difficult to give the devil his due, but Boston University grew in stature during his tenure. He was clinically a very good Periodontist, but clearly he got in his own way. He stifled his legacy in limiting his memory to those who embraced his obscure mystique or those tethered to him through business dealings. What Kramer failed to understand is that whatever distinction he garnered was under the shield of the school and university. Excepting this, his chairmanship could have been abrogated at any time. How brazen he was to misrepresent his authority. This disturbed Henry because of the passive aggressive way Kramer behaved. Henry continued his appointment because his merit at the time greatly seemed to outweigh the rancor his firing could and would foment.

When Gerry crossed his "Rubicon" (64), his faux pas brought an end to his tenure after eleven years. As part of the ongoing continuing education program, a group of French dentists had been taking advanced courses in Periodontology. When they became disenchanted (unconfirmed rumor) with the scope of the course at Boston University, Kramer, as only he would do, had the French to his office in Swampscott,

Massachusetts where, under his confines with his associates, he proceeded to continue the course(s) with them. He failed to comply with school regulations regarding continuing education courses, plain and simple. This course extended over 1979 to 1980. Henry had retired in 1977 and Dr. Spencer Frankl was the new Dean. Despite Henry being retired, the circumstances led to Gerald Kramer "retiring". He was fired, no doubt. Henry was still in control and the force behind the firing even if Dean Frankl actually was instrumental in carrying it out administratively. This was Kramer's Rubicon after which there would be no return. He knew he had been at Henry's brain since the time he had been hired.

Thus, to surmise, it was a shock to all people associated with the school in one way or another. Kramer was fortunate he lasted as long as he did. There was no doubt that he was a talented Periodontist. But, the truth is the fact that he was a legend in his own mind. He was a shame to all that believed in him. To this day, it is hard to reason his motivations. This was not the role of others to judge his knavishness even if he threw it in everyone's face. Many internationally known colleagues always questioned his one size fits all philosophy of therapy. For them he was a renegade, "a leader without a country" type. He was so severely at odds with himself. And, he covered it with bravado and a repugnant silky swagger.

It ended a period in the field of Periodontics that fortunately never rebounded. Coincidental or not, the teaching of Periodontology has deteriorated almost to a point of non-existence, being co-opted by the teaching of Implantology as if it were the Holy Grail. Almost as if saving teeth had lost its importance, a conversation with Gerry Kramer days before his passing confirmed his deep conviction that implants are not "magic bullets".

Today no one at the school save for one or two clinicians can really speak to his chairmanship at Boston University. His full impact will never be properly understood. He was too divisive and complicated. If he had lived in the middle of the 1600's in England, he would have been a vintage Shakespearean tragic hero. His hubris destroyed any of the good feelings Henry had for him as one of his early students. He felt he was a man of character, ability and talent. But, it did not concern how he baffled his residents into believing he was something more than he was. All Henry knew was that he gave him a long leash that lasted years until he finally "hung" himself. In his final conversation before passing he was very contrite and emotionally flaccid. He died at 77 on May 18, 2000.[43]

Much time has been taken with this highly controversial man. In another world, at another time, in the guise of a different spirit, he was a man who would have succeeded far beyond the irrational urges that took him down. His assembly of cult-like followers were and are selfish because they fed his ego, feathered his hubris, and immeasurably and consequentially brought his end. No one will ever know the truth of this man that could have been much more. Without the sycophancy, the unmitigated and deliberate contumacy, he might have acceded to the position of Dean. Periodontics as a specialty was burgeoning as the science for understanding tooth loss at the time he became Chairman. What a gift! So, the final question to ponder: what dwells within the heart and mind of such a man who has been handed the keys for success and did not possess the emotional control to not squander it?

The field of Endodontics did not train as many residents, but it was every bit a role player in the growth and development of the school. Henry hired a most unusual man to chair its department. Dr. Hertbert Schilder was "a man for all seasons"! He was a consummate politician, a brilliant orator, a superb clinician, and an academic maven. And, he was a nice man. He was obdurate with a bad temper. But, once over this excusable human frailty, how can anyone deny he was a helluva person! He was the best kind of friend, loyal as the day is long, and a talent of unfathomable reach.

He became well known for his clinical techniques he brought to the dental profession. His students were rightfully dedicated to this man who led with honor, respect and dedication. He was a luminary with

---

[43] Conversation with author.

very committed ideals and never compromised his ideas, be it teaching or practice.

Herb Schilder might have been the most all-around person on the faculty. He made his way to Boston like so many of the others through the very small dental pipeline of the day. In his case it was through Drs. D. Walter Cohen and Morton Amsterdam in Philadelphia via Temple University where he specialized. He came to Boston University in 1959 and spent his entire career there, also starting and maintaining one of the most recognized practices both in the city and nationally. He was a multi-faceted, inspirational man with an unparalleled perspicacity. He was tirelessly devoted to his professional responsibilities as a teacher and practitioner. But, some aspects of this respected man, not readily known, was his family, his religious affiliation, his cultural knowledge base and his ardor for running as a means of maintaining a healthy lifestyle. He was a leader among leaders in his field as well as politically savvy. He accede to the position of First Vice President of The American Dental Association.

In bringing Herb to Boston University, Henry really did not know the extent of this man's talents. That would be expected at that time because Henry was assembling a blend of very different personages based on recommendations firsthand with secondhand hoping and wondering. No one knew what to make of this new Boston University experiment, most of all Henry. But, as it turned out, Herb was more than solid gold, he was platinum. He did not add to the faculty as just another Chairman. He uplifted the entire composition of the school with his ambition, drive, and dedication to detail. He was innovative and communicative. If anyone could dispel the idea that the faculty would be splintered with each member confined to his own solitary responsibilities, it was Herb. He was a player, a unifier, and a coordinator. He was most gregarious with a very friendly, warm approach to his colleagues. He was stern, but with meaning and sensitivity.

He so not the lilywhite, pure type without human weakness. His temper made his handling of employees the butt end of intemperate anger when his perfection oriented personality took over. This was his

Achilles heel and the only demon apparent within a life of real decency. In spite of legendary reputation for losing assistants, he will be remembered as one of the great gentlemen leaders in dentistry.

As a Chairman, he was faithful to his recommendations which brought him to Boston University. He brought new, imaginative ideas to the treatment and management of endodontic disease. He had a penchant for basic science and approached his teaching with a sense that root canal treatment was more than a mechanical process. To be effective and for teeth to endure as functional entities in health, he was vocal about expunging disease bearing elements and rendering the root canal system sterile. Then, he devised the vertical condensing of warm gutta percha to seal the internal root canal system to the tip of the root. The "Schilderian Endodontics" as it became known reflected his passion for quantifying clinical procedures. He had an endless interest in probing the science of disease. The ultimate student his whole life, he never stopped reading. He was a fun man to engage at a scientific level because he was so alert and imaginative. He supported his residents with the image of "a father figure". And, they returned the favor reverentially with a lifetime of highly deserved love and respect. He ran a department that made Henry feel very grateful for having Herb as Chairman.

Unlike his colleagues in Periodontics, he was very politically active, both locally and nationally. He was recognized for the leadership qualities he brought to The Department of Endodontics. Additionally, he had the undaunted drive to actively want to assume leadership positions in organizations which would give him a stage to improve the standing of organized dentistry. He articulated his beliefs with simplicity, but with an eloquence that was impressive and memorable. He was so well-rounded and thought provoking that he was able to advance his political ideas cleverly and fruitfully. It was always very self-sacrificial for anyone to devote the personal time necessary for national recognition, but Herb accomplished this with great energy. The result was personal reward which reflected directly back on the school's good fortune. In this sense, he always maintained a profound loyalty to the school professionally as well as to Henry personally.

In addition he gravitated instinctively to what was decent. He had individual aspirations, but they were contained always within the matrix of advancing the school's needs. This is explanation enough for why his entire career manifested in not only his greatness as a practitioner but also as the forebear of the many great clinician teachers.

A final note about Herb Schilder. He was probably the most articulate man on the faculty. His curiosity went far beyond his profession. He spoke in the syllogistic manner of a Socrates. His deductive reasoning was quite inspiring and very precise. Unlike most, he was both highly cultured and cultivated. His passion for understanding the ways of the world, cultural differences worldwide, the political issues separating peoples of varying ethnicities, and bridging the divides which squandered geopolitical calm made his vocal presence quite significant. He was a very educated man and brought a definite sense of depth of character to the school faculty. It will be very difficult to supplant what he developed. His passing left a huge following of past students who ably foster his tradition with such stellar unity. He left with the universal respect of not only his consummate clinical excellence, but, more importantly, the manner he conveyed his message with such commanding respect. He would never countenance disparate feeling. He was most definitely a man who understood tradition, the building of a confidence that engendered long term harmony. And, boy if he did not fulfill this mantra! The tradition of the Department of Endodontics will have his finger prints for many years to come. He did things right.

Herb Schilder was diminutive in physical stature, but he was a giant in character. He exuded tremendous respect for Henry, and, he was always grateful for his opportunity. The Department of Endodontics was scrupulously well run. It was overall a cohesive component of the school. It reflected every aspect of Herb's personality. The residents were refreshingly competent and agreeable. Never a discordant issue of a substantive nature, Henry did not have to be concerned about Herb's ability to manage his department. He always maintained harmony and a quiet diligence to foster an agreeable, good-natured atmosphere. As a result, there was always a very fluid, easygoing daily expectancy of hard work, but never a tension or conflict that might alter the general interpersonal feeling of accord.

In contrast to the acrimony and uneasiness of the Department of Periodontology, Schilder's Department of Endodontics was shaped by civility and good will. Both departments reflected the intrinsic differences in leadership personalities. Kramer's vexatious manner brought too many contentious situations whereas Schilder did not exploit the school solely to personally advance himself. Their contrasting styles resulted in a lifetime career for Herb Schilder. Kramer's sterling innovative achievement was The International Journal of Periodontics & Restorative Dentistry. (92) But, it really never replaced the academic stage he cherished at Boston University. However, it shows how talented a man he was, if only he could have controlled his untamed petulance.

Herb Schilder was willfully honorable and immeasurably committed to elevate the clinical standards of his field. His hubris never took a front seat to his ambition. He found his destiny through the nobility of his character. He earned Henry's trust because the school's success was always his underlying determination. He was a team player.

In spite of scoping the backgrounds of all the projected faculty candidates, Henry would never have been able to forecast who would live up to their reputed reputations. In those days, people were hired more for their connections than their curricula vitae. Word of mouth from significant leaders in dentistry went a long way. Even though Henry had a great deal at stake the selection of chairmen was really no more secure than a bet at Las Vegas. In the end, it worked as a reasonable success story. Morris Ruben and Bernard Chaikin turned out to be solid journeymen. Gerry Kramer was colorful. Herb Schilder existed as if scripted in Hollywood for success. Gerry Kramer thought he was a "Minister with portfolio", churlishly embracing his multifaceted personality. And Herb Schilder was gifted and polished.

At the time Boston University started with planning most dentists who were treating children were general practitioners. The fortunate recognition that children require very different consideration compelled schools to expand the training into this very separate area as a defined specialty. That is not to say that there were not already small training centers, but they were very limited and usually without remediation of skill learning that is recognized today for its fundamental need. With increasing research into child growth and development came greater awareness and focus on training programs. In this regard, Henry knew that this department would require a conscientious person who would display the insight, hard work and personal interest. His choice was Dr. Spencer Frankl who came highly recommended. As a school of specialization, this was an expanding field with very different development requirements.

Dr. Spencer Frankl at first meeting was a most pleasant and personable man. Though quite serious, he had a very soothing way about him. He never displayed undulations of highs and lows, what most would describe as mercurial. He was quite temperate. He possessed a very steadying influence. In many ways he appeared similar to Henry, not having "self" as a prime motivating quality. At least, it was never a surface display. At the time, he had youth and vigor with a tinge of reticence borne of the newness of the position. Nevertheless, he took on the responsibilities with a serious yet very optimistic outlook. He had an outgoing, very gregarious appeal.

Spencer was the most diminutive man in the school. He was hard to read as his pleasance overshadowed all aspects of his character. He was always smiling. A cynical outlook, which is not out of the question in academics, would always send up red flags. No one could be that cordial and agreeable all the time. Ne never let his guard down. Indeed he was a steady-Eddie type, hard-working and dependable. Perhaps it was fortunate that Pedodontics did not carry the cachet that Oral Surgery or Periodontics did. He could carry forth behind a curtain of protection from the constant notice and flare of the other departments. It was generally not the most popular choice for specialization so Spencer's group was always in the background. As a result, he was able to concentrate on concrete matters that did not deter his focus. His quiet determination was particularly relevant because he thoroughly disregarded the ceremonious notice that came with his position. Just as the writer J. D. Salinger aptly described in his books, particularly "Franny and Zoey" (105), facial expression and appearance went a long way in revealing personality types. Somehow, meeting up with Spencer was always a very consistent experience, seemingly always gratifying. However, something did not jibe.

Unlike The Department of Periodontics, Pedodontics as a department was comparatively small in numbers. The two year residency had less than half the total number of one residency level in Periodontics. And, like Herb Schilder, he cultivated a strong following of residents who did not have to endure any "cult of personality" stress. One of the couched thoughts was that Pedodontics was merely general practice for children. Therefore, all the pretense of a more vigorous and significant training experience was belittled by many. However, this is where that type of thought process was shamefully ignorant. Pedodontics was paying much more attention to the psychological, congenital, periodontal and oncological implications embedded in study and treatment of growing children. So, this was rapidly becoming one of the more important specialties requiring very committed and responsible professionals. Also, children's dentistry was always considered the specialty domain for very unique people who could relate to children. In fact, from a stand point of training and practice, this was soon becoming the most intense training for dealing with a world which was rapidly integrating and therefore challenging the population with far greater dental needs. So those who would tend to invalidate this specialty off as an after-thought are naïve and uninformed.

Spencer's residents were very self-reliant and did not march en masse[44] with a herd mentality. He nurtured a sense of independent research and learning. The focus was on two years of exposure to as much remedial training and classroom time for acquiring new, or modifying and reinforcing, existing knowledge. Many new concepts were rapidly

---

[44] en masse: from the French: all together or in a group, or even literally: in a mass.

unfolding with regard to children's diseases and syndromes so that this was rapidly becoming a highly important primary care specialty. The result was allowing for a more thorough, purposive focus on tangible training endpoints. In this regard, Spencer was a student of streamlining didactic and clinical learning. His department was totally absent of a cult of personality and was dedicated solely on the seemingly sterile emphasis on bringing new residents into the fold and seeing to it that they left vastly enhanced from their experience at Boston University. Spencer's sense of purpose seemingly was committed to his residents.

Henry never showed favor, but his actions always spoke volumes. As the school developed from its initial opening, it was quite clear that its success would secure a spot for the school in dental education. The faculty was so exemplary that any of the chairmen could have ascended to succeed Henry at the appropriate time. However, Spencer Frankl separated himself from the others because his "soul" and character were settling. He was an extremely bright, hard working person with such an amiability that Henry drew him into his personal space with a conviction for his loyalty and leadership style. It was very easy as he provided calm amidst times of turmoil and rancor. At least this was the surface view.

Spencer came over from Tufts in 1964 and never looked back. Formally, Henry was Dean for fourteen years (nineteen including the five years as Chairman of Stomatology at Boston University School of Medicine in 1958). Spencer was Dean for thirty years (taking over at Henry's retirement in 1977). Most of everything he carried out as Dean was an inspiration of Henry's thoughts and pursuits. Like Henry he had a very liberal feeling for community and extending aid to those requiring support due the misfortune of financial circumstances. He was a compassionate man with purpose and conviction. He possessed an extreme sensitivity which always made him approachable. It was possible that Henry understood these virtues to be the necessary conduits to further what he had established. Spencer, once again, seemingly got the message and led the school through all the school's improvements with the style and class. However, it was not so cushy.

By the time Spencer Frankl passed away in 2008, he had left a legacy of major accomplishments. The timeline chronology of the school is evidence of his concentrated efforts. When most Deans are replaced, they are usually outsiders. However, Spencer was the ultimate insider. He had become almost ordained by Henry as he was groomed in learning all the political rope holding the school together. He needed very little, if nothing, in the way of advice from day one. He had already been a direct witness to everything as he so willingly followed Henry around for so many years. He was almost a puppy in a long training program. The experience was a daily laboratory for the do's and don'ts in how to handle the lonely position of Dean. Of course, the other chairmen would have had to be living in a closet not to be aware how tidy the relationship between Henry and Spencer was becoming. Of course, Spencer was thought by most to be Henry's favorite. It was almost an infantile bond. And, if Spencer were not so short, this nasty thought would never have been considered. It was most certainly being bandied about. Going back to the late 1960's there was a very mutual respect. Spencer was still new to the area and felt very secure in his new role. His general demeanor was both refreshing and sincere.

However, from the very beginning, no other faculty member spent so much time around Henry. But, it cannot be emphasized enough that Henry's weakness was to be overly trusting. If he were lumbering around the Serengeti, he would have been the first animal to fall victim to a hungry lion. That very carefully concealed temperament is what man him such a giving man. The numbers he shepherded through graduate education is legendary because of his caring personality.

The way Spencer moved so easily in and out of Henry's office it was so clearly apparent that one would have thought he should have been more discreet. The whisper refrain of his apparent motivation to stay so close to Henry was that he'll be the obvious choice to be dean. This was the talk in narrow circles, but it was heard with some justification amongst some very concerned people. But, as Henry got wind of the banter, he seemed to dig his heals in harder in pursuit of his intuition. But, this proved to be a costly decision. As wonderful a man as Henry was, his naivete and obstinacy cluttered his good sense. He was easily mislead by people who stayed quiet and obedient, but always around.

Henry did not deal well with any degree of querulous behavior or disagreement he misconstrued as pettiness. This is because he never fully engaged in back-and-forth debate. His approach was one-way, "my way" approach. He was so unique that he was more right than wrong in his approach to most decisions. It is not expected that leaders in the dental profession be "diplomats extraordinaire" Lawyers would characterize this behavior as "sua sponte"[45] because he believed everything regarding the school would be willed by his own acts, never questioned or undermined. Rather doctrinaire, but most likely a default behavior acquired from his upbringing by an authoritarian mother and very rigid high school environment. He developed a mentality that expected respect and obeisance.

Maybe Henry was naive, but he wasn't unaware. And, there is a big difference. He saw and heard everything, but his naivete only shone through when he refused to believe anyone would betray his trust. And, the brain trust at the school composed was composed of all who wanted to succeed him, and even the ones out of the inner circle who would refuse to deny that they also had a chance. If Henry had been more outgoing and more engaged in the process, he more than likely would not have become so openly vulnerable.

As it played out, Henry's attention was constantly being diverted by the tension that was the daily monotony with another Kramer comment or incident floating around the school. This really took Henry down emotionally. He was tired of hearing about the litany of problems in the Department of Periodontology. It was wearing, terribly distracting and terribly deliberate. The disturbing drumbeat of complaints were no small matter because it became unremitting. Henry was confused by the notion of any resident being tormented, jostled or used as bait to remonstrate others. He would have preferred if at least a month could pass without any noise about anything. Silence would have settled his emotions. And, this behavior was only a scintilla of evidence

---

[45] See website: www.latin-dictionary.org: "his own motion".

that the department's reputation was at risk for its incorrigible attitude and demeanor. In his wildest imagination he could not gainsay how ugly the prospective feedback might get. Individually and as a group Kramer and his team became so rogue in casting their proper deportment to the wind and behaving as if their philosophical belief system could be as a highbrow, cognitive cudgel to hurt others, be it selective residents or even at a national-international gathering or conference. However the feeling was taken then or now, the facts were the facts. The tragedy was that the rest of the faculty was in the dark, and Henry never expected that this is what "freedom of expression and leadership" would produce.[46]

In actuality, Spencer Frankl was not his choice at all to be the next Dean. He was craftier than ascertained. What quietly transpired became the workings of a very poorly directed soap opera. The amount of time spent behind the scenes on dizzying issues got to him. Frankl's craftiness and insights led him to aggressively play on Henry's heart strings. Henry was really at fault because he was getting older and kicked the proverbial can down the road. He actually never properly planned for his own retirement and replacement. His own brother who was a leader in the New England shoe industry's association told him endlessly that if he failed to prepare for that day, he should be prepared to fail in recruiting someone guided by his own mission belief system. But, Henry never committed to this advice. He really believed in his heart that everything would fall into place.

Kramer's unctuous character made him too hot and troublesome. For some reason Schilder was never in the picture, and for no good reason. This was mystifying. He would have been the perfect choice. He had all the qualities to lead: respectful, immaculately groomed for leadership, a transcendent educator, and a nobility for consensus building, all the virtues any institution would crave. Sitting right there in his presence, Henry truly never gave him consideration. It would seem that the daily outpouring of "Kramerisms" cluttered his brain so thoroughly that he couldn't think straight. It was awful to see how this

---

[46] Author's conversations in meetings with Henry and his brother.

quietly burdened him. In fact, at one meeting his lips were so flushed red that obviously his blood pressure was out of control, particularly the way he held his anger so deep within. The stress level was far beyond what anyone could imagine.[47]

Schilder commanded universal respect and his thinking comported practically with the good of the school. Henry's failure to probe this potential move to make Herbert Schilder the next dean might have been the biggest mistake of his tenure. It really is difficult to understand why this never happened. All the research shows so crystal clear that up and down from all the vetting information, he had the educational and political skills not shared by any of the others. Well, it didn't happen, and it seems that his choice would have averted a lot of the administrative challenges Spencer couldn't handle. And, just as a side, it would have been terribly amusing to view how he would have dealt with Kramer and his group (or, is it groupies)! A front row center seat for this would have been worth any price. It would have been Shakespearean, and the Las Vegas money would have been on Schilder in that battle! But, the thought hails a former news anchor, John Cameron Swayze, whose nightly enunciation: "Sit back and be an eye witness to the news that made history" (1960's 1950's and 1960's) would have been perfect for that entertaining contretemps.[48]

To continue, with Henry's ability to tap talent, Boston University was in fine fettle. The man he convinced to start the Orthodontic Department was Dr. Herbert I. Margolis. Like Henry's friend and colleague, Bernard Chaikin, Herb Margolis was an older practitioner who had already established himself both locally and internationally. After teaching anatomy at Harvard School of Dental Medicine where he got his dental training, he moved on to Tufts School of Dental Medicine. He established the Tufts Institute for Children with Cleft Palate and Other Facial Deformities. So, in coming to Boston University in 1963, he came highly credentialed with an ability to inject immediate credibility. This was an immediate advantage for Henry in terms of the specialty

---

[47] Sunday brunches at Henry's house.
[48] John Cameron Swayze, NBC News Anchor in the 1950's and 1960's.

recognition for matriculating graduate students as well as the experience Herb brought to lay out a teaching syllabus. This was convenient for the school as well as for Herb who was nearing retirement. But, in the interim, it was fortunate for Henry.

Herbert Margolis was a kindly, friendly man whose smile belied his depth of knowledge and serious approach to teaching. He had a very soft manner and was extremely open and candid. Like Henry, he was a trailblazer in his own field, highly respected and inventive (he designed the cephalostat, the head positioning device necessary to assure reproducibility of the x-ray beam). He was not an electric lecturer, but he was comfortable in small groups where he had always shone with great communication skills. Henry understood that he would be transitional. But, what a fortuitous experience for residents. For the day, he was a reputed leader equal to all his peers. He laid the foundation for what would eventually become one of the most renowned departments worldwide.

Like all the other chairmen, there was no remuneration as Henry couldn't afford compensation at the outset. So, like the others, Herb gave of his own time selflessly. He did have a well-established private practice in Boston on Commonwealth Avenue which flourished for many years. Although his most productive years were spent at Tufts, he gave significant years to Boston University in the same way Bernard Chaikin provided for the Department of Periodontology. Both of these men were coming onto a faculty with very much younger men. However, they integrated quite easily, serving the school at a most needed period. Herb was very easygoing, unlike the brisk, energetic pace Bernard Chaikin kept in a seemingly inexhaustible manner. There was a simpatico between them which went unregistered on the surface, but clearly there was a mutual sensibility and understanding. Herb had a calming affect while "Chick" was frenetic. But, just as Herb's smile was a cover to his depth of purpose, "Chick's" ingratiating demeanor disguised his wealth of talent. Of all the appointments Henry made, these two might have been the most serendipitous because of their cultivated, established work ethic. And with this interlude Henry had more time to ponder a more long term solution without having to be concerned with how each would manage their departments.

Probably the "diamond-in-the-rough" appointment was Dr. Donald Booth to the position of Chairman of Oral Maxillofacial Surgery. He was the embodiment of the traditional New Englander: quiet purpose, austere personality, tall and lanky, and wonderfully laconic. He was really the backbone of the entire faculty. Maybe he didn't reflect glamour and pizzazz, but he was ironclad and profoundly secure in his own skin. Henry also realized that Oral Maxillofacial Surgery was the buttress of any dental institution, and, its chairman would have to reflect a certain cachet that would advance Boston University's reputation. Booth did not come as a result of any previous distinction. Just a mainstream individual, he was referred to Henry through Spence Frankl, and left private practice when he decided to take the position. And, that might have been questionable at the time. Boston University being so new, he feared for his own future (a most natural feeling). To take this job came with many uncertainties. Henry was not a very convincing salesman: "like, son here is the job, take it or leave it" was his approach. Henry was in the military and had that mindset. At the outset, Booth was not enthralled by some of the important accoutrements of the Chairmanship: like where his personal office would be, salary and practical expectations. But, as was Henry's wont, he never presented a position with enthusiasm. Henry's concept was: Hey, here's a wonderful opportunity, take it because if you don't, it'll go to someone else who appreciates it. This paraphrases how Henry would think he was inveigling a candidate. Well, Don Booth was (and still is) an unemotional, very passive, straightforward shooter who doesn't mince words so he wasn't too overly enthusiastic. But, he demurred, took the position, and, as the saying goes, the rest is history. It was a great choice for a man with a "Cool Hand Luke" personality. (30) Don Booth's persona was very captivating. He was staid and stolid, not very extroverted, but unusually solid and dependable. If there was any sense of worry, he contained it well. Extremely bright and really cerebral, he was not jocular nor ever effervescent. Tall and thin with aquiline features, his rimless, spiny looking glasses always rendered an austere countenance. However, as he conversed, he immediately displayed a very kind and understanding demeanor. But, he was not wont for bloviation. He was very direct in a very reflective, approachable manner. Almost in a Lincolnesque stature, it was most certain that he rendered a sense of commanding self-confidence. If concern for his decision was flowing through his mind, his exterior never betrayed his thoughts. Even, as he relates, that the beginning offered no sense of organization, even with the need for his own personal office away from the mad scramble of a new position, he did not display any worry. Unlike all other faculty, he was most settling for a very unstable academic environment. His only match was Anthony Gianelly, but Gianelly was physically and emotionally his direct opposite. They both brought tremendous cachet and very undeniable talent[49].

In the midst of a very fluid environment in the years working up to 1963, it was very courageous that so many different personality types could interact and carry on with such grace. For a man like Don Booth, it was a quantum leap of faith and future for the sake of personal security, if the floor did not fall away, crumble or crack! No doubt, chance is for the young at heart and mind, but there were already two dental institutions (with tradition) in Boston. No doubt, Boston University was a school dedicated to specialization, but this was even more chancy. Credit to Don Booth when he first spoke to Henry about the position at Spencer Frankl's behest. In view of the ambiguity, the low salary commensurate with the position and work ahead, it is staggering that it worked out. As great a man as Henry was, he almost expected no one to ever question his offer. Retrospectively, however, it took a Henry Goldman to be such a categorical, laconic, pensive type to almost be above the fray and assume a "que sera, sera"[50] composure. This was quintessential Henry

---

[49] Conversations with Dr. Donald Booth.
[50] "Que sera, sera": no particular language: made up for a song for singer/actress Doris Day: "what will be, will be; can be in French, Spanish of Italian, but the language is different; closest is Italian: "Che sara, sara".

Goldman. When he came forth with Don Booth's proposal, he never would expect a denial. So, in this vein, there is a humorous as well as a piercing dazzle to this scenario. But, oh to be a fly on the wall in that initial meeting between two men who do not talk much! Their level of frivolity or scatter conversation would be no more eventful or eye-catching as the walls surrounding them. That must have been a laugh and a half! Not to dwell too long on this point, but it depicts so much of the incredulity of how the faculty was put together and, more importantly, the fact that it evolved and prospered into such a noted place in the history of dental institutions.

Boston was basking in the glow of a provincial ethos. Change was as difficult as reversing the flow of the Charles River. So, to put Don Booth in this context, it took a certain amount of confidence and youthful expectation that, in spite of not being able to totally interpret Henry's posture, all wrinkles would smooth over. In other words, it would work! Kudos to Don Booth that for whatever reason in grappling with such open-ended speculation, his instincts led him to accept this newly created position as Chairman of the Department of Oral Maxillofacial Surgery. And, he not only took up the mantle of authority, but he succeeded with aplomb and convincing distinction. Gradually growing with the position over time, he threaded the loose ends of fragmented details, defied the possibility of failure by virtue of his style, and eventually became the face of a highly recognized training program. He simply thrived eminently because of an easy manner and a respect he earned through a quiet competence. He would never broadcast or boast because he did not have to. He grew his department into a secure, very successful position among national residencies. The real question today is: now removed in retirement does he emote more feeling and speak with more ease and spontaneity? Well, it doesn't matter, he succeeded where all that mattered was hard work and dependability. Simply put, a really good man! And, a final thought: what a great Dean he would have made: ethically and morally clean, devoted to his work and position, and very resolute: all the qualities reminiscent to one of Henry's mentors, Paul Boyle (former Charles Brackett Professor of Oral Pathology at

Harvard School of Dental Medicine and Dean at Case Western Reserve University School of Dental Medicine).[51]

The Chairman of Prosthodontics was a most convivial, gregarious individual with the type of background which made him opportune. Prosthodontics as a specialty brought the practice of restorative dentistry into a much more defined realm in terms of its relationship with Periodontics. The man Henry selected was Donald Mori, who, ironically, went to Harvard School of Dental Medicine with Drs. Anthony Gianelly and Donald Booth. The existing friendships consequently created easy relationships among the various departments. And, as Drs. Mori and Kramer practiced on the North Shore of Boston, there was a pre-existing relationship which fostered interdepartmental teaching between Periodontics and Prosthodontics. And, Don Mori could handle Kramer because he was easygoing. Out of this grew a conceptual approach to patient management known as Periodontal Prosthesis.[52] Specifically learned techniques came into being as a result of the exchange of ideas between dentists who shared a mutual appreciation for a healthy supporting environment to teeth requiring functional restoration and maintenance. And thus commenced a new way of restoring patients with greater predictability and sustainable health.

It was certainly encouraging that Dr. Mori took over a department which garnered a most capable and experienced faculty. Two in particular, Drs. David Baraban and Leo Talkov, were noteworthy because of their clinical expertise and experience. Leo Talkov in particular was one of the great teaching clinicians. He was a humble man, a great communicator, and possessed an obvious love of his specialty. At the time, they were considerably older than Dr. Mori and brought immediate support and insight necessary to advance teaching concepts which were far more sophisticated and advanced. Periodontal Prosthesis became the watchword of the day.

The birth of this triad-Periodontics-Orthodontics-Prosthodon-

---

[51] See picture of Henry with Paul Boyle and Kurt Thoma.
[52] See Appendix #2, Periodontal Prosthesis at The University of Pennsylvania, School of Dental Medicine.

tics-was cutting edge for the day. And, it remains as a foundational practice tradition today. Don Mori was a teaching maven and possessed remedial qualities which smoothed over some of the overly conflicting arrogance his residents encountered with the Department of Periodontology. He managed relationships with simplicity and ease because he was steadfast and not mercurial. As a result, he was able to advance the academic experience of his residents at a time when egos were predominant. He was a salve, a most needed diplomat amidst mission bound educators.

Herbert Margolis retired in 1968, having given Henry five very good years. The man who succeeded him was the Harvard Dental School classmate of Donald Booth and Donald Mori, Anthony A. Gianelly. Probably more than any of the original faculty, he embraced all the virtues of greatness while gracing the people in his world with inestimable humility. He was a most genuinely talented scholar and one of the great communicators. And, in spite of his physically brutish, common appearance, he was very soft spoken, kindly, and sincerely caring. No doubt, he was the most credentialed man on the faculty, having received his undergraduate degree from Harvard University and his DMD from Harvard School of Dental Medicine. He did his orthodontic training at Harvard/Forsyth Dental Center, received a PhD from Boston University in biology and biochemistry. And, his last formal degree was an MD from Boston University School of Medicine in 1974. He took over the Department of Orthodontics and Dentofacial Orthopedics at Boston University in 1968. He stayed there until 2003, but returned as an interim Chair in 2007. He passed away of a heart attack at the age of 72 in 2009. But, in those years, he was revered and appreciated with profound devotion by all the people in his world. The man was universally characterized by excellence. It was veiled in incredible modesty. He was a lovely man, adored by everyone. It was impossible to find any negative opinions. And, if there was one renegade with an adverse opinion, he would have been run out of town. God help that person! Such behavior would have been sacrilegious! That is how this man was admired. The two-headed Roman God of "beginnings and transitions", Janus, would have Gianelly on one side and Kramer on the other: good and evil, right and wrong, etc.[53] If there was any weakness, it was his love of the hedonistic attractions in life which he embraced to excess: billiards, beer, rich food and sports. Maybe this was only his downfall because his DNA could not stave off a sudden demise. But, while his presence graced the school with his rather subtle erudition, there was no one on the faculty to match this man's sparkle and genius.

His robust energy and knowledge base was channeled with ease and simplicity. He created a mystique that was warranted by his breadth of scientific insight while never showboating even if challenged. Along with Don Booth, he contrasted decidedly to the rest of the faculty always remaining most obviously demure and focused to the needs of his residents and teaching colleagues. He was short on frills, long on substance. There was no one on the faculty who carried comparable qualities for teaching. Before he passed away he was honored with many acknowledgements and awards. When Henry brought him on the faculty, the sense of depth and inspiration that Tony revealed was masked by his physical appearance and the hard bruising type athlete he was. It seemed so incongruous that a man who played in the violent world of football and rugby could turn out to be so quietly resolute and thoughtful. He was able to reduce the complex to simple explanations with a unique skill. He fostered gratitude and recognition in his ability to convey the learning experience with utmost tact and pride in his work. He was patient and understanding while being jocular and easygoing. He was never dismissive or tendentious. If he wanted to make a point, he did it with his own sense of interpretation, never to humiliate or nullify. His skill was his breadth of knowledge and intellectual style. In so many ways he contrasted to the rest of the faculty by virtue of

---

[53] Janus was a mythical Roman God of "beginnings and transitions", but, mentioned by Iago in Shakespeare's *"Otello"*, and, as a result of Iago's chicanery, the two-faced God took on a more conflicting connotation between extremes; reader can refer to *"Janus is a Two-Headed God"* by Suzanne Marie-Knight, 2002, Awe-Struck.

his personality. But, because of the way he comported himself in such an undemanding and effortless manner, he was able to make the best of all his relationships. And, in this manner, he was always dependable and trustworthy.

Tony accrued a legion of dedicated students over the years he chaired the Department of Orthodontics. He was the only original faculty member whose virtues and likeability could be extolled by everyone with whom he made contact. Most people cannot pass through life without ruffling some feathers, even unknowingly. If he had enemies anywhere, they would have been hard to find. He worked his lifetime to develop such a profound understanding of both the purely academic and clinical side of his specialty. The only other faculty member who could match his intellectual grasp of his specialty was Morris Ruben. However, Morris did not possess the comparable clinical acumen to match. Just weeks before he passed he wrote a comprehensive compendium of clinical therapies framed in a syllogistic reportage that will be invaluable to all practicing and academic Orthodontists. It has been suggested that the stream of consciousness is very suggestive of a man knowing that his days were numbered.[54]

Tony was a very polite and extremely gracious man. But, to those who knew him well, he was a very hard liver. He loved his beer, his pizza, his pool, and his partying hard. He definitely got the most out of life, and really did what he wanted to do at all times. A devoted husband, father and grandfather, he was everything to the ones to whom he meant so much.

While the rest of the faculty was absorbed into the academic politics of the school, Tony was definitely above it. He simply did not care, was not interested, and would not waste nor trivialize his time. If you ask the legions of his former students to comment on their memories of him, it is mind bending how grateful they all are for being so fortunate to experience time with him. Tony had a "wow factor", no doubt. He walked through his time seemingly "as a very average, ordinary

---

[54] See Appendix #3, Gianelly's "Basic orthodontic Primer", courtesy of his widow, Ernestine.

man" that he wanted, but he departed having cast a bronzed image of greatness and gentility. No other faculty member projected a similar charisma. There was an easy mutual love and respect between Tony and Henry.

It is impossible to complete the story of the original faculty without addressing one of the more talented and inimitable teachers and clinicians: Melvyn Harris.[55] Mel is a very unique person and was a very interesting teacher and practitioner. Extremely bright and very well-informed on a vast array of subjects, he may be considered the most skilled of all the clinicians of the original faculty. A fully trained Board Certified Oral Maxillofacial Surgeon, he found his niche in retrograde periapical endodontic surgery and lecturing on odontogenic (tooth cells in origin) and non-odontogenic (not tooth cells in origin) tumors to graduate students in training at Boston University. He also served the biopsy service at the school for a great many years.

A product of Harvard College, Tufts Dental School, and specialty training at Boston City Hospital (a Tufts Affiliated Teaching Hospital at the time), he was an extremely self-assured, well-spoken individual. He served as a transition pro tempore Chief of Oral Surgery between Drs. Kurt Thoma and Donald Booth. He was very opinionated, but very rarely was he wrong. This is because he thought everything through very realistically. Quick, razor sharp and direct to a fault, he was a force. A great communicator with the facility to simplify and reduce complex concepts in a facile, cogent manner, he rates as one of the great teachers in the history of the school. He was never wowed by anybody or anything. For all the reasons Kramer dazzled with showboating, Harris was reality based. No showmanship, all authenticity. And, he would not like this said about him because he had a humble side to him. A very easygoing manner, he had a wonderful sense of humor. Joking around with him was an enjoyable time with him. He was not a full time faculty member as he spent most of his time in clinical practice. Nevertheless, his contributions to the teaching at the school were both irreplaceable and serendipitous. He blended the knowledge

---

[55] A colleague and friend over many years; a man of extraordinary character.

of a clinical practitioner with the diagnostic, theoretical considerations in a wonderfully interesting manner. His very direct and knowledge-able viewpoints were profound and teachable moments. He was as interesting as he was informative. He spoke quickly, forthrightly and convincingly as he conveyed information with fluidity and certainty. Not a brash person who performed with flair and pizzazz, he was me-thodical and laconic. He disdained wordiness and bloviating. He was a "straight shooter" personality. There was no way that he was going to get into the social-academic pressure cooker of institutional idiocy that make gifted teachers like Mel Harris turn away. He would never tolerate any pettiness or insipid behavior. It's hard to say because he would shake his head and look askance at the thought, but he would have made a great Dean. He was not made for academia, but he was perfect for it. Academia was replete with "plausible deniability", it was its daily sustenance, vitamin therapy, and Mel "would see blue" dealing with such nonsense. He was not the man who could deal with pet-tifogging or cradling the daily stream of administrative obligations. And, no way would he tolerate bureaucracy. But, if for one minute he could have been drugged to be counterintuitive, what a leader this man would have been. But, that is "the Cleopatra theory of history": coulda, woulda, shoulda if Cleopatra's nose had been shorter, maybe Marcus Antony's fate at the Battle of Actium would have been otherwise (not defeat). In any event Mel succeeded very well "thank you", and these are musings merely to postulate some possibilities retrospectively.[56]

Because of financial constraints, the departmental chairmen de-pended tremendously on the very part-time clinical instructors who gave a half-to-one full day of clinic instruction or short lectures. Without this type of support dental schools would not be self-sustaining. This has been the longstanding tradition for all dental schools. The only difference for Boston University was the need for part-time dental specialists was cru-cial to its survival. Mel Harris went far beyond this type of commitment, but it would have been almost impossible to get the same value out of

---

[56] Gleick, James:*The Information: A History, A Theory, A Flood,* Copyright 2012, Vintage.

someone else when there was really no one else with the same all-around abilities. To use a baseball analogy, if a team slotted extremely talented people at all positions on the field, some better hitters and fielders than others, Mel was the ultimate utility ballplayer that could play a number of the field positions while hitting for average as well as power. It was in this sense that Mel Harris was slotted into areas of key teaching where his utilitarian ability distinguished. The speculation could rightfully be put forth that proportionally his role was certainly understated to such a degree that, like Morris Ruben, the school would not have been suitably staffed without him. Indubitably great karma!

It was unanticipated where this original faculty was headed at the beginning. It was unchartered territory even in the most clear-cut, unquestionable perception. As if having been preordained by good fortune, a dissociative benevolence of unknown origin perhaps, the teaching qualities recessed deeply in these "characters" surfaced to throttle the world with an almost stately renown. All of them, and so complete. But, the part-time faculty in each specialty contributed in such an overwhelmingly reliable manner that their own star qualities reflexively bolstered the institutional distinction of Boston University. Such people as Alan Shuman and Gerald Isenberg (both in private practice with Henry), Richard Chaikin[57] (son of Bernard Chaikin), Hyman Smuckler (who was vastly under-positioned and terribly under-valued), J. David Kohn, Myron Nevins, Leo Talkov, Richard Cardiff (who died way prematurely; a wealth of talent in Prosthodontics), Howard Skurow and Herbert Yolin (both also died way too prematurely), and early on in his career Steven Anapolle (who passed away at 56 years old) etc., were teaching emissaries who represented the distinguished elite of Boston University. These full and part-time practitioners and so many others grew their own recognition, but all because of the bully pulpit proffered by a Boston University association. Deference should be made to Dr. Victor Dietz who taught and practiced in the shadow of Anthony Gianelly. But, Vic, now retired, was the consummate professional with the most kindly, easygoing personal style. He was a

---

[57] Author grew up playing golf with Richard and his father quite often; great conversations and memories.

reflection of the quiet, modest, and most capable standards Tony set. Vic clearly fit the bill with that very unstated competence that he contained with very little fanfare.

And, just as the older faculty grew into their positions, younger full time faculty were coming along who would latter assume the mantle of leadership. People like A. Stephen Polins and Frank Oppenheim etc., exemplified the future as their training in their respective specialties would sustain the tradition Henry was establishing. Steve Polins became a resource of skilled clinical wherewithal and the ability to convey his message to students. Full time for so many years, he represents a breed whose knowledge will be almost impossible to replace. He is a product of the formative days at B.U. when Periodontics mixed a clinical and basic science basis for the practice of Orthodontics, Endodontics and Prosthodontics. Steve represents the halcyon days of the coordinated conceptual thinking of the specialties for integrated treatment panning. No doubt people like him are not sufficiently valued, often because politics overrides sensible judgment. Just as well, Frank Oppenheim endowed Boston University with a sterling cutting-edge research mission over many years. He represents everything Henry had in mind when he conflated the importance of biomedical research with the clinical sciences at the University of Pennsylvania in the early 1950's. Frank's brilliant contributions and dedication to his years of inquiry reflect the original mission of the school. He is without doubt the very essence of what the school is all about. As congenial and loyal as he is capable, Frank is the perfect complement to those like Steve Polins in the clinical sciences. These men are the perfect match for what Henry had in mind. And, their reference here is to remember Henry's postulate that the research scientist and the clinician should embrace each other's talents. The three men, Hyman Smuckler, Steve Polins and Frank Oppenheim[58] are atavistic of true educators who brought

---

[58] All three individuals invested with a cornucopia of talent in their individual bailiwick: Smuckler in "Occlusion", Polins in the overall diagnosis, treatment planning and treatment of periodontal disease, and Oppenheim in the area of molecular and cell biology: very outstanding in their areas of expertise.

justification to Henry's ultimate dream for devoted and down-to-earth faculty. They stood in direct contrast to those who would have cast their influence by imagery and not substance. These three have brought honor to Henry's memory.

Mention must be made about a man who came early to Boston University without any perception of what his position represented, or, if there would be any tangible sense of his daily responsibilities. Very rapidly this man became the archetypal laboratory technician. To many his presence was ho-hum and an occasional yawn, that's until he was needed! And, very gradually he became the omnipresent source to whom all residents gravitated for their master's theses. He became a one-man army for all laboratory needs. His name, Arthur Bloom,[59] became a "household" name.

He came to work for Henry at the very beginning without any laboratory training whatsoever. However, in those days, the late 1950's, governmental regulatory commissions were not in existence. Therefore, coming out of the Navy without any particular direction, training on the job seemed like an acceptable proposition. As an Oral Pathologist among the many hats that Henry wore, Arthur would be his ideal person to bring to the laboratory. And, by the time Morris Ruben came on board in the early 1960's, Arthur would have the best for his training. He learned quickly and with that effervescent quality he brought every day. Always a sense of mirth and congeniality, he was a pleasure to be around. The unfortunate issue was his schedule became frenetic as the school grew in size and his responsibilities required additional help that never materialized. And yet he responded always with a "oh well, gee-whiz" as he proceeded into his work without fanfare.

Arthur Boom was a very hardworking, faithful employee who never shirked his responsibilities. He crafted his own corner niche in a laboratory which he kept organized, clean and always on schedule

---

[59] Arthur Bloom: head laboratory technician at BUSGD with whom I had a lot of contact when I was doing my Oral Pathology-Pathology training between BUSGD and Massachusetts Memorial Hospital (now part of Boston State Hospital and Boston University Medical Center).

for deadline obligations. He was a diminutive, well-dressed, always clean-shaven man who met anyone with a very broad smile and open greeting. He possessed a unique charm with the ability to mire through the academic weeds of controversy or interdepartmental conflicts. His office-laboratory became gossip corner. Over time he became very politically astute, and often he had to tiptoe very lightly through sharp edges swiping at his fee. He served everyone's laboratory needs in a timely manner, and his length of tenure was a testament to the wonderful success he had with all the demands made on his time. He started at Boston University when he was in his mid-thirties and didn't fully retire until he was in his early seventies. He became a lasting fixture of the school whose presence was most often terribly understated. Shamefully, there were some part-time instructors who casually pilloried him at times because he kept a quiet persona. However, this is the quality that made him an inviolable, dependable employee with Henry's endorsement and appreciation. In general, in the historical record of Boston University, Arthur Bloom will be honored because of consistency in length of service, never fractious, snarky or controversial. And, in any academic environment, this would be a singular achievement mostly for the often intimate setting which is commonly a depot for rumors, relationship issues and interdisciplinary rivalries. Often being in so much demand for timely laboratory preparations, he was very often the butt of anger, frustration, and casual irritability if he responded with objectivity. Over his tenure he had occasional aides, but none that lasted. Therefore, he was always dancing around the hot fires of demanding residents.

Arthur Bloom should be remembered as a man who came as a blank slate who transformed into a very deft technician. He had a great sense of humor and loved to joke around. Opinions will be mostly praiseworthy, but only those who really appreciated his circumstances will clearly understand how well he served Boston University. He represented everything Henry stood for: opportunity for anyone who could rise to the occasion. He always believed that if the opportunity is provided, people can merit their independence unless and until they demonstrate they do not have the maturity to be responsible. Arthur never let Henry down because he was always diligent. Most of all, he was wonderful to over-programmed residents because he provided them both emotional and technical support. Anyone who spent time his laboratory realized his easygoing nature, but he was always punctual and fastidious.

To some degree Arthur would have appeared to be easily replaceable. However, he gradually developed that intangible factor which made him so necessary to keep the laboratory functional, clean and always evolving. Most people really did not get to know his true personality, but he was always grateful to Henry for his job. He never took this lightly. There are not enough words to demonstrate how important he was to the school. It is unfortunate that, from a reality point of view, his memory will ebb very quickly. That is a fact of life, but hopefully these thoughts will serve to justifiably state how much his contribution meant both in the style and pride he manifested in his work.

So much more analysis of Henry's "cast of characters" would demand another book probing separately into each for their deep personal and professional contributions. Recapitulating thoughts of each in an overview conjures up so many thoughts about their growth and emergence as the "greats" of their specialties. But, the one fact that must endure over all else is they all served because of the opportunity and stage Henry M. Goldman provided. Without this none would have succeeded to the heights that they did. Yes, they initially gambled their futures on a whim that Boston University would succeed. But, they all knew that theirs was an investment in Henry Goldman.

It is important to realize that Henry was very proud of his faculty. He was as surprised as anyone with what happened to the Department of Periodontology. What is fascinating is how zombie like those that bought into Kramer's Jonestown-like mind-streaming did so because not one ever took the time to research Henry's stellar contributions to the dental sciences. To them, their total allegiance was to Gerry Kramer. What they did not realize was that Kramer was but "a false flag" fronting and attempting to obscure Henry's deep scientific background. They were exploited by Kramer's cult of personality, not by the substance which was very broad, but very shallow. Those that survive today foster this blind, illusory loyalty almost in the same way Socrates was condemned by men who were prejudiced by their own ignorance as they failed to probe his very open syllogistic reasoning in defense of himself.[60] If the residents thought for one minute that Henry was unaware what transpired during Kramer's tenure, they were terribly unaware. Kramer's behavior was tolerated with great dismay, but he was given a long leash to either mellow, back away or totally retreat to a much more elegant countenance. He did not attempt to punish Kramer for his insolence and impudence. Kramer's final departure was the result of his own failure to keep his defiant behavior untenable. He was a tragic person who just couldn't control himself for reasons no one will ever really understand. As La Rochefoucauld very cogently summarized: "Cunning is a poor substitute for sagacity".[61] Kramer's cunning wore very thin. Henry passed away having long put this behind him, but always mystified. No other faculty member was ever aware that this lasted for so long, at least by public or even private admission.

The history of The Boston University School of Graduate Dentistry shows that it was a very unique period in the history of dentistry. The institution came about because of only one person. Henry gave it its birth, development, and opportunity to flourish. The germination of ideas that he conceived was born while serving in World War II as a pathologist. The prescient ideas of the core science basis for dental investigation and practice blossomed during the war. If any other scientific investigator throughout the world could have willed a like institution, it would have been done. But it wasn't. Time has a way of creating alternate history, either opinion generated or mythical in feeling. As nostalgic or banal as it might be stated, clearly no man has ever endeavored to capture the spirit of such an overwhelming task and pragmatically engineer it to a favorable outcome. Henry, to

---

[60] Guthrie, W.K.C.: *SOCRATES*, Copyright 1972, Cambridge University Press.
[61] Rochefoucauld, Francois de La: *MAXIMS*, Copyright 1959, Translation, Penguin Classics..

Dentistry, was both the "Alpha" and "Omega", the man to whom so many are obligated.

All the original faculty chairmen: Morris Ruben, Donald Booth, Herbert Schilder, Spencer Frankl, Gerald Kramer, Donald Mori and Anthony Gianelly were the spokes in the wheel to spin excellence in education. Their eminence which grew in time was solely due to their free reign. Previously given noted significance, the late 19th and early 20th century American writer Henry James captured with vivid depiction in his novel, "Portrait of a Lady": "...he put wind in her sails.[62] Henry Goldman breathed wind in their sails to allow them to blossom as educators and endow their success through the freedoms of expression and development the school offered. To be part of a new opportunity was the greatest gift for any professional man at the time. He brought in these very raw neophytes never knowing what to expect and gave them a stage, a presence, a "total gift" in a very real sense. And as such, anything that should be acknowledged in terms of the future endowment and success of The Henry M. Goldman School of Dental Medicine should always default to Henry. He furnished a timeless gift that has no historical boundary. The future of the school will always retain his enduring imprimatur.

While he was still in good health, the torch of leadership was passed to Spencer Frankl when he became the school's second Dean. He bore the responsibility to live up to "a living image". Now under the third Dean, Dr. Jeffrey Hutter, an Endodontist, the mission statement of the school is moving forward under his guidance. As the first "outsider", the demands will assuredly be great over time and his decisions during growth will be crucial. To see what's ahead, let's summarize going back.

As Herbert Schilder was erroneously overlooked to replace Henry as Dean, consider that some people did not like him. It is a very narrow viewpoint because of his obvious legitimacy as a leader in education and a political impresario. He was perfect for the position. Kramer was a

---

[62] Henry James: *Portrait of a Lady*, Copyright 1961-Reprint Edition, Houghton Mifflin and Company.

certain no go. And, Anthony Gianelly, though a certain choice, frankly did not want the position. Tony was totally apolitical. He cringed at the thought of fighting political battles, for any cause. It was not in his blood. His personality was not made for the sly, cagey, distrustful people he would have to engage. And, he certainly would not countenance having to make decisions with deception and false pretense. It was far beyond his tolerance. As for Donald Booth, maybe his personality might have been too demure, but if offered, he most likely could have grown into the position. This kind of speculation works only at gambling tables, but he certainly would have rendered far more credibility than Spencer Frankl. Why Henry did not pursue an outside replacement is uncertain. But, in a sense he did by asking D. Walter Cohen, his first student and former Dean at The University of Pennsylvania School of Dental Medicine.[63] He reneged because he did not want to leave his father in Philadelphia. This was unfortunate. However long he might have endured, it would have contained the indwelling turmoil swirling about and would have made for a smooth transition. It would have also given time for a wise search between Walter and Henry after Henry's retirement. Walter regrets this decision. Henry lived another fourteen years and certainly would have slow-moved the process with time for careful pursuit. But, the reality was that Henry felt pressed, and, for no other reason, there was Spencer. He was the default choice. Was it right or wrong? Was it appropriate?

Spencer Frankl came in as his own man. His early refrain was quite deceptive. He attempted to change his stripes, but the stripes were still there. From a back, unassuming position he was cast front and center. From the diminutive man of congeniality and a friendly persuasion, he was suddenly blank-faced, thorny and aggressive. He took to the position Napoleon-like and jostled with anybody in his way. He came in as a man of self-interest and captious behavior as he pursued an expansion into programs that would benefit his goal simply to place his official stamp on his tenure and legacy. He fired Gerry Kramer in 1980 because he got in his way, though Kramer felt he "retired". So, perhaps

---

[63] Conversations with D. Walter Cohen.

by then, the feelings were mutual and understood. Frankl, however, was obliged after Henry's support. The interesting part of Kramer's post-script was the life he established after Boston University. He established his journal, he had his yearly conference, and his minions started his annual fund. But, for Gerry Kramer, it was never the same. He had a Chairmanship and full professorship in his hands, and, a prospect to become a Dean. But in his tragic inability to get by himself, he tripped all over trying to rediscover a professional life. It was a sad ending to a great deal of potential. And, as to Spencer Frankl, he spent the next decade while Henry was still alive, carrying on with angst in his heart and loathing in his eyes. His true colors surfaced. All in all, Henry might have still benefitted by searching outside the school when Walter was unavailable. In the end, all the back-and-forth was not kind to anyone. But, one thing is for certain, the ones with all the political ambitions forgot who got them there.

Just a comment on Morris Ruben. He never came into the conversation because he simply could not cover the necessary clinical needs as a Dean. He was never a clinician despite his excellence as an educator and researcher. No one will ever deny his academic qualifications, but he was severely lacking in clinical experience. At the end, he and his wife were severely hurt by this. They became surly, resentful and socially disagreeable. It was so unfortunate for a person who was probably responsible for holding the entire fabric of the early days together from completely unravelling. Morris was a good man with an honorable spirit. In his day, he was a gentle giant in his field of expertise, Oral Biology. He will always be remembered for his wonderful spirit, loyalty, and the deep void he filled so admirably.

In such instances there are "no rights and wrongs". The only true arbiter of controversial situations is time itself. There will always be sides taken, but it probably is best forgotten. But, Henry's tenure as founder and first Dean was tainted by this event, echoing even today long after his passing. Henry's failing can be compared in a way to a parent reprimanding a son. Depending on the manner in which it is done, there may or may not be blowback whether he is correct or not.

Henry was very public in his remonstration of Gerry Kramer, and this was costly. A listening public will never know the real facts and more often will voice an opinion based on innuendo and rumor. But, most will never knew the real facts. Such a consideration played right into Henry's very public statements. Henry was stubborn and did not reconcile the continuing bad feeling. He should have nipped it in the bud because he was Dean, and a leader must display the qualities inherent in leadership.[64] Nevertheless, Gerry was dishonorable in his complete failure to understand that he owed Henry for his entire career at Boston University. Kramer simply could not resolve in his mind that Henry put him in the position of Chairman. He was confusing his opinion with fact. Like the often heard truism: a person can provide his/her own opinion, but he/she cannot provide his/her personal facts. The fact was clear: Kramer was in his position at the pleasure of Henry M. Goldman. He could never understand that. His rogue behavior was neatly camouflaged from his residents and other faculty. And, he never came forth with how many conversations he had with Henry about his mischievous conduct. Whatever the words or lack thereof between them, his behavior was wrong. Like the reckless son, he should have treated Henry with respect and honor. It can only be speculated what Gerry's distorted interpretation was, but it certainly played out with misfortune and catastrophic repercussions for the faculty, the residents, the employees, the dental and patient community, and, most of all, Henry, Gerry and their families. It was despoiling and an irretrievable tragedy. Outsiders, and even insiders without direct appreciation of the circumstances, are left with a very oblique, distorted image.

Gerry Kramer was a skillful teacher. A very competent surgeon, a dedicated teacher graced with fluent and suave communication skills, he quickly attracted a rapidly expanding number of followers throughout the world. By dint of personality, he forcefully grew his legions. He had it all. Though he did not always have his way with other university chairmen, for the most part, he was sufficiently captivating

---

[64] Machiavelli, Niccolo: *The Prince*, Copyright 1995-Reprinted Edition, Hackett Publishing Company.

and mesmeric enough to draw in many followers. Henry simply did not possess the force of character to compete in this arena. And there lies the rub. The misfortune of being misunderstood versus the good fortune of gratuitous genuflection. It was a clash of personalities, never a competition between academic equals. Henry won that battle every single day of the week. Finally, Gerry was a very small consideration in Henry's everyday life. He had to deal with it because of some very disquieting events. In the grand scheme, however, there were too many factors in the management of a school for Henry to have raised his kerfuffle with Gerry to greater significance.

Retrospectively, the issue was probably mishandled by Henry. There is no doubt that the art of politics was never Henry's suit. However, it must be clear that any and every part of Boston University belongs to Henry M. Goldman. The building, the life that breathes vitality into the teaching process, the lasting improvements associated with the growing reputation are all the mirror reflections of the lifeblood energy Henry expended to bring Boston University to where it is today. This must never be forgotten. As (Valentin Louis Georges Eugene) Marcel Proust,[65] the French philosophical essayist and novelist, so effusively characterized in his very well-known novel, "A La Recherche Du Temps Perdu", elements of time, the present and future will always feel the pulse of times past as it leaves its footprint everywhere it passes. The people who will pass through now and into the future must remember who was responsible for what the school is today. Failure to remember the past history, Henry and his cast of characters, will be a grave rebuke of the vigor and true grit expended for such a venerable institution.

The original faculty emerged from a "nowhere state" of being, rough-edged, uncertain and dazzled to become one of the premier group of educators around the world. They were all engaged in asserting their wills on the developing institution. The times had a taste of quaintness because everything was very new and thoroughly undeveloped. There was an untainted quality of group effort that lasted

---

[65] Proust, Marcel: *In Search of Lost Time (A La Recherche D'Un Temps Perdu)*, Copyright 2013, Centaur (Republication).

through the early years until the reality of material benefits finally covered over the simple expectations that were quickly forgotten. Human nature being what it is, this was to be expected. As time marches on what will endure will be "the wow factor", the almost incredulity: that Henry did what he did, that he did it in the face of so much stress and daily challenge, and that he bequeathed the image of greatness with unswerving humility and honor, never to be forgotten. He was an icon!

CHAPTER 6

The Golden Age

Often, references to periods in history by a multitude of characterizations can be misleading. For example, Mark Twain referred to the latter half of the 19th century as "The Gilded Age". His reference was curiously and specifically chosen because on surface the glitter of wealth acquired with massive industrial expansion after The Civil War made rich people richer and poor people without a glimmer of hope. It was gilded on the surface, however, masking the perfidious industrialists, the so-called robber barons, who rapaciously ensconced safely away in their expansive royal domains leaving "the people" to suffer through very hard times as the country cascaded into severe financial crisis. The deception can be very misleading without the sensibility for the historical underpinnings. Between1860 and 1913 there were eight significant recessions and four outright Panics (1873, 1893, 1896, and 1907). (165) All were followed by rebound economic resurgence and lifestyle improvements. However, Mark Twain referred to times being "gilded" because they were limited to upper echelons of society with the brunt of poverty common to the waves of immigrants. Industrialization brought astounding wealth, but it certainly did not touch the people working for the great barons of the railroads, banking, manufacturing (textiles, printing, paper, shoes, etc.), importing-exporting, mineral exploration, etc. Massive domestic expansion did not trickle down to the laboring population until the birth of the middle class in the 1950's.

That being said, after WWII the country emerged into very

peaceful and auspicious times. Dreams could and were realized in the 1950's. Self-actualization for individuals aspiring to make do on their targeted goals was a reflection of the easygoing, neutral conditions of the era. Returning from a rather prolonged, nasty war on two fronts, people were ready to set about to the business of prosperity. People became engaged in all lines of factory work which grew out of the industrial advances specifically for wartime, characterized by President (formerly Allied Commander General) Dwight D. Eisenhower as "the military industrial complex". With the material growth of the 1950's came urbanization as the newly acquired wealth allowed families to escape the cloistered entrapment of the inner city to open spaces in rural areas where there was a greater sense of comfort and contentment. With this came advances in education, the health sector, and socialization (eg. YMCA's, country clubs, sports facilities, restaurants, hotels, etc.). In essence, the country was reaching out in every direction which would reap the benefits of unregulated hard work and the desire to secure an enduring lifestyle for many generations to come. The thinking was positive and the feelings were inspiriting. This age in our history was "golden" because all fears were transmogrified into a glorious and enthusiastic emotional rush infused throughout the country by "winning the war". The benefits were through and through to the potential of all society, not confined to the rich only. All the energy of negative worry and deep concern for survival suddenly converted to an indisputable surge of initiative and achievement. Dentistry was positioned fortuitously as a welcoming beneficiary of the new prosperity. In the modern era, which would be defined by the beginning of the industrial age, the profession would garner all the benefits from this swelling economic growth. It was a "golden age", not a "gilded one".

From the U.S. Bureau of Labor Statistics, (159) the Consumer Expenditure Survey, the U.S. Census Bureau, and the Statistical Abstract of the United States, it was very clear that living was affordable and comfortable as the country was rebuilding coming out of the most destructive war in human history. Between 1948 and 1953 unemployment was at a low of 4% of a population of 150 million as the country grew

10.4 %. The real key to point out is that the metrics demonstrate quite clearly that the five years right after the war set the stage for the growth spurt in the manufacturing complex which ensured and enabled a continuous wave of prosperity. Employment served as a basis for social well-being. The country turned back to the essential societal needs: health, education and sense of community. There was a turn back from national exigencies to local and regional necessities of life. The statistics reflect a balance between national, New York and Boston spending. There was an equal distribution between the requisite parameters of food, clothing and housing in the comparative survey. Though expenditures allocated for the miscellaneous category of "other" (as in what was of local community priorities), essentially they paralleled each other. But, the key was rising employment among both men and women (and the nation as a whole) allowing for a substantial rise in comfort, security and ambition. The interesting fact is that the harmony and productivity of the 1950's set the stage for the 1960's which became self-serving, more dangerous, culturally divisive and rebellious. The cultural revolt of the mid- to late 1960's somehow could not handle the gift of prosperity from the fifteen years after WWII. The overabundance, sudden wealth experience and inability to handle the social consequences made for a rebellious, renegade youth as government regulatory controls were inconsequential. Acquisitive materialism gave rise to a confused, indolent, listless youth. Self-reliance and appreciation for material well-being and social harmony were the keystones of the 1950's, but the 1960's unfortunately made the sudden prosperity unappreciated. But, during the 1950's, if desire was present, the world was anyone's oyster. The turbulent 1960's resulted from societal breakdown elicited by drugs, the emergence of inner city crime, a middle class leaving poverty behind in the growing ghettos, and growing labor unions which made for a welter of industrial strikes.

Henry's period of ambitious productivity was the beneficiary of the positive spike arising from redirected energies. His work at The University of Pennsylvania was timely. The socio-economic metrics grew in appreciable importance and sustained all through the decade.

Less than a decade from WWII, the times were rife for the academic planning which would set the stage for the eventual emergence of The Department of Stomatology at Boston University Medical School in 1958.

The economics made the changes possible. The initiatives taken were not fragile or of questionable value for long term planning. They were tangible and realistic. Henry M. Goldman was a groundbreaking example of this new era which was ready for innovative thinking. He had a vision which evolved from his education and practical experience. For whatever reason, he envisioned the change as a process, not a short term fix that might fall on its haste and lack of judgment. Continuous vertical growth was what he had in mind, not a series of lateral movement and change. One center, one change, one move.

The profession was stilted by what he saw as a continuum of lateral movement where programs all adopted new metrics in training without any thought to specialty integration. He felt this lacked purpose and educational perspective, merely stifling creativity and inventiveness. Henry once referred to the four years of dental education as a process inevitably leading to the acquisition of "a union card" for the purpose of practicing mechanical procedures which would never evolve. By the mere fact that they would be repetitive and desultory, they would stilt mental acuity and innovation. However, it was not the act of applied mechanical procedure that bothered Henry so much as the lack of co-ordinated investigational research in the biologic sciences. Restorative dentistry had become a dead end road without any consideration for the preservation of a healthy periodontium. Up to that point, the early pioneers of the 1920's, 1930's and 1940's were more engaged in the cleaning of teeth. Scientific investigation was quite shallow and blind to the causation of tooth loss. The early mutterings and ideas about therapies relating to soft and hard tissue therapies were still way off in the future. Henry's tutelage under Kurt Thoma instilled the sense that teeth are lost by chronic disease of the tissues supporting teeth. To effect change in the way the dental profession viewed the meaning of long term preservation of teeth for function over a lifetime thinking had to change.

His reversal of thinking emerged with an energy to lay the groundwork for change in a very dramatic fashion. He was to become the paladin of modern day dentistry by redirecting the business of graduate education to make this possible.

Henry was very in tune with the politics swirling within the profession. But, if he had to butt heads with the stultifying orthodoxy within the profession, he would. Many years later this would come to haunt him. But, for the time being, even with the most sanguine attitude, he knew change would be very politically difficult. Even the concept of the DAT he found to be overly perfunctory and deferential to mechanics as the profession's mainstay to extract the best candidates for dental school. For many years the people who went to dental school were those who could not gain admission to medical school. This was more fact than fiction. And very succinctly, the medical testing was far more advanced by the specific intent to measure reasoning skills as opposed to dentistry's emphasis on hand-eye coordination. Like Henry's admonishing dental education as a union card attainment process, the DAT was its screening–filtering mechanism. Showing that old standards die hard and long after his passing, the DAT (in its design) is pretty much the same despite tweaking its elements now and then.

Henry's timing was decisive, no doubt. Coming out of WWII, conditions in the country were ripe for an overhaul or, at least, an alternative thinking which would lead to tangible change. In the late 1950's when traditional practice was in its heyday, Henry was speaking quite often about rebuilding the bony apparatus around teeth which were being actively ravaged by ongoing disease. He articulated his ideas with an almost excitable tone, and picture this from a man who most often was usually overly understated.

The 1950 -1960 was historically the most unique decade of the 20th century. Many adjectives could describe it: serene, hopeful, simple but innovative, easy, friendly, predictable, stable, and productive. There are probably more, but the point is that the decade was ready for Henry's creative thinking. A decade later it might have happened, but the circumstances would have been far more restrictive. The country was starting to move in far greater government control. It was "golden" in the 1950's as growth was spurred by individuals with commitment and savvy, not from the bureaucrats in government which likely would have killed the entire concept. The post-doctoral program was planned and built with private funding. The university has always been a private institution in spite of the fact it carries the city name eponymously. It certainly made the entire project more complex to shoulder, but, in the end, its independence to ensure the proper result was mandatory.

When he returned to Boston after the war, his continued interaction with Kurt Thoma inspired a more intrinsic way of thinking about dentistry both as a profession as well as its scientific basis. Kurt Thoma was his mentor as a researcher-clinician. Henry could have easily set out to concentrate his energies in Oral Surgery to complement his career as an Oral Pathologist. Thoma was an Oral Surgeon as well as an Oral Pathologist at Harvard, and he became the first Harvard affiliated Chief of Oral Surgery at the Massachusetts General Hospital in Boston (66) But, as stated, his eyes were opened to the causative mechanisms for tooth loss. It certainly would have been convenient to follow immediately in Thoma's footsteps, and it would have taken him into a very productive lifetime of teaching, research and practice. But, as he so often said, there was such an opening for redirecting the biological sciences in fighting tooth loss that he felt choosing this life journey would be groundbreaking. His premonition was never questioned. From Harvard to Washington, D.C. and back to Harvard, there was certainly lots of time to contemplate what would be his life's path.

The contacts at Harvard, which had a very select teaching staff in Oral Pathology, led to his work at the Armed Forces Institute of Pathology in Washington, D.C.[66] during the war. The four plus years spent in this position was state-of-the art training for the day, and it was noteworthy that his position gave him exposure to a unique training center with educational opportunities on many levels. Maybe it would have happened in Boston as well, but Walter Reed Hospital was proprietary. Firstly, he gained exposure to top level scientific laboratory tech-

---

[66] See Website: www.afip.org (133).

niques which were cutting edge for the day. In the field of Pathology the laboratory learning experience was uniquely tied to the clinical behavior disease entities being investigated. Secondly, his on-site education in internal and oral medicine was a very rare opportunity. There probably is a preponderance of truth in the fact that had he not been in the Army his future life would have been very different. When he was discharged from the army, he had a clear-cut vision which would resound for the rest of his teaching life. The AFIP was serendipitous. On March 31, 2011 the AFIP stopped accepting consultation cases and in September of that year it was "disestablished". However, it transferred its operations to a different venue and re-opened on April 1, 2011 (that same year) under the new name: The Joint Pathology Center (JPC).[67] The AFIP was established during Abraham Lincoln's administration in 1862 and grew into the lofty reputation it rightfully deserved. For a pathologist, it was the place to be, be it for training or as a permanent position. It became the apotheosis in pathology. So, for Henry, his appointment to the AFIP in the United States Armed Forces was almost transcendent. How often is it demonstrated that in the lives of historic individuals one moment, one experience, or one relationship can be emphatically life-changing? But, in Henry's case the place was blue-ribbon, the people inventive and charismatic, and, the experiences seeded with dramatic teaching moments. There was nothing commonplace by what he saw on a daily basis. There is no question that it had a dazzling effect on him. From this period in his life a new reality set into his thinking that muffled convention and sparked a desire to be groundbreaking where others were blind. His life was classic for being in the right place at the right time, but, making the most of it was noteworthy. The only impediment would be to figure out where he would sell his ideas, make them reality, and demonstrate that his grand scheme was not just "pie in the sky".

In Meditation XVII, Devotions upon Emergent Occasions, the great poet, satirist, lawyer and cleric in the Church of England John Donne is often and appropriately referenced with these words:

---

[67] See Website: www.jpc.capmed.mil (180).

"No man is an island entire of itself; every man
is a piece of the continent, a part of the main;
if a clod be washed away by the sea, Europe
is the less, as well as any manner of thy friends or of thine
own were; any man's death diminishes me,
because I am involved in mankind.
and therefore never send to know for whom
the bell tolls; it tolls for thee.[68]

Even the classic, revered 20th century American writer Ernest Hemingway cited (and venerated him by so doing) John Donne with titling one of his great novels: For Whom the Bell Tolls.[69] In relating this to Henry Goldman, it is no stretch to see that he was suddenly returning home to Boston "…an island…" to some extent and yet connected to the mainstream by virtue of his new mission to promote and package the ideas he realized would reframe dental education. To the extent that the years spent in Washington, D.C. would conclusively redirect his professional life, that he would be a difference maker, and that he would separate from the prevailing direction of his profession was real but daunting. To this point, he was fortunately insulated from the mainstream. He was about to jump into a mix of different people and places where he would no longer be protected from life's little misfortunes, double-crossings, and just the "regular people" who might wish for bad things and hope for failure: aka "a reality check"!

Asked often if he really knew what he was going to do, and if he had this plan buried in his mind, he looked up with a very serious poker face and exclaim: "Of course"! Then, he would go about his business, pushing piles of papers around for a moment or two, and then turn around very vocal saying: "Are you nuts, I didn't have the foggiest notion"! The truth is that he went with his instinct, but he had a feeling that with

---

[68] Donne, John: *The Devotions-Meditation XVII*, Copyright 1624, (County) England.
[69] Hemingway, Ernest: *For Whom the Bell Tolls, Copyright 1995, Copyright 2010, Scribner (Republication).*

hard work there was a good chance his ideas would "cut the mustard" (an expression he and his brother liked to use).[70]

Somewhat overwhelmed by the challenging task to lure organized dentistry into a more progressive future, the task at hand was to step into this uncertain plan one step at a time. He must have felt like a one-man army, a singular voice trying to accomplish something that sounded preposterous in the breadth of its scope and planning. "No man is an island…" so he sourced his brother for ideas, business advice and a lot of comforting. No doubt, he instinctively understood that "…an island entire of itself…" would probably lead to a great story with a very poor ending. Tethered closely to his past, his education, and, his rather harsh and abstemious upbringing, his immediate objectives would have to depend on the distinctive nature of his training while effectively emerge from the quiet shell of deeply held thoughts and emotions to embrace a more outgoing countenance. This would not be easy because this was not Henry at all. But, he couldn't go it alone. He did not have to "…to send to know for whom the bell tolls…" it was now tolling for him as the years in Washington made him a different kind of Oral Pathologist. He now saw dentistry way out of its domain. Any hope to bring graduate dental education into a singularity with biological principles of science would be daunting. He did not have in mind to just lead with background, he wanted a full integration of cutting edge research and clinical innovation as the basis of all the specialties under the umbrella of one institution. This was a divergence from accustomed, traditional pathways in dental education, both in training programs and even at the pre-doctoral level. As transcendent as Henry's thinking was, this was not going to make converts overnight. So, for a great while he was what he realized he could be to succeed: "…an island entire of itself…." But, gradually, his force of his character would relentlessly persist.

There was a strange irony to all of this. Unlike his brother, he was very much a minimalist materially. Money never motivated him, be it in practice or what he would derive as a benefit from all his plans for

---

[70] Author's familiarity.

the school. It would not be untruthful to say that he really did not care about money per se. He was a very modest dresser, he never drove expensive cars, he lived in very "humble abodes", and never squandered his money in patronizing fancy restaurants. It would be most humorous to imagine that if he had lived in the 10th and 11th centuries somewhere in middle-Europe, he more than likely would have been the quintessential monastic cleric cloistered comfortably away in a remote abbey mumbling pastorals in an updated version of Middle French, and feeling quite dedicated to his mission in life. This was Henry Goldman, the learned, very quiet thinker.

This was a huge contrast to his older brother who, because he manufactured high-styled lady shoes and was immersed deeply into the fashion industry, scrupulously lived a much more embellished lifestyle. In a very conservative manner, he lived on a more material and capacious footing. Never ever gaudy or ostentatious, but never depriving himself of the benefits of his business associated accoutrements. Well, two men cut from the same cloth with diametrically opposed material habits. Clearly, without his brother to point out certain challenges that would confront him and to enforce certain modifications in his thinking and outlook, it would have been impossible to undertake what was a financial undertaking of major business planning. The irony is that without his brother this "floater", this brainstorm recessed deeply in his will and his mind would never become a reality. Henry needed Eddie to keep him focused away from the dream and into the reality ahead. As Nat King Cole sang in one of his songs from his "Unforgettable 1984 Album" (a reprise album), from the song "Straighten Up and Fly Right": yes Eddie had to get Henry "to straighten up and fly right". (29) What a strange irony for Henry who was always so independent to listen to a very successful older brother who would never say "boo" and dare to intercede in someone else's affairs, let alone his brother. How bizarre, really, how dramatic!

Henry was very much a dreamer, a man who was a deep thinker. Having trouble filtering miscreant or sycophantish people from his life was not due unawareness. He was dismissive because he refused to divert his energies and waste time. As Mark Twain intoned: "You can't depend on your eyes when your imagination is out of focus."[71] Well, Henry had a selective imagination in his ability to focus on things he considered important (the school), but not people who would persist in making trouble for him requiring his attention. Or, even, who was going to pay for all of his ideas? Like the infant who covers her/his face thinking she/he can't be seen, not caring or paying attention with much at risk was not wise. It was the kicking the can down the road disease in the face of "fear", so to speak, until all hell would break loose![72][73]

But, in terms of his school planning, he was like a kid with a new Christmas toy. His eyes observed every detail because his focus was so intense. And, the timing was very much a factor because the economic conditions were so favorable. It was a "golden age" because private industry had rebounded significantly. Gaining support was an onerous task, but it was very successful. Had it been just ten years earlier, it would have been extremely challenging, maybe impossible. From the time he left Washington to the time BUSGD was chartered was eighteen years. During those years a lot happened.

His networking with the early educators: Lester W. Burket, Paul Boyle, Hamilton Robinson, Kurt Thoma, etc. gave Henry access to the academic world. Leaving Washington, D.C., he returned to Boston where he practiced on Bay State Road near the Boston Common in Boston, Massachusetts. He was also on the staff at Harvard teaching and doing research in Oral Pathology. Perhaps this should be viewed either as his formative professional years, or maybe the period in time when his life completely changed. Very early in the 1950's he was asked by Lester Burket, then the Dean at The University of Pennsylvania School

---

[71] Twain, Mark: *The Family Mark Twain (Compilation of all his books and short stories)*, Copyright 1992, Barnes and Noble.

[72] Wise, Jeff: *Extreme Fear: The Science of Your Mind in Danger,* Copyright 2011, Palgrave Macmillan Trade.

[73] Amen, Daniel G., M.D.: *Change Your Brain, Change Your Life: The Breakthrough Program for Conquering Anxiety, Depression, Obsessiveness, Anger and Impulsiveness,* Copyright 1998, Times Books of Random House.

of Dental Medicine, if he would start a Department of Periodontolgy.[74] Lester knew of Henry's newborn interest in the field and he was interested in utilizing Henry's background to lend credibility to the idea that dental education needed to refocus the training of dentists. Lester Burket had as well become an early pioneer in the specialty of Oral Medicine[75] which blended with Henry's belief system. Through Kurt Thoma, Henry's mentor, a connection was established. And so, the seeds were planted for everything that followed. Henry's early lesson: It is nice to have imagination, creativity, desire and ideas to exploit, but it is also nice and most important to have associations and friends who trust and believe in one's capabilities. In tapping Henry for this position, Lester had extended his hand in fundamentally accelerating Henry's career, much in the way that Henry did for D. Walter Cohen, who trained as Henry's first student, became a Dean at the University of Pennsylvania, and became a tour de force in his own right. It's not as if Henry and Walter were not worthy of their access, it was simply an obvious fact of life that all people need someone and something to provide "that chance".

Henry was at that time the most talented young researcher in Oral Pathology of the day. In fact, the caricature drawn of the founders of the American Academy of Oral Pathology he was far and away the youngest.[76] But, it was through the benevolence of his mentor, Kurt Thoma (probably the most talented educator of the day in Oral Pathology, Oral Surgery and Oral Diagnosis), that he made the connection to Lester Burket. Nevertheless, Henry proved himself illustriously at the AFIP in Washington, D.C. so the cast had be set. It was then that all the wheels had been set in motion.

All these men who had set the stage for the post-WWII surge in dental education were the elite. They were noble, humble men of venerable

---

[74] See Appendix #2

[75] Burket, Lester W.: *ORAL MEDICINE*: Diagnosis/Treatment, Copyright 1946, Published by J.B. Lippincott Co.

[76] See "Caricature Photo" of the seven founders of The American Academy of Oral Pathology, now The American Academy of Oral Maxillofacial Pathology.

character. They spoke from their thoughts, but as Len Marrella pointed out in his book their destinies were a product of habitual thoughts and actions grounded in honorable ethical standards.[77] Yes, they acceded to the highest levels in dental education out of personal desire, but their accomplishments were rooted in virtue and exemplary respect for their positions. They possessed a profound care for their colleagues as well as those behind them who also were making the same effort. Call them naïve or unconcerned about any unconventional blowback, but it was plainly implausible. Rest assured that this was the very kind of feeling kindled in Henry's spirit to which he ruminated years later when very deeply tested by the unceremonious, urchin-like mistreatment by his former student, When D. Walter Cohen followed, the chain was extended without even a scintilla of question, and his lifetime achievements were of consummate pride and care acquired from those who came before, and as he so respectfully ministered to so many after him. These were people never challenged by ethics, they embraced it. It was a visceral reflexive tradition, not an exploitable quantum.

As described, Henry was socially very much like a fish out of water. He recognized, however, that his contacts were very meaningful. It was not easy, but he strove to offset his tendency "to hide". His aversion was the stereotypical social butterfly. As a member of a local country club, the tables were often turned on him because "the country club set" would be the ones to whom he would turn to financially support his school. He would never engage them in long term friendships because that was not his style, but his emerging reputation captured their attention. And, whatever be the psychology of the successful social elite, they naturally gravitated to one another. Therefore, Henry, albeit unintentional, did not rebuff currying favor in the social mix and always projected enough gravitas to warrant the following he garnered. This was definitely the heyday of growing wealth right after the war which made social gatherings vitally important to cultivate opportunities.

---

[77] Marrella, Len:*In Search of Ethics: Conversations with Men and Women of Character,* Copyright 2009, DC Press, A Division of the Diogenes Consortium, Sanford, Florida.

It sounds shameless, but it was just the way contacts were embraced. Project how much easier this would have been with the social media of today. From the mule to the turbo charged Ferrari, the horse to the Stealth F-18, the Pony Express to over-night FedEx, how things changed in less than a hundred years! In 1952, Henry started out on his pathway to being "a difference maker" with what seems like today as "stone age' communications.

Back to the decades during Henry's lifetime, there were always cyclical economic changes. He was born into serious down times, lived through many ups-and-downs, and died at the very early beginning of a tremendous economic boom. The very glaring difference, however, was the global enormity of the war which stimulated an immediate rapid growth. As tragic as the loss of human treasure was, the converse was very real for the surviving beneficiaries. It was not just the wealthy. It was, in the very true definition, the emergence of a tangibly significant middle-class. Today, real middle-class structure has been pretty much vanquished. The true quality middle class was the engine that galvanized the resurgence. The growing economy made a sense of security and goodwill palpable and long-lasting. The "Golden Age" projected substance and core value (and core values as well). It was a period to do or try anything because hard work most often defaulted to success. There was actually room to succeed. "The acquisitive urge" became easily accepted because of universally improved standards of living that everyone could readily enjoy. As the saying goes: "There is nothing like success to make people forget bad times". The very first middle class community of the 1950's was Levittown, Long Island, New York which reflected the emergence of this rapidly growing post-war middle class. It was the emblem of the day. Living in Levittown meant upward mobility and achievement.[78]

Tied very closely to this economic boom was the surge in dental school applications. Even though Henry's day as a youth was engulfed in a survival poverty mode, this new generation of dentists would

---

[78] E. Digby Baltzell: *The Protestant Establishment: Aristocracy and Caste in America (Aristocracy & Caste in America)*, Copyright 1987, Yale University Press, Paperback.

become the embodiment of this middle class from which Henry's Boston University School of Graduate Dentistry would eventually draw.

There was no template for what Henry contemplated. He was never vocal about his thoughts. But, emerging from his wartime celebrity was a flowering idea that there was a massive divide between his now very lofty mindset and the habitual nature of a general practice which had not been terribly excited by any major changes in patient therapies. But, the old expression of how "to teach an old dog new tricks" was nowhere more applicable than at this time in the natural progression of this time period.

During the war the average practice was in tandem with a "wait and see" mentality for survival conditions. Interest in embracing dental needs as a health benefit was not a significant concern at any level. The dental practice was not endowed with an extraordinary legion of selective measures for dealing with advanced dental disease. The approach was basic: fillings and extractions. To suddenly come upon the scene and convince people that teeth could be saved was a mission that would require changing the entire mindset of dental practitioners whose mentalities had to be reframed to emotionally make a leap of faith. That is why as much as it would sound ideal to bring dental health to a new found level of acceptance, it would require conditions that would enable dentists to convince patients to save rather than extract painful teeth. This would require patients to perceive the expense as warranted and worthwhile. In addition, it would also be necessary to re-educate the dental profession along lines of prevention-retention as opposed to the traditional mindset of extraction-function by contraction. This was the atmosphere into which Henry's civilian career would settle. He had one advantage: prosperity was increasing rapidly enough to enable him to gain a foothold at the base of this high mountain which he would have to climb.

History records events, but, on average, people are loathe to remember what does not have personal relevance. And, in good times, it is a rarity for people to have a vested interest to retrace the past. And, in this instance, the immediate past was so gruesome by virtue of the length of the war and the number of soldiers dead that any good feeling and cheer made the bitter memories soon displaced from daily conscious awareness. People were not so fast to forget, but the human spirit rebounded rapidly as V-E Day and V-J Day restored hope with a sense of exuberance and a return of high-spirits.[79][80] The industries that produced wartime supplies and the rudimentary capital expenditures in planes, warships, tanks and jeeps converted very quickly to peacetime manufacturing operations which supplied endless jobs for what was considered the "blue collar" sector of society. Thus began the wealth effect of a very quickly growing generation of hardworking people who would ultimately be the source of patients for growing general practices in dentistry. Thus, economists would consider this "wealth effect" as the impetus given to the private sector small business growth, away from the Keynesian big government control of the money stream. The "blue collar" working class was the under belly of the middle class. The middle class swelled with the newly minted white collar executives. This group was the beneficiary of higher education. The small businesses arising within this "wealth effect class" consisted of this new breed of executives who grew the rapidly expanding suburban outlying communities. This is not the middle class of today (which has almost disappeared). Without the growing middle class the general dental practice would not have succeeded with as much dynamism.

People of all ethnicities, religions and creeds heightened this expansion with newly minted court decisions. In 1954 the U.S. Supreme Court in Brown v. Board of Education of Topeka, Kansas outlawed racial segregation in public schools. This landmark 9-0 decision overturned the 1896 Plessy v. Ferguson state-sponsored segregation in public schools. (201) This became a reflection of this first new decade after the war which would free up societal constraints, the benefit being for all people through access to public education. It was by no means all hunky dory overnight, but it was intrinsically symbolic of a mentality bent on change. And, this was the same spirit which infused a fundamental energy and change in attitude. It unlocked enough prevailing attitudes to lay the groundwork for so many other social changes as old-guard thinking and rule was challenged, and in many arenas successfully changed.

So the world that Henry returned to was one of unrestricted opportunity. From a business sense the times were rife with growth and development in many industries. Top-down it was a "feel good" period. Some would describe it as a period of prosperity because of the numerous opportunities layered into all levels of society. But philosophically, it meant a measurable improvement in the quality of life. And, with this, there was a surge in productivity.

Henry's good fortunes were his connections with Harvard where he made contact with Dr. Kurt H. Thoma, one of the greatest of all dental educators at the turn of the 20th century. Not enough has been historically noted about this man. Swiss by birth he came to the United States to ultimately become a Professor of Oral Pathology and Oral Surgery. The most prolific author of very specific textbooks in several of the dental fields, Henry's association with him as a student at Harvard and later as a colleague was undeniably fortuitous. When Kurt Thoma was Editor-in-Chief of "Oral Surgery, Oral Medicine and Oral Pathology" (1948-1970), this was arguably the corresponding historical period of "The Golden Age". (131)(164) Kurt Thoma was 89 in 1972 when he died, but Henry was highly influenced by his genius and intrinsic academic pre-eminence. As pointed out, this experience set the stage for his dramatic change to dental education. Perhaps if the timing had not been so opportune, The Boston University School of Graduate Dentistry might never have happened?

When Henry returned to Boston, the economy was humming quietly but efficiently as the economic turn accelerated the growth of so many ongoing and established businesses. "Urbanization-suburbanization was a financial boost to the tide of growth. And so Henry was at the right place at the right time under the careful watch of the most influential dentist of the day. As The Charles Brackett Professor of Oral Pathology, Kurt Thoma attracted many key educators to Harvard. One was Paul Boyle who ultimately became the Dean at Western Reserve University School of Dentistry (aka now as The Case Western Reserve School of Dental Medicine) in Cleveland, Ohio. As a Professor at Harvard in Oral Pathology, Henry developed a close association and friendship. Ultimately, Paul Boyle would succeed Kurt Thoma as The Charles Brackett Professor of Oral Pathology after he returned to Harvard (and the Boston area) from Western Reserve.(160) These were Henry's very developmental and yet most constructive professional years. From 1948 to 1963 his leadership appointments at The Beth Israel Hospital, The University of Pennsylvania Department of Periodontology and The Department of Stomatology at The Boston University School of Medicine served as the culmination of his defining formative period at Harvard and in the Army. For at the waters' edge lay his ultimate prize, the 1963 Charter of The Boston University School of Graduate Dentistry. Everything that influenced his visceral feelings, thinking and sense for change would all be wound tightly like a compact ball of thread. As it would gradually unwind into a panoply of well-designed and programmed changes in dental education, there was an increasing citywide awareness of the school's entrée as a member of dental community.

It has been said that the interim period between the end of WW11 and The Korean War was almost hypnotic because people became entranced and limp-like from exhaustion. But, this was merely a five year interlude. In fact, The Korean War was a sectional extension of what General Douglas MacArthur was not able to do during WWII. (90) That is, he wanted to take The United States victory in the pacific and carry it past the 38th Parallel into China through Korea. But, his tete-a-tete with then President Harry Truman got him relieved of his duties. The point is that the conflict in Korea did not captivate the nation. The feeling of exhilaration, in fact, carried well beyond into the very early 1960's. So, from 1945-1963 when Henry chartered The Boston University School of Graduate Dentistry, the immense concentration he applied to his craft was only possible because of the great freedoms this period allowed. In all truth, it is most likely that what he so capably accomplished almost as a one-man army would not be possible today with all the regulatory federal controls built into bureaucratic agencies today. This was a period when networking among peers of like value systems could administer to and effect changes unbridled, and within a relatively predictable time period. Over-runs and cost overages existed, but nothing like in today's economy because private industry then answered to its own bottom line, not the government where waste has always been inestimable.

Up to this period specialty training was an apprenticeship either in a hospital setting or under the purview of someone who learned expertise through interest as opposed to specific method learning under the umbrella of a more systematic, programmed process. Henry had what many did not: the ultimate desire to capture opportunity and pursue it with undeterred order and purpose. Growing up very deprived, he did not construe leadership as exploitative. He was quiet, logical and very businesslike. Unlike "the robber baron", Gilded Age industrialists who were cynical and hollow, where wealth and opulent living was the endpoint, this fifteen to eighteen year Golden Age provided timely opportunity to propagate constructive ventures for a greater universal social advantage.

Such was the setting which set the stage for Henry's competitive nature. Nothing was going to hold him back. In fact, he could concentrate on his manifest plan because he did not have what could be defined as extra-curricular interests which might have deflected is energies from his intended blueprint. He did not share too much to anyone. When he did, it was an emotional outburst which was abruptly silenced by a shrug of his shoulders, and, a lowering of his head as he scowled. He was almost never ebullient. Most likely his nature was a genetic trait he inherited from his mother whose similar sullen nature pretty much never remitted. Likewise, Henry carried this trait which contrasted to his brother's more natural open and seemingly convivial exterior. Once in a while he lowered his innate defense mechanisms and joked around. But, this was a rarity. It was fortunate that Henry was not compelled to actively enhance his career with small talk and spontaneous communication. His deep concentration was not meant to appear anti-social, but it might have put a damper on all his hard work. He could not comprehend that people need to be "small talked", and he was most definitely the beneficiary of good fortune during "good times". The roaring 1920's were all about glitz, glamor, and gaudiness. The 1950's were all about a retreat to hard work. This suited Henry's personality. His mission required him to be a caretaker not a virtuoso in the center ring of a circus act. This was a very important distinction as he demonstrated his business-like networking skills as he traveled between Philadelphia and Boston blazing the trail for an emerging field. Periodontics would eventually alter the metrics of dental patient management

So let's recapitulate why this "Golden Age" was so significant, particularly for people who were not an eyewitness, or, the fact that the times are now so distant that even a description cannot capture its singularity, or even its "otherness". Firstly, from Francis Trevelyan Miller, Litt.D., LLD, an American Historian who wrote the first authoritative military history reconstructing all the war's battles in elemental detail, the statistics are gut wrenching. The foreward in this almost thousand page detailed document written with the able bodied support of legions of historical and military authorities as well as his wife, Ann Woodward Miller, summarizes some very chilling facts:

"We have lived through the most stupendous struggle in the 7,000 years of recorded history. The destiny of 70 nations and 2,000,000,000 people has been at stake. The homelands of more than three quarters of the population of the earth have felt the iron heel of war. More than 100,000,000, one out of every twenty human beings on the globe, have been engaged in the fighting forces of belligerent nations.

The records of WW11, as set forth in this volume, challenge the imagination. The official lists of numbers killed and wounded are a tragic commentary on civilization: more than 20,000,000 casualties; 30,000,000 more men, women, and children driven from their homes;

10,000,000 more massacred: hundreds of thousands of homes left in ruins.

The cost of this "War for Survival", with its destruction, devastation, and economic loss, is estimated at the sum of $1,000,000,000,000. The great wealth of the world of the world, with its resources, industrial power, and man power, has been concentrated on destruction. Nations have accumulated an indebtedness which far exceeds all the money in the world. The responsibility for meeting this obligation is placed upon future generations to carry the burden.

This is the price we have paid for human freedom. The amount of money consumed in this war is sufficient to build a home for every family in the world, or to give an education to every child on earth. It is far greater than all the moneys ever expended for schools, churches, and hospitals since the beginning of the human race...

This History of World War 11is dedicated to that great step in human progress. It stands also as a memorial to those who fought and died for this achievement...

May it never happen again."[81]

It is not strange how quickly wars have occurred with such facility since those sagacious words were written in 1945. Two graphic qualifying statements from the philosopher, essayist, poet and novelist consummately reflect on man's tragic inability to follow Miller's wish. In his soliloquy 'Tipperary':

"Only the dead have seen the end of war."[82]

George Santayana also poignantly qualifies the greatest of all human tragedies:

---

[81] Miller, Francis Trevelyan: *THE COMPLETE HISTORY OF WWII, ARMED SERVICES EDITION, Copyright 1948, Published by Ann Woodward Miller; Preface.*
[82] Santayana, George: *Soliloquies in England and Later Soliloquies,* 2012, Forgotten Books,"Tipperary".

"Progress, far from consisting in change, depends on retentiveness. When change is absolute there remains no being to improve and no direction is set for possible improvement and when experience is not retained, as among savages, infancy is perpetual. Those who cannot remember the past are condemned to repeat it. [83]

Unfortunately, Francis Trevelyan Miller, albeit a practical historian, was most likely quixotic in his aspirations for humanity. And, perhaps George Santayana was more cynical. Nevertheless, it is important to recall the wisdom of such scholarship to set all of us back a bit on our heels to understand our reality, an invocation of the hubris and lack of humility which seems to perpetuate cognitive dissonance. Our personalities get in the way of continued good fortune, and periods of creativity and success continue to be interrupted by forces of destruction which our more productive side seemingly cannot control.

Henry M. Goldman's time was one of these great interludes. He possessed the personality to engage the times, and the times allowed him to prevail in the construct of his dream, a specialty school in all the dental sciences which, up to the 1950's, had neither been contemplated nor fashioned into a reality. The "Golden Age" of the 1950's was robust in all the sustaining supportive measures: money, a sense of devotion to an idea, and a dedication transcending self-advancement. What a thought! These made Henry iconic, but, as Santayana noted, change has to be "absolute". The school's infancy and heyday were both immeasurably successful, but the paradigm change was not absolute by the prevailing powers controlling the American Dental Association, specifically The Council on Dental Education. The school morphed into its traditional existence as a school for general dental education. Perhaps for those sanctioning the manner of dental education, Henry's change not being absolute as Santayana would so define, that "...infancy is perpetual..." in undervaluing the continued merits of graduate

---

[83] Santayana, George: *Reason in Common Sense,* Copyright 1980, Dover Publications (Reprint Edition).

education. Yet, for the time and place it occupied for about fifteen years it was undeniably progressive in the thoughts and standards imparted to so many worldwide. It reached a zenith as a paragon for cutting edge teaching in advanced technologies and ideas from a central base where ideas could be exchanged and not simply through referred journals or an occasional colloquium. It was integrative teaching between all the specialties under one roof. Residents learned through trial and error, that is to say: remediation with the supportive wisdom and experience of their mentors (the shared exchange of ideas and philosophies of therapy). The setting was ideal in its progressive outlook. It was atavistic to Plato and his Lyceum It carried a substantive mission made possible by times that perhaps are never to be experienced again. Some would muse of the unfortunate fact that man continues to build on greatness then relinquish such success through indefinable thinking. Generations somehow can't remember the past long enough to retain its virtues. And, why does every generation seem to think it has to reinvent the wheel? Does synthesis mean anything? These thoughts will have to be left for the philosophers who relish such historical analysis. But, in the meantime, The Boston University School of Graduate Dentistry was seminal, its timing "golden", and its founder once-in-a-lifetime.

CHAPTER 7

The Winds of Change

In his memoirs, <u>Winds of Change,</u> conservative Prime Minister Harold Macmillan of the United Kingdom from 1957-1963 enunciated a major policy change for decolonization to the Parliament of South Africa on February 3, 1960. In the speech he said the following:

> *"The wind of change is blowing through this continent. Whether we like it or not, this growth of national conscious-ness is a political fact."* [84]

This famous description pierced the expanding balloon of grow-ing disenchantment on the continent of Africa involving so many of its colonial territories. The times were changing rapidly with political tremors advancing quickly toward independence as a feeling for na-tion-state status exploded during the Cold War. Macmillan contravened the majority extreme wing of his party who were against allowing British colonies in Africa from establishing independent governments. With his famous "Winds of Change" speech in Ghana and South Africa, he abruptly set in motion a political shift towards independence. The emphasis was notably on Apartheid dissolution. He courageously chal-lenged the policy disposition of his party for the sake of seeing global trends which were in the best interest of his country. His leadership

---

[84] Boddy-Evans, Alistair, Harold Macmillan: #Winds of Change Speech", Website: African.com: April, 2011.

thinking and action reflected on the economic and political changes negatively impacting Great Britain's financial health. The result was an individual initiative in going against the grain for the sake of making a categorical adjustment to changing times. Colonial territories were hell-bent on independence. Macmillan foresaw this despite parliament still drawn to longstanding policy status quo.

Key circumstances require key thinking, key evaluation, key courage of conviction, and key change when such circumstances require responsible leadership to make adjustments. Only doctrinaire thinking continues outdated paradigms and disallows forward movement in any industry. Henry, as a person of considerable impulsivity at seemingly incongruent times, sensed a change in the dental profession was impending and engaged the plans swirling in his head like a sailor jibing against the full thrust of stiff winds. He was impatient for change because he did not sense a universal acceptance of changing times. Understanding that tooth loss was primarily the result of an infective inflammatory process undermining the bony housing was still a totally obscure thought to most dental practitioners. Dental schools were for the most part only teaching hygiene as the essential "article of faith" without reference to underlying bone changes in disease. It was not crystal clear much more critical information was on the threshold of development regarding periodontal disease. Yet, the profession was still stuck with apparent intransigence on traditional teaching. Resolving this blind spot was going to be extremely risky and prodigious.

There were a number of educators and independent thinkers who had coasted along since the early part of the twentieth century with more awareness, but they couldn't totally put the pieces of the puzzle together. For the most part, dentistry did not organize as a profession 'til just before The American Civil War. Individuals who were trained physicians began to formulate ideas that perhaps oral infections were linked to physical distress, disease, derangement or dysfunction. The result was few individuals seeking out people of like thinking in order to apprentice and organize protocols for dental treatment. In Europe, dental education has always been linked very intimately with medical education. And, such is the case still today. Perhaps in the early founding of the American colonies and up to and after The American Revolution dentistry was practiced as a continuum of the Barber-surgeon days when apprentice trained medics applied their craft on battle grounds. Having learned through an on-hand training period with an older practitioner, the craft was rather primitive and often debilitating with the possibility of death. This was the state of dentistry in the early years of this country. However, some extremely gifted visionaries who, though having apprenticed as physicians, saw a definite need to investigate dental disease as a real threat to health. And, interesting enough, some of these inspired, imaginative thinkers argued their opinions in ways very reminiscent of their European predecessors. The linkage between oral and systemic diseases was not a novel idea. Yet, in this country, carryover from its European traditions never gathered muster. Anybody with the will and daring could apply his/her talent to people in need, mostly an art in the fashion of a trade, scientific method not yet ubiquitously understood nor practiced. Paul Revere, the famed silversmith and American Revolution provocateur, was one such example. The dawn of the very first pioneers whose work and influence would give rise to change came with remarkable and unexpected pioneering in applied medical science. They were disciplined and persevering, but their contributions were not without mixed acceptance for many years. Interesting enough, Henry M. Goldman's ideas were solidly based in the European tradition which guided this country's early pioneers.

Perhaps with prejudice it can be argued that until Dr. Kurt Thoma the two greatest influences in the field of Dentistry were Horace Henry Hayden, D.D.S., M.D. and Chapin A. Harris, A.M., M.D., D.D.S. Horace Hayden was a throwback to the Renaissance as he toiled in so many scientific areas of investigation: geology, mineralogy, and many fields of natural history. He published constantly on subject matter in all these fields. During The War of 1812, he gained experience from his medical training as a field surgeon. However, having trained as a dentist apprentice under George Washington's personal dentist, he went on to found the *"American Journal of Dental Science."* (69) His teaching and contributions to the interrelationships of medical/dental diseases compelled the Jefferson College of Medicine in Philadelphia to award him an M.D. degree. In 1840, his tireless work led to the founding of the American Society of Dental Surgeons. He became first President and served until he died. However, it is debatable what his great contribution to the dentistry might have been. On the one hand, along with Chapin A. Harris, he co-founded the Baltimore College of Dental Surgery. Today as part of The University of Maryland, it was the first institution to award the D.D.S. degree. (216) (But, in perhaps a much more provocative sense, he was the first American to see oral diseases as directly related to systemic pathologies. As a cross-scientific investigator, he ventured investigation and teaching into related sciences which brought dentistry much more biological perspective.

Chapin A. Harris was no less the articulate representative of the burgeoning field of dentistry. He apprenticed in medicine with his brother, Dr. John Harris, in Madison, Ohio. His brother also tutored him in dentistry as was practiced in rural areas of the young country. When he passed the Board of Medical Censors in 1824, he was officially licensed to practice in medicine. He acquired the D.D.S. degree from Philadelphia Dental College in 1854, but he turned to full time dentistry when, as a student of Horace Hayden, he moved to Baltimore and joined the American Society of Dental Surgery. When Horace Hayden died in 1844, he became its second president. He was a prodigious writer from 1839 to 1849, and of note was his founding of the first dental periodical, *"the American Journal of Dental Science"*. (69) He became the most prolific author of scientific papers and books for the day. They were provocative and extremely articulate. He was the primary influence in the founding of the American Dental Convention, serving as its president in 1856-1857. The year before his death in 1860 the American Dental Association was established, but, with the outbreak of the Civil War, it transitioned into The Southern Dental Association in the southern states. Eventually it united with the ADA after the war to become The National Dental Association until it was (again) renamed The American Dental Association in 1922. (137) The essential message is that early formal dental education carried their influence. They clearly demonstrated that the oral cavity was an organ manifesting a two way relationship with the function of the body organs in health and disease. Both Horace Hayden and Chapin Harris were the most serious, influential scientists delivering a message echoing even today, perhaps in spite of their influence totally lost in time.

As in all of life's challenges and grand blueprint, there are people of serious intent and those who may be adorned with a less than noble distinctiveness, perhaps charlatans or opportunists. But, all of human behavior is guided by character, and character type has its own development through upbringing, education, and peer relationships. In this regard, dentistry has been witness to much of those who have exploited the field for material benefits and those whose legacies have contributed markedly to furthering the science of dentistry. Harold Macmillan spoke about a "...national consciousness..." confronting societal issues swirling around a tempestuous political arena. In a like manner changing influences in dental education were rooted in men like Hayden and Harris. The "...wind of change..." blew with authority and notice. Had they lived longer their presence might have challenged their successors who emboldened the profession along a very different path. Such was the influence of Greene Vardiman Black, aka G.V. Black. (137) An argument can be made that he set dentistry back fifty years. He reduced dentistry to a mechanical science in upending the foundational influence of Hayden and Harris by limiting the profession to a formulated classification of carious lesions. He was a pure dental anatomist who failed to perceive the periodontium (the supporting apparatus of the teeth) as a vulnerable support system. This became the underpinning basis of dental education from after the Civil War up to and including WW11. His influence served as a basis of dental practice in spite of some early pioneers who ruffled feathers as they tried to impose their message about "Periodontoclasia" and "Pyorrhea" as the cause of tooth loss. They were lone wolves in a country fixed on very desultory techniques. Dentistry had been once again reduced to a perfunctory trade. Some of the wonderful pen-and-ink art caricatures are reminiscent of those days. Gillette Hayden, the great granddaughter of Horace Hayden, was one of the most noteworthy leaders of a science-based approach to oral disease and one of the founders of The American Academy of Periodontology. She served as President in 1916. A 1902 graduate of Ohio Medical University, (the precursor to The Ohio State University College of Dentistry) (204) her work in pioneering oral prophylaxis garnered a return to the days of her great grandfather. However, it was minimalist at best. Dr. John R. Wilson, who was Chair of the Department of Periodontology, formalized the Ohio State program in 1949 just months after The American Dental Association recognized Periodontology as a specialty. (137) Though instrumental in shifting dental education along a different tract, the field was undervalued and underappreciated. It would not have significant impact until afterWW11. It was compelling that the great advocates of oral biology and related sciences were delivering a strong message, but the sure firebrands did not march onto the national scene for years. Until then, G.V. Black's influence and practice methodology had become the basis for the primary predicate for the training of dentists. In a narrow sense, a theoretical belief that "Periodontoclasia" might/could affect teeth gained ground. But, how and how much? This irked and drew cynicism out of a normally solemn, soul searching Henry M. Goldman, one of the great American dental educators, to blaspheme repeatedly the G.V. Black standard with his standard blurt: "a dental degree is a union card". Upon hearing this for the first time it drew smiles that a usually taciturn man would be so bold. Mind you, Henry was communicating concepts in bone regeneration in the early 1960's. This concept would not practically take fold for another twenty or so years. It shows how prescient he was. He was not one of the firebrands and his public persona did not match his most inner thoughts. On the other hand, there was a gradual swing toward the field of Periodontics prior to WWII. The people involved would gradually transition dental education in a very significant and timely manner. They had their early beginnings in the 1920's and gradually got into the study of the basic understanding of tooth and jaw development. It would not, however, capture the curricula of the majority of schools for many years.

In the late 1930's with the rise of Hitler and The Third Reich (90) some of the future renowned dental scholars fled Austria and settled in this country. They substantially altered dental education by their research, writing and teaching in the field of Oral Biology. With the presence of Dr. Rudolph Kronfeld already established at Loyola University in Chicago, Illinois, he was instrumental in getting significant Jewish educators from The University of Vienna to expatriate to Chicago. This group included some of the early pioneers of American dental education: Balint Orban, Harry Sicher, and Joseph Peter Weinmann. Bernhard Gottlieb had a much more difficult time escaping the Nazi hold, but he eventually made it to Baylor University. In the same way that Henry's presence early on at The University of Pennsylvania affected the path of his protégé, D. Walter Cohen, to rise to pre-eminence in the field of Periodontics as an academic/clinician, likewise Orban, Sicher and Weinmann spawned the likes of Anthony Gargiulo as a viable standard for future Periodontists from Loyola. To a very real extent these early pioneers did not cut through the challenges of the traditional mechanically minded dental standards because their numbers were not yet sufficient. However, in time this would significantly evolve into a carriage of programs in Periodontology which ran their message right up the flagpole to be seen as early evidence for new horizons in dental education. Gerald M. Bowers was a product of both The Ohio State and The University of Michigan programs in Periodontics formalized by Wilson (started by Gillette Hayden) and Sigurd Ramfjord respectively. (204)(217). Some of the other emerging educators in the field of Periodontics whose impact contributed markedly to the raising of the ceiling in evidence based research and clinical standards were: Richard Pritchard, Saul Schluger, Clifford Ochsenbein, Irving Glickman, etc. Of course, there were many other rising stars, including international educator-research investigators such as Harald Loe and Sigmund S. Socransky. But, the granddaddy of all such periodontal educators rising with the tide of change, D. Walter Cohen directed the profession into new vistas of teaching and research as the curtain was lowering behind past standards of thinking and priorities. The rubric would change and become a model for great change in the world of technology. Some of the other notable pioneers who changed the landscape illustrate the intellectual shift: Lester R. Cahn, Paul E. Boyle, Donald A. Kerr and James Roy Blayney (all Oral Pathologists led by the "father" of all: Kurt H. Thoma). The point is that the numbers were changing the scope of influence in such a way that the biology of dental health was laying the foundation for the future of dental education. The mechanical sciences were not to be relegated into an obligatory back seat. In fact, just the opposite. The fields of Restorative and Prosthetic Dentistry and Orthodontics would fashion standards of care in tune with growing information for long term periodontal health. All in all, it was quite apparent that the talent pool was rapidly expanding. The face of dentistry was getting a very profound adjustment in appearance and expression. The key point, however, is that all the specialties as well as general dentistry were tuned into the preservation of periodontal health, the sine qua non of all dental education standards of teaching and practice.

Henry M. Goldman was an Oral Pathologist whose understanding of scientific method made him sensitive to the science and art of saving teeth. He fashioned his professional life around the fields of Oral Pathology, Periodontics and Oral Medicine. In a sense, he was a throwback to Chapin Harris and Horace Hayden, men of multidisciplinary skills and interests. His far reaching background in systemic medicine enhanced his ideas for The Boston University School of Graduate Dentistry much in the same way Hayden and Harris brought the concept of training and management of medical diseases into dental education. Their thought process for the proper training of a dental specialist and a general practitioner was eerily similar to that of Henry M. Goldman. Henry was very open minded when considering the importance of expanding the broad educational base all dentists should possess. He embodied the European tradition of the "physician-dentist". The general practitioner to this point could not look beyond the profession as an applied art of the mechanical sciences. Starting with Horace Hayden, "The Father of the Dental Profession", (216) tooth loss affecting health was effectively a dramatic shift in viewpoint. Radical for the day, his message was straightforward: the oral cavity was manifestly the starting point of both human body function and disease. If it appears simplistic, it was not because the blind spot of the profession restricted this most obvious perception.

It is very difficult to understand what motivated Horace Hayden to be so pro-active during the early part of 19th century. To gain the proper feel how remarkable his cutting edge thinking was is as challenging as the documentation is sparse. However, his personal writings and very public efforts reveals a man far ahead of his time. While he was centered on and intrigued by diseases of the oral cavity, the dentistry of the day was singularly limited to extractions and false teeth. And, for the most part, the people would go from day-to-day with highly infected teeth. It was in most cases an apprenticeship which educated the prospective dentist. Hayden came by his training during the time he spent with George Washington's dentist, Dr. John Greenwood, in New York City. But, when he got to Baltimore, he studied medicine. This fashioned his thoughts about the impact of oral health on system diseases in observing oral infections leading to septicemia from untreated blood borne bacteremias. Chapin Harris, a student of Horace Hayden, reflected his mentor's influence. The prolific and detailed nature of his writings were markedly advanced, reflecting a person of immense depth and measured expression.

The defining quality which staggers the imagination was the rigor of their dedication to education. Leaving very little to speculation, Hayden's legacy was a clear message: dentistry was not a trade the way he found it, it was a science embodied in medicine. The spirit with which he advanced this trade into a profession based on education (no longer tutelage) was reflected with his perseverance (along with Harris) to obtain the formal charter for the Baltimore College of Dental Surgery in 1840[85] (217) in spite of the contentious rival medical groups. It

---

[85] See Website, University of Maryland School of Dentistry

did not hurt that they were both equally trained in medicine, but there was nevertheless extreme resistance against a separate institution. With an appropriate sense of irony, their battle was very reminiscent of the struggle Henry faced early on in establishing and obtaining the charter for The Boston University School of Graduate Dentistry. In the same way that Hayden-Harris took dentistry to a new level within the framework of education and practice, Henry expanded the scope of dental education by singularly establishing an advanced institution solely for the training of dental specialists. Albeit circumstantially different, it was in the spirit of Harold Macmillan when he extolled that novel ideas translate into novel action when the winds of change appropriately measure the temperature of the times and there is leadership to bring about the changes necessary for the times and circumstances.

If Hayden and Harris were indefatigable in their pursuit of organizing the first dental school in the country, William J. Gies, Ph.D. came on the scene about a century after Horace Hayden. It is interesting to note that until just before WWII the most significant contributions to the dental profession were made by these three individuals in very unplanned ways. William Gies came to dentistry much the way Hayden and Harris did, very indirectly. Having been educated at Gettysburg, Yale and Columbia, his focus was in biological and organic chemistry. And, at a young age, he only gradually brought this interest into a very precise life path as he gravitated between the three institutions. Once settled in New York City at Columbia (where he received his PhD), he backed into dentistry through his research in chemistry. The zenith of his career, however, was twofold: 1) he laid the groundwork for the organization of the American Association of Dental Schools (the forerunner of the now American Dental Education Association-aka ADEA); and, 2) his landmark report on the importance of dentistry as a significant component of higher education in the health professions of The United States (funded by the Carnegie Foundation in 1926). These two most significant events were first in bringing all the dental schools in the country at that time into a coordinated oversight for the sake of quality in the advancement of the dental profession in the health sciences. To that time, they were disparate and without coordination. In addition, William Gies organized the first dental department at Columbia and founded the Journal of Dental Research in 1919 and the International Association of Dental Research (aka IADR) in 1920. (176) He was a key member of many significant boards, committees and political groups as they pointed to and weighted the importance of oral health and the oral health sciences in the development of dentistry as a profession. As a student, educator, researcher, activist and ambassador for the profession, he was in the minds of many the father of modern dentistry. Horace Hayden and Chapin Harris brought dental health and disease into the public focus in the early days of the country, but William Gies readdressed the direction of polarized teaching institutions into a unified profession with a focus on oral health research. He continued their historic contributions. Nevertheless, in spite of these dedicated men, the dental profession was overall still resistant to change. It was a profession with some very innovative segments, but it was very hard put to commit in toto.

The times made transformations essential in thinking and priorities. The core effort to improve from the benefits of professional education gradually was a difference maker. In this sense, William Gies bequeathed staying power by unifying research under the umbrella of the IADR as a means of furthering the quality of research. This had a most profound meaning in providing continuity to a most important component of dental education. To that point in the history of the profession, the meaning and importance of his accomplishments cannot be undervalued. The missing piece was a leader with a sense of organization. He set the stage for what was to follow.

William Gies died in 1952, the year Henry M. Goldman was setting up the Department of Periodontology at The University of Pennsylvania School of Dental Medicine. When Henry graduated from Harvard University School of Dental Medicine, the groundwork for the organization of dentistry as a profession and the specialties had been set in motion. Gillette Hayden, the granddaughter of Horace Hayden, was active in the formation of The American Academy of Periodontology in 1914. She was also its second President. The ingredients were present for meaningful change.

As Henry's mentor at Harvard, Kurt Thoma, was leading the way in fields of Oral Surgery, Oral Pathology and Oral Biology, the dental profession was transforming into a health science. His timely association with Kurt Thoma was unique because the focus of his education was on oral diseases. At Harvard Kurt was both Chief of Oral Surgery and Oral Pathology, combining specialties in the European tradition. (66) It was always thought that the most insightful surgeons had a strong background in pathology. The springboard for Oral and Molecular Biology was in the related pathology sciences: electron microscopy, cellular biology, nuclear medicine, microbiology, and biochemistry. These dynamic elements were beginning to come together as baseline unit modules for future coordination with an interdisciplinary focus.

If William Gies came into dentistry quite circuitously, Kurt Thoma came right into the mainstream. Growing up in Switzerland his roots in education were quite disciplined. Initially in research he returned to Europe after a brief early period in the United States. But, returning to complete his education at Harvard, he soon rose to the top, coordinating surgery with pathology. Into this milieu was a retinue of scientists who laid the groundwork for cutting edge changes in dental education. Amidst this group was Henry Goldman. Kurt Thoma was a Leonardo Da Vinci-like educator. He was intellectually multifaceted and clinically multitalented. He was spread out into such a wide range of contributions to the academic and clinical sciences that there remains a mystique to his memory. He is forgotten by most, but, he was singularly magisterial. Even though the technologies have reshaped the approach to treatment of oral diseases, his books in the fields of pathology and surgery are still packed with solid, pertinent information. If he were just coming into the profession today, it would be unimaginable to think what his accomplishments might have been. Probing his professional history is dazzling, but standing out was his election as the first President of The American Board of Oral Pathology (now

The American Board of Oral Maxillofacial Pathology) in 1947. He was the forebear of men like Henry.

Henry represented the culmination of all the great educators that preceded. He came along as technology ushered major inroads in both research and clinical practice. Studying the American historic record clearly reflects all the breakthroughs, developments and overall progress in the profession came into focus in the last twenty years. Overall, the country has benefitted from all the equipment and technical knowledge which has promoted professional enthusiasm and grown public awareness to dental health. The vanguards of this new era in technology uploaded dental education to a new plateau. They were responsible for the fundamental growth and development in the 19th and early 20th century. Today's vast array of educators are the by-products of this cradle of pacesetters.

Certainly, Kurt Thoma breathed life into Henry's professional career. He graduated Harvard University School of Dental Medicine in 1911, the year Henry was born, and twenty four years before Henry graduated. Kurt was the last of the renaissance men. He possessed a European flair bonded with an upscale Boston education. As a Harvard Professor in Oral Pathology and Oral Surgery, he wrote two separate textbooks on each subject. He succeeded Leroy M.S. Miner (a graduate of the Harvard School of Dental Medicine and the Boston University School of Medicine) during WW11 (on February 19, 1943) as Chief of the Dental Service at The Massachusetts General Hospital. So, his positions as The Charles A. Brackett Professor of Oral Pathology and Chief of the Dental Service at The Massachusetts General Hospital made Henry's association deeply meaningful for many years. (66) In fact, in 1960 when Kurt Thoma retired at Harvard and became Professor Emeritus, he became a Professor of Oral Surgery at Boston University and The University of Pennsylvania until very near his death in 1972. The legacy which dated to the late 1800's when Charles Albert Brackett was the first Chief of Oral Pathology at The Harvard School of Dental Medicine (established in 1867) was held by only three (Brackett, Miner and Thoma). This was a tradition which had a very significant bearing when Henry served as a graduate student under Thoma right after graduating Harvard in 1935. It is important to feel the history to realize that these were the men at the forefront of dental education. Both were every bit the forebears of present day dental educators. Probing with a reasonable depth into the background of those at the cutting edge of pathology and surgery, it is certain that Henry's post-WWII dream for a graduate school materialized from all these experiences. There is no uncertainty for this. The real question to be asked and examined was why Periodontology and not Oral Surgery? After all, his mentor was so keen and influential in every move Henry made.

To use Harold Macmillan's challenge to sense the winds of change was an oblique yet reasonable answer. In the same sense that Horace Hayden and Chapin Harris were pioneers, they possessed a stubbornness in pursuit of their ideals. Even William Gies was exceptional, poised to be an independent trailblazer. Even though he came to dentistry roundabout through a basic science history, he argued oral health as a necessary configuration of general well-being. It did not matter that G.V. Black was gaining a foothold with his own ideas. The dental profession was embarking in a direction which would absorb G.V. Black into a new paradigm.

When Henry came along from his very harsh upbringing, he learned very quickly that he needed something tangible to give his life meaning. The practical side of his personality would not permit him to settle for unchallenging and desultory endeavors .To recapitulate, he came from a public high school with private school work loads. It was a school where taking Greek and Latin wasn't optional. It was the only school of its kind where every student matriculated with the understanding that graduation demanded proficiency in these classical languages as well basic sciences. Thus, Henry's commitment to the depth and demands of advanced education had been established long before he got to Brown or Harvard. He took to Kurt Thoma because Kurt was invested in European traditions so reminiscent of his own youth. There was a mutual understanding and respect for intellectual growth. And, Henry identified with Kurt's prudence and intelligence. He was inspired and committed.

When Henry came out of the Army, he had a wealth of training which gained momentum at Harvard and was refined in the Army at Walter Reed Hospital in Washington, D.C. Returning to Boston as an Oral Pathologist, he was immediately attracted to the rapidly advancing field of Periodontolgy (aka Periodontia at that time). Why? Because he was invested in the biology of oral disease and he saw tooth loss as a major expression of the human struggle, like any other systemic entity. It was different from Oral Surgery because he was taken by the numbers of people who suffered from either complete or partial tooth loss. For the day, Periodontics was a growth field. He saw the challenges as well as the great need for this specialty. A great number of his neighborhood friends who went to dental school with him chose general practice as a lifetime commitment. His professional life thus far had dissuaded him from a similar course. There is no doubt that Oral Surgery could have been his directed path. He had the necessary affiliation and mentoring which could have made that commitment very tangible. But, very frankly, Henry saw that Periodontology was a viable opening with an enormous challenge and upside in teaching, research and practice. He saw so much potential. He would have made the most had he chosen Oral Surgery, but the timing was appropriate in every way to utilize his background toward the research and clinical basis for Periodontics in a teaching institution.

Winds of change only happen as a result of unique events, the committed passions of courageous men, the timeliness of such events, and the tenacious determination of leadership necessary to foster growth and expansion over time. With all the strangeness that adorned the birth and growth of modern day dentistry, Henry is celebrated for the dramatic change he brought both to graduate training and the continuing education experiment he grew and refined. The embellishments he inspired through such mechanisms provided the stage that has infinitely expanded at so many levels in all the specialties today. The experiment which was so new through the 1960's and 1970's was the forerunner of a profession today undoubtedly replete with the robust contributions of so many competent and dedicated educators today. Perhaps if they look to history, they will be challenged to find their worth in the inspirations that were those of a poor boy who grew up wise, clever and insightful. The winds of change which engaged Henry became the fortuitous legacy he left his profession.

CHAPTER 8

Henry's Hope and Design for Dental Education

If dentists were to reflect on their training and asked what major criticism they found, they more than likely would answer to the courses that were factually informative, but without a long term constructive purpose. Many a dental student has slept through either a physiology lecture on kidney function or on an abstruse subject in dental materials. And, even at the graduate level the repetitive lectures on arcane subject matter were no better. The managing of time was never common to dental course curricula at any level of dental education. It was woefully exasperating and incorrigibly expensive both in a monetary and training sense. It certainly did not make for effective organization and coordination. It seemed like a deliberate attempt to "gerrymander" the system to fulfill mandated requirements regardless of effective time management or meaningful learning. Everything about the pre-doctoral programs were an anathema to Henry's sense of purpose and pride. To this end he attempted to upgrade the rather wasteful and poorly coordinated course design with specific clinical development.

Mindless and throwaway course curricula were wasteful to the majority who were often critical, frustrated and resigned to despair because of excessive, improvident indifference. Keeping things structured with willful disregard of effective and meaningful course intent made Henry skeptical. Therefore, the thrust of his efforts was to proportion time effectively to maximize the learning process. But, even his tireless efforts were often lost despite noble intentions. Where in fact were the most glaring shortfalls? They were most often at the great intellectual divide between time relegated to didactic-academic and clinical training. Mark Twain expressed an opinion concerning education which fit intuitively and concisely into Henry's belief system:

"Education consists mainly in what we have unlearned". [86]

To the extent that he was always baffled by the continuous pursuit of a knowledge base that was generic, basic and without a constructive purpose, the first few years of general practice were spent "unlearning" information without bearing and "learning" what was not taught in dental school. This later became the very foundation of continuing education programs. That is, to teach what was unfortunately not taught (but should have) in dental schools. It is hard to believe (and to suggest) that this continues today many years after Henry has passed away. By the mere fact that Mark Twain wrote the above critique in 1898 sorrowfully suggests that what changes is that really nothing changes. Should it not be that education, as a living, evolving facet of human intellectual growth and development, be an awakening process instead of a manufactured accounting of splintered, unrelated facts? It is not necessary to memorize when day-to-day thinking evolves unfettered by unconnected facts. Memory cannot be a meaningful exercise if the knowledge base is a series of disparate experiences and events which do not project long term connected meaning. As Mark Twain suggested, education continues to be an unwinding, an unraveling of random, fragmented facts to make way for substantive, meaningful experiences. In this regard, Boston University would become a unique experiment, an exchange place for advanced, integrative specialties. Henry's dictum: residents must be linked by a need to know, working in tandem with a vested interest to develop skill sets supported by real science.

Henry recognized that dental school was a very rote learning experience. He felt the road to general practice was limited by learning

---

[86] Twain, Mark: *Pdd'nhead Wilson, The Family Mark Twain (Compilation of all his books and short stories)*, Copyright 1992, Published by Barnes & Noble..

mechanical techniques which would support basic patient needs. He considered the basic sciences as terribly exhaustive without relevance. At this level of training time was most precious to render the maximum essential learning without sitting endlessly in courses (like physiology, neuroanatomy, etc.) which provided an unrelated learning experience, soon forgotten. Two years of assembled time learning gratuitous information in the basic sciences should never be termed wasteful, but certainly very poor time management for effective learning. Henry certainly would have never minimized "a need to know", but he inveighed against its superfluousness. Being essentially nothing more than expedient, the unnecessary detail over a two year period could be condensed into one comprehensive review in the first year with specific relevance to the dental sciences. For Henry, learning details without utilitarian application was quite disturbing. Dental schools were mandated to produce scientists and yet the four years were overloaded where time could have been spared for relevant course construction.

Henry often sardonically referenced the dental degree as "a union card". It sounded strident, but it was merely critical of the bureaucratic system. The reference seemed perfectly defensible because so much inessential time was being expended delving into the weeds of physiology, biochemistry, pharmacology, anatomy, etc. He'd shake his head disapprovingly. He was convinced it was not the role of dental school to be formulaic generation after generation. This was the thinking of a true scientist. He wanted the sciences to be stimulating, relevant and authoritative. The political sway and corporate cronyism stood in the way of reform, but this unnerving resistance to change became the spark to his eventual "magnum opus". He felt education should inspirit, not dispirit.

Henry was a product of a high school where he gained an old-fashioned classical education. The Boston Latin School (154) was (and still is) reputed to be a 'trivium style" education. A trivium education is a three pronged linkage of systematic knowledge, reasoning and the acquisition of wisdom in realizing the ability for classical rhetoric. It sounds terribly abstruse for a high school learning experience. And, it was.

However, it produced disciplined minds with classical backgrounds. It was a very unique educational experience, growing up in an ideal learning tradition. Considered the number one public high school for learning in the country, graduates have always been educated with a rigor unparalleled in any other public institution. Learning traditional Latin as a graduation requisite as well Declamation (public oration) playing a vital role in the school's emphasis on training minds to think were unique to Boston Latin's great tradition. Graduates of such an outstanding background cannot help but consider education with a very different mindset. In addition, such depth would tend to embolden a student with a serious mindset. With this background Henry's perspective was rather serious-minded.

Yet, in spite of Henry's classical background, he never got to properly manifest any oratory skills. In fact, as has been carefully described, Henry was a very poor communicator or stand-up lecturer. He just couldn't develop a feel for public speaking. He was very diffident and pensive because his stuttering stifled his efforts to speak with enthusiasm and not in his languid monotone. Over the years he learned to smooth over this deficit. Gradually becoming more confident, he grew into a vastly improved public posture.

The very intense high school regimen certainly served to provide him with a profound intellectual base for his later scientific studies. Henry was like a number of notable intellects who grew up in poor circumstances only to excel beyond expectations. He was effectively no different than people who had to overcome a physical disease, a fear, or an inherent personality issue only to blossom somewhere along the way growing up. The combination of growing up poor and living in a home setting without a father relationship probably contributed markedly to his shyness and self-effacing manner. His real life caretaker growing up was his older brother. This contributed to making them so close during the rest of their lives. In spite of what he had to overcome, he was never held back from his career. He was never hesitant nor arbitrary. All his pursuits were measured and prudent.

The consequence of his background convinced him that dental

education had some real problems to which he would address with his own remedies. His accomplishments gave him credibility and he articulated very convincing arguments for change. He had a knack to easily parse "the gobbledegook" which he felt trivialized the real meaning in his message. The group of educators he eventually brought to Boston University reflected his gravitas and objectives.

Growing up in Boston, the city was segregated into immigrant districts. The South End-Dorchester area was primarily Irish, but it gradually became mixed with a heavy Jewish wave of newcomers. The North End was primarily Italian. Surrounding areas and the inner city (which was very small) was highly mixed. Friendships garnered lasted a lifetime. When it came time to embark on the all-important lifetime decision for the future, two influences predominantly held sway: parents and peer friendships (and, perhaps more so in Henry's day). Because Jewish immigrants were more educationally oriented, becoming a "doctor", an accountant, a lawyer, etc. always satisfied the need for making a living. This was all important, particularly to a Jewish mother. In Boston a sinecure position was secured for only the privileged and connected. The professions were popular because they represented steadiness, reliability and predictability. Therefore, Henry and his older brother, Eddie, were pigeonholed for medicine. The old saw: "My son the doctah..." gave a mother a sense of good feeling and pride in her accomplishment for the upbringing which was recompense for all the hard work and sacrifice. Therefore, in Henry's circle of friends, the majority embarked on a medical school education. However, when Henry left for college, he went out of state to Providence, Rhode Island where he attended Brown University. His brother, Eddie, stayed in Boston and went to Tufts College because that's where his friends were going. There was no hesitation. Peer pressure was never an issue, it was just natural by consensus. Someone thought it would be a good idea and all friends followed. Henry was four years younger than Eddie so when it came time for college, one of his friends heard Brown was looking for students in the Boston area. And, more important, it was not going to cost anything. So, to Henry, why not? Thought or consternation never came into play. It was almost blase. Their mother wanted them to go to medical school as was the nature of all Jewish mothers, but Eddie was afraid of blood so medical school was never a consideration for him. In fact, he disdained the feeling of being dirty or his clothes getting soiled. So, when he sat on the curb of a sidewalk, Henry told how he would carefully lay a handkerchief down before sitting. There's obviously a psychological component to that behavior, but it's silly to analyze because poverty and few clothes most likely accounted for this. He wound up at Harvard Business School because (yes) his closest friends applied. So, to Eddie it seemed like a good idea. Likewise, Henry did not pursue medicine because he had some close friends who were going to dental school because it was not going to take so long to get out and make a living. Interesting times. His friends applied to Harvard so it was a natural place for him also, and particularly because Eddie was still at Harvard. And, that is how Henry Goldman wound up in a profession that consumed all his energies for the rest of his life.

Interesting enough there was never anything more intrinsic or captivating to explain how he decided on a profession that at the outset had absolutely no meaning to him. It would simply be a living for him and his friends. They all grew up poor, some more than others. The immediacy of money was very enticing and determinative. How he graduated into the role he assumed for his life calling is another story. For the time being, it is sufficient to understand that Henry and his generation were indeed motivated by family and friends more so for need and comfort. There was no time or convenience to debate such an issue. Plain and simple, Henry was constrained in every way imaginable, and, it was a credit to him and his generation that most found their way to very productive and reasonably happy lives. They took what was given and appreciated what they received. They were not demanding because they were eternally grateful for anything that upgraded their lives and gave them hope for success.

Henry's albatross was the observation that so much required change. In rising to prominence, he had insatiable energy to succeed. At one time Henry wanted to be Dean at his alma mater, Harvard, but the politics did not work in his favor. Henry felt slighted and his thin-skinned feelings were hurt. It was a learning experience, but a blessing in disguise because it ignited his ambitions. The early 1950's friendship with Lester W. Burket and his University of Pennsylvania chairmanship finally gave him the perch on which to land. Lester W. Burket was the Dean and a very old school, hard-nosed personality. Both being part of a small assembly of Oral Pathologists at the time, they shared similar thinking about dental education. Both were convinced that Oral Biology and Oral Medicine had to play a much more significant role in dental education. But, their personalities were markedly different. Burket was quite phlegmatic and rather linear. Henry was dedicated to purpose with an easygoing, cooperative personal style. Henry learned a lot from his Pennsylvania affiliation and his friendship with Burket, both sharing in the long-range sensibilities regarding the future of the dental profession. (218).

Henry would never blow doors open in a bullish, headstrong manner, but he was purposive and steadfast. He often assumed the appearance of a busy librarian scuttling hastily through the book stacks. When he no longer traveled back-and-forth to Philadelphia, it was to become the Chairman of The Department of Stomatology at Boston University School of Medicine. This was his grand opening to a palpable change in leadership and management.[87]

The world of G.V. Black which seemed to constantly occupy his thoughts would become his motivation for change. He was not obsessed, but he definitely spoke of his historic influence quite often. The dental specialties were the springboard for the profession to move beyond and give meaning to integrative education. The Thomas, Burkets, and Boyles of the world were all similarly invested in like thinking, but none saw the greater picture as Henry did with such verve and telling conviction.

Henry's "design for dental education" was to eliminate the "union card" mentality. Oral Biology would transit thinking into this foundational advance. To this end, Morris Ruben served as the articulate,

---

[87] See Appendix # 2

tireless emissary for lectures, research mentoring, and intrinsic investigative animal projects on subject matter that was cutting edge for trending ideas and thinking.

Henry's message to Morris Ruben were composed of tacit reminders of his research and teaching responsibilities. Morris Ruben hardly required any motivation. He possessed exemplary standards. He was the master of scientific method and integrative research. He was able to accomplish what might normally require an entire group. Residents whose research would require a Master's thesis were fortunate to find refuge in Morris's wide range of competencies.

Henry would be the last man standing. His stringent classical high school education served as his inspiration because it codified his thinking. Over time his daily thoughts were consumed with anxiety because his target dream was so comprehensive. It is unfathomable the pressure cooker like course he chose for his lifetime achievement. It was not simply (and this is tongue-in-cheek because being a Dean is certainly not routine) assuming the role as Dean because he threw himself into a public arena where there was no time for failure. To Henry, tradition was not a lazy message. He saw it as a resolve to appreciate the very foundation of the human intellect. The very substantive nature of human biology would materially enhance specialization. Marching ahead, research would share the spotlight with clinical teaching. Periodontics would lend new meaning and importance to the other specialties because it represented in its totality the foundational message of dental health. Saving dentitions over a lifetime became the grand pursuit as specialty interrelationships expanded. To Henry, the school would become the domain for guided thinking and managed training.

So much of what was going on at Harvard and Pennsylvania cultivated great style and scientific method, but it lacked the full measure of integrative relationships necessary to make patient treatment comprehensive. Wherein Harvard or Pennsylvania (or other residency programs around the country like Ohio State, Western Reserve, etc.) might have one to three residents, Boston University had as many as six to twenty one at anyone year in any of the residency specialties. In fact, the programs were only limited in numbers at the discretion of each Chairman. The only specialty which remained traditional with very limited numbers from year to year was Oral Surgery.

Henry realized that size could never substitute for quality. For its time, it was a scientific pantheon of the dental world. Each Chairman brought a sense of enthusiasm and spirited conviction missing in dentistry. Henry's hope for change was not dashed. Boston University, once a thought and a plan, was an ideal. It was the ultimate colloquium on a permanent footing. The grand design which was years in the planning and development between 1958 and its Charter inauguration in 1963 was the culmination of one man in one era. Its noble vertex came in the decade between the mid-to-late 1960's into the mid-to-late 1970's. Peripheral to those years were either growing or problem years. But, for that one decade there was an ascendancy to greatness that dentistry might never achieve again. The programs functioned like a well-oiled machine moving with grace in a quiet, undisturbed atmosphere. Graduates of those days realized a unique style of learning that no longer exists. Class size ushered in a new concept. The idea of colloquia assumed the seminar format for an exchange of ideas and opinions. The piece de resistance was in its certainty, a living product of Henry's dream. It was Henry unceremoniously atop the dental world. Every contribution to the world of dental science each Chairperson made was not gratuitous. It represented the hard work and ambitious nature each possessed, but Henry gave each the opportunity to grow and realize a dimension of accomplishment unachievable without the forum Boston University provided. He was as the great late 19th Century writer Henry James articulated so wonderfully in his novel, *The Portrait of a Lady*, (79) by conveying the message as how his central character, Isabel Archer, matured into life's great offerings by expanding the wind in her sails (metaphorically). Henry "put wind into the sails" of his faculty and let them grow figuratively as far and wide as they willed. Henry understood the psyche of these great intellectual machines and he did not want to be the restrictor plate or governor to decelerate their progress. That was an art that enabled the greatness the school achieved. As stated before but bears repeating, his leadership was laissez-faire, hands off with regard to their own self-determination as educators.

Henry was a complex man no doubt, but he was unique in his cross training and practice between Oral Pathology and Periodontology. In addition, he came into dentistry when the fields of Oral Medicine and Oral Biology were springing from their status as "interest sciences" to full-fledged resourceful specialties. At first quite informal, they invoked very serious investigative study into diseases of the oral cavity. Henry was a very serious proponent of these burgeoning areas of study, research and practice. He was an intrinsic investigator as he viewed nomenclature to categorize specialty groupings as mere academic formality (and, in his view, perhaps mere frivolity). Nevertheless, his crossover interest between the pure investigative basic science of Oral Pathology and the rapidly growing specialty of Periodontology (and Periodontal Prosthesis) made him extremely unique. But, as explained, he was riding the wave of a newly expanding interest by many clinicians worldwide into causes for tooth loss. For the most part, the leaders in the field of Periodontology seemed quite numerous, but, in viewing the world landscape, they were a very select minority of research investigators and clinicians. For a time the trend seemed like an almost invisible swale in the grand valley of the more traditional dental specialties. But, with Henry's influence, the Boston University established a home where the dental sciences took on a position of considerable significance in the teaching panorama.

Ostensibly, Henry embraced a dream imparted by his own years of study. He established the fact that dentistry cannot be practiced without serious consideration given to periodontal disease as the leading cause of tooth loss. However, if the truth be known, as the ethical-legal considerations of dental practice were gradually catching up to the cutting edge knowledge of "tooth loss", general practitioners were forced to abide by and pay serious attention to license regulations governing practice. With that, a whole new world opened up which conflicted many a practitioner. On the one hand general practitioners had to be brought up to speed on advancing technologies for the benefit of their patients, but, on the other hand, they had to balance this with the practical resistive factors of patient acceptance and management. In Henry's ideal world, dental practice could not succeed if periodontal therapies were not tantamount to any kind of dental restorations. The result is that as departments of Periodontology grew throughout the country, its relationship with the other traditional dental specialties became "good cop-bad cop" in nature. Periodontists were becoming the new "bosses" imposing their will; eg. their science and practice skills. Boston University's cachet was its trend setting influence, perhaps because of its size and worldwide diversity. This was most definitely Henry's "hope and design for dental education" ad perpetuam rei memoriam.[88] As Henry was aging and feeling like the curtain was coming down on his active leadership, he never engaged the thought that there would be such a dramatic shift in teaching and practice priorities as the new field of Implantology came on the scene. (138) Rapidly growing and dramatically expanding like a new found toy in the hands of "babes", suddenly Periodontology lost its raison d'etre in the traditional sense. Commercial conflicts of interest began to compromise departments of Periodontolgy so that implants were substituting for the "saving" of teeth. This, for the most part, displaced priorities at the teaching level so that gradually the new "magic bullet" would rectify the conundrum of "what to do about the scourge of periodontal disease". At its peak, methods of treating periodontal disease became fundamental to dental education. The advent of implants eliminated them, so the naïve thought! After all, periodontal disease was eliminated and the lingering need to make dental practice direct its energies towards tooth preservation was extinguished. Like the baby who covers his/her face thinking the world can no longer see him/her, this "hide-and-go-seek" infantile deception gave practitioners the false sense of security that periodontal therapies were no longer vital considerations. After all, their energies resorted to implant replacement of vital teeth as "the deus ex

---

[88] Website: www.latin-dictionary.org.: "ad *perpetuam rei memoriam*": "*for the perpetual remembrance of the thing.*

machine",[89] or, in common jargon: "the magic bullet". The implant was the savior on the horizon, the panacea of man's dental problems. This was not Henry's "hope and design"!

"Education consists mainly in what we have unlearned", as noted by Mark Twain quite often in all his stories whether directly or by suggestion. [90] Henry would have seen implant therapies as just another modality to be integrated in the entire basket of knowledge. It would be a source to contribute where necessary, not as the final replacement of natural teeth. Henry would always use commercial sources to support a school's financial plan or a private practice need, but it would be an affront to let business considerations determine how and what to teach. (He certainly understood firsthand the expression: "money talks and '- - - - - - - - walks"!). (209) The serious implications of holding the profession financially tethered solely to corporate influence peddling was an anathema for Henry to embrace. He saw this as a burgeoning conflict of interest with irreversible consequences. He constantly upheld the belief that the overall template to preserve dental health was adaptive to what scientific investigation would provide in a common sense manner. Henry was not controlled by fiduciary opportunism yet he would utilize the tools of opportunity to support and enhance dental education and practice. His principles of teaching were guided by the evidence of proven scientific study. In times of war, subterfuge would be guided by "false flag" ruses and stratagems, but corporate support, to Henry, was just that, a support mechanism to advance and aid educational need. To use it like a "false flag", a neatly veiled deception, to hold up institutional need through financial control was self-destructive. As long as Henry was in control, Boston University would be governed by a purity of interaction between the business world and the needs of the school. He was the kind of person who would resist "unlearning" in phases in order to proceed in a fickle manner to co-opt "the latest and greatest"

---

[89] Website: www.latin-dictionary.org: "deus ex machine": "divine intervention" or "God in the machine".

[90] Twain, Mark: *Pudd'nhead Wilson*, *The Family Mark Twain (Compilation of all his books and short stories)*, Copyright 1949, Barnes and Noble..

therapy. Henry considered education a living process, advancing and refining through time, not finitely ending and changing in phases.

What about the ethical considerations regarding the purity of professional education? There are so many opinions that this is no place to belabor the considerations which impart a nasty taste to the entire conundrum. Refer to Len Marrells's views on thoughts, actions and character to extract reasons why the burden remains entirely with the person (or people) who purport to live by standards as long as the standards are their standards. The "gold standard" is set by the person who has the gold sets the standard![91] Henry believed it was vital to be inclusive of all beliefs, opinions and theories, but not to the total denial nor the displacement of established thought and practice in the name of "money" ("the holy grail" of life).

The greatest burden that Henry carried as an educator was the cost of dental education. Because there are generational differences in the cost of living, the managing of a dental education has remained relatively onerous since there has never been financial support save for training in the military services. The result is the strain it has placed on individuals and families to spend two to seven years in post-doctoral training (let alone what pre-doctoral education demands). This was a major weak spot in helping a good number of residents through specialty training, particularly those whose debt from dental school was still lingering in the balance. In certain situations stipends were available, but BUSGD was very different because enrollment into the residency programs was significantly larger than any training location in the world. Henry was able to gain low percentage loans for residents, but the expanding debt was an albatross for so many struggling to make the burden worthwhile. Because there was an age differential among the residents within the various specialties, dealing with the pressures manifested in many different ways. The graduate training was very intense and created a major sacrifice for the individuals making a profound commitment. The length of training varied among the various

---

[91] Marrella, Len: *In Search of Ethics: Conversations with Men and Women of Character*, Copyright 2009, DC Press, A Division of Diogenes Consortium, Sandford, Florida.

specialties, and especially for those combining clinical training along with advanced degree programs. The financial issues aside, this was the type of individual Henry had in mind when he considered the future specialist. It was to be a mix of clinical training, research and advanced masters' and doctoral degree programs. These individuals were going to be the educators, researchers, and practitioners who would carry the torch for future generations.

To develop a thinking, creative professional who would establish a profession more biologically in touch with the systemic health of the patient became the sine qua non of Henry's mission. To this end, there was clearly a standard below which he would never allow. His animus was the G.V. Black mechanical emphasis of erstwhile dental institutions blended with an American Dental Association so constrained in parochial, doctrinaire tradition that redirection, rethinking and recalibration of the entire educational process was not a convenience of possibilities, it was a compelling necessity.

Unfortunately, the encumbrance and the stress did not augur well at the outset. What Henry conceived was extremely ambitious, and yet the difficult undertaking was even grossly underestimated by his own admission. Admixed with his own imagination and projections was the daily, unnerving reality of deadlines and unexpected difficulties. He was truly the proverbial one-man army! Somehow he would distil a sense of purity in his educational project from the abyss of headaches and problems.

Henry's educational tapestry was an ebb and flow of rapid scrambling for a sense of order from the outset. It had no preset organization as Henry was making all the building arrangements, lecture halls, library usage, and especially class meeting areas literally on the fly. It was almost kaleidoscopic in that with each turn there appeared a different pattern to the basic design. But, he made everybody commit to the concept, and, with an understanding and faith in the long range plan, eventually everything fell into place. The work was different, the degree of pressure quite varied for each specialty. Periodontology was 24/7 drudgery. There was almost no time for personal issues.

The qualities which brought cachet to the program was the product of Dr. Gerald Kramer's demand for detail and excellence in teaching. Henry was very much aware of Kramer's hyperbolic charisma. His teaching skills were magnetic and inspirational. He was as well utilitarian as he was dynamic. He conjured up in his own mind the image of a clinically adept individual who intrinsically meted out an intellectually defensible thought process for clinical therapies. The institution was a model for change, a solution to sway the profession away from its wholly archaic tradition. He knew it would require a Hegelian-like thinking: a "thesis" for change which would curry an "antithesis"-like blowback, but eventually produce a "synthesis" of lofty refinement to deliver a more sophisticated, educated professional.

Henry learned early that he could not "cut-and-paste" his way through all the paper models which would eventually present the sense of organization and tidiness he craved. He had the business sense to understand that the culture medium comprised order, organization and opportunity. These were his "three O's"! What good would it do to cultivate a paradigm shift if he could not prevail upon top flight professionals around the world to come to Boston for their graduate specialty education? He only occasionally articulated what he had in mind because he was somewhat inexpressive. What he was obviously lacking in free-flowing conversation he compensated with meaningful, stellar planning. And, the majority of his faculty had the personality to front the public relations he could not.

Henry's prototypical dental specialist would be a blend of clinician, research investigator, lecturer-teacher and writer. In fact, although never discussed, he was projecting his own soul. He sincerely felt dental education was lacking in the well-rounded scientist. He sought a balanced, cultivated student of science. From a practical point of view, he made animal research part of a master's degree program. And, later on he added a Doctor of Science program which would bundle varying specialties for a minimum of three years to as much as eight years. However, at that time, he fell short because The Massachusetts General Hospital as a Harvard teaching hospital inaugurated a combined

MD-Oral Surgery Certificate program. Later it was expanded to other universities around the country. Henry flitted this off in an almost defiant manner as unnecessary. Fundamentally, this would have driven the graduate programs into a very select level of educational prowess. Not to say that it was a "make-or-break" deficiency in planning because it was not the case. Ironically, the man who instilled Henry with this thought was Henry's own mentor, Dr. Kurt Thoma. But, it was carried forth by Dr. Walter C. Guralnick, a Boston Oral Surgeon who succeeded Kurt Thoma. Guralnick instituted it at The Massachusetts General Hospital.[92] Perhaps it was simply more of the "perception-reality" argument, Henry never returned to this possibility. Henry was proud of the Doctor of Science program because only a few schools ever conferred this degree, The University of Pennsylvania being one. It was an atavistic degree to a long prevailing Eastern European tradition. In this regard, it represented a more clinically oriented fulfillment of training than the traditional PhD. But, it was not the MD program which may have been more practical. In all reality, it was really a "smoke and mirrors" issue and really did not reflect on the training. And, this is what really mattered. Perhaps Henry had it right, when in fact he most often did. Never caring what others would say or do, he always rested firmly with his own convictions. Therefore, the Doctor of Science degree manifested as his principal piece de resistance for those who would pursue it.

Henry's forte was his intuition, perhaps derived from his many years of experience. He did not want to while his time away trying to convince people or to worry about standards. He was not provocative, nor a provocateur. He was, for the most part, unassuming. Growing up and throughout their lives, Henry and Eddie were always silenced by their mother's very surly reproach not to talk about matters that were not for public discussion. And, mind you, always with a very acerbic

---

[92] Guralnick, Walter C., DMD: A HISTORY OF ORAL AND MAXILLOFACIAL SURGERY AT MASSACHUSETTS GENERAL HOSPITAL, Boston, Massachusetts: Massachusetts General Hospital, Department of Oral Maxillofacial Surgery, Copyright 2010.

Yiddish expression. Thus, it was very rare for Henry to be public about anything of personal importance. His opinions were always saved for very private conversations and particularly closed meetings. His views on dental education and the relevance of his concerns for change were fundamental to everything for which he worked so intrepidly and aggressively. But, rarely was there an exchange of ideas or conversation. His brother was of the very same stoic behavior. Sitting in a room with the two was often challenging. Which one was The Great Sphinx of Giza was hard to discern? But, he always said he had a feeling about this or that. And, how spot on were his de facto decisions. When he was certain, he proceeded without extraneous input. The only person who really ever stood up to him was his brother, but only if it was in his best interest, and if he thought Henry may be soundly wrong. Henry could be obstinate and that "immovable object" in the way of that "irresistible force"!

In his own inimitable way, however, he needed to bring his ideas into a very narrow focus so as not to be obstructed or deterred by all that was going on around him. Boston was a hotbed for gossip in the dental industry. Certainly, Henry and The Boston University School of Graduate Dentistry was the guest who came for dinner, but not necessarily with an open invitation. Harvard and Tufts were highly established in a very small city. Boston was always the figurative suburb of New York City.

Even though it was a hub for educational institutions, dental institutions were very territorial. So, in some sense, Henry's private demeanor served him well as Boston University's grand entrance into the dental scene in 1963, albeit expected by then, was hesitatingly accepted. No building, no gathering complex of buildings, most thought it would collapse being "hoisted on its proverbial petard" (209.). The other schools had small specialty programs, but not in all the ADA recognized specialties. As recorded before, in 1958 Henry organized The Department of Stomatology at Boston University Medical School with the sanction of The Board of Trustees of the school as well as President Harold Case. (173.) This was a specialty quite arcane as far as most people in and out of the profession would be concerned. Stomatology was a specialty that had absolutely no reference nor meaning to anyone, except for Henry. This unique word has always been part of the lexicon no one has ever cited. And yet it was part of the very language inherent in the verisimilitude of Henry's conceptual basis for change in dental education.

There is nothing proprietary about the field of Stomatology and yet, even today, it remains recondite because the dental profession has never advanced it privately or publically. It has been a part of the European (Eastern in particular) lexicon for at least two or three centuries. At its most basic connotation, it is the study of the mouth in reference to the entire human body and the reciprocal functions of the bodily organs. In fact, the Stomatologist of Henry's day was a dentist-physician. Some schools have embraced the construct of a Department of Stomatology serving as an umbrella for Departments of Periodontology, Oral Diagnosis, Oral Medicine, sometimes Radiology, and rarely Oral Surgery. And, Henry was very much aware of the fact that Stomatology as a field only rarely surfaced when it served a material, financially gainful purpose. Lip service was the only benefit provided by the mention of the word. In effect, a Stomatolgist is exactly what Henry M. Goldman was. An Oral Pathologist with General Pathology training, a Periodontist, and a specialist in oral mucosal, infectious, and tumorous diseases of the mouth. (143) He was a bone fide Stomatologist. There have been a selected few who ventured into the required years of training to be acknowledged as a sufficiently trained Stomatologist. But, today that is a rarity, albeit the field of Oral Medicine is growing within the hospital settings around the country. In Henry's mind, this was the paradigm the dental profession should have embraced with full ADA recognition. This was as important to the health professions as the metaphorical analogy to the Prime Minister Harold Macmillan's brave, independent turnaround colonial foreign policy cited before. (91) Henry's mission was certainly a full blown "wind of change", the creation of the physician-dentist. This was Henry's tour de force.

Even Pierre Fauchard, arguably known as the father of modern dentistry, had more to say about advancing the mission of the physician-dentist when he published his highly momentous and note-worthy book: *Le Chirurgien Dentiste, The Surgeon Dentist* in 1728. (83.) It was a capacious compendium of oral diseases that provided advanced considerations of oral-systemic interrelationships. They have been "ger-rymandered" by specific specialties in The United States today because of bureaucratic instability and resistance of controlling agencies and regulatory bodies. As the pundit philosopher, Yogi Berra, so wonder-fully anointed people trying to reinvent the wheel: "Déjà vu all over again"! (11) Pierre Fauchard's prescience was very precisely the very stuff of people like Horace Hayden and Chapin Harris. The material juxtaposition of Henry's philosophy and planning embraced their his-torical model, but he made it fundamental to the practice of dentistry.

Henry being the product of the Harvard School of Dental Medicine, a school saddled with the reputation that it has always produced re-searchers and not clinicians, conflated this educational model with his wartime experience to project the training programs for Boston University. Even his mentor, Kurt Thoma had fashioned this thinking long before Henry came onto the scene. But, it was Henry who would take this experiment in graduate dental education to a different level.

Most people knew Henry Goldman as a Periodontist, but, to re-iterate for the sake of emphasis, he solidified his reputation early on as a bone fide Oral Pathologist, both in training under Kurt Thoma at Harvard and then at The Armed Forces Institute of Pathology in Washington, D.C.. Even though he spent many years as a clinical practitioner, he had the luxury of highly recognized partners, Alan Shuman and Gerald Isenberg, who provided him the time away from the office so he could administer to the graduate school. Henry's repu-tation among his international peers was inviolable. Therefore, every department was based in evidenced based thinking he experienced at the AFIP. Henry, by virtue of his education, training and experience, was able to design a unique pattern of training for all the departments. At its peak, Boston University turned out uniquely trained and highly sophisticated physician-dentists.

The "Education consists mainly in what we have unlearned" Mark

Twain[93] refrained suggested beyond its primary meaning that with every generation the relearning process is only manifested by the staggering manner by which core knowledge discarded must be relearned. A mystique was created that concerned Henry. So, perhaps Mark Twain should have added that "unlearning" may be a lifetime enigma of the educational process. The responsibility for retaining continuity in education has always been the educational institution. Today the field of Periodontics has been decimated by institutional diminution, an academic reductionism where the sum has been continuous bastardized by the parts which, for too long a time, do not add up to "their sum total". The specialty has been undermined by the erroneous validation of implants over saving teeth. It is as sinful as it is unfortunate. Periodontics at the graduate level has been a virtual three year implant program with Henry's paradigm having been supplanted. The fact that an implant company can irresponsibly co-opt a graduate department with its financial canoodling to sell its system reinforces "the great unlearning" of fundamental Periodontics. This has now evolved over many years now so that even a return to the original paradigm shift Henry promulgated decades ago would require a total relearning. William Bendix playing the role of Chester A. Riley in "The Life of Riley back in the 1950's characterized this so very aptly when he said: "What a revoltin' development this is"![94] The problem is, however, that it is not funny at all. It is the true reversal of fortune, more for John Q. Public than Henry Goldman! As the famed literary giant and coquettish beauty, Clare Booth Luce, observed: "No good deed goes unpunished"![95] Oh, how this quote has become the staple of so many conversations and references. Yet, in most circumstances, it is appropriately used. For Henry's great accomplishment, only the aging mortar remains of its original construct. Long gone is the intellectual patina that served to

---

[93] Twain, Mark: *Pudd'nhead Wilson, The Family Mark twain (Compilation of all his books and short stories),* Copyright 1992, Barnes and Noble.

[94] Brecher, Irving: *The Life of Riley,* Copyright 1949, Published by Waverley House in its First Edition in 1949.

[95] Shadegg, Stephen C.: *Clare Booth Luce,* Copyright 1970, Simon & Schuster.

gracefully represent the institution's grand mystique it possessed for a very long time. It was laughable at times to observe the petty jealousies or even bitter resentments battering the school for absolutely the most juvenile reasons. The energy Henry expended putting the school to-gether before opening was minimal compared to the amount necessary on a daily basis to hold everything together. While big business has a laundry list of middle management administrators to execute daily con-cerns, Henry was the administrative overseer of all departments. His Chairmen attended to the educational care in their daily activity, but Henry was on top of everything which manifested any financial issue. His legendary reputation amidst residents who never came to know him was one of "a not-so-present" Dean, not often seen and when so was standoffish. Nothing could be more far from reality, with a twist of the ironic. His demure, quiet persona was remarkably confused with absenteeism or detachment. In actuality, the very opposite was true. He was very hands-on and actively involved in doing so much for so many. His pleasant and highly refined manner with which he so often interceded wherever he could facilitate the life of a resident or staff member was very selfless, yet memorable by those involved. It was just performed in his style, unassuming and quietly. His mentoring and attention to those in need was a reflection of a man who took measure of the most important part of his leadership: coming to the aid of a student resident wherever possible. He did not wear this behavior as an emblem as he was intrinsically so very altruistic, generous and self-ef-facing. Many seemingly could not perceive this, perhaps due to poor judgment skills, naivete, or their own self-centeredness which impeded their own perceptions. Nevertheless, Henry had a most benevolent and protective side of his personality which was awkwardly sealed in by his unexpressive personality.

Long after his death many may have neglected to remember the institution and the gravitas it imparted. Their mentors were the sails through which wind billowed words of knowledge they carried for life. But, as Henry James so artfully displayed with Isabel Archer in "*Portrait of a Lady, (79) "...the wind in her sails"* which saw her through growth and maturity came in the person who provided her protection with very pleasant domestic surroundings. Henry Goldman built a school that guided so many through the good fortune which provided for their future and all that they derived. In whatever measure, each took a little of this man who gave so much in his most humble and inimitable way. His legacy is in fact the monolith he "built".

CHAPTER 9

Dental Education and the Teaching Institution

Education is an abstract embedded in reality. That is to say, theories abound on what education means, how they should be applied, and, as abstractions, how they become meaningful applications. Their factual basis becomes the tangible take-away of every student at every level of the learning process. Along the way considerable theories wash away for one reason or another, but most often because they are not important or do not relate to long term needs. And how information is retained markedly depends how it is conveyed. And this depends on how, where and when it is presented as well as the degree of emphasis. And so education is thereby very subjective in nature. Aldous Leonard Huxley, the great metaphysical thinker-author of the 20th century stated in *Proper Studies*:

> *"Facts do not cease to exist because they are ignored".*[96]

Therefore, for education to be just and purposive with long term meaning it has to be thoroughly and objectively refereed for those that would benefit from the process. In this regard, Henry wanted to produce professionals who could think on an intellectual plane with a very high level of sophistication. The graduate level was to be transformative in that "the facts" would be evaluated, challenged and interpreted. To

---

[96] Huxley, Aldous: *Proper Studies,* Copyright 1957, Chatto & Windus (originally published in 1927)..

Henry, relevancy of fact conveyed the basis of the learning process. The conveyor belt-like approach to learning techniques like an automaton frustrated him. He wanted to bring a higher meaning to the investigative exercise of testing research ideas and vetting principles which would then present intelligent and viable clinical applications. These are the "facts" which pre-doctoral dental education did not inspire because of a pathway lost in training "mechanics" with very narrow exposure to the biology of oral health and disease (the very area which attracted and inspired Horace Hayden and Chapin Harris centuries before). Somehow, the dental profession was off the track where Henry thought it should not have been for so many years. If he were still alive, he would solemnly recoil at Huxley's statement because he effused his entire life the importance of opening up to facts because denial does not make them go away. When residents matriculated at Boston University, they finally found themselves immersed within an exchange of ideas related to clinical training and research projects. It was like a scholastic repechage in raising them to a level of far greater clinical achievement.

If each member of the original Chairmen are examined, for the most part they all broadened their focus and raised their goals. They captured the empirical teaching methods and raised the level of interaction. The measurable was immeasurable. This is not to intellectually dispose of and diminish other institutional teaching methods. Boston University was different. It separated itself by the mere fact that it was a graduate institution with a far more sophisticated mission, both qualitatively and quantitatively. More was expected from the residents, and, conversely they expected more from the interdisciplinary learning process. Henry created this approach because he was chagrined by the first two years of dental school. Basic medical sciences being served up like soporific doggerel only accountable to satisfy compulsory credit obligations, but certainly not contributing to stimulate or influence the learning process. The truth is that blarney would have had purpose in providing entertainment, but preachy facts of the basic sciences only served two objectives: firstly, to satisfy compliance with examination formalities constructed by PhD educators to measure standard learning of esoteric facts; and, secondly, to perpetuate outmoded regulations which essentially wasted the first two years of dental school. Remodeled, the four years would be far more educationally productive. The incorporation of one comprehensive basic science course over one year would be far more productive and free up much more time to offer many optional clinical-research seminars. The failure to bring dental education into a new age format has gravely limited the four years to exactly how Henry described them: conformity to requirements to obtain a "union card". Another way of expressing this: tradition is a thing of the past!

Boston University was indeed an experiment. It was never fully tailored to a one purpose maxim: that an ideal works when mutual cooperation of all departments exists. This was never achieved as a measure of harmony among faculty, but practically the residents got the message and worked cohesively. In this sense, the environment was always learner friendly. The optics were quite revelatory in maximizing communication.

The faculty member who commanded the most attention was Gerry Kramer. Henry originally hired him for his conscientiousness and will to teach. He demanded so much of himself that it was easy to understand how and why he transferred this to his graduate students. He taught with style and brio. However, his sophistry was notorious because he wandered into areas way beyond his expertise. But, he got away with it because of his theatrics and impressive display of personality. This approach obviously percolated with other faculty. He over-embellished the prosaic. He manufactured facts from basic pathology which were often far-fetched, but sounded smooth. His lectures were jaw dropping, his personality charismatic, and his attraction magnetic. At the beginning, Kramer represented to some extent what Henry was looking for and required. A man of complicated depth and energy, his lectures were like a Socratic dialogue in the production of his presentations.[97] He mesmerized his residents and totally captured their attention. He loved the limelight and postured to his audience. He

---

[97] Guthrie, W.K.C.: *SOCRATES*, Copyright 1972, Cambridge University Press.

was a real showman. Nevertheless, he must be credited for elevating the teaching process with energy and substance. He squeezed everything possible from all his residents. And, in so doing, he was responsible for so many Periodontists who could reason with probative insight. He may have been a character of extreme behavior Henry never could imagine, yet he thirsted for knowledge and aimed his sights squarely at clinical excellence. The old euphemistic saw: "give the devil his due": Gerry Kramer accomplished one of the most essential goals which is almost completely gone today. He very clearly showed that periodontal therapy is the best "insurance" against tooth loss in most circumstances. And, in so doing, he scrupulously demonstrated that the field of Periodontics is the "mother's milk" of dentistry. And, to think, that both the ADA and the AAP have allowed periodontal care be apportioned as a casual afterthought buried with a premeditated nonchalance away from notice and in deference to the "mystical gold-plated gods" of implants and crowns"! Credit Kramer for driving home the importance of periodontal health as the basis of a maintainable dentition. Were he to have enjoined with science devoid of theater and sanctimony, he would have been long lasting and not eventually marginalized.

Henry simply found his treacly, condescending manner very unnecessary and exhausting. Although he seemed to carry a lot of angst and did not show any respect for Henry, he inspired so many to achieve so high. The department grew in stature in spite of Kramer's heightened reputation, not what Henry ever imagined. Henry had put together a team. Kramer, without doubt, was flying solo without any deference to others when it was not in his singular interest. It was as if he saw himself as a mythological figure, like the original King Midas. The Greek historian, Herodotus, depicted King Midas believing everything he touched would turn to gold.[98] Kramer possessed this self-image and carried himself with an air of self-confidence that trickled down to so many of his "flock". He was a man of unlimited potential who foundered on the issue of personality, not ability. Stripped of his compulsion

---

[98] Burn, A.R.: *Herodotus: The Histories*, Copyright 1972, Published by Penguin Classics.

for "show time" and an insatiable need for recognition, he possessed all the elements necessary to excel. He was simply too high on himself, utilizing Boston University as his connection to people and places that would advance his good fortune academically and materially. Why he assumed this tact no one will ever know. His innate capabilities were so overwhelmingly excellent that he would have achieved anything he desired. Yet, he couched his resentments with bravado, but it was not hidden sufficiently as he also seemed to be a friction point for most of the other faculty. To the faculty that did not have to engage him on important subject matter he was a gentleman, suave, stylish and so-phisticated. This was most certainly a betrayal because he was shrewd enough to lend a stately impression to those he might need but did not represent any immediate need. Frankl cajoled in a similar manner, but, at the time, gave the appearance that he was more dedicated to the school as a team player. Certainly Henry had more than he wanted to handle. He was burdened by the waste of time it all presented. It was only Kramer's personality, however, which spilled over throughout the Boston community. He was certainly becoming everybody's pin cush-ion very quickly. Was it deserved? Yes, it was because it was deleterious, combative, and certainly priggish. He was a gifted man who did not have to scheme the way he did. All he had to do was live and let live. He could not. The question which could never be answered was why. He sold his own problems on the open market.

The world outside of Boston University really had a misconceived impression of the inner workings from the 1960's to the end of the 1970's. The big question floating around was why did the city need another dental school? The Boston dental community did not have a clear picture at all. Rumors abounded because Boston was a small city where gossip was ever present. Henry's reputation was so unblemished that its image could not be called into question. The bravado of some faculty, however, added a dimension. The personalities of Kramer and Frankl could be over-reaching. They were not wallflowers and with-ering vines. They were aggressive and opportunistic. As their profes-sional reputations mounted, they seemed to have wrought an overly magisterial image which did not bode well in a very competitive pro-fession. Henry endeavored to be respectful of the other schools and to cultivate sound working relationships, which he did. The drawbacks of some faculty surfaced in time. The spotlight was an aphrodisiac.

When his mentor, Kurt Thoma, came over from Harvard to as-sume the head of the Oral Surgery department, Henry was able to embrace him as a family-like member. This was also true of Bernard Chaikin (from Harvard and The University of Pennsylvania) as well as Herbert Margolis (from Tufts). All three were the traditional, old-guard educators. They softened all the hoopla around town. They projected substance. And, Henry was definitely comfortable with their more modest composure. "The misery index" was very much on the low side. So, for a time, all was quiet and smooth. Because they were seasoned ed-ucators their presence was timely and very much welcome. They were transitional, but they brought experience when it was most needed. As previously stated, Kurt Thoma was replaced by Melvyn Harris. The balance was still maintained as Mel had a solid reputation. So, at this point, the school's presence was very much low profile.

This graduate school model was an idealized center. One would think it would be a pantheon of dignity and grandeur with universal ac-ceptance. But, as the expression intuits: no good deed goes unpunished. Changing financial times and government regulations eventually made survival as a school only for specialization too onerous. Conceptually, it was scripted for the long term. However, insurance programs, regu-latory requirements, research money, and accreditation politics made this impossible.

It has flourished as a pre-doctoral school for general practitioners as well as programs for specialty training, but the memory of a once inti-mate communal setting where a very profound colloquium atmosphere flourished is but a fading thought. Without having been witness to that graduate environment, it would be impossible to fully convey what the seminars and lectures from some of the greatest educators of the day (who visited from around the world) meant to all residents. And, not to be forgotten, other local school research faculty like Sigmund

Socransky from Forsyth (today the Forsyth Institute) (203) enhanced the learning experience with his sheer brilliance and remarkable communication skills. It was a different time and most certainly worth more to remember than just a historical footnote.

Consider what the public does not fully grasp. General Practitioners are simply the caretakers of the publics' dental health. This is not to be confused with dental public health which is another discussion matter. The entire purpose of the graduate school concept was to fill in the gaps where general dentists were limited by training to manage patient care beyond their insights. This was certainly a workable model for addressing population changes and demands.

In 1972 when Boston University initiated the DMD (Doctor of Dental Medicine), it was for specifically for foreign students who came for specialization and stayed in the United States. For them, adding the DMD degree allowed them to qualify to take state licensing boards for clinical practice. This event was the forerunner of the final conversion of the school from a graduate to a pre-doctoral institution. There was a transitional phase into the early 1980's resulting in the final disassembling of the Boston University School of Graduate Dentistry, but the late 1970's marked the end of "the graduate era". For those too young to be aware, it was simply an era so short that it did not have time to inure. Boston University has graduate departments today, but the atmosphere and raison d'etre is vastly different. What happened and why?

To repeat Yogi Berra's illuminating malapropism: "Déjà vu all over again". (Ibid. Berra) The reasons for its collapse were complicated, but as the ADA Council on Accreditation determined, the school had to serve a more demanding need: the training of general practitioners. But really, one would have to be living in a cocoon to buy into this. The issues: money and more money.

Now let's examine the secondary reasons. It was no longer possible to prove to the powers to be in the ADA and in Washington where grant money for research was appropriated that graduate education could remain as a de facto entity. It became financially impossible to satisfy this demand and justifiably qualify for federal grant research money. The ADA had determined that independent specialty programs would suffice, and that pre-doctoral programs would be universally the proper model for accreditation. No change, no money nor research grants! This was feigned in far more lofty verbiage, but essentially these were the same kinds of people who never grasped Henry's idea in the first place. Henry remitted as the back-and-forth became an endless loop of repetitive buncombe veiled in highbrow analysis. At the end of the day, it was thought too expensive to train a few specialists "caged" like birds flying around in a protected aviary. So, it was all about money and how the bureaucrats wanted to spend it. Matching funds did not make sense. And so, back to square one.

A return to conventional teaching with a pre-doctoral traditional format and protocol was a return to "same ol same ol"! (220) There was nothing wrong if this is what Henry had worked on so assiduously. But Henry understood that his was the only way the school would survive and endure. When Spencer Frankl became Dean in 1977, it really sealed Henry's glory days into the past. Spencer had nothing to lose as "he had no skin in the game" as the saying goes.

The teaching model at the graduate level reflected panache because it was a paradigm which produced "the thinker types" who reasoned therapies because they were well-versed in the dental literature, trained in advanced clinical techniques, and, more importantly, had learned "to think"! Maybe some would consider this a luxury. In Henry's reasoning it was just the opposite, a sine qua non of a more science oriented dentist. The generation which benefitted from those days of exception and singularity is dying out. There remains only the halcyon memories and echoes of a past fading quickly and consigned to a history which may never be remembered or appreciated. Perhaps Gerald Kramer, Anthony Gianelly, and Herbert Schilder will be the most heralded for their deep wisdom. However different their personality types were, these were the real eloquent spokesmen of their generation. To think, to reason, and speak intelligently on a given subject was their calling. They were purveyors of unbridled knowledge in very different ways, but they conveyed the essence of the school's raison d'etre. These men were the paladins of an erstwhile generation faded in time. Let's invoke a reprise in respect to what made Henry enlightened.

Henry perceived the teaching institution as a forum for sounding out ideas which would stimulate the mind, not as a conduit for rote learning. In this sense, Henry had a very hands-off approach to his faculty. Spencer was not of this mindset so that after Henry stepped down there was a major separation of philosophy and leadership. And, very specifically, he did not have the scientific background Henry had. Over the years a lot of emotional energy expended went under the radar because of Henry's overly private way of dealing with daily administration and management issues. Intellectual development was central to Henry's planning, and, the faculty intuitively supported this.

To extol his greatest attribute, Gerry Kramer was the perfect example of the proper mindset and teaching skills to implement Henry's paradigm. His intellectual depth was not matched by anyone else on the faculty. He was a perfectionist with an insatiable curiosity. And, he matched his depth of imagination with impeccable clinical skills. Only if his zeal in pursuit of dominion and sense of superiority could have been attenuated! On the other hand, Spencer was definitely not in line with this thinking. In fact, because he was Henry's choice to follow as Dean, most people instinctively thought there would be a linear follow-through without any changes. But, Spencer came with his own style. They conflicted dramatically as their philosophies were dramatically antithetical. The political jockeying reflected strikingly on incompatible belief systems. This issue became a head scratcher because Spencer simply did not have any competition in spite of the talk. It bothered Henry insofar as he waited too long to be proactive. This whole issue could have been sensibly averted if Henry had gone outside the school in search of a more accomplished educator. Because he did not it was quite clear that there would be a complete overhaul that would almost put complete finality to Boston University as an institution of integrative learning.

In its day the teaching institution amped up the spirit and enthusiasm like nothing before. Who would ever want to see the air suddenly burst from the expanding balloon of such prosperity and success? Well, the medley of political infighting, differing views, reputations challenged by pettiness, and a sudden loss in continuity spurned what was once a mutual admiration society. The school came to a crossroads of the past and future just as Henry was passing on the leadership baton. His teaching institution which intuited his dental education philosophy was suddenly in flux. Why?

No family is ever completely harmonious. And Boston University had become one big family in spite of the place being satiated with egos. When the head of the family is young, vibrant, on the upside of any possible downside, and tightly grasping all the good fortune which comes with prosperity, thoughts about succession and to whom should the torch of leadership be passed are only casually addressed. As thoughts of Henry's possible retirement surfaced, it was almost as a "force majeure" took over. Suddenly, a good number of the faculty made their ambitions apparent. For some there was great impetus. Just as this very timely change was fomenting there were also impact changes being made all around the country in every dental school and specialty training facility across the nation. The field of Implantology was inching into the academic teaching format of every school across the country. It would be a new and consequential revenue stream and was being commercially driven by every implant company which could make schools financially invested in their products. They tethered schools to the sale and support system for their product line. Initial capital money brought schools into their corporate fold by "a pay-for-play" scenario. As long as schools would allow them access to students, they would provide capital investment to the school in the way of chairs, implant kits, implants, and other items which would enhance their presence. It meant contact with pre-doctoral and graduate students who would use these companies for their own office set-ups upon graduation. This was the beginning of a fiduciary pact which would negatively impact dentistry forever. It meant that dental schools became so committed to corporate support that before long these companies had major control into every mechanism by which they could survive and function. Corporate donations took over teaching at every level, and was even responsible for the evolution of the continuation education cash cow. It was a marriage of deans and corporate oligarchs. This momentous shift in financial support spoke volumes for two issues: who would succeed Henry as Dean, and, why corporate intrusiveness angered Henry so deeply.

Long before outside corporate influence grew to what it is now, Henry's particular dealings were quite local. But, like anything in life, major change has to start somewhere, and it is usually gradual. Only when change has evolved into such corporate largesse does its fretful impact begin to be acknowledged as irremediable. Even the most ethical and purist of great dental educators fell to this state of affairs. For the dental schools to financially survive they genuflected understandably to corporate relationships which would help pay the bills. It was as simple as that.

It all began in the early days of Boston University when Henry engaged a local dental supply company run by an individual who was both mercenary and covetous. At the beginning, he was the only game in town who was able to control all business at all three dental schools: Harvard, Tufts and Boston University. In the 1960's, however, Henry's worldwide reputation gave such credibility to this company that it grew into international celebrity and financial power very quickly. The company, Rower Dental Supply Company, and its primary owner, Meyer Cyker (102) contributed immensely to the growth and expansion of Boston University. This influence was so great that it would be naïve not to acknowledge its impact on dental education and the teaching institution. Henry felt a financial relationship was worthy and important, as long as he was in control. To this extent, he always held Meyer Cyker at arm's length. Meyer was a WWII refugee who hustled for survival. He was very aggressive and innately charged into anything and everything that engaged money and control. He was a very hungry man. For a long while a story suggested he consummated a rather large business deal by holding a gun to his opponent's head. People who knew Meyer well swore as to its authenticity. But, it was never verified. It merely supplied insight into what to expect from this man who was bold, abrasive, and spoke in a guttural Germanic lilt that unnerved anybody. His overweight diminutive size was very deceiving. He was a bully who tried to con anyone in a saccharine manner until he defaulted to a bestial behavior when he realized his "victim" was turning. How Henry tolerated this uncomfortable relationship was a credit to his tolerance. But, Henry also knew Meyer carried influence with banks, other vendors, and socially prominent business people. He was a character, but he was also the only game in town. Years later, Meyer took his company globally under the name Healtco International. He eventually sold out for millions until Henry Schein came on the scene and put Healthco out of business. An interesting business story, but certainly one Henry would have wanted to forget. This was understandable, but Henry needed this connection for the sake of the school. Fortunately, Henry fashioned a blank countenance so that it was difficult for anyone to read what was on his mind, even Meyer Cyker.

By contrast, Spencer had a more frivolous mindset and submitted to any and all financial deals that would enhance his "power, position and privilege" at any cost. Henry clearly saw this and was very dissatisfied, perhaps disconsolate. In actuality, all the disharmony made Henry sick inside, but, sensing he was a default choice, he demurred. All the true men of character on the faculty kept silent and away. The old saw: "The Napolean Complex" suborned the politics. He was "frothing" to be Dean. The school was discernibly dichotomized. Spencer's unsettled feelings, however, compelled him to erase Henry's memory as much as he could. This complex behavior of resentment and betrayal crescendoed when the school was renamed eponymously as the Henry M. Goldman School of Dental Medicine. When Henry died on December 9, 1991, a real icon of the dental profession passed. His battles with adversity were immense, but the one over succession reflected a certain irreverence which seems to linger today. So many of the alumni just cannot grasp who truly laid the groundwork for their ability to achieve with such good fortune. He was a man of very few words, but of great honor and take-charge accomplishments.

So, once again as Huxley railed:

"Facts do not cease to exist because they are ignored".[99]

The facts were very clear: corporations began a pro quid pro fiduciary connection with dentistry as pharmaceutical corporations coddled medicine. Long gone were the bedeviling days of Henry Goldman wheeling-dealing with the carnivorous Meyer Cyker. As bad as they were, they were structurally innocent compared to what was to come.

The times saw the lines between schools (and, specifically, departments) and large crony corporations become very blurred. The line in the sand which demarcated the separation of corporate influence peddling blew away. No one would argue that capitalism provides a platform for growth in all industries. Yet, proprietary measures became so inordinate in proportion to need that it became easy to allow a "buy-in" at every level of dental education. It became an octopus with such fine interweaving that "the die was cast". (A wonderful metaphorical comparison was in Caesar's Civil Wars which transitioned Rome from a Republic to an Empire. When Caesar crossed the Rubicon river (in 49 B.C.) separating Cisalpine Gaul and Rome, there was no turning back. (64) This marked the commitment to wage war against the conservative element of the Roman Senate leading to a dictatorial hegemonic government. It marked the beginning of the end of The Roman Republic.)

By comparison, a seemingly innocent marriage between business and education served a mutual need. Dental education was the beneficiary of what innovative business arrangements could bring to the profession. And, the dental business industry was able to grow with the consequent gain in prosperity from so many different individual and institutional arrangements. However, as no good deed goes unpunished, in time the relationship was overtaken by commercial overindulgence and influence. The fact so overtly ignored was the beast had grown so large that it had to be fed on the backs of dentists and every phase of dental education. And, this resonated with one of Henry's grand conundrums. How would the school benefit without losing control to

---

[99] Huxley, Aldus: *Proper Studiess*, Copyright 1957, Chatto & Windus (originally published I 1927).

the dental supply and banking promoters (and their hand-carry interests)? Unfortunately and very innocently, a price would be paid many years later.

Henry had a very purist outlook. Maybe naïve, maybe defiant? He wanted to bring the best in terms of quality. He was never beset by negativism, and he proceeded on his mission without any sense that he could not complete it because of anyone or anything. So, just as his business relationships grew into a very large organization for the day, he believed he would always be in control. Therefore, maybe part naivete and part defiance brought him to his line in the sand. It is very difficult for most people to understand this very point because it took an extraordinary person with an extraordinary personality to take on such a burden, absorbing all its relentless impact and hurdles. Most people would want to ride the coattails of someone else's hard work, but very few would take up such an initiative. This was a fact that was invariably ignored because hubris stood in the way character. Reputation couldn't be sacrificed nor compromised. In Henry's mind it would be a curse to see this happen.

Henry was in a sense foiled by the very people he put in high places. They perceived a man who would never meddle into what might have been considered too picayune to be worth the effort. He never kept his faculty at arm's length. He wanted them to flourish with a sense of pride and accomplishment. To Henry a teaching institution was a living, evolving experiment in which the day-to-day progress of students was the responsibility of his chairmen. He respected this by keeping his distance. By allowing the department to grow and integrate within the overall Boston academic community, he believed this would consolidate the school and breed harmony. Henry always wanted to lead by example with the highest of ethical standards. He would never think of imposing his ideas on others without consent or desire. What he got was pretty much the opposite.

Tufts and Harvard interposed small specialty programs into the conventional pre-doctoral design. It was obvious that Boston University would immediately stand out by virtue of it being different. It would have been like a yellow ochre three story ante-bellum Charlestonian home constructed amidst the Boston Brownstones. Faced with a stand apart circumstance it was imperative to be steadying and stabilizing, not imperious and aggressively assertive. But, in search of quality, he additionally acquired some personality types who survived on trouble, conflict and antagonism. Realizing that only one attempt at a first impression governs "the world of community", Henry was wise to know that making a negative splash would boomerang and eventually create unneeded and purposeless blowback. Therefore, what was the Boston University myth?

Probably the apotheosis of dental education in Boston University's decade of world acclaim was the achievement borne out by the seminar configuration for learning. It was an intellectual experience which brought together the intimacy of inspirational teachers with challenging residents. In addition, the constant parade of other educators visiting the school to lectures and meet in seminars served as a great opportunity for residents to be witness to cutting edge research and clinical thinking.

The individual Chairmen developed into highly resourceful and determined teachers. They were men of Augustinian-like quality. Sincerely devoted to the highest levels of the learning experience, they became more than just purveyors of clinical techniques and "how-to-do", recipe-like information. They sensed their unique positions in being at the forefront of history gradually ushering in a period during which trained clinicians thought through literature and learned to intellectually test, question and challenge conventional thinking. Henry saw the dawn of a very different therapist. The beauty of all the specialties under one roof availed them the opportunity for integrated exchanges. Learning how to question and discuss concepts which blended with individual research initiatives was Henry's innovation. As an advanced graduate education center it went beyond the other specialty training centers of the day. At the outset it could have been likened to a quasi-religious experience. Albeit somewhat tongue-in-cheek, it really co-opted that sense of a belief system for scientific learning and dialogue.

Residents of the day even humorously averred to the experience with deference to its singularity and distinctive quality. It was appreciated because it was as advertised. It was a dream which evolved into a very unique brand, unprecedented and unequaled anywhere else in the world. Henry brought together many clinicians who were raw and totally inexperienced. They grew into the role models he had surmised. They became noted for individual clinical ingenuity, thoughtful and provocative minds, and outspoken leaders within their own specialties. They reached the zenith of professional standards because of their very vocal and knowledgeable opinions and ability to lead with authority and conviction. The residents were like apples from the proverbial tree falling all over the world, but never too far from the tree that permanently secured them to Boston University forever. They became the devotees of a linear thinking that was as superior in its worldwide acceptance as the clinical supremacy it established. This truly was a period of excellence and tradition that seemed artfully established and incapable of fracture. Yes, the residents in a very lofty sense conferred "disciples in nome"[100] upon themselves in a way that justifiably mirrored a religious-like reflection of a more spiritual following. It was a feeling gratuitously sensed, never voiced, but certainly very real in their feelings and universal awareness. If it seemed mystical and yet real, it was. Such stout thinking is hard to convey, but the times were very telling because of this very quality which grew over time and sustained inviolably over that decade between the mid-1960's and mid-1970's. The sustained awards conferred yearly by The Academy of Periodontology for Gerald Kramer and Richard Lazzara are emboldened as memories for what Boston University meant to one of its residency programs.

In conversations with many who spent two, three or even multiple years for both clinical certification in one of the specialties as well as an advanced doctoral degree there were very interesting results. For the most part, those who were not part of the Department of Periodontology did not know much about Kramer. In addition, when urged for a comment, they had none because they had little contact

---

[100] Website: www.latin-dictionary.org.: "in nome": "in name".

with him. Even their fellow periodontal residents never really got into conversations with them except to comment on the amount of work. The periodontal residents were the most vocal. The majority were in support of Kramer to a fault. However, two very clear observations: firstly, almost all had no understanding what transpired behind the scenes between Henry and Gerry; secondly, all, to a fault, were completely ignorant of Henry's past or credentials, nor even aware superficially about how and why the school evolved in the manner it did. Some assailed Henry with an incomprehensible venom, some were fortunate to engage and realize his warmth, and others did not know what to say as they were disturbed by all the rancor. The interesting finding was how the other faculty never saw Kramer's very dark side and were completely duped by his congeniality. Some faculty, albeit only two, refused to return numerous phone calls. These people were not pressed because everyone else were most receptive. One thing was very obvious, those that fashioned an almost worshipful, religious disciple posture were part of a trend in Kramer's heyday that were drawn quite purposefully in like "Moonies" of the Unification Church of Sun Myung Moon. (170) It was obsessive and curiously mystifying that grown men (and very few women) lacked basic discernment. This is what makes for "groupies", "follower religious or political types", etc. those that follow, do not and cannot lead, or are not capable of individual thought. Credit to a human being who can generate enough psychological succor in becoming a refuge for the emotionally wayward. The phenomenon was real, and, this following remains intact even if it has ebbed to some degree over time.[101]

What about Henry? Among faculty and residents there have always been criticisms of the typical full time academic politics issues, the kind that no institution is able to resolve. But, none have anything but kind and deeply appreciative things to say about him. A great number had no comment because they never got to meet, interact with, or had

---

[101] Conversations with alumni of BUSGD over five years, including many with Kramer himself. The conversations with Kramer were quite cordial, but extremely frank, specific and revealing.

a longtime relationship with him. The only pejorative commentary about the evils of Henry Goldman came from the Kramer domain. And, it was clearly anger or spite never generated from any personal contact, but from a disliking to the way he commented from a distance.

In digesting all the commentary it was evident how juvenile and foolish it was. But, it was also disturbing to see how long it has lasted with such an internecine undertone. If nothing else, it clearly evinced how disturbing Kramer's underlying pursuit was cloaked in innocence, yet with a vicious behind-the-scenes attempt to dismantle and purloin Henry's image, all in the same meretricious behavior. It is truly incomprehensible, but anyone who cannot fathom this should go back and read a little Aldous Huxley.

A final comment on Kramer. There is no rhyme or reason why, given the proverbial "keys to the kingdom", he would knowingly undermine his own future. He consciously went up against one of the most respected scientists in dentistry with the bold, ignorant defiance of a threated bull. It should be emphasized that Henry spoke to him so many times that it is incredulous that he could not tone down his behavior. At the height of this issue were some unfortunate incidents that have no place in this biography, but it is necessary to mention that they were so corrosive that Henry had to dig his heels in deeply to prevent a complete school upheaval. In the end, his drawbacks so heavily outweighed his contributions that his dismissal became necessary.

What is the conclusion? Is there really one? Is it even worth the ink on this paper to reprise? None, none and no! The only clear reality is that it is tragic in history to record egomania that overtakes goodness, meaningful endeavors, or kind-hearted people. Any student of history knows that there are people who fail to understand history. And, for one reason or another, even educated people who can't control themselves and perpetrate a type of nastiness that willfully undermines harmony, are simply bound to continue until reigned in. Sensible people will just sit back and say why? But, there is no blowback to historical turpitude strong enough to shake evil from the tree of life. (26,37,44,45,84,87106)

As far as Henry goes, it has been repeated endlessly in these pages what the institution meant to him. He was creative, endowed with an imagination he shared with innocence, and so giving in a forever manner that he did not deserve the unmerciful thrust of backhanded distrust and susurrations. He deserved more of the opposite.

The pinnacle in dental education that was reached at Boston University was also unique because its worldwide reputation attracted so many noted researchers, clinicians and academic administrators. Call it for what it was. It was defined by one quality: commitment. Professionals came from all over the world because it was more than a place. It was a center for unique learning. It had an institutional quality that harkened back to what Plato developed after his mentor, Socrates, initiated. Plato took the metaphysical learning experience to a Lyceum from the streets of the marketplace where Socrates discoursed over subjects of challenge to man's human experience. (21, 67) In the same vein, Boston University became an updated center of developing advances in dental education. It was neither sophistry nor buncombe. In fact, conversely, it became a hub for evolving therapies and research ideas that challenged all the standards of the day. Like the spokes on a wheel converging to the center, Boston University was the convergence point for diverse thinking and opinions. The most talented people around the world at one point or another came to present thinking that challenged or anointed the most avant-garde, cutting edge thinking of the day. It was most certainly atavistic in its bearing and direction. One of the great days was listening to one of the greats of the day: Jens Waerhaug. He spoke at Boston University to a "sold out crowd"! It was 1978 when combat was established by the people who followers of the "Kramer Theocracy" and everyone else. His brilliance was as blinding as a sunlit diamond glare. This is what Boston University enabled. The likes of legendary researchers and educators like Harald Loe, Fermin Carranza, Robert Schallhorn and many others made it so obvious that Henry was an extremely respected leader.

Like the duck on the water surface blithely gliding along, the furtive, frenetic turnover of its tiny webbed feet is obscured. This is how

Henry conducted business as he was most calm and undisturbed on the surface.

When Gerald Kramer and his coterie flouted their loyalty to the school by taking French dentists to their personal office in Swampscott, Massachusetts, a very public rift ensued. A welter of back-and-forth ill feelings surfaced that merely represented the tip of a deep-seated iceberg fracturing and whirling out of control. The gist of the matter pointed to a group of French dentists who were taking continuing education courses in advanced periodontal surgery and seemingly grew disappointed with the effective content for their expenses. So, contending that they would be lost, they were quietly wrested away from the school to Kramer's office.

In Henry's mind, this was an action representing the final shock wave from a litany of shenanigans that merely peaked with this event. Like a wave thrashing a seashore of sharply angled rocks with, it was endless nightmare. In the end, Henry fired Gerry Kramer along with his unwitting followers. He felt betrayed far beyond what he deserved. Any Dean will admit that there will always be someone who will try anything to knock "you" off your perch. This was very different.

History will clearly show that Boston University was the sum of many parts, and yet in a very real sense, it was many times greater. Gerald Kramer was no ordinary man in ordinary times. His mission was not the school. It seemed from his profound intellect that he resented dentistry as beneath him. He rejected the common and savored only the elegant in any form or expression.

He was impeccable in appearance and stature, imbued with clinical capabilities well beyond most of his contemporaries. The residents were gradually transfixed by Kramer's charisma into a clone-like state. They lost sight of who was in charge, who was the real leader, and who provided the platform for their training and opportunities. The residents were not inexperienced, innocent and unworldly. For the most part, they were either approaching middle-aged or well into that stage of life. Their loyalty was very much misguided. It is understandable that mentors are respected and remembered passionately. But, in this case, their allegiance was very abnormal (almost as if to a deity in Greek Mythology). They matriculated purely and simply at the pleasure of Henry M. Goldman. And, Gerald Kramer was at best the fortuitous recipient (as were the other chairmen) of a responsible leadership position. There is no doubt that he was a wonderful clinician who inspired by his intellect and sense of art as a vehicle for science. But, it was not hard to plainly see that his personality got in his own way. His ambition and sense of self was only exceeded by his clever, manipulative style. It is suggestive of malignant narcissism. Can a bad apple really spoil a barrel? Yes, if it remains hidden or unrecognized.

To reprise what Aldous Huxley so profoundly captured in a very terse manner that: "Facts do not cease to exist because they are ignored" speaks volumes about Gerald Kramer's unpardonable behavior.[102] Most of his sycophancy was such lost and wasted energy. The residents became "his residents", and his only. He snookered a lot of teaching colleagues around the world. If not for the students he keenly adopted as clones in different parts of the world, he would have lost all friendships. As his stardom grew, he became known for pillory and cynical public behavior. Residents gloried in his thespian antics like children around cartoon humor. It was mostly pathetic. There was nothing admirable watching him publicly "undress" colleagues who did not possess his stage-like command. Conversely, he possessed skills, unremitting energy and a driven thirst for knowledge. It was manifestly a true "Dr. Jekyll-Mr. Hyde" scenario!

When reflecting on dental education and the teaching institution, he would have been a perfect fit to continue Henry's dream well into his remaining lifetime. But, as his residents never took ownership of the reality, he knowingly lost sight of respectability and propriety. He was singularly responsible for allowing his residents to falsify their allegiance when he knew better. Was it a shame? Yes. But, what is more shameful is the flashy way his great following fashioned his mystique (and continue to do so) as amnesiacs disavowing everything else.

---

[102] Huxley, Aldous: *Proper Studies*, Copyright 1957, Chatto & Windus (originally published in 1927).

In the 1950's and 1960's it was rare for professors in the profession to have education backgrounds. And, even today this remains somewhat a lingering void. This is most notable in the dental profession. Henry had both inspirational and self-trained mentors, but none were versed in education per se. For the most part, leaders in dentistry were devoid of any background in the humanities. Whatever exposure to the arts was captured on the fly. However, they all learned very quickly and overcompensated.

Henry truly appreciated the fact that the lay public could never (and most likely would never) discern a dentist's proficiency. He understood that the trust garnered through time between a patient and a dentist was an emotional connection because a person did not possess the knowledge necessary to make such a value judgment. To this end, the paradigm shift he engineered in dental education became all that more important. And this became the basis of what became a much more serious, in-depth approach to continuing education. Laying out the template for the basic sciences and the clinical management of patients became very quickly a basic essential of teaching.

In 1958 when The Department of Stomatology came into being under then President of Boston University, Harold Case, Henry commanded immeasurable respect from the medical faculty who understood his background. As a result, he was able to institute the most advanced curriculum for the dental specialties. At that time he did not have a building, but he formatted the contiguous teaching program which embraced all the basic dental-medical courses under the umbrella of the medical center. This served as the basis for what would eventually become the outline for the graduate school. Personality issues aside, the entire faculty embraced this format with a limitless enthusiasm that Henry organized through his well-earned connections. When most of his faculty came on board in 1963, they were pretty much all neophytes in the teaching world. Under Henry's assiduous guidance they all developed into confident, very capable educators in their own right.

Daniel J. Boorstin writing an article in Newsweek Magazine on "A

Case of Hypochondria", July 6, 1970 characterized education in a very bold, most pertinent manner, saying:

> *"Education is learning what you didn't even know you didn't know."*[103]

Boorstin was contemporaneous with Henry's living years, though he was born three years later and passed away thirteen years after him. He was a national treasure through his accomplishments as a professor of law, Librarian of Congress, and a writer of twenty very accomplished books that were very profoundly impactful on the national culture. His views on education were eerily similar to those Henry vocalized with a very determined conviction. That is why in light moments he referred to a dental degree as "a union card". In coupling principles of medicine to the proper training of a dental specialist, he wanted the end result to be an analytical thinker, not a mechanical robot. He explicitly remonstrated against the very average practitioner whose training was so limited that he didn't know what he didn't know. Daniel Boorstin's observation goes directly to this thought. In fact, Henry understood that the mind was expandable and moldable. It was not as Dan Quale hypothesized: "What a waste it is to lose one's mind. Or not to have a mind is being very wasteful. How true that is". (194) Very funny, but not what Henry had in mind. An intercommunicative exchange of ideas and knowledge became the highlight through which all residents were trained. The following idea: "Eyes will never see what the mind has never been made to know" [104] underscores what Henry considered the basis of his thinking for curriculum change. Advanced dental skills would have to be end points of probing, inquiring and analytical minds. The bare bones of Henry's mission went right to this philosophy, to wit his faculty was specifically groomed. As a result, this faculty grew into a very intellectually robust, vigorous group.

---

[103] Boorstin, Daniel J., Librarian of Congress, historian, attorney, writer & adviser: *Newsweek Magazine: "A Case of Hypochrondria"*, July 6, 1970.
[104] Rochefoucauld, Francois de La: *MAXIMS,* Copyright 1959, Translation, penguin classics.

Henry was not one to overthink nor challenge others willy-nilly. Henry was a very complex man, but he lived by simple methodologies. Anything that became layered in obtuse thinking he quickly and sternly deflated to simple conversation and understanding. His decisions could appear draconian, but they were not. There was always a soft touch behind them. When he had to, he was perhaps more forthright and bold, rendering a more stern impression.

In retrospect, it is hard to find anyone else who might have undertaken such a maze of challenges. He had everything in his master plan all properly scrutinized, arranged and executed. He was like an architect who lived in the present, but constructed with a futuristic vision. He had the capability of seeing "the big picture". He was a visionary with guts. For this reason, he should be ultimately remembered as well for his courage as for his stroke of genius.

In his brilliant book, *In Search Of Ethics: Conversations with Men and Women of Character*, Len Marrella[105] takes measure of what role character plays in the life of a person. For, eventually character defines how a person lives out his/her life, and, within that role how that person's life is defined and the impact that life makes within community and relationships. He spends time interviewing people from all social strata to draw attention to the importance of "character". The book attempts in a very comprehensive way to demonstrate how getting along in life successfully, both qualitatively and quantitatively, is governed by tiered components of one's persona. That is to say, the way a person thinks will ultimately determine how they speak their thoughts, that how they speak will translate into a consistency of actions, that such actions become viscerally repetitive and habitual, and that this will define this person's character. Marrella very clearly shows with all his examples of people throughout history that their destiny is uniquely governed by such character development over time. People cannot be categorized like Zebras so that their external appearance obscures their true nature

---

[105] Marrella, Len: *In Search of Ethics: Conversations with men and women of Character,* Copyright 2009, DC Press, A Division of the Diogenes Consortium, Sanford, Florida.

and personality. His book is an excellent reference to take measure of and size up Henry and his faculty.

In the hierarchy of strategic planning, this line of thinking would never enter into Henry's decision tree. Nevertheless, character would play a major role in what brought down the school as it was conceived. It would determine how the faculty would be judged and Henry misjudged!

How comfortable any of these men were in their own skin is very difficult to precisely measure because they possessed biphasic personalities. They all had their stage and private presence which were much more accentuated than the average person. To understand their emotional stability is not for this analysis, nor for Marrella's vivid analytical and insightful personality types. What was very certain was how this original faculty could have easily jumped right off the pages of Marrella's book because of their dynamism, determination and decisiveness. They were not indecisive nor shrinking violets! These were highly aggressive, mission-bound men of "character"! Thoughts, words, actions, habits and character are as Marrella so vividly defines "life's tape measure". Assessed against this "tape measure" these individuals became far greater than the sum of their aggregate personalities. Their destinies were circumstantial to some degree, but their personalities were so overwhelmingly undeterred and centered on "control, power and legacy". Frankl, Schilder and Kramer definitely wanted to succeed Henry as Dean, but Booth and Gianelly were neither consumed nor driven to expend the energy to tunnel their ambitions so open-endedly. They really did not want anything to do with the position. The uncertainties of such a "sardine-can-like" atmosphere was far too front loaded with too much collateral unpredictability.

The missing component in some of them was revelatory as a character gradient that was calibrated according to its level of "humility". Only in Kramer's instance did this gradient become so acute that it crushed his stature within the intimate circle who perceived this troublesome character flaw. His hubris was wonderfully camouflaged because he was a brilliant thespian of inscrutable dimension whose chameleon qualities could wonderfully lay cover when he found it necessary. To a large extent, this was such wasted energy for a man who had the potential of a Gianelly, but lacked the latter's strength of character and power of resolve. Kramer's destiny was self-limited when, by any other measure, he should be noted as an academic powerhouse who slowly, by an almost Greek tragic hero, slowly blew out his own candle. There should have been the comforting "deus ex machina"[106] which could have interceded in his behalf early on for, shy of this un-disciplined inclination, he would have made a quality Dean. During this eventful decade an ethicist like Len Marrella would have had a field day trying to come to grips with all the personalities that smiled at each other with shiftless but frank disdain. Melvyn Harris alone sized up the realities with the greatest insight and simply stayed away from personal over-commitment to the school. He rightfully used the school affiliation to his own advantage, staying away from the frontline politics. He might have been the most versatile man on the faculty who had no permanent standing. He had a very steadying influence. He was too clever to cozy up to the hot, "smoldering coals" atmosphere. His stellar intellect belied his "streets smarts" insight.

For all the traumas in Kramer's department there was never any danger that the school would ever derail. During all this time it wit-nessed the greatest success of any institution in the world. In the city of Boston, however, there was always subliminal rivalry and acrimony with the other two schools, Harvard and Tufts. It is difficult to pin blame on a specific institution. It just seemed like a sustained clash of egos. And, Boston University's faculty did not attempt to dampen the heat. Henry's minions liked to intellectually rattle cages. It was cathar-tic for them. Who knows why? It was both jejune and troublesome. Tufts and Harvard always returned the inveigling with gossiping and their own trickery. It was self-perpetuating gamesmanship. Adults act-ing like children.

Henry understood at some level the psychological parameters of

---

[106] Website: www.latin-dictionary.org: "deus ex machine": "divine intervention" or "God in the machine".

ego and what happens when it gets out of control. He always put money and control aside because his focus was always pure and constituted from a very deep, indwelling sense of unblemished purpose. Pettiness and trouble-making did not concern him. The idea of "power", "position" and "privilege" was too much of a time waster to draw him away from more important concerns. His innocence was almost admirable, but it lost any advantage over time. For a man who understood the pathogenesis of physical disease as well as he did, he could not transfer this understanding to more weighty and far-reaching events.

If Henry had been more authoritative and proactive a person, the repercussions would have never adversely affected feelings people had. Even years afterward, people are in the dark about the grief Kramer, his partners and those close to him delivered on a continuous basis. The initiative Henry did not take gave too many people an opening for finding him guilty of a situation which bled the vitality out of the school, and most particularly the Department of Periodontology. No one in a reasonable frame of mind, understanding what prevailed for so long would not have given Henry the benefit of any doubt in firing Gerry Kramer

Brave or craven? History should reveal that there was no other choice for Henry, and, as the man who cited him for excellence after WWII, President Harry Truman, stated: "The buck stops here", referencing his desk. (194) And, when no one else could have properly interceded to protect the integrity of the school, he most certainly did the absolute right thing. And, since others could not understand or acquiesce to this decision, it reflected most simply on their not being privy to a group who had a cold, self-anointed disregard for their behavior and the general good.

Henry never allowed all the notoriety to interfere with the build-up and continuity as the school grew in size and reached to all corners of the world. Fortunately, he had a practice being run by truly admirable partners who understood his mission. They sustained the practice allowing Henry to be absent for the sake of obligations that related to the formidable details in the daily governance of the school. Alan

Shuman and Gerald Isenberg were Henry's partners who endeavored so faithfully and forbearingly in soldiering the long hours necessary to support a very busy practice. Henry's reputation made for an exceedingly large patient community. They both worked many years under extreme demands. But, this allowed Henry to perpetuate a dream that otherwise would have been impossible had these men not had the good sense and understanding that Henry's success would spill over into theirs as well. They were stalwarts of immense support and rectitude. Their contributions should never be forgotten.

As to what the teaching institution constituted in Henry' mind, most indisputably it represented a watershed period in the history of American dental education when specialty training and technology, laboratory and clinical research, and the integration of advanced biological sciences with dentistry unfolded into a bold new world of investigation, ideas and teaching methods. The integrative relationships between basic science research and cutting edge technologies started and grew with thrust and financial support under Henry's sphere of influence. He grew a respect worldwide that made Boston University a hub of universal acclaim in all phases of the profession and related industries. As the first and only graduate school ever, it will be remembered for manifestly laying out the groundwork for centers that emerged as examples that integrative modalities were the future for the profession. Drawing from elements of his unique education, war and teaching experiences, his prescient ideas were telling and timely. Maybe Boston University lasted only about a decade in its most vital capacity, but it forecasted what could and did develop after his passing. His journey was never deterred, never constrained. Yes, he was tested by events adventitiously acquired, but, if people who were present then fail to realize who unmistakably made it all happen, then they are unfortunately defined by their stultified sense of the big picture. A splash is not a wave that propels dynamic change, it is merely the glitter that seemingly sits atop the wave as a mere noticeable spume. Henry was that wave. His faculty was the spume who rode his energy. He overcame a lot to give certainty and longevity to a profession in all its substance.

CHAPTER 10

The Money Tree: The Myth and Pity
Of Continuing Dental Education

At one time it was fashionable to learn just to learn. Today, there is continuing interest in learning, but it has lost its luster. There was a time when it was a treat to sit and listen to someone with insight render an interesting opinion on an intellectual plane which would encourage thought and maybe stimulate the learning process. Learning, however, is a lifetime exercise. It is invigorating and grounding. Just when it seems the educational system has seemingly saturated society with content, it should be even more evident that education is an endless adventure. An every individual should determine for herself/himself how far is far enough.

But when there is a defined end on this basis, it conveys that there is a glitch in the system. There should never be a cog in the wheel which turns away interest, thwarts the desire to learn nor dissuades a person's interest to express an opinion which could be contrarian. Therefore, in the open forum, impressions gathered through the learning process should be a barometer of its ability to instill enough interest that it may not shut down the will to share intelligent conversation nor the creativity which it unleashes. As ideal as this may sound, let's read what one of the great scholars in the fields of Mathematics and Philosophy had to say about this: Bertrand Russell (1872-1970):

> "Almost all education has a political motive: It aims at strengthening some group, national or religious or even

social, in the competition with other groups. It is this mo-
tive, in the main, which determines the subjects taught, the
knowledge offered and the knowledge withheld, and also de-
cides what mental habits the pupils are expected to acquire.
Hardly anything is done to foster the inward growth of mind
and spirit; in fact, those who have had most education are
very often atrophied in their mental and spiritual life." [107]

It is the inward growth that allows people the benefit gained from all aspects of the educational process. A loss of interest restrains and retards that process and people just become androids of a technocracy-based society as merchants of materialism and its primary benefit: opulence.

Henry Goldman understood the benefits of advanced education in the so-called "ideal". He was certainly not a philosopher in the measure of a Bertrand Russell. However, he understood "intellectualism" as a conveyance of exchangeable ideas which would broaden interest while offering a platform for the give-and-take of opinions and criticisms. He was not one to take interest in the historical background of "liberal" thought (not to be confused with politics of liberalism, aka progressivism).

Open expression is the byproduct of the intrinsic thoughts which govern communication. He felt that the only way to advocate for a "thinking man's dentist" would be to gear the science of dentistry to those with a willful desire to interpret ideas based on the science of health and disease. Education that purely merchandizes changes and advances in technologies bothered Henry to no end. Being confined to the dogma, orthodox tradition of mechanical dentistry boxed in the profession and did nothing to instill the openness of creative research (which was the true definition of "liberal"). The "...inward growth of mind and spirit..." was the full expression Henry articulated in a very different way, but with the very same enthusiasm.

---

[107] Russell, Bertrand: *Principles of Social Reconstruction*, Copyright 1916, Published by George Allen and Unwin, London, England;175.

Continuing education became the cornucopia of the dental profession in all conceivable ways possible. In its beginnings it was the proverbial "cash cow". Early on it provided subject matter on interests which were practice appropriate. So, getting to the point, what was the great myth? It would serve the practicing dentist an affordable means to keep in step with research that advanced clinical techniques. The incentive was in its most pure sense almost atavistic to the 19th century thinking of an Oscar Wilde, as in "art for art's sake"! (41) It was a period of a very idealistic state of thinking. A busy clinician would approach continuing education with a Bertrand Russell sense of idealism. Unfortunately, and totally without any cynicism, that was/is not real world thinking. At least in the dental profession, the myth is that continuing education would be the forum for bridging the gap between growing stale in practice and being able to benefit from advances coming forth from "academia". The myth was learning on the basis of an ideal: a motivation to learn without having to benefit in a material way. Turning Oscar Wilde on his head: learning for learning sake, the spirit and sense of gratification that is engendered from within. There is a benefit to instill enthusiasm with learning. Great educators so wonderfully display their own passion that it is easily perceived and is a source of heightened energy. It's all about communication in a thoughtful, meaningful style.

However, the dental profession "lost its virginity" to the proprietary interests of corporate manipulation. This is a layered statement which requires explanation insofar as Henry laid out his plan for continuing education.

At the outset, continuing education fulfilled two major needs: a venue to bring all practitioners together in an academic setting for course study, and, a cash infusion for the teaching institution. How could this not be to the benefit of everyone concern? Well, it depends how one analyzes its origins, growth and development, where and how it changed, and seeing it in the light of day for where it is in today's world?

The first dental school founded in The United States was The Baltimore College of Dental Surgery by Chapin A. Harris in 1840.

Harvard became the first university affiliated dental school in 1867. The University of Michigan was the first state school and second university affiliated dental school in 1875. In 1891 a two-year dental school curriculum was required. And, with the formation of The National Board of Dental Examiners in 1905 came the first continuing education courses with school affiliations. By 1909 The Dental Education Council of America was established by a consensus of the national organization of dental examiners, dental faculties and dental practitioners. In 1910, graduation from high school became a prerequisite for dental school admission. In 1911, the Army Dental Corps was founded. In 1913, Dr. Alfred C. Fones initiated a dental hygiene program with thirty three students. By 1927 two schools of dental hygiene began: one at The University of Buffalo in Buffalo, New York and one at The Forsyth Dental Infirmary in Boston, Massachusetts. The American Dental Assistants Association was incorporated in 1925. Dr. W.H. Stowe open the first independent dental laboratory in Boston with his cousin, Frank F. Eddy in 1887. Finally, The American Dental Association was founded by twenty-six dentists at Niagara Falls, New York in 1859. This chronology offers an overview of the beginning of dental school education (along with its affiliated organizations) in The United States. The outgrowth of all these organizations was the basis of continuing education and gradual re-licensing based on school and non-school programs. (137)

Interesting enough, the first school to get into the serious education business was The Baltimore College of Dental Surgery. Chapin A. Harris, as outlined previously, was a product of a physician apprenticeship in Ohio and gradually got interested in oral diseases. He was the very first to draw a relationship between physical health and dental-oral disease. Moreover, Horace Hayden, who is also noted for making note of oral disease as a viable threat to general physical health, joined Chapin Harris in Baltimore within the year of its founding so he is credited with the school's pioneering attention to and treatment of oral diseases. Although these men were instrumental in educating the dental students and practitioners well into the very early 1900's (Horace

Hayden had died by then), there was a tremendous slide away from the biology of oral diseases. Chapin A. Harris had published numerous papers and textbooks on the subjects of systemic disease relating to oral health/disease. (216) But, its emphasis fell off, and particularly with the influence of G.V. Black in the 1920's and 1930's. His textbook publication on operative dentistry diminished any impact Horace and Hayden had. In fact, even though they had a major impact with the founding of The Baltimore College of Surgery, the remote attention to oral health and disease really took a back seat to what the general practicing dentist considered on a daily basis.

Entering the 20th century, it was sufficient for a practitioner to limit his/her practice to a specific area of interest (not necessarily expertise). This gradually changed as the dental profession was becoming more organized by more highly trained individuals who took specific interest in one or more areas of practice. With the first dental school opening in 1840 and The American Dental Association chartered in 1859 just before the American Civil War in April, 1861, a long period prevailed during which time there were no specialties and a practitioner could practice ad libitum. However, with the number of dental schools opening through the 20th century, the profession became highly more organized and regulated. Today, encompassing the public dental schools, the private dental schools, and, the private and state-subsidized dental schools, there are sixty-five by figures listed through the American Dental Association. (137) With the number of schools and practitioners increasing, there was a surge in what dental practitioners chose as areas of interest. To a large degree this was the result of where practitioners were: cities, growing suburbs, rural (but near a sizeable city), and rural territories of remote locations. Concomitantly, as specialty interest groups developed at the turn of the 20th century, they became increasingly organized. By mid-century (1940-1950's), defined specialty organizations came into being: The American Association of Orthodontics was unique in getting certified and thereby recognized by The American Dental Association. This was in 1929, the year of the great stock market crash in the United States. But, the other eight were not certified until the 1940's and 1950's, the exception being The American Association of Oral and Maxillofacial Radiology in 1979. Therefore, of the nine officially recognized, seven formalized mid-century. (137) Interesting enough economists debate as to how the country grew out of the depression, whether by a change in the business climate or the manufacturing surge from the capital needs to fight WWII. Whatever be the causes, the 1930's were years of severe, protracted economic and financial depression. Its social effects were dire and gruesome. The number of suicides were expressions of lost hope and a national emotional low-point. The National Industrial Recovery Act of 1933 was President's Franklin Delano Roosevelt's first attempt to stimulate the economy. The social-economic ills of the 1930's into the war years through 1945 were a veil of silent distress during so much of the changes in dentistry. (61)

After The American Association of Orthodontists was certified by The American Dental Association in 1929, over a decade ensued until The American Academies of Pediatric Dentistry and Periodontology were certified in 1940. The economic data reflected very depressed social and economic conditions as the war heated up with troop mobilization in Europe and Japan's expedition into the pan-pacific areas of China, Manchuria and Mongolia. With the groundswell of economic productivity conditions in the military-industrial complex, there was a rapid growth spurt in all phases of social-educational networks. This was a by-product of factory output and jobs created as a consequence of the war effort. Domestically, the effect on dental education was an increasing number of dental schools, dental organizations, dental curriculum changes, state dental societies with local affiliates, and the very early emergence of informal continuing education in the form of short lectures and presentations. (159,212) There is a plethora of historical information relating the complex growth of dental education paralleling the social-economic changes in the country as it emerged from a series of interconnected fallow, remote lands to giant cities of warren-like labyrinths. In short, today it is comparatively a mega-enterprise.

The dental profession grew on the coattails of the medical profession and its related industrial resources. Yet, interest in oral diseases predates the Sumerians (circa 5000 B.C.) to The Indus Valley Civilization circa 7000 B.C. Even in a six volume treatise on the British Empire, Samuel Pepys in the middle 1600's delves into dental maladies and speaks of a Mummery tooth (internal resorption). Pierre Fauchard in the late 18th and early 19th took dental treatment to its most modern level for the times in which he lived by ushering in orthodontic, operative and limited minor oral surgical techniques. In between, dentistry and the various civilizations (the Greeks, Egyptians, Romans, and Chinese) mirrored each other utilizing some very primitive tools and techniques. The one common observation was a desire to formulate a consistent way to relieve pain, oral infection, and fill holes in teeth with uniquely devised tools (as in the case of the 14th century surgeon, Guy de Chauliac, who used a pelican-like peak to extract teeth). (27) It all historically reflected a very early indwelling sense to want to know more about oral-dental problems which may have basic treatment remedies. The common theme that the historical record shows is a compelling human curiosity "to want to know."

Perhaps the more primitive periods in world history reveal "fascinations" with dental and oral diseases, but they parenthetically all reflect the same human interest that existed in the United States from colonial times well into the Civil War when the relief of dental pain and the repair of holes in teeth (due to decay) resulted in primitive but inventive techniques to remedy some of the most ravaged mouths. The history of the barber surgeon is also that of the dental pioneer who first relieved local and systemic disease by treating extremely debilitated patients. (27) The history of dentistry somehow draws attention to shared common historical thinking: that there have always been people of similar thinking and interest to diminish pain as well as to conceive of ideas to advance treatment methods. Long before the industrial age there were scientists of all stripes whose thinking managed to be prescient because they either imagined or dreamed ideas which far exceeded their times. Staged advances throughout history reflected this common thread: people think beyond their surroundings and have a calling to discover, to experiment, and to remediate their mistakes. (18) The modernization of the dental profession as it mobilized methodologies to nurture and forge new ideas in dental education is a reflection of the same kind of people who but for different times were similarly challenged intuitively and sometimes without rhyme or reason. Creative thinkers transcend times, but the times in which they live may make their contributions benefit to a greater extent from innovative technologies and cooperative support systems. Otherwise, the history of mankind clearly demonstrates that the desire to relieve dental pain and treat disease is a shared experience.

The advent of the industrial age no doubt accelerated the modernization of the dental profession much in the same way that space age technologies have enabled cutting edge equipment and instrumentation to be adopted. This is both good and bad depending how the good serves and the bad detracts.

The early pioneers of the dental profession had their own issues, but the incentives of the post-industrial age saved them from some of the human pitfalls: fear to explore new horizons in research, lack of curiosity for the sake of immediate material success and, worst of all, opportunism. There was a will to learn and be productive. Continuing education was part of this will to become better informed and skilled. It was a mandate that made education a manifest destiny. It escalated in popularity because it promoted self-image and prosperity. It started to bridge old practice with new techniques. It was early evidence that dentistry was becoming a more science based profession.

The dental profession matured exponentially through the late 19th and 20th centuries, perhaps because it was not yet overly complex and lost in regulatory issues and controls. Everything accomplished by the great early pioneers set the stage for Henry Goldman being able to fulfill his dream. This is in no way to suggest that his accomplishments flourished solely on the heels of his predecessors. His ideas and achievements were unique and groundbreaking, always balancing the practical and the ideal.

There was most definitely a void in dental education that he was able to fill by virtue of the fact that specialization in dentistry was not only coming into its own, but it was expanding very quickly as an umbrella-like presence within the framework of the existing pre-doctoral institutions. Henry's idea to integrate all the recognized dental specialties (which were eight of the nine because Oral Maxillofacial Radiology was not certified by The American Dental Association until 1979, sixteen years after Boston University was chartered as a school of specialization) into one building was quite dramatic for the times

A large measure of the lectures and seminars were open to all the specialties. It was an intellectual universalism in which understanding of the biological sciences as a basis of patient care and management common to all the dental specialties evolved from a commonality of thinking and an expression of evidence based opinions in a useful exchange of analytical thinking. In effect, Boston University reflected the highest degree of integrated thought for the day. It was unique for the times, but its express purpose was conceptually a throwback to the Greek Lyceum where in an open air forum the free expression of ideas revealed unscripted thoughts, viewpoints, motives and intentions so they could be intellectually challenged.(19,21) Perhaps today's general practitioners are aghast at such hard to reconcile "ho-hum" innocence and candor. For, after all, if it can't earn money immediately, where's the value? Well, the answer is that Henry never refuted "the ethos of capitalism" (82) Continuing education, at the outset, was not meant for: "teach me and I'll go back to my office and earn a million bucks" mentality. However, for the majority of general practitioners this is what it has become. Not all, but most. The smart ones realize the inherent dangers, the majority that do not set themselves for complaints and malpractice litigation down the road. In today's world, there is no doubt that there exists a vocal group of general practitioners who either casually think specialization is a waste or, over time, think they know as much as specialists if they take enough continuing education. Unfortunately, Henry showed the system does not and should not work that way.

Continuing education today, in fact, has burdened the elite

specialists more than any segment of the dental population. The higher up the ladder in dental education the more deliberate are the re-examination and licensing procedures. The general practitioner answers to only his state license, yet astounding numbers practice with the self-assuredness of specialists. The art and science of basic periodontal therapies has been lost in the cascade of "magic bullet" implants placed. Sophisticated soft and bone grating procedures are being done by general practitioners with the very casual "because I can do them" attitude. A great deal of Oral Surgeons have been forced into the facial end of the Oral Maxillofacial portions of their practices out of diminished referrals. And, the granddaddy of them all: when did "the restorative dentist" supplant the Board Certified Prosthodontist? And, whether it is "the cosmetic dentist", "the restorative dentist", etc. the prism through which Prosthodontics was once measured has been rendered opaque by the "cataracterization" of continuing education.

The original thesis for specialization and the virtues of continuing education as a measure of advancing ideas has been irreversibly corrupted. Henry always thought continuing education for the general practitioner was essential, but never to summarily vitiate the specialties. The thought that in 1952 Lester Burket called for Henry to start a program in Periodontics at the graduate level is irreconcilable as the true private practice has become expunged by implant dentistry. Henry would be aghast, and say something to the effect that overly simplistic methods will eventually turn them on their own swords. The "God given being replaced artlessly by the man-made" attitude was just coming into vogue as Henry was aging so he never had the strength to rebut the new trend. Even Gerry Kramer in days before he died was rightfully bemoaning "the magic bullet" attitude that had over the dental profession.[108] Gerry, in his very demurring emotional state, was tragically miffed at seeing the field of Periodontics not only being reduced to an afterthought of hygiene and use of topical antibiotics (the definition of "supervised neglect") but that the guardian of the specialty, the American Academy of Periodontology, doing nothing and merely

---

[108] Conversation with author.

lay down while the American Dental Association has condoned this eventuality. In the end, both Henry and Gerry had a common meeting ground.

Henry, unbeknown to most people, had a very pristine view on education in general. It harkened back to his formative years at The Boston Latin School. His conditioning to very classical learning most likely (and, very privately) affected all his future thinking. He possessed a very fair-minded approach to all aspects of the teaching environment. The structure of the school was a unique construct, but he never interfered with the way each department was managed by its chairman. He gave them a complete wide range of expression and leadership. And, it was in such a manner that residents were able to benefit by this sense of identification. The academic interrelationships emboldened all the residents and defined the unique environment of the school. At the same time, there was always a sense of independence and free expression. Each resident felt self-reliant, secure in their learning progression, but at times very anxious due to the overwhelming amount of work. Being older and more experienced, however, the residents muddled through the process understanding that it was manageable. And, these department chairmen had become just incredible mentors to their residents. It was as an ideal learning environment as could have been fabricated even in a dream.

To the same extent that Henry wanted a sense of free expression to the learning process, he was similarly consistent when it came to continuing education. Historically, it was very different when it came into being. It was fairly free-wheeling and loosely configured when it came to scheduling. There were no mailing of brochures, nothing was permanently scheduled, and even last minute lectures were easily arranged. At this point in time it was not a sideshow or an unimportant consideration. To the contrary, it was very noble in its intent: a pure education benefit at a very inexpensive rate, or free when it was being supported by the local dental supply company. There was no permanent faculty, and most often faculty members were enticed at the last minute with some promise of a favor. Henry was good at that, but no one would ever think of refusing his entreaty. The dentists who attended really benefitted from the lectures and clinical on-site demonstrations. There were no continuing education credits, no relicensing requirements, and the school did not have to maintain any administrative records. And, by the way, there were no liability considerations when it came to any of the clinical presentations. In essence, it was a very relaxed atmosphere at a time when bureaucracy was never a burden to anyone. But, of course, there was/is no Shangri-la in the real world. So, administration and bureaucracy got married, and, like marriages, things got more complicated.

Some of the most well-known lecturers/investigators/professors would give of their time without any honorarium. It was beneficial to them because it was a great way for them to become recognized. In those days the teaching was not bromidic, it was original, cutting edge and with meaning. This kind of learning process was optional, and never from a compulsory obligation. In those days it was genuinely a learning experience that was idea oriented with techniques used to defend clinical thinking. They did not have to complete forms critiquing anything or anybody. And, they felt fulfilled by coming away with some pearl of knowledge. Such simplicity devoid of any encumbrance would be hard to imagine for any clinician today. Those halcyon days of voluntary learning, by any stretch of the imagination, would be virtually impossible to revisit.

There is an old saw: "You can never go back"! And, this is true. However, "extreme ends of trends" are not likewise productive nor healthy. And, that is where continuing education has migrated, to the opposite of Henry's spectrum: where the "teach me so I can make money in my office" attitude has run the profession into a dangerous rabbit hole. When a general practitioner graduates, takes a one General Dental Practice Residency, and then goes into practice believing that through continuing education she/he can supplant the need for specialization, the mental attitude demeans the standards for which the specialty programs stand. It is a sad reflection historically of all the genuine erstwhile educators in specialization. Their dreams and hard work has been buried in layers of bureaucratic drivel which has allowed this to happen.

Getting older and wiser is one thing when considering a person's journey through life. On the other hand, such a description can't be applied to a bureaucratic process which loses control and direction at it ages. At the outset, Henry valued continuing education as a need, not a luxury. He always preached that the learning process was a lifelong commitment. Honorable, yes. Practical, well let's report and then conclude what Henry began to realize.

He earnestly felt that a continuing education system would certainly add to Boston University's outreach to local dentists just as the graduate program did for those who came from all over the world to train in one of the eight original dental specialties. Yet, as the program grew, dentists from all over the world started to matriculate in the continuing education courses. The faculty commitments became so overloaded that gradually other "experts" would join the continuing education faculty. The courses got more expensive. In fact, they got overly pricey. Several basic factors began to play into the program (which was typical of other institutions throughout the country as well):

1. The continuing education faculty increased in size very dramatically.
2. The honoraria paid to the faculty varied with experience and reputation.
3. The program (which grew to international status) required administration.
4. Administration costs were so high that registration fees went up.
5. Continuing education became tied to relicensing, complaints and state board punishments.
6. The advent of competing private education businesses certified by The American Dental Association to teach continuing education. With their own faculty, they faced the same financial issues as dental schools.
7. Dramatic increases in the cost of courses.

8. Biennial relicensing established an entire cottage industry of businesses which arrange courses at "discount prices" for home study and recertification.

9. Licensing began to be tethered to Drug Enforcement Agency and penalties. This has resulted in increased cost renewals for DEA numbers.

10. Increased liability insurance underwriting.

11. Increased penalties and punishments for liability-for any reason-has made continuing education a default solution along with financial retribution.

12. Continuing Education is no longer just a supplement to university based education. It has taken on a life of its own, competing directly with university based programs.

13. Continuing education programs are now competing to train general practitioners in weekend courses of extended periods (two to four years); a very significant financial and time commitment;

14. Continuing education as a requirement of state licensure by credentials;

15. The American Dental Association regulates Continuing Education Programs so that their increased costs are passed right down the line to the terminus: the dentist.

16. Corporations' fiduciary co-opting of continuing dental education as well as dental schools (especially specialty programs) in a "pay-for-play" relationship to sell equipment and new products.

Over time continuing dental education has expanded in geometric numbers. There seems to be courses on any and every subject, from technical "how-to-do" courses to those on business related ones. Snail and internet mail is replete with an endless stream of course advertising. The costs are other-worldly and the faculties are advertised as the last word experts on seemingly everything (perhaps to justify the costs). There is no doubt that it is such a money opportunity that it has taken on a life of its own. "The money factor" has escalated so dramatically in recent years that it almost needs "a truant regulator". They are ADA approved insofar as course content and the person/dental business organizing the course, but the consequential issues are not. That is to say, whether the expertise of the clinicians to handle the level-appropriate courses in behalf of the patients who will become the subjects of their newly condensed and abbreviated training is not regulated. There are very advanced bone regeneration-bone block clinical grafting courses to "all" dentists. Many have numerous general practitioners who really have no business being there. But, that is just a microcosm how out of control the continuing education business has become. This has nothing to do with making a great living, but it has everything to do with ethics and the defense of the general public against charlatanism and pretense. The great specialists and their training programs stand for something, and their stature should not be trivialized.

Several aspects bothered Henry with respect to the growth and earning power it generated. He saw continuing education as what it suggests: "continuing", not "foundational". Whether right or wrong, he had a very fundamental outlook, feeling that essential learning should be university based and that continuing education programs be "supplemental". He was not averse to anyone wanting to lend their expertise, but he was thoroughly against opportunity transitioning into opportunism. He realized that the larger the business end expanded the less it would retain the quality so essential to be successful: "thought provoking". Well, since his passing, courses have taken on a new dimension: certainly no longer just supplemental/informational. For the most part, the courses that are more attractive are the ones which teach techniques that are profit bearing. The misfortune as Henry so often admitted is that honesty or ethics cannot be legislated or regulated. The subliminal message is buried in political correctness and acceptance. The inherent virtue of graduate education at Boston University was the time available to think through the mechanics of treatment planning and the hidden ideas beneath the surface. "Supplemental" education has become "elemental". Therefore, to a large extent, it has allowed a general practitioner to compete with "legitimately" trained specialists with impunity. The issue has also generated ramifications of a tendentious nature: liability, liability insurance costs, and state licensing board activity along with its autocratic and thoroughly over the board imperious power. It is an endless loop of self-perpetuating contention. Had continuing education remained as Henry conceived, a supplemental stream of keeping dentists "au courant" (and nothing more), perhaps so many practice violations would have never become so much fodder for malpractice lawyers.

In summary, the most consequential feature of continuing education is that it has transformed from something of value as "an ideal" to a "myth", a false belief that it would be the ultimate resource for keeping both general practitioners and specialists up-to-date without blurring ethical codes of practice.

Several things transpired of which Henry openly disapproved. Firstly, it gave general practitioners the opening to take advanced courses that made them feel capable of providing services equal to that of specialists. The old adage that "a little bit of knowledge is dangerous" has never been over-repeated when it references this conundrum. The "greed factor" disturbed Henry to no end, particularly because he thought it not only disingenuous, but he knew it would signal so many issues relative to malpractice and liability. And so "the virtue" became "a myth", and evolved into "a pity". It had a snowball effect which became an avalanche.

The pity is that continuing education has become so part of "the dental bloodline" that it's a wonder why anyone would want to take the time and endure the costs and sacrifice to specialize anymore. The profession sanctions it and the law defends it through anti-trust legislation. But, somewhere ethical standards must trump the law. As Henry so often inveighed: "Who's the loser? The patient"! The ability to self-regulate demands great self-discipline. And, money is the greatest aphrodisiac known to man. Well, maybe the second! In any case, there will always be sound thinking people who will recognize the virtues of specialization and the sacrifice necessary to be as committed to a sense of excellence that Henry always expounded with deep emotion.

One of the greatest rejoinders to anyone who would question the value of an advanced learning center or residency would have to understand what is missing from a weekend continuation course, or even the series weekend courses given for implant study. All the lecturing and chairside laboratory time spent for learning such an advanced process can never ever replace the one aspect that teaches the intangible a person gets in a graduate program: the constant "remediation" on a daily basis, the openness to make a mistake, reconfigure, try again, make another mistake, and so on, so forth. But, all the while being properly monitored and remediated accordingly.

The repetition that a resident gets by an intellectual-mechanical interchange with different professors and hands-on staff while be challenged by literature and discussion seminars can never be replaced or easily by-passed by a quick or foreshortened program. Yes, it is legal, but is it ethical? The answer is emphatically "NO"! And, yet the profession has condoned this from the day that continuing education expanded. Implant Dentistry is merely an example, but it is a multi-specialty issue. A general practitioner writing an in-depth article in a journal or magazine (refereed by a "legitimate" editorial board) on a recondite issue as an articulate expert is like the lawyer who represents himself/herself: he/she has a fool for a client. As Bill Parcells, the erstwhile great football coach said emphatically: "You are what you record says you are"! (151,152) Henry, in all his tolerance, believed that the general practitioner should be availed of every opportunity to learn, but the misrepresentation as a specialist begs the question how this is condoned. Perhaps the ethical issue of "political correctness"? Mark Twain in his immensely wonderful imaginative manner succinctly concluded on this education state-of-affairs in his book that was a magnificent compilation of irony and ironic commentary, "Pudd'nhead Wilson" (1894): he took measure of the issue this way:

> *Training is everything. The peach was once a bitter almond. Cauliflower is nothing but cabbage with a college education.*[109]

---

[109] Twain, Mark: *Pudd'nhead Wilson, The family Mark Twain (Compilation of all his books and short stories), Copyright 1992, Published by Barnes & Noble.*

In a most terse and almost brash manner he said it all. The remediation process of a graduate program cannot be duplicated by any continuing education program if a dentist is in search of the knowledge that will fulfill his/her quest to excel in bringing the foremost in treatment chairside. If not, all the practice experience gained over time from continuing education will not be the same. It will only make him/her more experienced at making the same or different mistakes. And, as the saying goes: repeating the same procedures expecting a new result is the definition of insanity! But, the profession condones this while looking away from the ethical considerations in the name of corporate and financial influence. So, what began as an ideal has ballooned into considerations which disturbed Henry when he was alive. However, it's best that he is not still around to be an active witness to how continuing education has become a giant consortium, an unholy alliance between mutually dependent entities: corporations of the dental industry-advertising and marketing money complex and the growing numbers of practitioners whose proprietary interests may be direct or indirect.

One of the most staggering, mind-bending examples of shooting oneself in the foot is what Departments of Periodontology are doing. Because Implantology has become such an integral factor in dental practice, dental schools are profiteering from their fiduciary relationship with implant companies and the cottage industries built up in association with them. The most glaring reflection of this is what these companies are doing for university based teaching specialties to capture their business. Supplying them with equipment and supplies captures the business of residents. Is it illegal? No. is it questionable? Most certainly. Yes, schools will gloss over this point by intimating they get sufficient training to warrant their financial support. In all phases of dental training and education gratuitous commercial benefits are "accepted". But, with a price, be it subliminal or overt. One glaring example is how the implant companies have virtually taken over graduate programs, mail based private teaching courses, and academy affiliated lectures and courses. Whether the qualifications to deliver implant therapies (placement of implants inclusive of bone and membranes as well as sinus augmentation) with university trained specialists are ensured matters not. Some programs have general practitioners teaching in graduate programs. It is very problematic to say the least. In addition, implant therapy has so overtaken dentistry that sound teeth are being lost either for failure to treat or because of the inadequacy of training programs. Realistically, the commercialization of dental practice is so complete that it cannot be remedied. And, it has befuddled the patient who really is totally confused on issues of training and qualifications necessary to practice in very specialized areas of dentistry. To a patient it is a blur.

It is not just in one aspect of dentistry. General practitioners are performing botox and other facial sculpturing procedures for which they are not trained. Oh wait, wrong, they are trained in ADA sanctioned courses (137) The question that it is out of the educational domain of a general dentist and drifts into the legitimate expertise purview of an MD specialist in Plastic Surgery has never drawn public attention. Oral surgeons are crossing over into territory once wholly sacrosanct for Plastic Surgeons as well (blepharoplasties and facial reconstructions, etc.). And, every general practitioner is a cosmetic specialist, once the purview of the Prosthodontist.

Everything that once had an almost pastoral allegiance to the university system has been frayed so dramatically that it is simply impossible for patients to determine which dentists are fully trained to provide a proper service without a compromise of trust. To a patient, most of the time, that a dentist is a nice woman/good guy is sufficient. The law distinguishes, but does not limit the difference. There is no legal consequence within the framework of licensing. The law skates over it. The ethical concerns may alter interpretations, but the general public is left hazy and bewildered on the subject. To "Joe Q. Public" a dentist is a dentist, and her/his smile and comforting way is more important. That's until something untoward happens. If a Prosthodontist is in the same "pool" as a general practitioner as far as a legal issue, the patient and the general dentist are responsible for revealing the difference only if asked. But, there the lines are blurred and glossed over. As an ethical issue, it affects the Prosthodontist because the general dentist is not held to the same standards. It is a giant net under which practice, continuing education, liability and patient communication issues remain in a state of confusion without resolution. When a complaint is filed by a patient against a dentist, the entire process is so bereft of clarity that the legal decision tree becomes muddled and protracted with misunderstandings. Attorneys do not care about ethical consequences and limit their actions based solely on their mission: defense or prosecution. These situations are going to happen merely as the result of human nature, but the dental profession has not protected itself adequately. And, in good measure, it has seemingly evolved from "the cash cow" of continuing education. It is now a cottage industry for lawyers who benefit from the failure of the dental profession to self-regulate. And, for licensing boards it is also "a cash cow". "Idealism" is a very narrow path. With old-fashioned common sense regulating its behavior, it is in its own best interest for dentistry to revisit this absurdity. But, it is so far beyond the pale today that it doesn't seem that the people who should care (the leaders of the industry) care at all. The body politic is grossly and brazenly impolitic.

To summarize, the idea of continuing dental education was a very vital and significant contribution to the long term health of the profession. It truly is incumbent on every practitioner to want to continuously read and learn. With the noblest of intentions and a very firm conviction, Henry took it upon himself to initiate his program with the purest of intentions. It blossomed into a money tree and provided a needed source of revenue from a very practical point of view. Dentists came from every local area to take courses, and eventually from all over Europe, parts of Africa, a good deal of countries in South America, a great deal of people from the Pan-Pacific rim, and even from Canada and Australia. The school ambitiously grew into a megaplex-like domain under the aegis of a highly skilled faculty. Today the program has flourished with outstanding leadership in all phases of dentistry and industry related topics. There is no question that like Boston University, all the other sixty-four dental schools have prevailed with the same proviso that they all serve to keep the profession abreast of all research and clinical information as it abounds at any time.

And, as to Henry and Gerry Kramer, they really clashed over attitude. Gerry sold his beliefs with selfish egomania. At the end of his life, particularly with the way he voiced his deeply held beliefs, he profoundly resented how implants blew in like General Sherman into Atlanta during The American Civil War, ravaging the principles and practice of a once glorious specialty. No doubt, Gerry took this to heart because the science of Periodontics had become his easel on which he painted his very personal interpretation of treatment planning and therapy. He artfully translated views with his uniquely imaginative style. It was his energy and firmly held beliefs he felt were crushed by the haphazard, careless implant gurus who virtually threw the era of orthodoxy in Periodontics to the dogs like scraps of inedible meat. He was rolling "sevens" in this his last conversation against a backdrop of "snake eyes" cast against all the belief systems that defined the great teachers/researcher in Periodontics. The tragedy is that the clash with Henry could have been averted if his brazen youth had not gotten in the way of his very capable mind. But, history can only forgive, it cannot forget or rewrite itself.[110]

Knowledge is a powerful tool. Abused and used for the wrong reasons can be a danger. Henry saw this coming on very early. But, for the most part, it has sustained as a very useful part of the entire complex of dental education. Boston University was the sole proprietor of a school founded for the express purpose of specialty training. In this regard, there was always deference paid to the importance of the biology of health and disease as a basis of clinical training. The repetitive process of probing into the whys and wherefores of therapies in relation to research studies, clinical projects and seminars involving point-counterpoint discussions made for the highest degree of the remediation-learning process. It is thus possible to conclude that by today's standards the major problem is the greatest number of continuing education courses (which are no longer university based) are

---

[110] Conversation with author before his passing.

minimalist by comparison. Being ADA approved, it is within the letter of legally accepted practice, but it is clear that "supplemental" courses cannot raise the level of the general practitioner to perform at the same skill level of a specialist whose training far exceeds that of a continuing education level course. Not to be overly repetitive, but the remediation process in education is the one intangible that any continuation course cannot provide. In a true sense, this is what specialization provides. The so-called pearls of the education learning process are embodied in those intangibles which come with daily interactive seminars and open forum discussions. Remediation requires a continuity over many years provided by an ADA recognized training institution. Thus, when the money element became a controlling factor, as Henry easily fore-casted, inconvenient and unexpected drawbacks in the process started to glaringly loom large. And, allowing the pool of the practicing body of dentists to comingle, it has affected the patient population and its right to expect the best of what is humanly possible in the delivery of care. But, clearly with everything delineated above, this is a "myth". At the time, this chagrined Henry to no end. The system is in overload and irreversible. The purity of education cannot be restored even remotely to any degree with so many levels of trained dentists delivering vastly different standards of care. The "pity" is that the profession is frayed like an old, overly used blanket. Can it be repaired? Yes. But, it would take a mind and a doer in the embodiment of a Henry Goldman, with his perspective and resolve. As he stated so often: "You don't know what you know until you know it"! [111]

---

[111] A repeated proviso to the author. His most repeated maxim, usually in a re-sounding, but humorous, tone.

Figure 1: Henry as a Captain in the United States Army during World War II during which time he served as Dental Chief in the Armed Forces Institute of Pathology in Washington, D.C.

Figure 2: D. Walter Cohen, former Dean at the University of Pennsylvania School of Dental Medicine and Chancellor of the Medical College of Philadelphia.

Figure 3: Henry standing behind his mentors: Kurt Thoma and Paul Boyle, both former Charles Brackett Professors of Oral Pathology at HSDM, and, Founders and Presidents of the American Academy of Oral Pathology

Figure 4: Henry as Dean of BUSGD, 1972.

Figure 5: BUSGD named for Henry; 1977; Dean Spencer Frankl making presentation; Henry to left; President of Boston University, John Silber, to right.

Figure 6: Founders of The American Board of Oral Pathology; Henry is at far right.

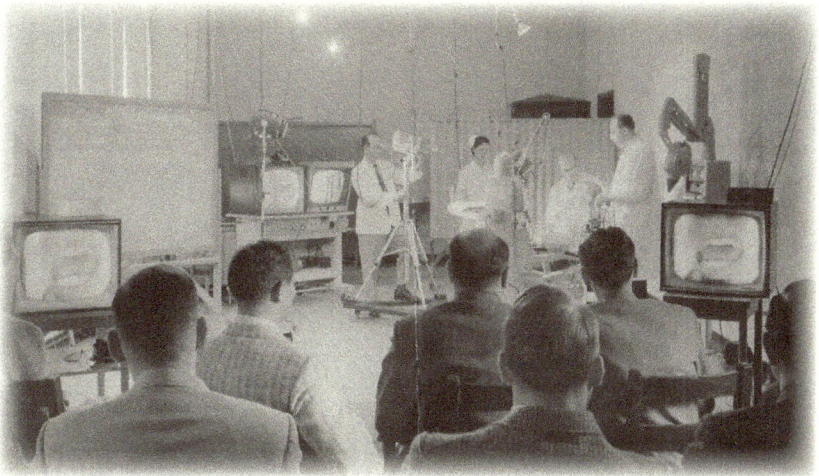

Figure 7: Henry giving a class demonstration with D. Walter Cohen standing next to him on right, circa 1950.

Figure 8: Henry giving a
lecture, circa 1950.

Figure 9: Boston University Centennial, 1969; Henry seated lower
row to left; seated atop second from left to right: Morris Ruben, Leo
Talkov and Mel Harris.

Figure 10: School is renamed the Henry M. Goldman School of Dental Medicine at Boston University in 1996.

Henry M. Goldman, D.M.D., F.A.C.D., F.I.C.D.

Figure 11: Henry received the Alpha Omega Achievement Medal in 1968.

Figure 12: Henry receiving a special citation in Atlanta, Georgia, circa 1950.

Figure 13: Henry receiving an honorary doctorate from the New Jersey College of Medicine and Dentistry in 1977.

Figure 14: Henry receiving a special commendation from the United States Army in 1954.

Figure 15: University of Pennsylvania School of Dental Medicine Graduation; Henry is fifth from right; D. Walter Cohen is at far left.

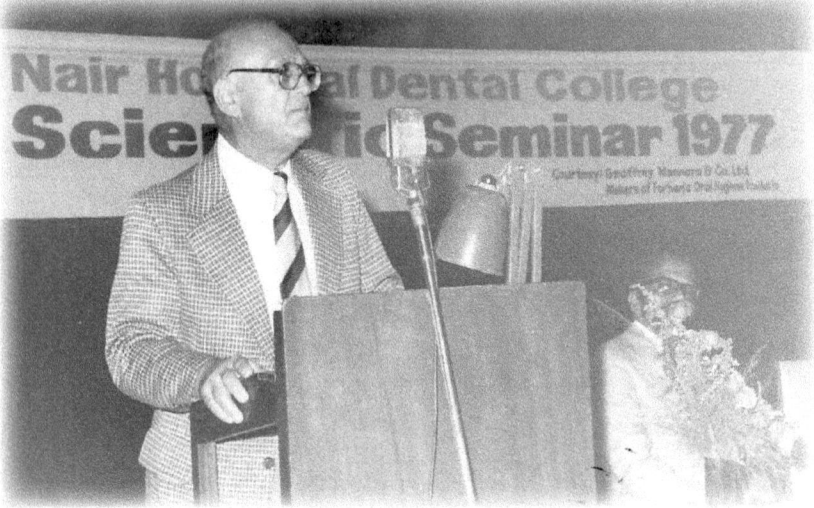

Figure 16: Henry lecturing at Nair Hospital Dental College in Mumbai, India in 1977.

Figure 17: Henry receiving an honorary degree from D. Walter Cohen in behalf of the University of Pennsylvania School of Dental Medicine, circa 1970.

Figure 18: Conference in Boston, circa 1960; Henry is third from left; Bernard Chaikin is second from right; and, Leo Talkov is at the end on far right.

Figure 19: Harvard School of Dental Medicine, Boston, Massachusetts.

Figure 20: Henry received certificate for lecture at the U S Naval Dental School.

Figure 21: Henry made Honorary Professor of Stomatology in Provence, Cote d'Azur, France, October, 1977.

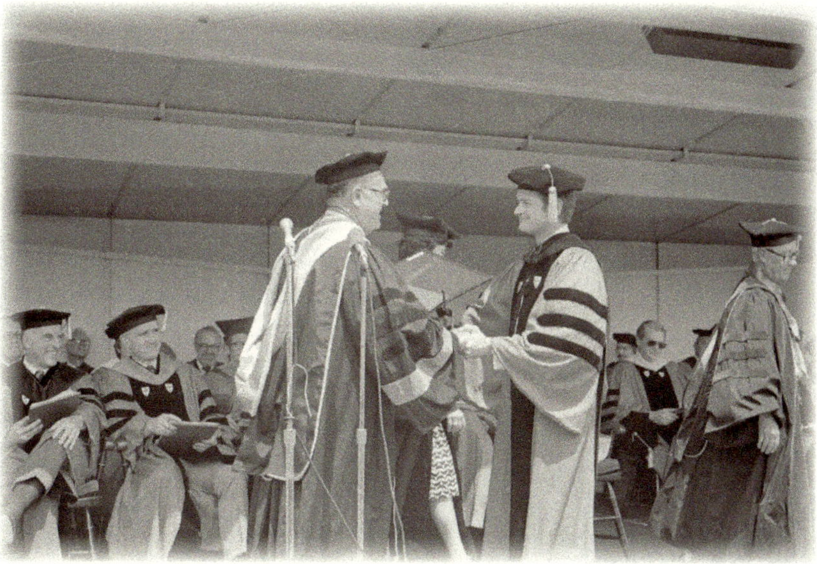

Figure 22: Henry receiving an honorary Doctor of Science from John Silber, President of Boston University, circa 1977.

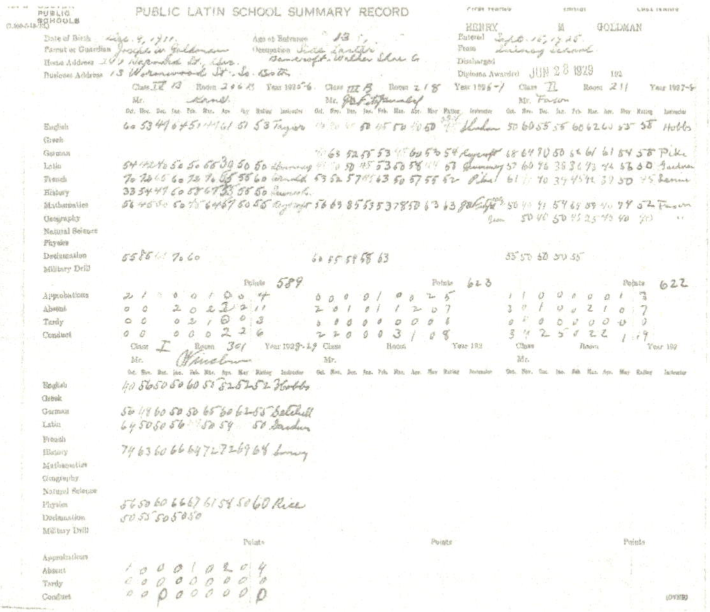

BOSTON PUBLIC SCHOOLS

PUBLIC LATIN SCHOOL SUMMARY RECORD

HENRY M GOLDMAN

Date of Birth

Age at Entrance

Entered

Parent or Guardian

Occupation

From

Home Address

Discharged

Business Address

Diploma Awarded JUN 28 1929

English

Greek

German

Latin

French

History

Mathematics

Geography

Natural Science

Physics

Declamation

Military Drill

Points

Approbations

Absent

Tardy

Conduct

Figure 23: Henry's Four year report resume at The Boston Latin School, Boston, Massachusetts.

Figure 24: Henry as a dental student at Harvard School of Dental Medicine, 1933.

Figure 25: Henry, seated to the left, as a member of The Phillips Brooks Association at HSDM.

Figure 26: Henry Maurice Goldman in 1935 at Harvard School of Dental Medicine.

Figure 27: Kurt Thoma, Oral Surgeon and Oral Pathologist, Henry's mentor at HSDM.

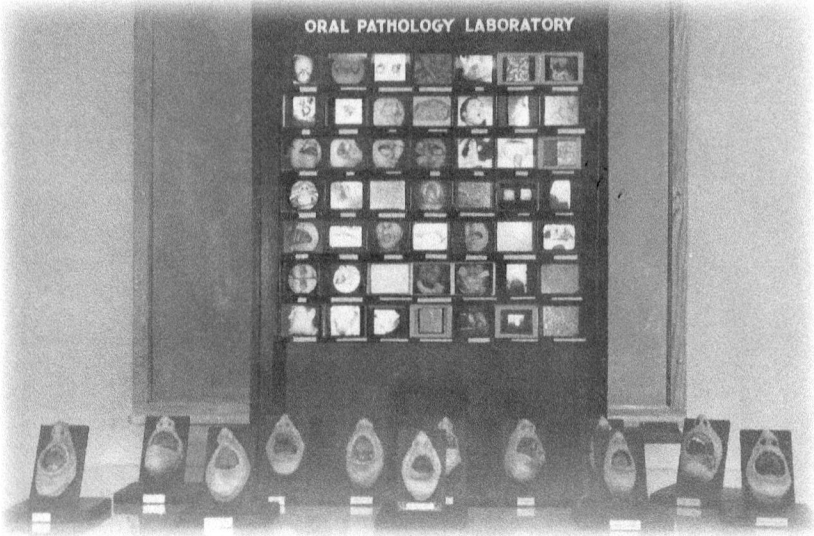

Figure 28: Kurt Thoma's Oral Pathology laboratory at HSDM, circa mid-1940's.

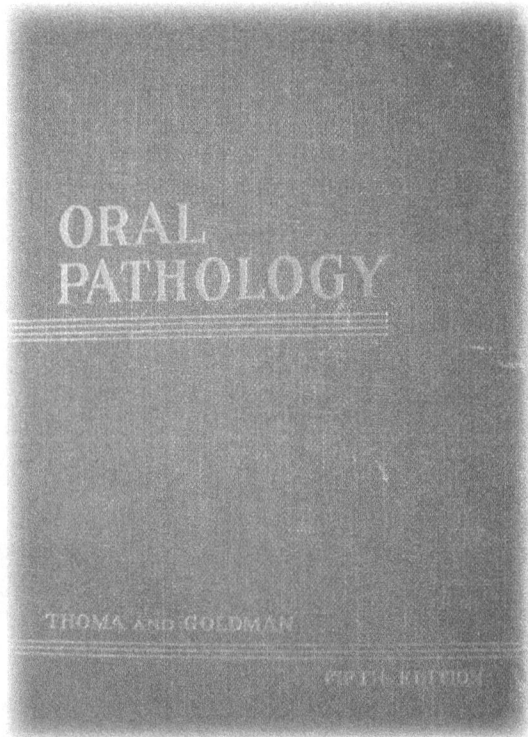

Figure 29: Oral Pathology by Kurt Thoma and Henry Goldman, Fifth Edition, 1960.

Figure 30: Chapin Harris: with Horace Hayden started the first dental school in the United States, the Baltimore School of Dental Surgery, now the University of Maryland School of Dentistry.

Figure 31: Gillette Hayden, 2nd President of the American Academy of Periodontology and Great Grand-daughter of Horace Hayden, founder with Chapin Harris of the Baltimore College of Dental Surgery (now the University of Maryland School of Dentistry).

in the news

HENRY GOLDMAN, Alu '35

WALTER COHEN, B '50

The Graduate School of Medicine of the University of Pennsylvania in association with the Beth Israel Hospital of Boston, Massachusetts, has established a two-year postgraduate course in Periodontology. The first year will be spent at the University of Pennsylvania and the second year at Beth Israel Hospital. Henry Goldman is chairman and professor and Walter Cohen Vice-Chairman.

Figure 32: Henry and D. Walter Cohen announcing a two year graduate program in Periodontics between The University of Pennsylvania School of Dental Medicine in Philadelphia and the Beth Israel Hospital in Boston, Massachusetts.

Golden Scroll Awards to Leaders in Education

The Jewish love of learning, respect for the intellect and quest for educational excellence is exemplified in the quartet of eminent academicians whose distinguished achievements will be recognized with the presentation of Twentieth Century Golden Scroll Awards. The presentation will take place Thursday evening, May 4, at the Eighty-Fifth Anniversary Banquet of *The Jewish Advocate* in the Grand Ballroom of The Park Plaza Hotel in Boston. Noted scholars Dr. Abram Sachar, Dr. Alfred Gottschalk, Dr. Henry Goldman and Dr. Stephen Jay Gould will be honored for their leadership in educational administration and in the classroom.

Dr. Abram L. Sachar

Dr. Stephen J. Gould

Dr. Henry Goldman

Figure 33: Henry received a Golden Scroll Award for his contribution to education.

Figure 34: 94 Esmond Street, Dorchester, Massachusetts 02121, where Henry lived in dental school.at HSDM.

Figure 35: Street where Henry's father, Joseph Goldman, worked as a side laster in a shoe company, only two miles from where the dental school is today at 100 East Newton Street, Boston, Massachusetts.

Figure 36: Henry with wife, Dorothy, on a lecturing-teaching trip to China in 1980.

Figure 37: Bunny and Alan Shuman. Alan practiced as a partner with Henry in a periodontal practice in Brookline, Massachusetts for 50 years.

Figure 38: Helen and Edward Goldman in 1951. Edward was Henry's older brother by 4 years.

Figure 39: Helen Ruth Rubenstein Goldman-
-Dorothy and Henry's sister-in-law, married to Edward, Henry's older brother.

Photomontage of Henry M. Goldman

CHAPTER 11

The Passing of the First Generation Of Dental Educators: Reinvention of the Wheel Or New Wheels on Old Vehicles

Very few of the post-WWII educators are left. The ones still alive are retired and out of the mainstream of active practice and the education connection. Their legacy is the bedrock of advanced practice techniques they passed on. Education is now in the hands of their former students. However, over the years the history and philosophy of treatment has either been forgotten or marginalized. The greatness of dentistry's early modern pioneers is remembered for their dedication to their work and pride in being the best that they could be.

Boston University was unique in its founding design, but it was certainly not the only institution where some of these people were to be found. Boston, as a city, merely had a great concentration due to the presence of three institutions so close together. There were also formidable educators all over the world. Their contributions were remarkably trailblazing, and, their publications and collaborative efforts not only made them standouts but infinitely respected for their enduring research and clinical work. Residents in those days were first hand witnesses to fundamentals which explicitly developed their thinking and permanently spearheaded an enthusiasm for practice, research and teaching. The vindication for their unique opportunity was the inspiration they embraced and disseminated.

After the war there was a sense of newness and a feeling for what was possible and an appreciation for the opportunity to succeed. It was a "Golden Age." (Chapter 6) It was a Voltairian time: *"All is for the best in all possible worlds"*.[112] With that thought Voltaire, the great French philosopher-writer-spokesperson in the early "Age of Reason" (aka "Age of Enlightenment") cast a sense of optimism. (43)

Productivity was measured in desire and hard work. Springing forth with eagerness and "an anything is possible" conviction would give man a chance to succeed at anything. "Golden" in a Voltairian sense conveyed the best that life was going to be. In this sense, dentistry in the 1950's was in a state of "the ideal". It was a period when educational pursuits were in their most unadulterated, pure expression. This was the world of first generation educators. Retrospectively, life was pretty calm and uncomplicated. People were not chasing rainbows, they were merely enthusiastic and fairly optimistic. It was as close to Voltaire's "El Dorado" (a perfect society) as anything could be. The world was free of regulatory controls: no insurance overlord governing treatment plans, no OSHA, HIPPA and liability worries. Those constraints were years down the line, office overhead was realistic, and encumbrances in general were non-issues. All in all, it was an uncontentious, freely driven lifestyle. The times were certainly not as "ideal" as what Voltaire described in his historic tome, "Candide" but they were special and almost providential for dental education's coming out from the shadows of its quite low-tech, rudimentary past. (121)

In an unfettered environment the culture of learning was a reflection of great leadership. Whatever the personality drawbacks, the residents gathered what they most wanted to learn and cast aside what was unappealing. Some were overwhelmed, some underwhelmed. But, in all cases, they all came away with a feeling of accomplishment and satisfaction. Each Chairman had so effectively set such a high standard that the ladder of success made the climb a day-to-day effort all the way through. Whatever personality issues prevailed, somehow these teachers embraced the convictions of their students upon which a lifetime

---

[112] Voltaire (nom de plume) aka Francois-Marie-Arouet: *Candide (Translated by Lowell Bair)*, Copyright 1959, bantam Dell (Reprint Edition).

allegiance developed. In general, the esprit de corps was extremely high. In spite of the hard work no one languished from fatigue or stress. Most felt nervous about the length of the days, maybe twelve as much as sixteen hours some days. The general takeaway was a feeling of satisfaction in spite of the high degree of tension and work load. Some of the pitfalls were political infighting around the school, talk and trivial gossiping. These were cast off as frivolous and inconsequential. But, after all, these were human beings in an oft competitive atmosphere which was relentless in one department trying to stand out above the others. There were criticisms, complaints and a lot of acrimony in pursuit of the ultimate goal: to drain these well-known icons of every bit of what they had to offer for all that it was worth. And, they all did.

Before the curtain came down on this first generation of teachers, they succeeded in producing model clinicians. The training became a self-perpetuating learning process of traditional clinical therapies. It was honed for continuity.

It was such an unusual time that without being a firsthand witness it would be impossible to gain a full appreciation of the differences between the various departments. They were similar by virtue of their commitment to detail and pride in the learning process. The periodontal department set a frenetic pace all the time, what with all the deadline commitments from seminars, documentation of patient treatment plans, lectures and meetings all foisted upon an already heavy course load of basic and clinical sciences. It was like a feeding frenzy of boundless information. The endodontic department seemed much more relaxed, but their chairman set a very high standard as well. The prosthetic and oral surgery departments were certainly the gentlemen scholars who worked very hard but were never overburdened with similar library research work. They seemed always soft spoken and never flustered. The pediatric dental department was never integrated as it had its own section for children. The orthodontic department was always around, but the residents were comparatively a very easygoing group. They were always industriously at work and never challenged by the unremitting demands which beset the periodontal and endodontic residents. Particularly the periodontal residents, no one could afford the luxury of relaxation. A tense feeling was common to a periodontal resident merely from so many daily commitments that personal or family time was almost impossible to find. Gerry Kramer's department was overly regimented and produced an extremely high degree of scholastic achievement. He demanded excellence, and he got it. Some were stretched tighter than guitar strings. And the sounds coming out were not melodious.

In his "A Tale of Two Cities" (1859), Charles Dickens captured the tone of the times around the French Revolution in Paris with an opening to the story which, in its unique felicity of expression, renders very descriptively a sense of the atmosphere so predominant at Boston University in its heyday. It shouldn't be construed that it was warlike. It is the masterful wording that is so appropriate that reflected well on the disparate conditions and emotional tenor

> "It was the best of times, it was the worst of times, it was the age of wisdom, it was the age of foolishness, it was the epoch of belief, it was the epoch of incredulity, it was the season of Light, it was the season of Darkness, it was the spring of hope, it was the winter of despair, we had everything before us, we had nothing before us, we were all going direct to Heaven, we were all going direct the other way—in short, the period was so far like the present period, that some of its noisiest authorities insisted on its being received, for good or evil, in the superlative degree of comparison only." [113]

This text just perfectly describes the department of Periodontology under Gerry Kramer. For people who were not witness to the decade that made Boston University so superbly the architect and inspiration of so many well-trained clinicians, it would be impossible to comprehend that it was a living contradiction. The quality narrative above

---

[113] Dickens, Charles: *A Tale of Two Cities*", Copyright 2007, Published by New American Library, a division of the Penguin Group; opening paragraph to book.

covers almost every detail of feeling and emotion that it could not be described any better. It resonates so well with the tide of up-and-down mood swings that reflected daily with the changing intensity of work. It was in fact "the best of times" while it was "the worst of times". It was so in fact "the season of Light" while it was disturbingly "the season of Darkness". The departments mentioned above were programmed to turn out some of the most accomplished clinicians of the day. But, for some there was a price. There is no doubt that the department of Periodontology was the most burdened by the rigor. Any "joie de vivre" was suppressed. Many residents were thrown back on their heels with deeply felt internal stress.

When Henry Goldman opened Boston University, he did so with his focus on the education format. But, it was clear from the outset that the welfare of each resident was first and foremost in his mind. He was very aware of what it would take to get new residents acclimated in each of the specialties. A smooth transition was foremost in his mind, but it was difficult because nothing jibed at first. Between 1963 and 1969 (1970) there was just a series of old, dilapidated brownstone buildings which had virtually no heat in the winters and no air-conditioning in the summer. Installations were present, but they were minimally functioning on a good day. The one advantage of such old buildings was the thickness of the stone foundation as well as the walls. Varying from a foot to two feet, the building retained the dank, musty smell from the cooling evening so it took a while to heat up the next day if the ambient outdoor temperature shot up. But, listening to technical information did not coordinate well with Maslow's basic pyramid on education. (202)

The old medical library at Boston University was overly decrepit and almost physically untenable. It was so old and dingy that the book stacks barely stood, but taken in stride with sardonic humor by most residents. And, getting around the medical center was an experience: a meltdown in the Boston summer heat, and, almost freezing in the windblown Alberta Clippers of the winters. Was this an artic marine training center or an august educational center? Some kidded around about whether to laugh or cry? But, it was also a different era when complaining was never standard fare. Joke but don't complain, toughen up, and carry a stiff upper lip. That was the mantra. These were the accepted disgruntled feelings in those days. Everyone was in for the long run to completion. That was pretty much established thinking. Grind it out from day-to-day almost in an existential bearing. There were always wannabe comedians so the one-liners flew around endlessly, even during the lectures.

In spite of all the weather issues in a completely skeleton-like, makeshift environment, things were running surprisingly in a most cohesive manner. Anyone still alive from those days would smile quietly with a brief shake of the head to inwardly acknowledge those unimaginable times. Sitting in a Morris Ruben lecture in an incomprehensibly small, rickety room in a down winter jacket (with a shirt and sweater—or may two), earmuffs or a winter hat pulled over the ears, and winter gloves while chattering teeth disturbed actually hearing what was being said. There was so much CO_2 being blown off with each breath that it was like a car exhaust jettisoning from an accelerating hotrod. Taking notes of complex ideas coming from every one of Morris Ruben's utterances was as ridiculous as trying to digest why this was even happening when trying to sort out how a pen or pencil would stay in place while wearing winter gloves as it wandered everywhere on the paper except where it should have been. Yes, "it was the best of times, it was the worst of times…" Morris Ruben was like a mechanized doll that was wound up from somewhere in the back and began until it stopped with sudden loss of force. He had the sustaining power of a Detroit Lions linebacker like Dick "Night Train" Lane (195) and the motor-mouth virtues of a filibustering Washington, D.C. senator. He never dithered, relented to the obscene weather constrictions, nor ever, ever complained. He was rugged and hardnosed to the nth degree. And, he was knowledgeable beyond imagination. He was a walking encyclopedia of dental-medical trivia, and seemingly poised to outrun weather conditions, moaning and groaning residents, and, really, anything else that might impede him. What would Henry Goldman have done without this heavenly-sent, mission impossible character who was like a Hollywood set creation of special wonders? It is not an underestimation to conclude that these early years would have collapsed on themselves without him. He served a very primary need in Oral Biology and the basic sciences. He was every other chairman's outreach for year one in the different graduate programs. He was the Yang to the Yin, the foil to Sherlock Holmes, Tonto to The Lone Ranger, or the straight man Bud Abbott for the comedian Lou Costello. (118) Henry could never have weathered the turbulence of the startup to the opening of the new dental school without this indefatigable "intellectual behemoth".

When the smart alecks greased their tolerance points and mar-shalled up their gumption, attention to the din from the outside blast of frosty New England air coming in like a freight train in the form of an Alberta Clipper (149) was diverted by the indoors idiocy. It became solace so that intemperate behavior could rescue everyone's sanity. Morris Ruben kept on lecturing in spite of the rather juvenile laugh-ing coming from grown men. If he heard it, he never let on. He just kept on spieling out the pearls like the wound-up doll he seemed. The material was so esoteric that it was hard to believe anyone was re-ally listening. And, in those days there were a lot of smokers so that the tobacco smoke billowed around in competition with the CO_2 and like the smoke stacks from the engines leaving North Station on the Boston & Maine rail line. So, between Ruben's cacophonic effusions of "whatever", the bitter artic air, the radiators belching heat once in a while in between their persistent crackling, the tobacco smoke choking the non-smokers, and the cackling from the interminable jokes flying around, it was amazing anything came out of this experience besides distant memories years later! But, the real joke was Morris Ruben's per-formance. It was a stand-up monotone, unconscious of the goings-on and with his traditional wide spectrum of literature references trying to catch an occasional ear. He was like the old red and white pole outside barber shops with that spiral motion to which no one paid attention, but certainly kept it recessed in the grey matter of the cerebral cortex forever. To the early days may the humor of it all sustain instead of the excruciating mind games which almost made that period in the school's history collapse on its "trial by torture"! Today's residents could never imagine what staying power was necessary to survive. It is better to keep the memory "light and campy"!

This was a prelude to this original faculty composed of upstarts who were grouped together with blind expectations. And, by the time their intellectual machismo had grown into their spiritual beings, and, their confidence had wrested them from total uncertainty, they had assimilated like oil and water. They didn't. They were grouped, and that is about all that can be said. The exception was Don Booth's friendship with Don Mori and Anthony Gianelly from their dental school years at Harvard. It took a while before there was an established comfort zone. However, in time this faculty grew into each other and harmonized with ease and cooperation.

In Voltaire's utopian world, everything would have turned for the best. However, Voltaire was part of an age when thinking through things with common sense for the sake of orderliness, harmony and even-handedness would make sense. This was "The Age of Enlightenment", the 18th century view that man could be the master of his own fate. Benjamin Franklin was America's most significant example and proponent of this period which stressed individual initiative, scientific inquiry, and the belief that personal conduct could improve a person's lifestyle while having a positive impact on society as well. It was a kind of thinking that fostered human endeavor, hard work and mastery of one's own fate. Franklin's witticisms pillorying behavior which promoted laziness and allowing others (like religion and government) to be in control laid out an outline for personal conduct. This reasoned analysis for individualism as the basis for human initiative and scientific investigation accounted for the era known also as "The Age of Reason". In a sense, it was imbued with idealism. Structure, purpose and order were essential for success in life. Franklin's *"Autobiography"* (43) described conduct becoming of a gentleman. He extolled the virtues of daily living, and detailed as well the manner and behavior becoming of an honorable citizen. For the most part, he was the very quintessential scientific and humanistic student (writer, printer, lightening experiments, promoter of the post-office, founder of The University of Pennsylvania, etc.). Like Isaac Newton, John Locke, etc. (33), he represented an age that clearly showed human progress through individual initiative. He projected a romantic idealism in some sense because of his detailed day-to-day living in "the ideal". However, it was not rooted in "Idealism". To the contrary, lucidly reflected a belief in barebones self-reliance. His path to success: attention to detail, careful planning, living a life of self-discipline, and, most of all, the assiduous reinforcement of oversight on a daily basis. These were the sole criteria for not only getting things done, but, most of all, reinvigorating the process. This was Franklin's yardstick by which to measure individual resourcefulness and accomplishments.

Well, of whom does this remind the world? Would it be Henry Goldman? Was he a throwback to an earlier time? What about his faculty of aspiring teachers? Yes, they were the first generation of dental educators who were assembled for the express purpose of forging Henry's blueprint. They all entered coming from the mainstream milieu with very modest pursuits in their objective sights. Never imposing, extremely unassuming, these were all well-intentioned clinicians with glaring uncertainty how their transitions would play out. They all came recommended by a very small inner cadre of dental educators whose friendships promoted their group needs. This would become a collection of politically savvy leaders. Henry had a firm game plan worked out in his head, it was just laid out on fallow, untested ground.

That is why the days of enduring a Morris Ruben lecture in the artic, windblown, subfreezing, heater-less, timeworn Brownstones on East Newton Street were so memorable. Only a few miles away on Commonwealth Avenue by The Boston Commons these same buildings were the verisimilitude of 19th century lifestyle images of largesse when inhabited by the Boston Upper Crust, aka The Boston Brahmins. (2) But, this was East Boston and since Henry spent his youth within a block or two away, the area fell into blight and ecological submission due to the very near pass-through of The Massachusetts Turnpike with a connector through the area known as The Southeast (Northeast) Expressway. To locals it was more of a "distress way". It was central to merchants of crime as well as graduate students listening to the wafting of arcane science being discharged in an uninterrupted rhythm from Morris Ruben's seemingly unaware lips to the frozen tundra around his biologically inert body. Missing only the metronome, those around him recoiled into semi-consciousness as their minds were frozen into submission. Some felt it may have been one of Boston University's early live clinical investigative studies into cryonics! Humor aside, this was one brilliant man.

As unsure and clearly apprehensive about whether they were making the right decisions to change their direction in life to full time teaching, they had nothing more to trust than the full faith and credibility of Henry Goldman. The gamble was a two way commitment. The question is: were these men Voltairian-Franklin types, or, were they uncertain hopefuls just taking measure of a possible gamble that may or may not work out? Or, based upon Henry Goldman's already established reputation, were they given a chance at something others would lurch at even with such uncertainty? It was a little bit of it all. But, certainly, Henry's reputation had a lot to with it because the overwhelmingly effusive, engaging and jocular nature they might have expected never came into play. Looking for that personality was clearly as rationale as a youngster digging a hole on the beach hoping to reach China. The most they ever got out of him was the opportunity as he probably implored: "Ok, you got it, now go do it"![114] This was quintessential Henry Goldman. He was categorically the most stoic man they would ever confront. Feedback being hard-pressed, they nevertheless accepted with great askance and worry. But, something inside every one of these aspiring educators compelled their inner ambition to scratch that indefinable itch. The gamble appeared timely.

It is impossible to adequately judge whether any of them ever sat back to fully consider how bold and courageous such an innovative

---

[114] Another Goldmanism!

move Henry made to even consider a graduate school, let alone pursue its fortunes with such a measured pursuit.

Why not just another dental school with specialty programs like other dental schools? This is a question which most likely was never asked directly in those words. But, he often expressed his reasoning for the school. It was fairly simple as Henry was very forthright in his ability to reason out his motivations. To the extent that he never expostulated on the details, terseness reflected his directness and impatience with prolixity. He was by every means a very taciturn person. If there was ever any question as to his commitment, then just ponder this relevant fact: he lectured all over the world in pursuit of marketing the newly established school. The new school became a magnet highly educated dentists from the four corners of the world. The peripatetic nature of Henry's ambitious lecturing worldwide probably set a record for travel miles logged over any other Periodontist. The example he set should be enough to dispel any thought that would call his determination into question. In fact, this accomplishment translated into a heightened reputation of both the main campus as well as for the medical center. Never as highly recognized as Harvard, M.I.T. and Tufts, the general surge in applications to Boston University's schools was a singular consequence of Henry's efforts to disseminate the university's worldwide presence. The School of Graduate Dentistry became a lightning rod for its very dynamic growth.

Henry's teaching, writing and lecturing no doubt served as his philosophical basis for graduate dental education and, later, his views on continuing dental education. He appeared aloof, but he was merely quiet and introverted. He was also easily embarrassed so it seemed like he was short on social graces. This was his Achilles heel, but he was never going to change his core personality. To prejudge him on this quality was solely for relentless critics who could never imagine the burden he carried.

On the other hand, the "riveting" question is: Was the faculty disposed to appreciate the enormity of Henry's undertaking? Or, for that matter, anyone in dentistry? The answer to this is quite simple: Probably yes, but most certainly with a sense of bewilderment! Whatever the personality traits each of the faculty shared, they all grew into talents with very different styles. Each developed a presence over time due to the imagery of their language and the captivating brand each brought to an international audience. The growing reputation of Boston University emerged from their dynamism and leadership qualities. Boston University eventually became their bully pulpit. The school provided a stage upon which to grow a style, an image, and, most of all, a following. But, to answer the question, it was Henry's dogged tenacity to bring Boston University into being, and then to international notice and fame that gave purpose for this emerging group of aspiring intellects.

Of all the people with the perception, Morris Ruben recognized his good fortune from the outset and took accurate measure of his circumstances. He knew and often verbalized the extent of Henry Goldman's background. To the little informed, Henry Goldman was a longstanding Periodontist with some teaching background. And, this included the faculty which, for the most part, was unaware of Henry's background. Amazing, but true!

To Morris Ruben who knew Henry as a famed Oral Pathologist and a longtime scientific investigator, he was thrilled to be associated with such a venture. Morris's background as a journalist was good fortune because it gave Henry a "man for all seasons" type in someone who could impart the science with an explosion of "the gift of gab". Morris did not have Henry's background, but he so calculated what his position demanded that he adapted very quickly. Assuredly, he could weave a verbal discourse like no one else, but he effused an alacrity to bring order and immediate recognition to his responsibilities. His contributions were so fundamentally

a part of the school's success that he became an immediate attraction. He raised eyebrows, got people shaking their heads, and captivated audiences by his free-flowing lecturing style. His reputation grew with an immediacy that was as convenient as it was so very opportune. And, Henry was very well aware, though his personality disallowed any public display of emotion. All the Boston dental schools venerated Morris' style, competence and humility. No doubt a diamond in the rough, he always credited Henry's learned depth of knowledge as his inspiration.[115] Morris being very unaggressive, somewhat socially awkward, even somewhat of a political ingénue, he always dreamed that Henry would have considered him a worthy successor. Unfortunately, as gifted in the academic realm, he was grievously unpolished. No, he was not a philistine. He was simply a very endearing, honorable man who was clearly deficient in the attributes so very necessary for the position. It was unfortunate because he was not shy about speaking about this in the years after Henry died. In industry he would have been slotted to a high level advisory position, but he could never have been a CEO. In academia where he was comfortable, his enthusiasm and expertise defined his long term success. There was no person who captured more respect for the virtues of his teaching skills and compassionate manner than Morris Ruben.

Unfortunately, his wife, neither sheepish nor self-effacing, got involved late in his career and with very public entreaties made herself a very tacky and sloppy embarrassment. Her intentions were quite bold, even confronting Henry in public to his obvious chagrin and distress. She clearly wanted the lofty position of Dean for her husband. She unfortunately made so many awkward overtures that it became intolerable and made Morris feel so begrudging and unrequited. Yes, it would have been nice to have seen him rewarded as such, but she could not let it go. The mere finding that he would never even be considered weighed very heavily on him because he was severely challenged by the idea that Henry was ungrateful for his years of devoted service. Had his wife not pressed this idea for so long Morris would have capitulated. Morris was a very refined man who submitted to his wife's aggressive and very public pandering. The letdown eventually strained his once very endearing relationship with Henry. This was a shame. Upon Henry's passing, the distance that had grown between them evolved into outright acrimony with Henry's widow. Almost Shakespearean in nature, the goodness and mutual respect of two of the most honorable people left the legacy

---

[115] Private conversations with author.

of their years highly tarnished. It was clearly cultivated by Morris's most concealed thoughts that only came to the fore when Henry commenced his search for his replacement. Henry always embraced the good fortune of having Morris in the most needed, yet probably the least public and maybe the most thankless, position on the faculty. He certainly knew that Morris was irreplaceable, and particularly early on. It was a most sensitive kerfuffle that may possibly have been obviated if Henry had possessed greater communication skills. And yet Morris's wife allowed her normally courteous, pleasant personality transfuse into the likeness of a harridan. There was nothing that would have mitigated this misfortune. The bitterness swelled as the decision for Henry's replacement grew near.

The rest of the faculty, albeit talented, successful and politically savvy, never fully appreciated how well in command Henry was when they first started at Boston University. As Dean he was fully in control, albeit going about his business in a muted way. In most circumstances this journeyman appearance would have sufficed. However, Henry, in his wildest imagination, was too much of an "idealist" to understand or even see that Gerald Kramer was on a mission to run "his" Department of Periodontology parallel to the rest of the school. From the outset, his behavior was very carefree. He was going to run his department completely without deference to Henry's original charge. It would have been no different than a newly appointed CEO of a major corporation on a methodically contrived scheme to upend the Chairman of The Board. Unfortunately, his rogue behavior cultivated a sense that his domain was above the everyday school spirit. He was completely absent of any esprit de corps. Henry represented the bedrock of the dental profession. If Henry had taken Gerry early on to the proverbial wood shed and schooled him as to his proper comportment, he would have forestalled a lot of heartache. In a very realistic sense, Henry attempted to avert serious action, but Gerry fell on his own sword like a fallen, wayward Shakespearean character.

In his own inimitable manner Henry Goldman was atavistic of the prototypical "Franklin persona". Henry very easily could have been considered part of "The Age of Enlightenment". He arose from very humble beginnings to become founder and Dean of Boston University. It was not at all a gratuitous, simply a lucky endpoint owing to good fortune, networking and the collaborative efforts of others. To the contrary, it was the day-to-day, persistent attention to hard work, perhaps with a touch of defiance. It was his tenacious self-reliance and his independent spirit, a throwback to the late 18th and 19th centuries. It was not the acquisitive urge bundled from the great wealth of the early industrial age of growth that came in the late 1800's. To the contrary, Henry's inner guts and glory came from the spirit of a man who worked "tooth and nail" to see an idea through knowing the hard reality of what it would take to succeed. He knew very realistically it could simply play out as a dream or melodrama, and, that it could fail at any point. His determination overwhelmed his sense of fear, some personal setbacks and open fears of public speaking (due to stuttering overcome with therapy). Instead, he embraced the slew of unending hardships to construct the support system necessary to establish a groundbreaking institution. His unambiguous results at The University of Pennsylvania and Boston University reflected the core essence of "Age of Reason" mentality: self-sufficiency, determination, resilience and strength of character, and, most of all, the sinew and the will within to prevail over the fear of failure. This was the spirit of Benjamin Franklin outlined in his *Autobiography*. (43) Henry's whole life was subsumed in his struggles against insufferable odds. If anyone considers this hyperbole, then they do not comprehend the Henry Goldman who, in his very unassuming, quiet manner, carefully calibrated everything and anything that needed to be done, and always came through. Never vocal, no splashy headlines, he always produced. He truly possessed that quality of character which garnered respect and appreciation of his peers.

He was a foundational spirit. The innovators, the pioneers, the entrepreneurs and the great architects of dental education accounted for the grand matrix of the business of dentistry from which society is the beneficiary today. D. Walter Cohen undeniably is cast in this historical pantheon. The teachers are never to be under-esteemed or under-appreciated. They have always served to ensure next generation learning through their dogged perseverance.

The original Boston University faculty of that illustrious period from 1963 to 1978 means very little to dentists today, the second generation to whom the historical record means nothing. It is axiomatic that two generations after death a person is forgotten unless there is a convincing subset of reinforcing reasons.

However, in the world of short span memory today, this is a shame because this was a group of worthy significance. To Endodontists, Herbert Schilder is their icon. His prodigious accomplishment of taking root canal therapy to a new historic status where it is practiced today was groundbreaking. It was a historic transformation: eliminating silver points, establishing the proper preparation of the root canal system, emphasis on the internal anatomy with emphasis on lateral and accessory canals, the proper sterilization of canals, and the introduction of the warm gutta percha technique for filling treated canals, and other formalities related to x-ray diagnosis in relation to pathology. He was genuinely deserved of all the acclaim of his past students. He was truly transformative in every sense. Highly articulate, innovative and a perpetual student of his craft, he possessed inexorable energy. As one of the original faculty, he was a giant in his field. And, he warrants all the respect he has garnered over the years. Gerry Kramer as well was a legend among his former students. He was faithful to his purpose as a Periodontist: a dedicated teacher, journal founder and editor, and always in search of excellence in diagnosis and treatment. Allowing himself to shortchange his legacy was as much an enigma as it was self-destructive. For comparison of the two most dynamic faculty members, Schilder was a tremendous consensus builder whereas Kramer was divisive and brazen. In the true Charles Dickens descriptive manner, Kramer was Pecksniffian, a man of unfortunate sanctimony and narcissism.[116] Schilder possessed idiosyncratic behavior as he tended to be self-centered and irritable at

---

[116] Dickens, Charles: *Martin Chuzzlewit*, Editor Patricia Ingam, Copyright 2000, Penguin Classics (originally serialized in 1843 and 1844).

times, but he was never condescending nor combative. His conduct was always forthright and straight-up. He was a man of manners and had a noble air. Certainly not as flamboyant, Anthony Gianelly was a giant among giants. He was a man of the people, the most genuine man anyone would possibly encounter in any lifetime. He stood out, not because of his dress or his external perception, but because of his spirit and class. His knowledge oozed like a continuous flow of sap from a ripe maple tree in summer. It was effervescent, uniquely organized and profound in meaning. He was easygoing, friendly, and deeply supportive of anyone he could help. He was simply a teacher's teacher. Without being overly repetitive, it should be repeated (and maybe not enough) that it was unfortunate not to have seen him replace Henry. He possessed all the qualities of leadership, character and the uncanny ability to bring people together with his energy and rather deeply layered sophistication. He died far too early. never wanting any part of being the Dean. With his perception and insights, he probably knew a great deal that his cohorts did not. But, had he been of a different mindset, he would have made a great leader. And, more than likely, the school would have remained undeterred from its original charge. It is interesting to note that the preponderance of his residents carry the same mindset, and, save one or two, are of the same refinement and rectitude. Both Don Booth and Spencer Frankl were very different. Don Booth was very much averse to controversy and would have more than likely found being Dean too much of a perverse position. Spencer was very purposive and driven. As a Pedodontist, he commanded the genuine respect of his students, but the dynamism of the other departments was lacking. It was linear and very methodical, but that was a virtue not a drawback. Don Booth, on the other hand, was as refined and determined as any of the faculty. A tall, gentle man of purpose and intellect, he was without flair or showmanship. He was all about importance and meaning. Like Frankl, his residents came from a different direction, less of the doting types, more of the appreciation for the residency they expected and received under his chairmanship. Spencer Frankl became Dean only because the men who would have been the proper choices (Anthony Gianelly and Don Booth) never showed even the slightest taste for the position. The two men who would have cradled the position like Atlas carrying the earth on his back, Schilder and Kramer, were never options, but for very different reasons. And, finally, the man never mentioned, Don Mori, was not special in the sense of unusual leadership and educational background. He was more convivial and led with a more open, laissez-faire style that was totally devoid of demands and stringency. He was an interesting person who complemented the faculty around him, but, despite his clinical competence was lacking in administrative acumen.

What this discussion does illustrate was a very detectable level of tidiness which characterized all the residency programs. And, each department reflected a discernibly different quality, be it the result of cult of personality or the core course content. The school's vested commitment to excellence in teaching was reflected in the charismatic faculty. Was this like a baptism, mind control, or blind genuflection? There is no doubt that it was a little of all for the majority. It would seem some were blinded by their mentors' hypnotic wizardry. And, there were numbers who frankly never capitulated to this jejune behavior. In some classes over the years it became an outright herd mentality. The training left them very self-assured with a very sanguine outlook and self-confidence. This was a very positive legacy, but, unfortunately, a good number became extremely self-promoting, quite intolerant and somewhat holier-than-thou. It could be almost considered very overbearing and tedious. It was a self-centered trait in the manner that many developed a willful disregard for others. There is no doubt that for a long time graduates of the varying programs had to tolerate reputations that preceded them on the national scene.

From an educational point of view, Boston University produced many specialists who were inclined to feel thankful for the detail and relevancy of their training. So many expert clinicians, researchers and teachers went on to fashion their own careers, all with varying emphasis and affiliations throughout the world. It was an endless stream of highly skilled clinicians adorned with their mentors' insights and traditions. Maybe they were set apart from other programs where the regimentation and coordinated programming may have been less stringent. Because Boston University had larger class sizes the atmosphere was perhaps more serious and demanding, but less chummy. In that regard, there was a definite group sense of identification that other training institutions did not share. In another sense as well, the mere size difference engendered a continued connection that the smaller programs did not foster.

As life at Boston University changed with Henry's retirement and the swirling politics surrounding his replacement, a very clear picture of change in the quality of dental education began to take notice. All the rich tradition that grew would dilute and change forever. Things would never be the same. It was almost as if the school lost sight of its past genius. In lock step with the rest of the country it was as if information transfer was lost and teaching had lost its way. Every new teaching methodology had lost its link to the near past. There was a swing to refocus with emphasis on new ideas and methods, which were not new at all. Old ideas were patched with new insights. It was very strange to see that everything which was believed to be so technically avant-garde was not at all. What was once a teaching priority was not, and people with new ideas were just recasting old ideas in newly bundled forms and different ways of expression. Yes, instead of a continuity and a flow from one generation to another, newly minted educators were attempting to reinvent the wheel. Some were inexplicably trying to refurbish "old vehicles" with "new wheels" in the sense they embraced new technologies without all the consideration given to the periodontium in health and disease. It was as if time had stood still and a new "brave world" emerged without consideration of all the hard work from its glorious past. New technologies have come and gone, almost totally replacing the "thinking dentist" with the "systems-procedure dentist".

Very early in his career Henry Goldman practiced general dentistry. With all his subsequent technical training he formulated some very definite feelings concerning the inherent inadequacies of dental education. This was his prime motivating consideration for Boston

University as a pure graduate school. The reason for his rather casual, yet quizzical smirk when he referenced dental school as a "union card" process was just this point: that somewhere, somehow, someone had to bring dentistry out of "The Stone Age", a lengthy period of "trade-like" training. His mission became that of a one man army. It was not an obsession, merely a clear understanding of the difficulties he would encounter. He was not so naïve to think he could win a battle over a rather staid, phlegmatic organization like The American Dental Association, but he felt there was enough support to enhance the graduate specialty programs.

He therefore put the negative criticism behind him and progressed with a very positive game plan to ameliorate the dental curriculum at the graduate level. By doing so he elevated the entire profession. The old saw: "that a high tide lifts 'all' the ships in the harbor" was indeed a reality. It forced other dental schools to upgrade and be more fastidious even in their pre-doctoral core courses. Even though the teaching of Periodontics was already an ongoing part of dental school courses, its improvements on a pure informational level were dramatic. Very early on there was once a rather negative suggestion that Periodontists were general practitioners in skirts. But, as curricula acquired a far more serious tone with investigative research and rapidly advancing technologies this allusion soon disappeared. The attention to course detail warranted advancing the didactic presentations to more critically scientific documentation and data collection for all the journals worldwide. By the time he had retired, he had seriously called attention to the need for "the biology of oral disease" being front and center in all course curricula. This would certainly change the face of dentistry.

One of the greatest oversights in the history of the dental profession is the fact that that he clearly elevated every other school in the world. Many will not see or recognize this for one reason or another, but his many changes most certainly propagated "a rising educational tide" in the paradigm shift he brought to dental education. Looking at the very broad picture today, it is easy to see how the entire face of dentistry has become much more of a biologically driven profession. Scientists now retired but still alive would support this observation in spite of some defiant naysayers who would be in denial. But history will ultimately justify the timeline. Henry's accomplishments herald his academic distinction and will validate his standing amidst great American scientists. Bringing to fruition an American "private" institution and energizing a profession is a mission statement of incalculable magnitude.

In his short story, *The Outcasts of Poker Flat* (70), Bret Harte surmises parenthetically that there is a little bit of good in the worst of us, and a little bit of bad in the best of us. Commenting as a writer of the western scene in the late 1800's, he apportioned human character quite rationally and appropriately. The message is obvious: there are no perfect people, but situations are never cast ideally as well. Even though he was writing in the rough and tumble of the early post-Civil War west, his perceptions about human nature and life issues remain quite valid.

Human nature is a very fragile component of personality. Its nurturing depends on environmental influences that can alter the behavior and thinking of anyone, even grown women and men. To recreate a flat-out conclusive flow chart of how and why things could not have been taped together at Boston University in the late 1970's would require a Bret Harte-like psychiatric analysis. There were so many ingredients in play that made the emotional tide too overwhelming to hold back Henry's angst and deep-seated, dogged disgust. In the end, Gerry Kramer went and Henry endured in a Bret Harte shootout of warring souls. Only an intellectual exercise would dare get into the weeds of the "whys and wherefores" of such a deliberately perpetuated testing of wills. Suffice it to say there were no winners, simply a man who lost his way and a man who was taunted for years and finally compelled to assert his will out of necessity.

That was the ugly. The good: Gerry Kramer saw this in a religion-like message to restorative dentistry: periodontal health must be the sine qua non of all its applications. The message was appropriate, the delivery was very preachy. His public flair and debonair quality was so holier-than-thou that he perpetrated disgust and aspersion upon himself. His bullet-proof and cleverly crafted, sanguine presentations were embarrassing for anybody with a sense of dignity and respect for the heart and soul of the specialty. Interesting enough, it made anybody with sound thinking to ask "why"? He had position and power, why would he want to project such a nefarious image? It didn't make any sense. The single greatest skill he possessed was exquisitely realizing "the historical moment" of his chairmanship and exercising complete control at the helm. Henry had no idea how his choice would backfire. Gradually, Henry saw him as a recalcitrant rogue without common sense for right and wrong. Was he right out of *"Candide"*: That "All is for the best in the best of all possible worlds"? [117] The Charles Dickens imagery seemed to waft like an air of the paranormal about his persona: "It was the best of times, it was the worst of times, it was the age of wisdom, it was the age of foolishness, it was the epoch of belief, it was the epoch of incredulity, it was the season of Light, it was the season of darkness, it was the spring of hope, it was the season of despair... we were all going direct the other way..."[118] Nothing could more artfully describe where Gerry Kramer was in that decade when Boston University was ascending so prodigiously high into the academic stratosphere. Here was a man with so much promise who gloated in his own ability to capture the attention and allegiance of people who, like he, were immature enough to be so incalculably duped and amused. The greatest pity was it was almost a little boy game to him in a big boy world. It was brazen and unforgiveable.

In *"Maxims"* the Duc de La Rochefoucauld made a comment that highlights the essence of Kramer's incomprehensible misbehavior with the following succinct axiom:

> *"It is not enough to have great qualities; one must know how to manage them."*[119]

---

[117] Voltaire (nom de plume) aka Francois-Marie-Arouet: *Candide (Translated by Lowell Bair)*, Copyright 1959, Bantam Dell (Reprint Edition).

[118] Dickens, Charles: *A Tale of Two Cities*, 2007, New Amer.Library, div.of Penguin Group; opening paragraph.

[119] Rochefoucauld, Francois de La: *MAXIMS*, Copyright 199, Translation, Penguin Classics.

There is no doubt that personal conduct determines character, and as Len Marrella aptly describes, legacy is never parenthetically determined. It is in fact the direct result how people "manage" their character through "personal conduct".

Gerry Kramer seemed to be at odds with himself in the category of "reality": he simply and completely lost sight of how he got to his position, and he unscrupulously undermined the man who endowed him with his trust. Worst of all, he was so willfully manipulative that he cradled his residents like newborn ducklings. Their devotion to him was excessively misplaced. Devotion often implies a religious experience. An academic environment should not displace the idea of respect as a sign of "disregard" for leadership in the name of "devotion". That is why Kramer's behavior was even more reprehensible. He took advantage of emotionally vulnerable people. There is no place for demagoguery in academics. His conduct was dishonest and deceptive.

The aftermath of Boston University's metamorphosis into a pre-doctoral program with independent graduate specialty departments was hardly unsettling. It happened and that was it. Spencer Frankl became Dean in a relatively unchallenged transition. But, the teaching climate was far different than the way it was in Henry's day. In consideration of that highly elaborate decade, some of the quite acknowledged and accepted thoughts are:

1. Acknowledgement of the intimate relationship between periodontal therapy and restorative dentistry in the preservation of teeth in function;
2. The place for Oral Biology and Advanced Dental Materials Research in the school setting;
3. The elevation of continuing education to a more significant role in meeting teaching objectives for practicing dentists;
4. The plethora of new clinical journals that continue to come on the market as communication vehicles;
5. Advancing technologies and their dissemination in graduate programs and continuing education programs;

6. Cottage industries which emerged to encourage faculty participation in advanced teaching methodologies; eg. ADEA/AAL: Institute for Teaching and Learning; started by N. Karl Haden, PhD; an in-depth compendium of courses offered to teaching faculties to fine tune their skills and self-awareness; a very awakening experience that should be on any dentist's agenda going into teaching! Truly a must in this regard![120]

7. Increased participation in professional association meetings with more meaningful continuing education programs for practicing dentists;

There are many other upgrades in dental education which have emerged since the BUSGD days, but clearly Henry set the stage. This was his greatest contribution which was incidental at the time, yet monumental.

Unfortunately, along came "...the epoch of incredulity". As Charles Dickens implored when he clearly expostulated his reasoning for man's pitfalls when power, greed and wealth take control and behavior leads to collapse. In this line of thought, Henry set standards so high that like the outgoing tide, the ships in the harbor would settle with the water. Over time standards have been lowered due to changes contrary to the health of the profession. In a review of The Marquis of Halifax (1633-1695), George Savile presents one of his most relevant statements:

> *"They who are of the opinion that money will do everything*
> *may very well be suspected to do everything for money."*[121]

With that in mind, dental education has lapsed into an eternal divide. Assuredly, what Periodontists were once they are no longer, and

---

[120] Hayden, N. Karl, President and Founder of ADEA?AAL, Institute for Teaching and learning, *Article by N. Karl Hayden, PhD*, Copyright 2009, Journal of The American Dental Association.

[121] Savile, George: *Miscellanies by the most noble George Lord Saville, late Marquis and earl of Halifax. Viz.I. Advise to a daughter. ...VII Maxims of state*, Copyright 2010, Published by ECCO, Print Editions (Paperback); opening.

what they are today they should not be. What general dentists were they are no longer, and what they are they should not be. It has become literally an income generated profession. Dentistry, as a profession, evolved through the gradual refinement of educational standards. As practiced today and seen through the eyes of Henry Goldman, it has devolved by virtue of the wayward application of technologies. The technologies have become thrust upon the public through fiduciary interests aside of formal training.

It is a triad of controlling entities: technology companies-continuing education-general practitioner. Specialty programs in Periodontics and Prosthodontics, once the purveyors of periodontal prosthesis (and even implant prosthesis) are no longer a financial investment for the future when repayment of educational specialty expenses and loans will be generated in competition with the general practitioner whose investment is paltry and academically inadequate by comparison. Why would anyone make this financial commitment in today's world? Even Endodontists in many locales have experimented with implant placement to generate more income. As stated, Oral Maxillofacial surgeons in many areas are competing with M.D.s (Plastic Surgeons) for similar reasons. Orthodontists are niche protected. The point is that the dental profession has become monetized since falling victim to corporate intrusion into both the academic milieu and the marketplace. At some point, a return to quality will require the profession take back control. And, this will require leaders of the profession to have "a come to Jesus moment" with themselves for the sake of the future. It is important to realize that when children act improvidently, it is the fault of the parents. And, as Henry said over and over: "You don't know what you know 'til you know it"![122] It is very disturbing to see how general practitioners practice today way above their training when they do not know what they do not know! And, specialists, the well-mannered victims of this boondoggle, continue on often "bailing out mistakes" as opposed to treating the dental public in ways for which they were trained. And, this is not the complete story, but one of the major reasons why

---

[122] Conversations with author over many years.

liability actions are increasing. Henry foresaw this as a consequence of continuing education abuse, but it is way beyond "the Rubicon"! (64)

As the Marquis of Halifax reflected about money, dentistry has become a money pursuit. Dentistry is a profession run as a business, not a profession purely run as a business. And, dentists understand money as their basis of financial survival, but often confuse their success being measured solely in terms of their wealth. Money is certainly not a bad thing, except when it becomes the be-all and the end-all of one's raison d'etre. A good definition is: the sixth sense that keeps the other five functioning. Money should be a means to an end, not the end pursuit devoid of the means to provide value. If a dentist is in business to make money, then he should be in business. As Warren Buffett, financier and industrial mogul, so admirably expressed so well in what must have been a reflection of "the ideal": "Price is what you pay. Value is what you get" (177) In short, dental education today is commercially driven, similar to the lobby effect on Congress. Commercial enterprises lobby institutions with their products and provide equipment, services and materials to exploit their presence to capture the business of future dentists. This is especially common to continuing education programs, journal advertising, and anywhere whereby commercial enterprises can front dentists for their attention and business. This would not be totally nefarious except that general dentists have forgotten who they are. They are no longer "general" anything, at least in their own minds. They indulge in all things "special", at least if it will bring more business and more "money". In the fond memory of the Marquis of Halifax, they can and will "…do everything for money". (109) It is certainly legal, but often very unethical. The advent of Implant Dentistry has vitiated the field of Periodontics to the point where they are either in an endless loop chasing for their share of the business with "general" dentists who take continuing education courses solely for the money it brings. Saving teeth has been diminished: savable teeth are lost to implants, implants are often placed inaccurately, and eventually treated for further remuneration by techniques developed for its widespread occurrence under the category: "failing-ailing" implants. Unfortunately, this has even been driven by continuing education courses marketed for anyone, and sometimes by dentists who coat-tailed with an oral surgery department never actually qualifying in a certification program. This is disturbing at all levels, but it is the result of the loss of integrity. It cannot be just fluffed out as forgetfulness or arrogance. Specialists are benefiting from increased quality of training, but at a cost. General Practitioners are very limited, but enjoy the politics of acceptance. Unfortunately, the end-game victim is the patient.

There was a time when Henry Goldman was proud of the direction dentistry was going. But, the profession has lost its way, and "political correctness" does not permit its direction to be corrected. Like the rearing of a child, if there is not enough timely discipline, eventually that child will grow up to be an out of control monster until enough mistake making compels them to "grow up" in "an ah-ha moment". Perhaps in some cases there will be some with an indwelling measure of sound common sense and they will defy the odds. Severely undertrained for what they do, "general" dentists are over-trained for what they do not want to do. Getting back to Mark Twain's allusion: "Training is everything...", thus the "general" dentist should remain within the purview of her/his education or return to training to "remediate" for what she/he would like to do in her/his practice.[123]

The profession owes it to the public domain. It cannot gloss this over, keep a blind eye and hope licensing boards and attorneys will do their job to clean out the overreach and problems. In a sense, it is good for the legal business. Continuing Education and litigation are not the solution. They will always be part of the problem. However, the system is over-cooked with "plausible deniability". Dentistry is today still an honorable profession, but it is confounding to see the "general" dentist as the "special" dentist. This was not what Henry planned. For the most part, all patients deify their dentists, not because of their competence, but because: "Oh, she/he is such a nice person"! They have become legends in their own minds, and, to the competent restorative dentists who

---

[123] Twain, Mark: *Pudd'nhead Wilson, The FamilyMark twain (Compiltion of all his books and short stories)*, Copyright 1992, Barnes and Noble.

still realize their limitations, they are a competitive nightmare. Some of the consequences: increased liability exposure, patients not knowing who is adequately trained, continuing education geared emphatically to either a relicensing need or another revenue enhancement medium, and nice sounding dental school curricula. Those that go into specialization come out in tremendous debt without any certainty that it can be paid back. And by the way, the debt pressures lead to societal issues: higher divorce rates, alimony debt, child education debt, etc.

Is "All for the best in all possible worlds"? Voltaire[124], without commenting on society in general but just taking measure of the dental profession, would more than likely say no. If Henry Goldman were alive today, he would be chagrined by the lack of idealism that captured his imagination. Continuing Education has replaced "true" graduate education to advance the "general" dentist beyond "the union card". This was never Henry's intention when he initiated continuing education programs to inform and to perhaps stimulate the minds of those who would be motivated to go into advanced training graduate programs. He never ventured that they would become "proving grounds" to learn and execute techniques with blind indiscretion. And worse, there is the head-on collision of arrogance and the "I do that syndrome", and also "political correctness" not to spoil a potential referral. That is to say, the "general" dentist no longer feels general. He is buoyed by the feeling she/he is now "special" particularly after a few procedures enrapturing her/his ego. The end result is the lofty feeling that "I do that" and why do I need the specialist, who will never say anything (except to moan to her/his specialty colleagues) as the true guardian of "political correctness". And, of course, this "political correctness" goes right up the food chain to The American Dental Association and the specialty organizations. In this "maddening" behavior, everyone is a loser. Henry Goldman's continuing education premise was not "plausible deniability", it was a "positive affirmation" of the integrity of the education process. The leaders in dental education today would be very

---

[124] Voltaire (nom de plume) aka Francois-Marie-Arouet: *Candide (Translated by Lowell Bair)*, Copyright 1959, bantam Dell (Reprint Edition).

hard pressed to understand. Either by living in the proverbial "white ivory tower" protected from the realities of practice, their perceptions would be limited by their exposure. In a sense, dental education today is a throwback to Oscar Wilde's "art for art sake" (123) and not its core intention: the generic scientific inquiry which emboldens the advancement of knowledge. This wisdom is pursued only at the highest level of the profession: in the research laboratories and in all the specialties. However, to the "general" practitioner it is a figment of her/his imagination. In the world of the "general" practitioner if it there is no financial gain, it is a total drain. When throwaway dental journals are presenting evidenced-based articles by generalists who can derive their information from a medical textbook or journal, it's insulting to those who have been through remediated training programs. When they demonstrate techniques specialists do commonly without fanfare, it is "political correctness" that prevails and plants the seeds which furthers the continued compromise of the profession.

There is enough validity with seasoned, masterfully trained educators to push back against continued mediocrity. So much is the foundation of what became germane to teaching institutions generations ago. The 'reinvention of the wheel" is a pattern in all aspects of dental education today. Classic literature has been buried like Styrofoam in trash facilities. It doesn't biodegrade and will linger in perpetuity if resourced productively. Today's dentists are counter-intuitive. They simply want to replace "old materials" and create a new spin for marketing new cosmetic presentations with "new materials" on "Old Vehicles". This is truly Oscar Wilde's world of "Art for art's sake." Lost in the mix is what a Boston University or a University of Pennsylvania trained Prosthodontist, trained fully in Periodontal Prosthesis, would consider in a full diagnostic evaluation of the patient's stomato-gnathic health or lack thereof.

Henry had his day in the sun, and it was not without meaning and historical importance. His guidance was inspirational, his wisdom sobering, but his untiring message was consequential and timeless: study and learn the ideal because it projects value forever. Henry was never one to condone cutting corners. He rejected quick fixes and short term solutions. He saw the big picture and sacrificed everything for quality. His guide was his intuition. But, his legacy is his honor and high ethical standards by which he lived. Ultimately, this was always his tape measure for success.

CHAPTER 12

Dental Practice Today: Progress? Hidden Secrets and Issues: Malpractice, Regulation, Cost Cutting, Technology (ies), and "The Clinics"!

So much has changed in dentistry since Lester Burket, then the Dean at The University of Pennsylvania School of Dental Medicine, approached Henry Goldman to lay the groundwork for a Department of Periodontology. The early 1950's are light years away from days when dental practitioners enjoyed very simple times. Perhaps this juncture may be considered the watershed moment in the modern historical record for the dental profession. It was the beginning of the end of "old time" dentistry and the maiden voyage into horizons never even imagined prior to the war. Up to that point, Henry's entire professional life involved his work in general and oral pathology. The major gift that his rather reclusive past could never have projected was his fortunate timing to meet Kurt Thoma. There were pathologists in the dental profession, but Kurt Thoma was the clinician who strengthened The Massachusetts General Hospital when he instituted the residency program in Oral Surgery. (66) Even though the field of Periodontology had been around for many years at that point, it had not become the focal point of a dental practice. Though it had conceptually set the stage for changing where the emphasis of dental health should lay, it was not until Henry came around and established the full blown administrative foundation for a certified, credentialed department with its first graduate students.[125] It is hard for dentists today to imagine what Henry must have been thinking. Someone could suggest that perhaps he wasn't thinking that deeply nor projecting thoughts to the future. Well, then they did not know Henry Goldman because his thinking never idled. Assuredly, he was most likely in the moment, but his expectation was not "ho hum". Lester Burket was also an oral pathologist with a clinical interest in the field of Oral Medicine which, at that time, was unfortunately only an "interest field". Truly a problem! He wrote the original great textbook in Oral Medicine but it was not a fast growing field because it did not have its own department as a recognized ADA specialty. (17,137) Even for those days it was too scientifically based requiring more of an educational study for the average practitioner. And, for the general practitioner it is a "specialty" without money making value. And, it requires very lengthy technical training. However, Henry and Lester had a common interest that would be the wellspring for clinical advances which would be actively forthcoming. The greatest influence on Henry's interest in Periodontics was the very man who had a network connection with both: Kurt Thoma. It seems historically that no matter how big the world expanded it always defaultedto just the few who always seemed to be the trendsetters!

History can be written with so many slants and opinions, sometimes losing the facts in opinion or from some argument that springs from prejudice or misconnected evidence. There are also people who believe that what they create or do will earmark them for a very special place in the annals of their particular niche. Simply put: being pegged!

Dentistry has its share of the latter. Henry was too plain and unconcerned to even remotely think like this. Throughout his whole life he enjoyed doing what he did but always seemed to avoid the limelight. He embraced more of the refrain of a Pathologist than a Periodontist even though he was heavily invested with both. The former was the true academic, the latter engulfed by the fanfare and show which gave this specialty more public presence. By the time Henry got to Boston University it was easy to see that his personality was more comfortable

---

[125] See Appendix #2.

away from the limelight. He was not the philosophical type who reflected ever on his purpose. He mused over principles and possibilities. And, if it had any meaning, Henry was never driven to comment or engender a serious discussion on its history. He certainly had a very acute sense of where was headed and what the future would bring. He did possess a very informed, analytical side which made him easily conversant on subjects like public health, liability, government regulation and interference with healthcare delivery, technology advances in reference to teaching and practice, private clinics and their effect on the quality of care, and the advertising/marketing which opened up private practice competition (influenced by trends set forth by the Supreme Court decision in Bates v. The State Bar of Arizona in 1977). (215) For a man who was always so laconic he always had an opinion on this subject matter. To this end, it would seem only fitting that he would because of his firmly held opinions he always held with regard to the importance of continuing education. The depth of his thinking was quite significant, particularly in view of his rather also-ran fluency with words. He was never thrilled with flimflam, showboating or cavalier behavior. He had very firm opinions so he had a very short attention span and tolerance for nonsensical ideas. The medical aspects of oral health and disease sparked his greatest interest because they were the heart of where he wanted to focus dental education. This was truly his intellectual center of gravity, framing the oral health-disease association with metabolic organ system flux. It was his feeling that so much of the phlegmatic, disinterested behavior of dental politics contributed to the snail's pace in reshaping old guard curricula in dental schools. Even today the upgrades are very slow and shallow. He was always bothered by a lack of vision to reformat the four year dental curriculum to reflect where the specialty training programs are. His concern with the great divide between the "general" dentist and the "special" interest dentist would be very upsetting today. It seems that the more things change nothing changes. Stodgy denial and complacency bothered him as if it were intellectual entropy.

Chasing change with blind faith can be very destructive, particularly if the change feeds on one of the more cynical aspects of human personality: greed. When advertising became a commonplace standard for all professional-business marketing, it ran "the proverbial horse out of the barn" undeterred and unbridled. To the more respectable, more reserved personality, this seemed aberrant and risky. This seriously concerned Henry whose reflections on ethics starred down this unfortunate change. It was difficult enough to hold the practice of dentistry to a reasonable degree of self-restraint. Open advertising, like the ambulance chasing lawyer created open season for the "general" dentist to advertise to a public always more concerned with cost rather than the health consequences. The responsibility of the dental profession to educate the public beyond advertising and marketing of products has always been inviolable. However, "the greed factor", "the selling of product", and "merchandising" has also never been ethically regulated, even it has meant educating the public. The "monetization" of everything related to health has always been in the "catbird seat". To Henry, it was the profession working at cross-purpose with the public health in mind! Also, and very unfortunately, liability lawyers have never adjudged imperatives based on ethical subtleties. They only see "risk" as an equal opportunity business. The enticement through advertising just created another vehicle along with continuing education "technique courses" to inveigle dentists into treatment options without due considerations to required specialty training. No single event in the law worked more to conflict with what Henry was trying to achieve in terms of advancing criteria as guidelines for all levels of dental education. Advertising and marketing became the invisible "800 pound gorilla in the room". Balancing opportunity with the very alluring financial incentives was imposing, especially with the putative "quality control" continuing education courses sanctioned by the ADA working at cross purposes. The world of implant dentistry is the most obvious example, particularly when a third year was extended to the training of Periodontists to implement an advanced formal training element of quality control. However, it was designed to offer implants as an alternative, not as a replacement to periodontal therapy. This was (and continues to be) the ultimate in hypocrisy: make specialists train longer, yet "general" dentists can take weekend courses! Where is the ADA? It's not a matter that someone is asleep at the switch. It all about "the monetization of society"! Recalling Mark Twain once more: "Training is everything...." The panoply of ethical questions this has opened up would not make a very cogent argument for "progress". This conundrum is tacitly suggested in Bertrand Russell's *Authority and The Individual*:

> "*Progress...requires the utmost scope for personal initiative that is compatible with social order.*"[126]

The social order here is just simply in disarray and disorder. Professional organizations, licensing boards, and personal responsibility seem to be all in a maelstrom.

This sounds pretty harsh, but most defense attorneys will admit that dentists are their own worst enemies. When seeing new patients, they're known for comments to them like: "My gosh, where did you get that work done", "I can get you out of trouble from your failing dental work", "If you don't replace the work in your mouth, you are going to lose all your teeth", "I haven't seen that kind of work ever, I think we ought to discuss replacing it all", etc.. The commentary is purely detrimental for everyone. It's pure troublemaking, and nothing very good comes of it. And yet, these are the same individuals who practice blithely way beyond the scope of their training until they are caught in a malpractice transgression. Then their life turns on itself and they become "born again reformers". Henry always spoke about the irreverence up and down the dental profession food chain. The very transformation of Boston University to a predominantly pre-doctoral program was illustrative of the "hypocrisy of educational standards". The practical side of this thinking unfortunately is similar to the public outcry for murder rates in the country. It does make a difference whether someone is pro-guns or anti-guns or whether someone believes gun control will

---

[126] Russell, Bertrand: *Authority and the Individual*, Copyright 1949, Simon & Schuster.

lower murder rates (or, that people kill, guns do not kill). What matters is that murder is monetized as a practical circumstance. The control of murder rates will always be an endless loop argument! This similar line of thinking is similar in dentistry. As long as ethics takes a back seat to the monetizing of all dental education issues as they relate to practice, there will never be a modus vivendi. Henry was not so naïve that he could not see this, but he was a consensus builder and he continued to fight for reasonable thinking both in specialty education and proper regulation in continuing education.

This is not the domain for a discussion on professional deportment, but it is important to realize that there is a food chain which is layered as any business. The American Dental Association is at the very top for anything relating to the governance of education for dentists, accreditation of dental specialties, providing supportive programs for dentists, and providing assistance in many ways for schools, public programs benefiting the general public, and other features to further the national dental public health. It is not a legal sanctioning body and a dentist does not have to belong to practice within the 50 states. But, in its purview, its oversight enables a reasonable control of practice through The National Board of Dental Examiners. Through the administration of exams to would-be dentists, their exams must be passed to take a state licensing board examination. So, there is an interchange of responsibilities to which both practicing prospects and existing practicing dentists must adhere. Ethical behavior is something out of the realm of control, except in the mind of the practitioner. But, certainly, a pattern of unethical conduct can promote misguided commentary and reactions which can lead to liability complaints. That is why Bertrand Russell's statement is so pertinent. "Personal initiative"…must be "compatible with social order". (104) There is no governing body in existence which can regulate stupidity. Ethical misguidance and misconduct fall back on issues related to the social order: family, good parenting, peer pressures growing up, teacher guidance at all levels of education, and a positive spiritual feeling for human values.

Henry Goldman was the product of a broken home, but he had

a smart, very forceful mother. She had working class sense with an appreciation for hard work and respect for authority. The sense of purpose and drive for achievement derived from his mother remained very evident throughout his entire life. He knew that if he worked hard he could open up the doors holding in all the possibilities for success. His older brother would always say: "Good looks and good personality will get you in the door, but it won't keep you in the room".[127] Well, Henry will never be remembered for his ebullience, but he was one of the most pleasant, unassuming people of his stature. He was keenly aware of his brother's common sense rallying cry. And, as a young man, he was lean, athletic and good-looking, but his mother would never let him think good looks would advance his prospects. In addition, his mother would never allow even the slightest transgression or occasional laziness. His brother would always preach that there are two personality types which are intolerable: "a liar and a cheat". The direction he received as a growing youth and through his professional training compelled him to dismiss unethical behavior and what he called "quick fix" education. He view that with dismay and concern. It was antithetical to everything he felt about life. It was a violation of his upbringing and sense of "right and wrong". Perhaps too much simplicity, but Henry was as fundamental as a person could be. To really understand how Henry Goldman was able to achieve so high, then it is important to understand that all his thinking was derived through his mother. He was naturally attracted to people like Kurt Thoma and Paul Boyle because of these perceptions. His home life conflated with sense of purity he derived from his mentors as he climbed up the academic ladder. It was almost pre-ordained, but certainly conditioned, that he would respect education in its spirit to allow shortcuts, tolerate charlatanism, or a cult of mind control. In lecturing all over the world as a Dean, he was all purpose with the ultimate integrity. He was of the mindset that to achieve "do it with legitimacy".

If Henry were called today on issues like malpractice, regulation, cost cutting in educational support, technology and private dental

---

[127] Conversations with author.

clinics, it should be understandable at this point where he would come down. Realistically, he would never expose himself to public recrimination or commentary so he would be silent. He just would never put himself in the crosshairs of the collective attention on such sensitive subjects. That does not mean he would not have nor share his opinion because he held very definite opinions on the subjects. "The father of Russian socialism", Alexander Herzen (1812-1870), also a highly respected philosopher wonderfully captures some of these thoughts in the following:

> *"Human development is a form of chronological unfairness, since late-comers are able to profit by the labors of their predecessors without paying the same price."*[128]

And, late-comers in dentistry today are very much unappreciative of their predecessors. If they held a deeper respect, they would respect educational training with a far deeper meaning.

So much of this kind of inequity manifests in dullness and lethargy. There are many ranges of thought to define success, but the first and foremost is monetary. And, likewise the inference of the "gold standard" of hard work and unwavering ethical conduct in the pursuit of monetary gain is a back seat argument.. This is most discernible in a "general" practice where nothing is "general" and all is about "specialty care" where the financial reward is much higher. Misrepresentation and unfairness are veiled in many disguises, but often underneath the false mask which feigns skills to patients. Inevitably, Henry would see this pure and simple for what it was, and continues to be: misrepresentation, simple and clear.

Understandably, "the buck" stops with the business professional: the dentist, not the professional businessman. However, examine the circumstances when a dentist meets the patient for the first time. This is known as an initial patient exam and evaluation, or more appropriately a consultation. In an ideal world this allows the patient-dentist

---

[128] Arendt, Hannah: *On Violence, Copyright 1970*, Harcourt Brace-Javanovich..

time to assess one another in terms of communication and manner of mutual comfort. The reality is though that the general practitioner is going to perceive it as a business transaction, the byproduct of which is the dentistry she/he produces (sells). Too cold to accept. It's reality. The expectations may be very different as the perceptions are construed through conversation. Patients generally do not understand what they are told because they are not channeled into something as foreign as dental treatment. In this regard, it is so imperative to be basic in communication and to be a good listener. It is unfortunate that there are a great number of practitioners who clearly fail this.

The reality today is that most general practitioners practice way out of their skill levels, education achievement, and experience. In today's world of private health clinics this is a rampant problem, and, it is escalating the numbers of complaints and liability settlements. This seems to be a desultory scenario as the world of private practice is tiered according to neighborhoods and their socio-economic structure. At the lowest level are "dental mills", and, the highest level the refined, high level quality practices. The divide with shades of differences up and down the economic ladder are greater today than ever. But, even in Henry's day this was proportionally a similar narrative. The reality is that a general practice should be like an information center as well as a source of care for the sake of informed communication and treatment. With so much economic distress in the world today, it is not practical to assume this real life patient-dentist relationship. At the lowest level it is pure business and poor dentistry. At the very top of the economic ladder, practice is elegant and pure (and, responsibly remunerative). The majority in between these book end conditions is a medley of numbers none of which operate similarly. Evidence shows an elevated number of liability cases which suggests a great decrease in quality care. (171,161,211) Henry tried to marginalize the dilettante who was pure business and locked into low level care with indifferent concern. His solution to this was through education at the most formative level: thus his basis for curriculum change in dental education. Patients' expectations have always varied in dental IQ as per their life experience, but dentists should not vary their standards: education-communication-fealty should be universally applied. Henry always said the burden should be on the dentist to make this commitment.[129]

How many practitioners tell their patients how they derived their training; eg. from a series of weekend trips over a nine month period? Beguiled because "my dentist is a nice woman/man", the unwitting public is not expected to assess differences in training. The public depends on a culture of controls built into the continuation education-licensing board-academic axis to properly referee themselves in behalf of the lay public. But, as Henry always proposed: the glow of money is blinding. And, the specialists who are self-serving enough to teach the courses have a rather impassive, arrogant stake in this very remunerative venture. When specialists teach "procedures" on weekend courses, they are providing the neophyte-the learning general dentist with sophisticated information who have not been schooled enough to understand nuances of case selection, the depth of important background science, and the decision making tree analysis. When information on surface is simple, but very complex to its core, the superficially educated are blind to risk and consequences. Unfortunately, the more someone learns the more that someone realizes what she/he doesn't know. Therefore, the dentist diving into complicated therapies does so without that limiting threshold of risk. Henry was very aware of the dentist wandering blindly into procedures learned the weekend before. Truly one of the great conundrums and ironies in advanced dental education is: The higher up the ladder in quality education, the greater the responsibility for recertification to specialty boards. The less qualified who take weekend courses in very sophisticated specialty areas are responsible to no person or entity until they are exposed for malpractice. That is the cold, blunt reality!

Most general practitioners are congenial enough to squeak by and sweet talk their patients out of their mistakes. This is the kaleidoscopic picture in that cavernous divide between the top tiered dentist and the very bottom where the unfortunate are "milled" with misfortune.

---

[129] Author's communications with Henry.

Some people may call this akin to "the real public dental health", the average person not the fortunate who are well served in financially comfortable communities where they are more than likely to be availed of a higher standard of care, hopefully?

Is this progress? Henry would suggest no, but he would fault the bureaucratic system through its own fashioned "Peter Principle" whereby the most unskilled, uncaring and unprincipled rise to the top through their own unsavory social-political attributes. 'Political correctness" as in "pure politics" makes it unfashionable, too truculent and suicidal (for its own financial harmony) to make even the most minimal reforms in the complex system. Henry would always comment that it's too far gone to canoodle the politically connected. Then he would guffaw out of frustration (like a frustrated twitch) if no one was around. Henry was not, most definitely, a crusader campaigning and fighting for reformation. Hardly. No laws are broken, practitioners are well within licensing regulations, and institutional programs (as well as the massive numbers of private continuing education companies) comply with all administrative requirements as well. Alluded to repeatedly, it's all about ethical standards and the way society embraces codes of honesty, honor, and integrity, everything Len Marrella [130]discusses in his writings. The very linear upbringing Henry derived from his stern mother, who was short on patience, unforgiving and unsympathetic for deceit or dishonor, emboldened him to an almost saintly respect for virtue and clean living. People today would call him very old guard. However, a small measure of return to "an ideal standard" would be constructive.

Malpractice is one area that Henry projected as the great anathema because it defiled a person's honor. Dragging a practitioner through the injustice of the legal system was like exposing the king without clothes. If only dentists understood this weighty and punishing experience enough to reform their attitudes and the way they practice. Unfortunately, they are very naïve as to the true nature and onerous nature of the legal process. The preponderance of hard working dental

---

[130] Marrella, Len: *In Search of Ethics: Conversations with Men and Women of Character,* Copyright 2009, DC Press, A Division of Diogenes Consortium, Sanford, Florida.

practitioners are not without some soft area that can be easily victimized by a patient with some misguided ill-intent. The best defense
against this is education. And, Henry often said that risky practice is
no different than putting out a fire with bare hands. Even though there
are a number of dentists who set a poor example for the honorable
majority, the legal system is rigged against the practitioner. This has
never changed. The licensing boards clearly constructed to protect the
consumer are aggregates of venal and ignoble vigilantes masquerading
as sagacious dental practitioners in service to their compatriots. They
are political opportunists who savor their power and willfully demean
the spirit of any dentist, specialist or generalist. Dentists are very, very
naïve to this, even the arrogant ones. Guilty and never innocent by any
measure is their mantra. "The legal process" and the venturesome, tan-
talizing "game of chicken" a licensing board plays with a practitioner's
professional life the majority of the time is both dehumanizing and serpentine. For the true villains, it would benefit a little devil's den therapy,
but, for the most part, dentists are forthright and undeserving of such
medieval-like mentalities who mete out their punishments with a very
cold disposition. It's almost as if these urchin-like misanthropes appear
generationally from some dark place below the mantle of the earth. The
truth is that if dentists were more educated about the true nature of
malpractice litigation, they would keep their noses clean in all regards.
This does not apply to the very isolated case of misfortune. However,
dentists are generally as uninformed and sadly naïve as Sunday school
choir girls at an exorcism for amusement. Having to endure the length
of the legal process is so draining that it is not only disruptive to a practitioner's daily practice schedule for years, but it also breaks up marriages
and contiguous relationships. And, by the time some legal endpoint
brings the curtain down on some form of monetary agreement that
was forever in the coming, then the licensing board is then given its
"good-ole-time" to extract its own "pound of flesh" from what's left of
the practitioner's emotional bearings. (182)

The dental practitioners are sold a bill of goods by their insurance
risk management carriers with all the frivolous, soft-peddling pap they

serve them with their courses for premium reductions and license renewal. This is their self-serving way of pretending they are in control of practitioner's propensity for misguided violations of practice standards. Well, the truth is that dentists would be very circumspect about their malpractice susceptibilities if they were truly lectured in no uncertain terms about what really happens as cases play out. The fault of the system is they are terribly uninformed and tragically in the dark about its "dirty secrets" ex post facto. One day of informed lecturing every biennial licensing period would "scare them straight". There will always be some that will taunt the system, but so be it and let them learn the hard way. Henry was always fraught with disgust the way the system was constructed, foisting "the innocent" so cavalierly up to a hot barbecue of salivating, egomaniacal henchmen so ready to display their privilege of power. Henry would decry this as a horrible abuse of power and far less than a sense of progress. The interesting aspect of this is the brazen dentist will always be brazen until he knuckles under to his likewise brazen peers, but finally being demeaned enough to finally submitting to "a come to Jesus moment" with the reality of their imperiousness and emotional battering. Dental Licensing Boards are composed of self-serving "dental piranha" who assert their lust for power by seemingly enjoy the process as a sport. This human regression is well depicted in C.S. Lewis's *"Pilgrim's Regress"* (81) as his puritan central character, John, searches for his "ideal", a utopian island of sanctuary, which is seemingly more elusive as he is taken down by all of life's obstacles. The man-to-man evils are quite telling. It would be educational to understand how the pain of facing the legal system is not worth the transgressions in which dentists find themselves so often, and quite naively. Well, Henry, if alive today, would see all the elements involving malpractice as a sordid mess. He would, as he so often did, see it as a mindless pit of endless theatrical sorcery without any benefit to anyone. Or, maybe the lawyers, who always get paid! Anyone with experience with serving as an expert would make this suggestion: anyone can make a mistake, but anyone who makes a mistake must at least be properly trained for the level at which she/he is practicing. This was (and continues to be) Henry's thesis for specialty education.

Regulation is like a constantly shrinking girdle with its oppressively burdensome demands and constraints. Jokingly, Henry would say: "good for some, bad for others"[131]. It is the eternal Brett Harte tug-of war: some good in the worst, some bad in the best.[132] Consolidation of power in too few hands for the benefit of the majority is overly onerous and is the ultimate source of corruption. The grievous misfortune is that some need oversight and the greater numbers do not. Some controls are good in life to remind people to walk "the straight and narrow" when others are affected. It is a safe assumption that human nature is such that a little coddling and a bit of indulgence like a parent to a potentially wayward child is necessary when the greater good is at stake. Yet, at some point, overreach and vexatious intrusions become intolerable and unproductive. Enter stage right: government controls and regulations! Did anybody say or hear "government revenue enhancement"!

Be it local, regional or national, before Henry Goldman died on July 23, 1991, the dental profession was well into being drawn into the ever increasing regulatory controls of government. The trial of Dr. David Acer[133][134] a dentist with AIDS practicing in Florida, brought national attention and focus to his infecting six patients. One of his patients, Kimberly Ann Bergalis, died on December 8, 1991 at age 23 and was the subject of a CBS "60 Minute" program which created pejorative fall-out to the dental profession. Soon thereafter with the Occupational Safety and Health Administration Act of 1970 for the monitoring and safety controls for business, OSHA regulations were launched heavily into health and safety controls and monitoring of every dental practice in the USA, be it private practice, clinics, schools and hospitals.(192) Most of what OSHA brought in its very large monitoring notebook to the

---

[131] Another Goldmanism.

[132] Harte, Bret: *The Outcasts of Poker Flats,* Copyright 2013, Create Space Independent Publishing Platform.

[133] www.nytimes.com/1993/06/06/weekinreview.

[134] Ciesielski, C.A. et al.: *"The 1990 Florida Dental Investigation, The Press and The Science,"* Copyright 1994, Annals of Internal Medicine.

dental practice in the way of infection control utilized the Acer-Bergalis case to co-opt control out of the hands of the individual state licensing boards to a multilayered federal system. This was a watershed moment for the dental profession. "Big Brother" was now everywhere watching over every dentist in the United States. Like a contagion, its effect was to induce a flurry of other aspects of enhanced controls in dentistry: state relicensing requirements, continuing education programs as cottage industries, enhancement of coverage for ADA site visits for dental schools, specialty board certification requirements were markedly upgraded, etc. Another federal money grab, "the monetization" repechage! The point is that there was a welling up of controls within the dental profession which began to reformat the entire structure of practice and institutional requirements. Every year or with legislative periodicity new (and not necessarily qualitative) changes were in the offing. HIPPA (Health Insurance Portability and Accountability Act of 1996) (174) was another example of government asserting its power to regulate patient information, record transfers, fraud involving insurance, etc. Edward Kennedy, who, as Massachusetts junior senator, always wanted a one-payer medical insurance system (from the early 1970's) was its legislative power source. When he gained influence years later as senior senator, he was a prime power behind HIPPA being passed in 1996 (and, being otherwise known as The Kennedy-Kassebaum Act after the two political sponsors of the original congressional bill) (169) This law passed and became known as HIPPA.

The bottom line is that it is prudent to have controls for the welfare of society at-large, but the federal government exercises power with overreach and the longer its burdensome laws expand over time, the people (and, in this case, dentists) are victimized by their regulatory harassment. And, of course, it is another overreach of government which increases office overhead which transfers to increase costs for the patient. Government regulation has become the ultimate albatross for the practitioner.

Henry was a longtime Democrat and always supported more public policy which favored healthcare delivery for people who found it unaffordable. He therefore believed it was the role of government should have a role in support of facilitating legal support structures, but with strong limitations. He believed strongly in free market capitalism. That is to say, that the market place should determine the free flow of business. Unfortunately, those were days of "true liberalism", not the progressivism of today. Edward Kennedy's brother, John F. Kennedy was a throwback to the liberal who believed in limited government and fiscal conservatism. Today the term liberal is confused with progressive. OSHA and HIPPA are only two examples of the regulatory noose around the necks of practicing dentists. Of course, at the time Henry was Dean the national debt was 309 billion, and at his death in 1991 it was 3.6 trillion. Had he lived to see 18.3 trillion in 2014 he might have sung a different tune. His liberalism in the 1960's in his prime was founded in profound center-right sound business principles and socially liberal philosophies which favored opportunities for people who needed supplemental government assistance. Today's progressivism is not 1960's Liberalism by any stretch. From 1965 to 1974 the food stamp program (revived in 1961) went from one-half million to 15 million people. In that same time period the population of the USA went from 194 to 213 million people. But, these people were working and receiving supplemental food stamps (especially the farmers for whom the program was founded). Today with about 317 million people there are approximately 48 million people on food stamps (who are not working). The numbers show about 7% of the population supplemented their incomes with food stamps and today 14.5% of people who do not work and are completely out of the work force are on food stamps These facts plus the debt and all the other problems associated with the country would have jarred Henry's thinking with bold pushback. He was a fiscally sound thinker who was totally reviled by supporting the bad habits of laziness and dependency. His impoverished growing up made him sympathetic, but not so foolhardy to anoint government "Big Brother" oversight like a forever stamp. The inevitable overhead increases for a dental practice make professional life continuously burdensome, particularly with the reality there will never be retrenchment. (159,209,211)

Regulation to some extent plays a vital role, but the more the "Beast" (Government) is fed, the more it sees, needs and demands. A sow will eat interminably unless the food is taken away. As well, the more opportunity to regulate, the more regulations will come into being. The process becomes interminable because power feeds on itself thinking that a silk purse can be made from a sow's ear!

Most disturbing is the fact that the delivery of health care parallels the numbers displayed above. People at the top will always receive the best that's available in dental health care if they are fortunate to find the right person trained to minister to their needs. The people at the bottom contrarily are not so fortunate as their choices are limited to private, public and institutional clinics where care is suboptimal. In the *Oral Health, U.S. 2002 Annual Report* (191) age, gender, education and poverty correlate with the statements above quite accurately. With increasing education and decreasing poverty, there is an increase in the numbers who visit a dentist. However, there is no evidence for the numbers who will be able to pursue even the most modest treatment plan. Common sense must assume that, fear aside, affordability will also correlate with increasing educational levels and financial security.

So what is the point? Over-regulation disturbed Henry to no end because he saw that with increasing participation of government into the delivery of health care, there was a spike upwards in visits, but this was self-limiting. This again was the educational level factor which was never improving among the segment of the population tethered to the public clinic system. Even in neighborhoods where lower middle class people lived affordability was very constrained. Even though at the most highly regulated lower tier, the predicate of educational level determines if the patient completes any dental work. Rising upwards through the matrix of caregivers, highly regulated private offices pass on the costs to their patients. Thus, the self-fulfilling prophesy of "the wealth factor" determines delivery of dental care, but it does not reflect quality. This will always be directly related to proper training, practitioner commitment and ethical resolve.

Henry was always bothered by the platitudinous, grandiloquent federal grants to schools which on surface made for wonderful press in the spending of the tax payer dollars for various social programs. But, "the head shaker" was always the wording, "the devil in the details": to study, to evaluate, to compare, to draw attention to, to project, etc. Such wording meant a slow churning of the process where dollars upon dollars were spent with bewilderment years down the road when the money had effectuated very little, and, "they're still pondering, evaluation, considering, etc., etc. This is not to negate, to decry, or to debunk research and the role of government. As a man who spent his life in education, he felt there would be a point when the role of government would be too invested in its bureaucratic weightiness. There had to be a balance with the private sector where rising up the pay scale and getting things accomplished demands self-reliance, initiative and persistence. Like the runner, his legs must move to run, the private sector commitment stops once "the legs" stop.

Jonathan Swift (1667-1745) said in "Thoughts on Various Subjects" in *Miscellanies in Verse and Prose*":

"Vision is the art of seeing things invisible."[135]

This was Henry Goldman's greatest attribute. The invisibility of a stand-alone graduate school for the specialties in dentistry is the salient feature of his legacy. In 1962 he was drawing sketches of three dimensional pictures of soft and hard tissue regeneration in periodontally compromised teeth. He was twenty to twenty-five years ahead of the world of dental investigators. He ruminated on technologies that would embolden a good number of the specialties. He also believed that their applications for the purpose of positively impacting man would ultimately be determined by man's sense of purpose. He saw "use, misuse and abuse", the latter totally dependent on man's ethos. Joel L. Swerdlow writing in the *"National Geographic"* in an article in the October, 1995 edition on the " Information Revolution" said:

---

[135] Swift, Jonathan: *The Collected Works of Jonathan Swift,* Copyright 2009, Halcyon Press Ltd (First Edition-Unexpurgated); 19.

> *"The law of unintended consequences governs all technolog-
> ical revolutions."*[136]

No more vivid nor meaningful example in dentistry than this lies in the field of Implantology. This might be the most meaningful modern day technology in Dentistry. To some this may be historically arguable and profoundly rash. However, it is a technology which has rescued dental cripples, both physically and emotionally. The medical effects are quite numerous in the dietary and nutritional improvements that untold numbers of people have experienced. Yet, akin to the intrinsic weakness in mankind with the love of money, power and control, it is hard to anoint all of dentistry bearing down on the spiritual center of the universe. Hardly, for as stated, with every use there is misuse and abuse. To a great extent, implant dentistry has been "the golden calf", the ultimate "money grab". Without delving too deeply into the intellectual depths of a debate, it suffices to say that the alarming abuse lies in savable teeth (but, with infective periodontal disease) being extracted without treatment for the less time consuming, financial immediacy of implants. In general, a person is better off with "the "God-given" as opposed to "the man made". Obviously, the virtue of implants lies in its properly designed treatment plan when saving a tooth (or teeth) is not possible. In dental education today teaching implant dentistry has leap-frogged the teaching of saving teeth. No greater example in dentistry captures "The law of unintended consequences..." that Smerdlow identifies in his article. Henry and all the early pioneers in Periodontology saw (and still see) this as a very slippery slope. Implantology has reshaped school curricula, both at the pre-and post-doctoral levels within the domain of restorative and periodontal teaching protocols. There are areas of the country where root canal specialists are doing implants even though, most assuredly, they are way out of their training milieu. The financial incentives are too tempting. "The Clinics" noted before are notoriously heavily invested in this money making advantage. Where quality and bottom line daily

---

[136] Swerdlow, Joel J.: *Information Revolution*, Copyright 1995, National Geographic.

printouts override any patient concern, the outright business intentions make these clinics steeped in ongoing liability problems and a very high misery index for the patients forced to be there. But, the most outrage should be placed right in the laps of the powers to be in the ADA and AAP (137,143) for allowing educational institutions to vouchsafe this practice behavior. The teaching principles of Periodontics are virtually extinct with the teaching of Implantology having been relegated at all levels of pre-doctoral and post-doctoral teaching institutions. It is sinful for the patients as well as for the future of dentistry. For the immediate future, people will be born with teeth, not implants. Failure to educate future dentists in Periodontics will result ultimately in blowback, particularly as stem cell therapies and nanotechnology have a preponderant influence on dental therapies of the future. In the meantime, the extraction of savable teeth for the sake of implants is a reverse of the inviolability of precepts invoked by the pioneers of Periodontics. Worst of all, the AAP (143) should be ashamed for not standing up to the ADA in allowing this pattern to become a trend, which will have the profession condoning it the accepted method of choice to preserve the stomatognathic (oral-jaw) system in health and function. Henry would take measure of this as an educational transgression for which there is no intellectual defense.

Henry's comment was: "the pollution factor". He was, as stated, not a reformer, but he found the indignity of it all quite concerning. It is the business of the dental profession to once in a while get off its lofty perch and make good on the more pragmatic, grounding issues which are certainly a stigma, an undeniable black eye. The attraction is no different than the denture clinics which run people through on a daily basis for full mouth extractions in the morning and the insertion of full dentures in the afternoon. Their ethical defense is that they provide for the poor in the most affordable manner possible. This is very complex treatment that in Voltaire's world of "the ideal", Eldorado, would expose the ultimate self-imposed intellectual wound: "All is for the best in the best of all possible worlds" suggests that man endeavors to the maximum extent of human capability. (121) Henry would, in a moment of reflection, argue this, then sigh and say: "Soft-peddling what's important, typical!"

It is very hard to argue the politics because Henry was not interested in "the politics of life". Henry's brother, Eddie, was President of The New England Shoe Manufactures' Association for many years, always butting heads with labor unions. He proffered always: "If there is anything of extreme consequence that demands very meaningful action, never, but never, ask a politician to do it"![137] The conversation when the two got together would always involve in some manner the unsolvable issue of "cost cutting". Of course, to a shoe manufacturer this was the lifeblood of survival. The industry was unceremoniously run out of the country by high labor costs (starting in the 1960's). This was the first of a very prolonged history of manufacturing loss over many years that is poignantly seen with much chagrin today. To Henry "cost cutting" involved part time teaching appointments without pay and full time teachers working for as little as he was able to commit. To Henry's brother, Eddie, cost cutting affected the lives of hundreds of employees who lost their livelihoods when in the 1960's and 1970's shoe companies vacated the north for the southern United States where labor was affordable and "right to work laws" were in effect. That's until the unions changed that, and then factories migrated in search of "cheap" labor to Lebanon, Italy and Spain, and then eventually to the Pan-Pacific countries like Thailand, The Philippines and Malaysia. And, now today, China. However, to Henry running a dental school at the graduate level was very different from the manufacturing of a product. Like all dental schools today, part time faculty played a very big role as he curried favor with local dentists to donate their time. And, no chairman ever got rich on a full time dental salary. Such a person could augment her/his income in other ways (like lecture fees), but it was certainly not like private practice.

"Cost cutting" to Henry was "a cat and mouse" game because of the loans, grants and private donations he had to continuously chase to

---

[137] Author's note:Growing up he repeated this continuously, and within the context of a very serious declamation.

keep the school afloat. The underlying feeling Henry shared with a very deliberate stare was the fear he had for the demise of dental education if Deans of the future would all universally continue to be victims of the rarely discussed complexities of managing financial operations. This could be considered one of the great unspoken miseries Deans suffer. If there are contiguous issues which translate into a money issue (like building replacement or expansion, clinic additions, research laboratory add-ons, etc.), then the Dean becomes a fund raiser with committee management burdens. All in all, if an argument can be made for "progress" with regard to the all-around health of administration, searching for the appropriate words would be hard to source. Nothing has really changed in all these years. Dental schools are still operating under a "sword of Damocles", and, though it might seem glorious to be a Dean, it is hardly. It might be the hardest, most thankless job in dentistry. A Dean has to smile in frozen pose so often that it is a wonder their facial muscles are not in a numbing spasm. A Dean dreams of the prestige, and then one day looks in the mirror thinking "What prestige" as she/he counts the wrinkles, furrows, crow's feet, and gray hair. Whatever they are paid, it certainly is not nearly enough for all the pressures and hard work they endure. Henry's little "cat and mouse" game still survives.

It would be a casual remiss not to make a very germane, contextual comment about the impact Henry wanted to make on "the progress" of both dental education and dental practice. He held no allegiance aside of family and education. He was quite narrow in the focus of his life. But, he was dedicated and centered like no other educator. The hardscrabble of his youth really hardened him to a very Spartan life. He never grew out of that feeling. Most people from meager circumstances fantasize about what they'll do with the money they'll make. Not Henry. This was an admirable quality, but the drawback was his lack of compassion for others who were full time faculty who felt needy. It was not from a meaningful slight of their needs. He simply overlooked them quite inadvertently in concentrating his focus elsewhere. This was his habit. Any sense that his behavior was deliberate was a general misinterpretation of his intent. But, in spite of how it was perceived, full time faculty more often than not misjudged him. The people who knew him best were Alan Shuman and Gerald Isenberg, his partners. They would agree that Henry did not have one mean fiber in his body. He was so committed to the fortunes of the school that money lost personal value. Its significance to him was whatever justifiable, purposive cause it would serve in funding the school.

Ronald Reagan, former President of the United States of America, was also an actor in Hollywood (among other vocations). He once did an ad on television for a cleaning product called: "20 Mule Team Borax" (Borax being the cleaning agent, sold today by The Dial Corporation). (130) He cuddled the box in his hands near the end of the ad, looked all smiley and said very convincingly as only Ronald Reagan could do so very convincingly:

Progress is our most important product. [138]

General Electric Corporation claimed this as their motto so it is hard to know its real origin. The real factoid is how much this was buried so deeply into Henry's raison d'etre. Both Alan and Gerry would most sincerely concur how dedicated Henry was to BUSGD. It was the centerpiece around which everything revolved. In one way or another he faced head on for a very long time all the issues that have so profoundly impacted dentistry: continuing education, core course curricula, advances in laboratory investigation research, technology, appropriating the finest faculty, and railing against issues like malpractice, over-regulation, the eternal overhead conundrum, the good and bad of technology and public health. He was very often overwhelmed by the direction of dental education. Yet, with all the ups-and-downs, it would be fair to conclude that with all the creativity in the science of dentistry no man gave more and took less than he. He gave of himself like no one else. The irony is that so few really knew him, and the few that did would all agree that he was a wonderful man to know and have, particularly in all that he had to give.

---

[138] www.20muleteamlaundry.com.

CHAPTER 13

Healthcare Today: The Education Conundrum: A Return to Henry's Thinking and Proposals

If Henry were to return to the world as it is today, he would find that all is well at the university level in the education and training of young dentists. There is a general feeling throughout that dental education is de rigueur. No question about it. In fact, an argument can be made quite readily and with confidence that it is more rigorous, demanding, and productive than ever. The stringent entry requirements, the DAT (Dental Aptitude Testing) administered by The American Dental Association, and the parity among all dental schools across the United States bodes quite well for the profession. It is actually interesting to see The ADA and The ADEA (137,132 respectively) are expanding and that applications reflect an ongoing interest in the choice of dentistry as a lifetime profession. Well, now let's awake from the dream and come back to reality.

Associations are bureaucracies and do not reflect the marketplace. In the real world, job opportunities are very difficult to find today except in very up-scaled communities or major cities. If a graduating dentist with a year residency program behind her/him is lucky enough to find the rare associateship in one of these locations, then the future may be more propitious. For everyone else the chances of finding a professional home somewhere are not nearly as possible. If a young person wants a very rural community, a state not as populated, public health, an AIDS clinic, the federal prison system, or some other place where the odds are not stacked much higher, then employment may be achievable. However, income will be marginal comparatively. And then there are educational loans to be repaid.

For those who can afford to go on to specialization the future will be brighter. The metrics will be similar, but there are specialties that present more hope for a reasonable future. For example: Oral Maxillofacial Surgery, Pediatric Dentistry and Endodontics (pending location). Sadly, Prosthodontics and Periodontics are passe! In today's world, with the exception of those that practice in very highbrow areas, Prosthontists will practice like general dentists to make a reasonable living. And, general dentists, aka "restorative/cosmetic" dentists do not recognize the Prosthodontists with the respect they are entitled and deserve. Save for very niche circumstances, Periodontists have become implant specialists. Treatment of periodontal disease has become an outlier practice. That is to say, within the general practice the preponderance of patients are treated with chemical and limited surgical therapies. The Periodontist, once "the King of Diagnosis and Treatment Planning", is the dinosaur rapidly dying out. Orthodontics is a specialty unto itself. It has a life stream in its own world which flourishes on its own. It is the perfect home to those graduating dentists who want income predictability. The caveat: it is a specialty that attracts a unique personality (a very pure mathematically related science), and in very limited circumstances interrelates with mainstream practices (eg. adult orthodontic treatment for implants or bridgework). Oral Pathology is a great area for specialization, but positions are limited with very occasional turnover. Oral Medicine is finally finding itself in some hospitals as staff positions, but this is still a growing circumstance. The future will be bright is the specialty ever gains recognition. However, in spite of the capable people who have been mired in this effort, they represent a very fragmented, unaggressive leadership. Their objectives are legitimate, but their long view is skewed, off target, and aimless. Therefore, although this is an area of primary concern for the dental profession to address, the leaders necessary to effectuate the specialty's recognition are woefully disorganized, lacking purpose and laggard. Finally, academic positions, the services (Army, Navy and Air Force), and public health present reasonably remunerative lifestyles, but a dentist has to be comfortable emotionally with such a choice.

Because the dental profession is so bound to the tides of economic change, then it is imperative for any young person to be alert when it comes to life choices. The professions and some businesses fluctuate with the times. In burgeoning city growth, engineers, architects and city planners would be secure professions. In the 1950's when suburban growth exploded, general dentistry was a timely niche. However, nothing is permanent, and social-economic parameters can be very fragile so as to incur sudden upswings or downturns.

Today, the economic recession that has hung like an immovable cloud over the country. Though dental schools seem to be getting the application numbers, it is still difficult to get the prime private practice opportunities. Numbers of "chain clinics" offer opportunity, but the quality of care is inferior. Specialization is consistent in numbers, but solo practice or group practice opportunities are highly diminished. Those that find an office pay heavily to buy in with no future guarantee. Business conditions today do not predictably guarantee long term security. So, even though applications to dental schools are steady, the payback on tuition and the future practice openings are very tenuous. Even though the health of the dental profession appears to be reasonably holding in terms of applications, the private practice job opportunities do not correspondingly reflect well. The metrics for dental schools show that without foreign matriculation, many schools would be closing. All the demographics do not bode well for this generation of graduating dentists. Whether dentistry can be considered a worthwhile choice as a livelihood today is very debatable. Because dentistry is directly dependent on economic upswings and downturns, careful thought must be the sole determinant for choosing this future. Low quality clinic settings for employment are not ideal, and they have sprung up nationwide as a default choice for employment. The flurry of ideals which embrace a young dentist's ambitions can be thoroughly squashed when having to resort to this rather lowbrow, totally compromising and business driven ownership. It can really stifle a young dentist's will and impart emotional turmoil to be in what is such a hot area for litigious activity.

The quality of student is apparently well prepared for the training that is exceedingly demanding. The ADA site visits are real fitness tests to ensure the high quality level the schools purport. The facility and technology teaching upgrades are quite impressive along with exceedingly well trained faculty at all levels, be it at the pre- or postdoctoral levels. There are still important considerations that must contribute to the unfortunate disconnect from school to dental practice. Somewhere along the line there is a very significant drop off. In this regard, Henry Goldman would be very critical and bothered by how this divide can be so evident. It is necessary to examine and address this reality. Even though the education and its rigor reasonably prepare future dentists along traditional lines, the world they are entering has become so more overly complicated, regulated, and costly that financial survival has become a reasonable assumption for many.

Education at some point becomes a luxury because most practitioners are busy making a living. The world is a far more complicated place today so choices play a significant role when integrating advanced training for practice advancement. The problem is that the format of dental education has never changed I spite of Henry's very earnest entreaties during his life. It is never too late to learn, but it is late to learn what dental school has failed to teach.

The reason Henry always referenced the dental degree as "a union card" is due to the amount of attention paid to highly traditional courses that do not enhance practice competence. The amount of time spent on basic science courses during the first two years has never changed in the modern era of dental education. For years Henry talked about one comprehensive course which would take all the courses (anatomy, physiology, biochemistry, histology, etc.) and subsume them into a general review. Henry suggested a name such as "Comprehensive Basic Science Review". His idea was to integrate such a course over four years. The content would advance from basic to a more clinical adaptation over the four years to make it more practically oriented. The amount of time it would free up to allow for more enhanced clinical sciences (Oral Diagnosis, Oral Medicine, Oral Biology, etc.) in tandem with the four year schedule would result in the graduation of a far more sophisticated and better prepared dentist. Upon graduation, continuing education programs would be far more sophisticated, transcending the traditional cookbook style today that mere prepares dentists as "technique programmers" (without sufficient science based understanding). This would put students way ahead of the curve upon graduation. Henry acutely understood that dental schools educate defensively as they have long been subject to PhD educators who have been instrumental along with dental scientists planning the four year program without deference to change and adaptation to changing times. Dental schools are not preparing physiologists, pharmacologists, biochemists, histologists, etc. It is sufficient to integrate these sciences compatible with the clinical applied dental technique courses for far greater meaning. And, the formatting of the National Boards should be changed to adapt to the curricula reprogramming. Henry often suggested how much more prepared and refined the graduating dentist would be for clinical practice.

Even graduate programs belabor residents with basic science reviews that could and should be replaced with incisive comprehensive reviews. Henry always bemoaned the ponderous, parochial nature of the ADA not to refine and modernize course curricula. Whatever be the reason: laziness, egomania or vested financial interests, it is simply a lost opportunity. Dental students graduate, take licensing boards, go into one year general practice residency programs, or go into specialty programs, all spending more time re-reviewing all the basic sciences they will all forget again. It is insanity, the repetition of the same scholastic process thinking a new result will be in the offing. There is no benefit and contributes very little to enhance the dental student's overall clinical acumen.

In Henry's day, this was as much reaching for the stars as it is today. Incomprehensible as it may be, the thinking was that if the regular basic sciences in their classic format are stripped away, the result will be a severely diminished dentist. Not so fast, this is exactly what makes this continued thinking so obsolete. "The stodgy, recalcitrant old guard" seemingly will never adapt their thinking to a new dynamic and for-ward-looking viewpoint.. There is no doubt that learning is a wonderful luxury, but why spend so much time studying kidney function, the sensitivity of beta cells in the islets of Langerhans, etc.. It is not anything that a comprehensive science review given with input by a wide cross section of faculty could not satisfy in a stunningly more perspicacious manner. "Science for science sake" is the Oscar Wilde "art for art's sake" (124) equivalent. The problem is that clinical direction is far more im-portant. Unfortunately, dentists graduating today may be educated for what they are taught, but they are not sufficiently knowledgeable to a very significant degree for what they should be. These are intelligent people who should be biometrically programmed for far greater profi-ciency and understanding of the clinical sciences.

The key to education is in information transfer and to ensure that its value is retained with "periodic updating". This is the very defini-tion of "continuing" a professional's educational experience through-out life. For the most part, the four year dental curriculum has stifled this. It is unquestionably more rigorous due to more information avail-able to learn. Yet, the graduating "general" dentist is still pretty much "the mechanical" operative dentist well short of understanding the periodontium in health and disease. Most general dentists have a cav-alier attitude about periodontal disease. They will shrug it off like they fully understand its pathogenesis and treatment, but as Henry so often said: "They only know what they know when they know it." All the throwaway journals in the world are no substitute for upfront clinical teaching based on classroom instruction. This confluence is what is inadequate at the pre-doctoral level. And, it is typically brushed aside. The truth is that the mind must absorb information which will direct eyes to see and then allow the mind to recalibrate for interpretation. Reading throwaway journals and attending continuation education courses are insufficient unless dental schools "train" students making eye-mind coordination as important as hand-eye coordination. When the former conflates with the later, the result is a far more intuitive dentist.

As an educator who always pondered the imponderables, Henry found the absence of this perception totally indefensible. He always urged a total reformation of the four year curriculum for this very reason. He always joked that "the dental union" should be stripped of its powers in the interest of new "right to learn" laws. Then he would snicker. Was he wrong? Gosh no. He was inventive, and, always looking ahead with very progressive thoughts. The ADA, on its best day, would never give this a nanosecond of consideration!

This enigma as to why the politics of dental education has failed to meet the challenges set forth by dentistry's early pioneers is going to require some merchant of common sense. The problem is that people in the profession who are responsible for change are "the politician-caddies". As Henry's brother, Eddie used to repeat endlessly: "If change is necessary, never ask a politician to carry it out because politicians are self-serving not true policy wonks"! I presume he was right because loathe all these years it's still "same ol same ol"!

There will come a day when people will require less mechanical replacement therapies as the biologic-based needs increase. With the tremendous surge in research and education today, the dental specialists have acceded to levels of competence with such remarkable proficiency that the chasm between the "general" practitioner and the "specially" trained dentist is wider than ever. As it stands today, the standard approach to clinical therapies are soon to be challenged and revolutionized by advances in stem cell science. There will come a time, and probably very soon, when implant science will give way to tooth regeneraton with stem cell technologies, nano-robot technology (currently in development) along with 3-D printers. Existing therapies will supplant the classic implant-prosthetic therapies, casting them to their rightful place in some museum for dental artifacts. Crazy? Right! No, it is going to happen and dental institutions are going to need curriculum modification to keep pre-doctoral students au courant! Imagine microscopic nano-containers filled with antibiotics or chemotherapeutic agents and delivered intravascularly with specificity for bone and soft tissue locations to treat infective periodontal disease, tumors, swellings, ulcerations, etc. They will have cell specificity for effective treatment.

The academic level researches, teachers and practitioners would make Henry Goldman proud. He would, however, be quietly discouraged to see private practice somewhat of the charade it has always been: the general practitioner as the centerpiece "doing it all" while the specialists expend all their pride and self-worth with a politically correct posture in search of referrals. Henry would probably comment, with a wink and a nod, that it's good to see political correctness still alive and well in the circus game of "referral practice". Its continuation has perpetuated all the elements which contribute to the negative aspects of what is right for the patient. The under-treatment/over-treatment issue is a legacy problem of this referral game that is both stunningly bad for patients' dental health and for "unrighteous dominion" of the general practitioner (the least capable in the dental hierarchy of diagnostic acumen sitting in the catbird seat determining what's best for the patient). The incongruity continues in spite of the fact that this should be the purview of a Board Certified Periodontist, the dental specialist sitting highest in the dental hierarchy with the overall diagnostic training and insight for treatment planning. Just to recapitulate, this is what gave Henry the impetus to formulate the original program at The University of Pennsylvania over sixty years ago. How far the righteous have fallen!

The culture of "plausible deniability" at the highest level of dental education keeps this myth, political correctness, and irrational comportment alive and well thank you! The most hurt is the patient, the consumer. It is no different than the insurance carriers keeping the outdated practice of seeing a specialist only through "a primary referral". Even that had to attenuate. In dental education, the graduating dentist (even after a one year general practice residency and all the continuing education courses known to man) cannot accede to the level of a Board Certified Periodontist in justifying the true dental needs of a patient. That is just a fact that traditional practice cannot and will not accept. This drove Henry "crazy" for years. On a golf course he could be ablaze with conversation on this subject during the entire length of a round. Normally very laconic, this subject always got him going.[139]

In assessing the huge "education debt" that exceeded well beyond the ability of a newly anointed private practitioner to handle, further training was out of the question. This spelled the beginning of her/his sudden welcome to the world of a sudden reality check. Beyond the cost of education (college and dental school), the office equipment and the rest of the financial investment made to underwrite a practice, the newly burdened graduate started out way behind financially. And today the economy prevents most from setting up solo practice. Income capabilities are no longer like it was in the 1950's through the 1970's. It is more of a compelling issue today than when Henry was alive. This has markedly contributed to the "over-treatment/under-treatment practice" issues which are more common than ever. Will the elements of this lingering "politically correct" upside down culture of dental practice ever be resolved? Henry believed "NO"! Human nature and dental politics allows "monetization" to override changes in dental education. This is just the way it has been and will continue to be. Change comes hard, and when it does, it will suit those at the controls, "the dental power brokers". And, if history means anything, the self-serving probably will not help the dental student and dental education.

A review of the "Council on Dental Education and Licensure: 2011 Periodic Review of Dental Specialty Education and Practice" is insightful in terms of the tremendous disadvantage for a dental specialist today, some more than others. (137) Firstly, demographics show that most dentists want to practice in relatively large city environments, be it urban or suburban. Therefore, the nature and referral tendencies of a general practice will be totally different than for a city oriented versus a rural practice. And, specialty practices will almost totally be in or near a city because a rural practice as such would not financially survive. Of the nine American Dental Association recognized specialties, only four have a dependency for referrals: AAE, AAOMS, AAP and ACP. Of these four, only the AAOMS provides services so advanced

---

[139] Within conversations with author, and with a very meaningful tone.

that a general practitioner would not dare explore their intricate procedures. On the other hand, the AAE, AAP and the ACP are financially in direct competition with the general practitioner. Of those three, the Periodontist (AAP) has become the most vulnerable as the periodontal practice today survives by placing implants. In spite of the ideologues, without implants a Periodontist would not survive. The emphasis on implants in the institutional training centers reflects this. In fact, the traditional periodontal training is buried in its clinical emphasis on implants so Periodontists are certified with very little proficiency in the rudimentary tooth oriented surgical techniques. And, of all the nine specialties, five reflect members who are Board Certified as Diplomates. Their percentages are not impressive: as a percent of the membership, the AAOMP is at 81%, the AAOMR is at 63%, the AAOMS is at 57%, the AAO is at 51%, and the AAPD is at 50%. The others (AAPHD: 32%, AAE: 23%, AAP: 42%, and ACP: 36%) are comparatively low. And, it is not compulsory to be a member of any ADA recognized specialty to legally practice in a dental specialty once licensed. What this shows is everything Henry confirmed in his thinking. Why would a dental specialist want to grovel for survival in a setting where his referring dentists are their competitors? In Henry's time the numbers were very different, but the general practitioner's mindset was the same. Today for a young specialist, the issues for survival in a competitive market are more acute. And, as stated, the most vulnerable are Periodontists. (138-146)

There is a "quality factor" in dental training today that Henry would continue to eschew because of the curriculum factors which make for great academic discipline at an extremely challenging level. But, when information reaches a relevancy factor so low that it merely satisfies some academic mindset and not reality, the time consumed could be otherwise used more expediently. In addition, the way continuing education programs are today, why would a sensible individual want to sacrifice so great a financial investment in most of the specialty training programs, unless for an academic position, research, or a life in the military (particularly for Periodontists, Prosthodontists, and

Endodontists)? The payback would be too long and stressful, and that's if there was an eventual payback at all!

When Henry opened the Stomatology Department in 1958 at Boston University Medical School under the then President of Boston University, Harold Case, the heavy emphasis was in Oral Biology and Oral Medicine. As referenced before, his influence was his own training and practice early on as an Oral Pathologist with his formative years training under Kurt Thoma at Harvard and then heading the dental section of the AFIP (Armed Forces Institute of Pathology) in Washington, D.C. during WWII. This set the stage for Oral Medicine. Early on, realizing that the study of disease would make for a more informed clinician, he felt that the singular importance of Oral Medicine was crucial to the education of all dental specialists. As an Oral Pathologist and Periodontist, he firmly believed Oral Medicine should have been become an ADA recognized specialty. It has never. Be it a political or academic threat to some of the other specialties, or simply out of its competitive threat within the hospital network for the AAOMP, there is no doubt it satisfies a public outreach and need. Going back to the 2011 Periodic Review noted above, its last section on "Requirements for Recognition of Dental Specialties" it lists six areas whereby a sponsoring organization must satisfy all. Here is a paraphrase summary of the last page of "The Council on Dental Education and Licensure" from 2011: (137)

The requirements for recognition of a dental specialty have to fulfill six approved requirements: (1) the specialty must wholly be relegated to the specifics of the specialty and it must have a certifying board selected from its membership; (2) the specialty must supersede the expected training skills acquired in dental school; (3) the specialty must demonstrate a uniqueness that doesn't draw from another or shared likeness to anyone or combination likenesses of the other specialties; (4) the specialty, in research and clinical practice, must enhance its own strengths as well as the profession and benefit the general public in a manner of service that a generalist cannot; (5) the specialty must satisfy a direct patient need; and (6) a specialty must be a minimum of two years to fulfill ADA required standards.

Without any replication of the ADA language (a rephrasing), the above is a suitable template from which to make some significant points and generate some needed thinking. The world today requires that knowledge be accepted as an unending process that exploits no one's benefit and simply contributes to the greater good. To expect a generalist to be the refuge for all dental-oral-systemic knowledge is willfully sanctimonious and culpably exploitative of dental public health. One of the reasons Henry propounded Periodontics as a necessary specialty was the barebones reality that periodontal health is the very basis of tooth retention for health and function. To repeat, it is "mother's milk of dental health"! He knew general dental training was insufficient and ill-suited fulfilling this goal. It became quite obvious that advanced training would produce a type of dentist that could determine what and how patient needs could be served. General practitioners simply did not have the training to determine such needs, particularly at the most demanding and intricate levels of thought. No doubt continuing education has tried to close this gap, but a little bit of knowledge is dangerous and, in general, commercial lobbying has effectively eliminated a once proud tradition in periodontal practice by replacing savable teeth with implants. Like the implant has been nurtured and cradled as "a magic bullet", a now more profound and serious dental public health issue has been unveiled. With the loss of the traditional Periodontist, the generalist has become the "implant suitor" to the public. Forget that it is far more involved as a didactic and training skill, the commercially driven continuation programs are implicitly and explicitly condoning insufficient learning to benefit public need. The basis of The Boston University School of Graduate Dentistry was to enhance, not vitiate the standards of dental education. It is essential that a general practitioner and a specialist practice to their highest level of training. Weekend courses, long range weekend courses, and learning centers do not replace full time commitment to institutional learning where remediation and course interaction predominate on a daily basis for the length of a specialty program. There is no doubt that the six points paraphrased above not only violate its own precepts, but, in addition render their requirements for defense of specialty recognition pretentious and effete.

That being said, a few thoughts must be considered if, as the will of the profession is so universally directed, pertinent markers and indicators of oral disease are to be linchpins in bringing systemic afflictions into focus. That is to say, if oral-systemic health and disease is such a draw for so many journals and continuing education venues, then it is also necessary to understand that this is an area of specialty training demands that parallel very closely all the other specialties. And more so. It is rooted in all the basic sciences that impact the understanding of physical disease. To pretend that the learning process doesn't deserve the same recognition of the other specialties is basic "plausible deniability" at the expense of rightfully serving the best interest of the public need. The more that is learned from remedial institutional training in oral-systemic medicine the greater the collective benefit. Simply put, the only restriction is misguided politics.

Let's try to briefly take a look at these requirements and, "en plein air",[140] try to assess them. Why? Because the very being of Oral Medicine underscores the very raison d'etre for Henry's lifetime achievement: that systemic medical health and oral health are mutually inclusive and mutually affected.

Point 1: If an effort has ever been made to attend an annual meeting of The American Academy of Oral Medicine, it is patently observable to see the entire membership is totally reflective of professionals whose business is to advance the diagnosis and care of issues related to Oral Medicine on a regimented daily basis. The American Academy of Oral Medicine is the sponsoring agent to promote its specialty recognized status. Its members are either trained or are training to limit their practices or to take hospital based positions in Oral Medicine. The AAOM has had a certifying board for many years. (141)

Point 2: Let's synthesize the mission statement of The American Academy of Oral Medicine: essentially it exists to render educational

---

[140] "en plein air": French for: "open air"="open discussion".

standards of teaching and training to advance research, bring more effective therapeutics to patients, raise educational standards in the field, and enhance public awareness of trained specialists.

Very clearly dental school graduates hardly measure up to the standards of existing board certified members and teachers, nor those who are in the process of preparing themselves to limit their practices or predominantly practice within the scope of oral medicine for their patients. Their knowledge and skills are unique to the highest standards of the academy (which, by the way, has been in operation since 1945). CODA by this time must be aware that its Accreditation Standards for Dental Education Programs are exemplary on paper, but, in practice cannot purport to compare a dental school graduate to a person who has followed AAOM guidelines in preparation for board certification. There is an ocean of difference. And, to use the words of "Requirements for Recognition of Dental Specialties": the AAOM "requires unique knowledge and skills beyond commonly possessed by dental school graduates". CODA's standards are of the highest possible level for a pre-doctoral program, but certainly cannot be taken to equate with the standards of the AAOM. (141)

Point 3: To point (a): the wording is spurious because any reasonable dental specialty would and should impart some level of oral medicine to both its training and board certification process. It is also judicious owing to the fact that any specialty work within the oral cavity should be responsive to any pathology with its working environment. But, here's the key, such general knowledge of a dental specialty or combination does not measure up to the standards the AAOM demands for its didactic and clinical learning process of highly advanced details that a superficial overview cannot impart no matter how many times it is repeated; and, to point (b): any kind of accommodation cannot be enough to equate with an existing certifying board (like the ABOM) unless it wants to be the ABOM. It would be a feckless attempt just to make a presumptive point. And, the comparison is "apples to oranges" as the AAOM and its certifying board, the ABOM, are not "new kids on the block". (141)

Point 4: To point (a): The AAOM is continuously producing "valid and reliable statistical evidence/studies" contributing to new knowledge in the field by virtue of members who are in research as heads of departments or working within recognized departments of sanctioned American universities around the country; they publish in the OOOO Journal on a continuous basis; in addition, the AAOM's publications can be seen on its website; its members are engaged in research relating to significant topics in oral medicine that no other researches do on a totally limited basis; to point (b): all factors mentioned in point (a) all contribute to an ongoing education process in addition to the two meetings held by the AAOM (which are quite unique and topical, realizing that no other specialty groups cover them); to point (c); as stated above, members in academic settings have ongoing research dealing with pertinent issues which relate both to academic and clinical issues of ongoing importance, be it issues of antibiotic sensitization, advances in steroid usage, optimization of treatment of oral ulcerative conditions, etc.; to point (d): it is important to be quite clear on this point; as in all the other specialties, not only are general dentists and other specialists engaging in practice areas in which they would not otherwise be engaged if they were busier; eg. general dentists surgically placing implants, doing advanced periodontal surgical procedures; oral surgeons doing routine botox applications, face lifts and blepharoplasties, etc.; so, it would be egregious sanctimony not to realize that general dentists and other specialists are spending very limited time treating some oral medicine issues (irrespective of the success gained or not); it cannot measure up to the members of the AAOM whose practices are specialized and focused in oral medicine.

Point (5): "A specialty must benefit some aspect of clinical patient care": given cancer patients who manifest all types of intraoral ulcerations, erosions, hyperplastic tissue responses, etc. due to their treatments or as a consequence of their medications; another example would be autoimmune disorders like SLE (Systemic Lupus Erythematosis) which could and often do cause severe intraoral tissue changes due to altered kidney function, loss of basic minerals, or chemical imbalance, etc.; all of these examples, and a litany of other medical dyscrasias, require oral medicine treatment which quite clearly "…benefit some aspect of clinical patient care".

Point (6): This has been a very specious argument for anyone within the leadership of the AAOM for many, many years. There are advanced programs already in existence in hospital settings or schools with Stomatology Departments. But, the legions of time the AAOM has spent trying to get CODA recognition is quite minimized and obscured by the intent of the statement. The elemental intent of all the hard working members of the AAOM who have been seeking Advanced Specialty Education Program status through CODA presupposes that its long awaited elevation to that status would allow for ubiquitous installation of formal advanced education programs. Point 6 is inherently denotative of a new specialty. For Oral Medicine, around as an effective organization since 1945, it would be like telling an established builder of homes that a building permit cannot be granted for a new home in a new area, but that an example in the area must be shown to get the permit. For Oral Medicine Point 6 is like a self-fulfilling prophesy that there is a preordained blind spot within CODA's vision destined not to see what AAOM and its members can offer by way of specialized care to the public which haphazard attention by others within general practice and other specialists cannot and will not.

To defend the indefensible is senseless when the prejudice is quite obvious by virtue of the years the proverbial can has been kicked down the tired road of obfuscation and hypocrisy. The point-counterpoint above is like intellectual gerrymandering to co-opt fiction from reality. When it comes to the AAOM, anyone who has been down the continuous rocky road of deceptive intentions tires in a dispirited manner. It is clear that the process is wearing very, very thin. And for the AAOM, the message is clear. But, the public need does not change. So perhaps where public health is concerned some sagacious person of an alternate reality will prevail over the political minds who seem to act like "Cigar Store Indians", as in "no see, no hear"!

It is important to delineate what the requisites are for recognition,

but suffice it to say that back in the early 1960's some of the very imped-
iments to full recognition still exist. The only difference today is the
vast increase in the number of members, the upgraded quality Board
certification process, the numbers of training centers, the increasing
numbers of dentists who want to make this their life's work, and the
ever increasing public need. In examining all six points, Oral Medicine
has both qualitatively and quantitatively satisfied CODA's requirements
for many years. It is a shame that despite the ever increasing public need
that the specialty serves, and, the quality of dentists who have trained
and continue to train in Oral Medicine that it has still not been duly
recognized. The political barriers are unfortunately discordant and
gratuitous.

Particularly in view of the global presence and impact of population migration patterns the need for Board Certified specialists in Oral
Medicine is greater than ever. Its leadership is outstanding and endures
the bureaucratic demands with patience and persistence. Henry's belief
in this as a specialty was reflected in the fact that not one of the original specialties at Boston University escaped the training without a full
dose of lectures in Oral Medicine and Oral Biology. To Henry a dental
specialist could and should not practice without a formative exposure to
oral diseases. As a specialty the public need demands recognition which
would warrant greater participation through applications to future
recognized programs. To think that general practitioners can serve the
public need defies common sense as to their very limited exposure and
training. And, to think the other dental specialties can act as spillover
default agents to serve the public need dilutes and undermines the very
understanding for specialty training. The whole basis of a specialty is
to delimit an individual's concentration of time, not to further dilute
its importance by ministering to the need in a general manner. Finally,
fully defined departments first demand recognition in order to make
schools creditable and worthy of applicants. It has long been overdue
and the evidence seen for its hospital staff needs are readily apparent. It
cannot be solely a private practice based orientation for Oral Medicine
as a specialty. It must also be a collaborative hospital based specialty

with a complete laboratory research funding program. Had Henry Goldman lived and Boston University survived as a pure graduate program, this was the direction for Oral Medicine as a distinct specialty.

When it came to healthcare and public policy, Henry had an altruistic compulsion. His reality check was his inability to accomplish what he really wanted. Most people remember him as a Periodontist, but he was an accomplished Stomatologist. His mentality was of a different era. He served a lot of masters in his early years so he was able to synthesize his thinking with the benefit of his endearing relationships with so many of the great educators in Dentistry (Kurt Thoma, Robert J. Gorlin, Helmut A. Zander, Lester Burket, Harold Loe, Hamilton B. G. Robinson, Paul E. Boyle, Sigurd P. Rampfjord, etc.). He was not a born politician so fighting the prodigious political forces throughout his academic life was a testimony to his fortitude and range of ambition to get things accomplished by his standards with the least amount of provocation. He found out very quickly that despite his animism for politics nothing gets accomplished without some degree of involvement. And, for someone whose formidable distaste for influence peddling, he learned to quietly get more accomplished through whatever and whomever he needed. He would supersede anything for the sake of doing what was right. At the end, the school became too much of a drain with everything tugging at his spirit. He knew and engaged all the great educators of his day, but none could put together what he so deliberately achieved. There's no doubt that if Boston University had not consumed all his energy that he would have acted peremptorily to effectuate Oral Medicine as a distinct specialty. He saw it as a liaison between the hospital-based dental specialist and medical specialties such as Oncology, Dermatology, and Radiology. He was fervent about this need, but his other responsibilities as Dean and founder of Boston University embraced all his commitments.

He wrestled endlessly in his mind with the inextricable finding of over treated versus undertreated patients. This was a clinical conundrum that he was never shy to discuss. It was like the carpenter who seeing a nail always instinctively and without thought took a hammer to it. The eternal battle between full mouth restorative dentistry without even venturing any treatment for ongoing periodontal problems was (and continues to be) the ultimate cornerstone of this tug-of-war between dentists with different opinions, training, and insight. And, the converse, though not as common, was also problematic as many patients persevered through a questionable need for periodontal surgery. Coupled with today's bromidic overreach with implants to replace savable teeth, this continuum of questionable decision making for patients' needs either due to "one size fits all" or dental treatment continues without pushback. It is impossible to always moderate extremes because of human nature. The hammer is never far from the nail. As long as there are people, there will be attitudinal differences based on factors out of the range of dentistry and more within human discretion. Greed and lack of ethical concern feed into this unending saga which often gets dental practitioners into liability problems. This is the Achilles heel of the dental profession Henry often discussed very openly because it was the most palpable finding.

If a patient was penurious, most often dental needs went untreated. And, be it in public clinics or in private offices, the quality of care was substandard. On the other hand, money could access "the best" the profession had to offer. However, money did not always conflate with proper care. In general, the under-overtreatment healthcare plight will be eternal. And, this returns this thought as to why there is such a divide between the academic setting and the reality of private practice. Though Henry, given the privilege, would have completely turned pre-doctoral course design on its head. He would have emboldened the general practitioner to be cautious and judicious in all ways of practice. The same mindset should apply to the specialist, though it is less commonplace. Sound judgment and ethical behavior are rooted in upbringing and reflect the family traditions but which unfortunately cannot be the responsibility of professional training.

What the dental profession can ask itself is why the specialist is so more carefully scrutinized with oversight than the general practitioner? The more exams and boards, the more monitor and watchdog compliance with periodic relicensing exams. General practitioners who should require far greater scrutiny have the least. Most overindulge far beyond their training through the good graces of barebones continuing education programs which delude them into a false confidence level of practice. So given these circumstances, the specialist would question the value of board certification and all its maintenance. And today with the cost of education, why specialize and fall victim to a life of competition with general practitioners while playing "the politically correct game of referral dentistry". The economics do not work. This is the fault of organized dentistry. As Henry would be the first to admit as often as he did, a car can't brake while hydroplaning nor accelerate on a sheet of ice. The greater the effort to fight the laws of nature is no different than trying to remove blinders that cannot be removed. The numbers of board certified diplomats being at a constant low is a byproduct of all these realities. As often tritely stated: "There is no justice, just us"!

Finally, to consider the status of dental healthcare in a negative light was never a byproduct of Henry's deprived, rather sterile upbringing. Just the opposite, he was a perfectionist borne out of a very disciplined, highly parochial education. He never accepted short cuts, nor achieving without proper guidance. Accepting that he was a victim of a very doctrinaire lifestyle, he never relinquished his sense of humor nor forced his disciplines on others. He honored the differences in other peoples, but merely required a sense of respect for the advantages that were the benefits of graduate education.

Henry Goldman had been discharged from the Army at The Armed Forces Institute of Pathology about the time The American Academy of Oral Medicine was founded. He was very friendly with a good number of the people who were at the helm when it became a viable organization. Lester Burket, Dean at The University of Pennsylvania School of Dental Medicine at the time was one of the pre-eminent authorities in the specialty at the time. There is no doubt that in his friendship with Henry they were very like-minded concerning the AAOM. As pointed out in prior discussions, Henry was one of the early founders and

Presidents of The American Academy/Board of Oral Pathology and he was getting ready to organize the first Department of Periodontolgy at The University of Pennsylvania. Knowing this timeline, he hardly had the time to be active with known colleagues in The American Academy of Oral Medicine. However, the mission statement of the academy was at the essence of everything he supported as a dental educator. His vision went beyond the integration of medicine and dentistry. He believe the knowledge of medicine was a sine qua non of the practice of dentistry. He integrated Oral Medicine into lectures for all the dental specialties at Boston University to bring attention to the milieu in which dental specialists would be applying their skills. Beyond this however, he proffered the need for Oral Medicine being a separate dental specialty because of related oral cavity dysfunctions and dyscrasias which would require very specialized training. He spent his lifetime sounding this message. He knew that physicians were familiar, but not adequately versed in Oral Medicine. He also realized that a mere cursory background in Oral Medicine for dental specialists (let alone general dentists) would hardly suffice. He always said that "a little knowledge is dangerous". All his clamoring over his lifetime for specialty recognition was futile. He had no "ax to grind" as he did not possess any ulterior motive other than what was good for the dental profession. But, Oral Medicine is the bridge between medicine and dental specialists adequately prepared to treat patients with oral pathologies.

Over the years he mentioned all the politics that served no useful purpose other than to be self-serving and defiant. At once, no one in the profession seemed to care because eventually throwaway dental journals came out as opportunistic replacements for the real need. The OOOO Journal was an effective dispatch for research and clinical articles, but highly arcane for untrained dentists. The throwaways were written by general practitioners who seemingly wrote articles that appeared as excerpted information directly from a textbook. And, the articles would always repeat over time. Clearly, there was a subliminal message at every turn that the time was long overdue to formally recognize Oral Medicine as the tenth dental specialty. Willful pessimism could be a reasonable reaction for all the unholy disregard for recognition by CODA (and ultimately by the ADA). A wise man would say that it's no different than stabbing oneself in the back to show the knife cuts and kills. It could only serve to upgrade the dental profession in respectability. There are no negatives of subliminal intent for anyone.

To dwell on this subject is only to heighten its importance and honor the memory of Henry M. Goldman whose lifelong mission was to bring dentistry out of the hallmark "barber surgeon" era into a scientifically based profession. Not unlike Horace H. Hayden and Chapin A. Harris who both realized the direct relationship between the oral cavity and medical health/disease. Henry heavily invested his lifetime in the transmogrification of the profession from a trade into a medical-based science. Perhaps the powers to be in The American Dental Association's Council On Dental Accreditation will have an epiphany one day and see that the ipso facto history and future demand its recognition. If Henry were left in a room with Hayden and Harris, the harmony of thought and emotion would distill all the nobility of mutual intent, in hopes that the less rational of today could learn. "Healthcare Today: The Education Conundrum..." This is it!

CHAPTER 14

Henry's Legacy: The Future through the Rear View Mirror: The Uncommon Finding of Common Sense

Henry M. Goldman was born in 1911, opened the Boston University School of Graduate Dentistry in 1963 and died in 1991. He was 52 years old when the school opened. And now, almost 52 years after the school's opening, a century's worth of the most dramatic social and economic changes in modern civilization have unfolded. The 100 plus years since his birth have been witness to more significant innovation and diversity than all earlier times and cultures. From the agrarian period of The American Revolution past The American Civil War and the industrial period of the late 1800's, major developments dramatically altered man's relationships with his environment and his fellow man: the railroad, electricity, industry and the ship. Social change accelerated with all the physical gain. And, at the turn of the 20th Century as Henry was growing up, he lived through the most fluid period in the young life of the country: the dynamic growth of the cities, the birth of the car, the gun industry, the airplane, the growth of industry (the telephone, computer, telegraph, post office) and aerospace technology. But, most of all, it was all the very rapid transitions which heavily altered the healthcare industry: the diagnosis and treatment methodologies in uber-spin mode. Henry did not live to see the frenetic culture of social media, and maybe that's a good thing. His temperament and ever serious pursuit of only the positive meaning of creative technology would have limited his attention and tolerance. His indifference to frivolity and entertainment culture he kept very personal, but it was ever present. However, he was wise enough to find a way to convert the technology for some scientific application.

The year 1963 was a watershed year in a time that was going to revolutionize dental education. The most significant changes which came were in research: establishing causes of infective periodontal disease borne out of research in biofilms and bacteriology, research in modern ceramic restorative materials, applications of radiology advances in CAT Scan, MRI and Cone Beam technologies for clinical diagnosis and patient therapies, prosthetic reconstructions of jaw(s) and faces from tumor destruction, and the advent of the entire implant business. There were many others, some not so dynamic in the resounding way the above impacted society. Ultimately, it would all fall on educators to formulate teaching experiences which would unfold in the most sensible outlines possible. It could not be formulaic like a biochemistry chart because it was too subjective, but the manner had to be purposive and correctible as the process played out.

At a time when great change was set in motion after WWII, it was quite evident that leadership would reflect the thoughtful attention necessary to lead like a tour guide and relegate authority to trustworthy, ambitious academic types who would carry out the grand mission of education: to mold thinking minds, to instruct in the art of technique applications, to stimulate research investigation, and, most of all, to be exemplary in every manner that the teaching position required. People in history who were responsible for initiating great change are remembered for the change, but not necessarily for the difficult manner by which it evolved. Henry was a pioneering master in the dental-medical sciences, but his genius was right at the friction point where all the decisions were being made for a new and as yet untested experiment in postdoctoral dental education. It was a revolutionary concept in the nation's historical record. Similarly, how overwhelming it must have been for Horace H. Hayden to put together the design for a first of its kind dental school in Baltimore (The Baltimore College of Dental Surgery in 1840). Very soon after the initial undertaking, Chapin A. Harris came into the fold to aid Horace Hayden so he is considered one of the founders. Hayden was more of the clinical mindset while Harris was a prolific writer and research minded teacher. They complimented one another, but both with stout medical-dental backgrounds of significance for the day. Wherever there was someone or something to observe and learn they traveled to enhance their understanding and sensibilities. It is important to appreciate the difficulties of opening up a dental institution in such primitive times (even as challenging as they were).

For all that Henry accomplished to further the dental profession, Boston University is and will always be his legacy. It stands as a living symbol of his brilliance: The Henry M. Goldman School of Dental Medicine at Boston University. Today it has grown into a private pre-doctoral institution with graduate departments, but its aura continues through its line of graduates. As enumerated before, there are sixty five dental schools (forty public, twenty private, and five private with public support) of which Boston University is the only one that evolved as a pure post-doctoral institution. It is unique in origin as it carries Henry's name to reflect his primacy in its founding. He was first and foremost a scientist, and second an educator. In the same fashion that Max Planck (Max Karl Ernst Ludwig Planck) revolutionized theoretical physics as the discoverer of Quantum Theory (Nobel Prize for Physics in 1918), all the institutes throughout the world are all independent, but they fall under the research umbrella of The Max Planck Society. (187) But, in honor of his grandeur, they all carry his name. In similar likeness, Henry's name continues the school's eponymous heritage because of his contribution to dental science and its founding.

Among some very astute observations, one of Voltaire's most glowing, "common sense is not so common",[141] imparts one of man's most exposed psychological shortcomings on a routine basis. The dental profession, for all its great educators, has been a long time reserve of competing leaders who controlled school teaching fundamentals, with site visits for academic compliance. Though very

---

[141] Voltaire (nom de plume) aka Francois-Marie Arouet: *Candide, (Translated by Lowell Bair)*. Copyright 1959, Bantam Dell (Reprint edition).

rigid, it was mostly a demand to further some teaching standards that were often lacking in common sense. This was part of Henry's sense that a fundamental change in the approach to dental education was so key to meet the health demands of the future. But, as it pertains in this writing, much of the profession was a haven for dental educators who were resistant to change. The pursuit of constructive modification was like chasing windmills similar to Cervantes' *"Don Quixote"*.[142] The persistent finding of excessive hubris and egomania was self-replicating generationally. It seemed to follow both men and women of superb intelligence who could not accommodate their thinking and outlook. The world was changing and the format of education had to adapt. It was just stifled by stubbornness and lack of political opportunity.

As Aristotle observed

"There is a foolish corner in the brain of the wisest man."[143]

Decision making is one of man's most significant everyday behaviors which carries consequence. It incorporates the making of mistakes within the living experience. If people did not make mistakes then they were not living. Mistakes are made by people with the most practical living sense, but they are correctible. It differs markedly from the slow churning calculation(s) which lead to uncorrectable, mindless or politically motivated actions which are unproductive and most often the result of a bias, an angst, or a political conflict. Hunger for power and control can manifest in some of the most blatant "common sense" errors which are as much self-destructive as they are senseless. But, it falls under the heading of decision making and emanates from that special "foolish corner in the brain" of which Aristotle spoke. The glaring examples involving Henry's life involved injecting the teaching of the medical sciences into the dental profession as well as the issues he had

---

[142] Cervantes, Miguel de: *Don Quixote*, Copyright 2005, Harper (Reprint Edition).
[143] Carnes, Lord, Translator and Introduction: *ARISTOTLE: THE POLITICS*, Copyright 1984, University of Chicago Press.

with Gerry Kramer over continuing education. Both were so protracted that they became turgid and self-defeating.

Henry spoke often about understanding failure, the accepting process, and then moving on. He was always amazed by people who couldn't realize the uselessness of not coming to terms with mistakes or failure. The result was the foolish redundancy of their mistakes. To recall what Santayana warned:

> *"Those who cannot remember the past are condemned to repeat it."*[144]

One would think that some persevering scientist is going to find a genetic link to this human inclination with every successive generation? Whether it is an intellectual blind spot where pride grows wild matters not, it is more important to the people who may be the victims of the pettiness and sleuthing.

Henry thought dentistry was a wonderful profession for many reasons, but most of all the independence it afforded him. He wholeheartedly felt that anyone who couldn't transform this into the high comfort zone it provided was spoiled and unappreciative. But, it was only the bureaucracy of leadership he could not understand nor tolerate. Only in private would he expand, and he did so with his typical shake of the head when coming to a highly sensitive point. In general, he was resistant to anything that interfered with free-thinking and independent action. But, he was convinced that his work would never be easy because of the politics in the dental profession. His angst: the control of bureaucrats and the regulations that subordinated every dentist in every walk of the profession. He never relented in his decisive animus for this. It is certainly a reflection of today's insanity that has elevated regulations to a whole new level of despair.

Going forward, Henry upheld his belief that medical sciences would play an ever increasing role in the teaching of future dentists.

---

[144] Santayana, George: *Reason in Common Sense:* Copyright 1980, Dover Publications (Reprint Edition)..

He was convinced that a much more dynamic leadership within the American Academy of Oral Medicine would be required to promote the case for ADA recognition. Before he died he felt the leadership was too preachy without any real zeal and energy to be effective. It is not a new perception, but he realized that the leadership was too lazy, uncertain and buoyant. He felt the leadership in Oral Medicine operated in a rudderless boat, drifting aimlessly. He was otherwise occupied with the school, but he would often comment that it would take the same kind of conviction and commitment he brought to Boston University. There is no doubt that if Henry were alive today, he would be beating down doors until it got it done. He would be clear and simple as was his style to say bluntly: "It is the future going forward, get it done already." He understood very, very well the stonewalling by swollen egos. However, typical Henry, he would say that even the political effete die from hearing the truth. He knew the answer was to keep rattling their cages.

Let's come back for one more look at one other overdone behavior which just perpetuates the most egregious situation affecting dentistry today. It's the little boy running around in a field on a hot summer day and runs right into a hornet's nest. Once again the eight hundred pound gorilla in the room for the dental profession is the rather blatant commercialization of dental practice. Whether it's implant dentistry, the topical placement of antibiotics into periodontally diseased and swollen gums, Invisalign orthodontics, treating mouth ulcerations and other soft tissue diseases, or other less general problems related to the TMJ or the salivary glands, the dentist is marketed and controlled by companies which drive their business instincts. Whether it's good for patients or not the dentist rarely cares or understands. It is common for a sales representative to support the merchandise with a research article which supports the claims they foist on the dentist.

Another example is the implant issue which is an accident waiting to happen because general dentists are simply not properly trained at the university level to do the invasive surgery they are doing. It's classic "plausible deniability", Peter Principle, and Ethical relativism all wrapped tightly into one protected holding pattern. It is an example of mediocrity climbing up the ladder of dental health care, and ethics aside, general practitioners push product in deference to profitability. The loser: the patient. The cover article of the July, 2014 issue of The Journal of The American Dental Association by leading academicians in assessing many criteria of implants placed with both the surgery and its restorative component done in many general practices conclude: "These results suggest that implant survival and success rates in general dental practices may be lower than those reported in studies conducted in academic or specialty settings (178) This is statement of fact which will be read by few, but, in fact, it is a lot worse than this article purports. In the "real" world of everyday practice, there are implants placed which are unfortunately so substandard that it makes a mockery of specialty training which remediates to a 97% standard. But, the general practices are overwhelming higher in numbers catering to the general public. This is simply a reflection of not controlling what should be controlled (and allowing less significant issues command the attention). Is this something new? No. In Henry's day it just manifested with other important public concerns, like the failure to diagnose and treat periodontal disease.

Today the difference is the availability of more technologies available to find trouble. For example, generalists taking continuing courses in advanced bone block grafting without any graduate study in advanced surgical training. Even oral surgeons teaching continuing education courses to general dentists because it is a powerful money making business is a major ethical issue. In the end, organized dentistry enables it. Legally it is permissible because of anti-trust laws governing restraint of trade, but when are professional organizations going to be ethically responsible to control their membership to protect an "unknowing" public. Is it universal? No. But, it is rampant enough to be a major dental public health issue that liability can't begin to control. It's only the ones that slip into a liability violation of practice that are exposed. Even then, there are numbers still practicing who have been sued endlessly and unconscionably. Henry tried to have a prevailing influence to clean up this problem, to no avail. As explained, there are too many more technologies available today which increases an abundance of issues multifold. Today the problem is an endless loop. Unfortunately, it is a major part of the patient's blind decision making because she/he chooses a dentist based on "how nice they are", not on training and competence. Finally, it should be clear that there are a minority of very ethical, sensible and highly competent general dentists who never get engaged in this slippery slope. As an opinion from what can be construed from the historical record, this will never be solvable until the ethics of educational standards of practice are upgraded to a palpable reality. The chances of this pipedream being realized are slim to none. As long as ethics are not a staple of human behavior, money is too much of an aphrodisiac. It's just life as Len Marrella clearly describes. "Follow the money" when a reality check is in order. (87)

Conversations with Henry over the years carry interesting projections for the future: The most significant change in the dental profession will be in the area of stem cell technology and genetic coding. With globalization, there will be an increase in exposure to new diseases and old ones which were once eradicated by seminal immunization. There will be an enhanced need for dental specialists in Oral Medicine who are trained in infectious disease, immunology and the medical based sciences related to oral health. This is even more reason for its recognition as an ADA specialty. At that point there will be a need for hospital based services whereby their expertise will be needed on both a consultative and treatment based participation with in-service physicians. This is a clear reality and hopefully there will a level of intelligence within the governing powers to recognize this need. It is not a novel concept as Henry discussed this more seriously than anything else.

As much as dentists can, they adorn their practices with the latest in technologies as exemplified by their advertising for tooth whitening, botox, dental implants, Invisalign orthodontics, veneers, laser therapies, and as many as they can as the market changes. The statement made concerning stem therapy will also come true as its applications will eventually find their way into dental care. It will displace the ultimate golden "toy" today, dental implants. There will come a time when lost teeth will be replaced by genetically engineered replacements with biologic compatibility. Stem cell therapy will impact temporomandibular joint disease and dysfunction. Be it from arthritic or biomechanical bite changes from injury, periodontal disease and tooth loss, or factitially related habits, stem cells will eventually become a treatment modality. Wherever there will be a need for tissue replacement to restore a function or a loss in esthetic appearance, stem cell science will play a major role. The real issue will be what it is today: to ensure its use is in the hands of properly educated professionals, and, that the advertising and marketing does not overreach in its expectations. How far down the road this will happen is impossible to predict. It was Henry who in one seemingly "mystical moment" predicted bone regeneration therapies over twenty years ahead of their appearance. So, why not stem cell therapy? The science and individuals involved in the research are quite optimistic. The use of 3-D printers for organ replacement are already cutting edge realities. Advanced genomic testing for cancer will become a conventional biometric modality, the likes of which is presently used to screen families for the breast cancer gene. The entire concept may be just a generation away from becoming a universal and predictable convention in screening.

From a theoretical vantage point, Henry would be awed by the level of erudition at the very pinnacle of research trained scientists in dentistry. Without doubt the PhD/DSc level dental scientist is producing wonderful and very connected information, linking the practice milieu with success rates for patient therapies. Some of the most remarkable, pragmatic research which essentially changed the way dentists look at ongoing infective periodontal disease was in biofilm research. The misfortune is that it served as a vanguard for how to misapply a technology. In a sense it exemplified how "supervised neglect" (by virtue of topical antibiotic therapy applied to very advanced bone disease around teeth) by general practices who still garner great financial return as pointed out above. It is profoundly disturbing in its misapplication; another example of "monetization". However, as stated, it is propagated by corporate sales representatives to practitioners who are virtually without the academic training to validate its proper application (if any?). Unless and until many teeth are lost to this reality, then the guffaws over the costs for time consuming, expensive retrenchment make for angry patients when they say: "But, I've been dutifully going to my dentist on a regular basis, why am I now having such costly problems"? When Henry was alive, this was called "supervised neglect"! This is the heart of what bothered Henry for his entire professional life. It cuts right to the heart of the great disconnect between the highly trained specialist and the average journeyman general practitioner who is restoring broken-down teeth, doing implant surgery and all the other treatment modalities which are quite financially remunerative, but out of synch with their most essential professional responsibility: the recognition and diagnosis of all the levels of infective periodontal disease. It is a public dental health dilemma which has transcended generations of modern day dentists. The profession has extracted this poison from practice by removing savable teeth for implant placement rather than apply established modalities of periodontal therapies. Those days are over unfortunately. To repeat, the chasm between the lofty, super-specialist and the general practitioners of the world continues to widen. In fact, with inattention to this state of affairs, there is no guarantee it will ever be corrected. A shrug and ho-hum is the shroud of askance in looking away to other more au courant, revenue enhancing issues of the day to be addressed in cutting edge continuing education programs. Yet, this lingers as the most basic dental health conundrum today. Who knows how much money has been squandered in giving advanced surgical courses to general practitioners over and over, overlooking the most primary needs of the public. And, periodontal disease of more inveterate concern is ever present today with globalization creating an intermingling of refractory diseases induced through drugs, poverty and the most universal pandemic of all: neglect.

Henry did not live long enough to witness this play out. Globalization was not a major concern at the time of his death in 1991. He might not have adjusted his mindset to diseases like Ebola, SARS, MERS, Anthrax, Small Pox (again), Measles (again),Tuberculosis (again), Dengue Fever, Scabies (again), BSE, Enterovirus68, etc. The point is that grouped with poverty these diseases (along with grand-daddy of them all: HIV and AIDS) present a major public health issue. As the upper middle class gets older (along with the very wealthy) and dies off, and as the lower classes increase in size, there will come a time when the general practitioner will have to know much more than a four year education with a one year general practice residency will provide. Henry always said that to adequately reshape the mentality of the future general practitioners "the great divide" will have to be compressed and the dental curriculum (in general) must be reshaped to become much more purposive and applicable to the rapidly changing culture in the United States. And, he never got to half of what exists today. It was once ok for a nonchalant nod and sneer from a reality that was once a different environment thirty and forty years ago. It was possible to kick the can down the road, deal with the hush-hush liability issues of malpractice and unfortunate aversion to reality based dentistry, but now and going forth this cannot be veiled in forgetfulness, a "who cares-no money attitude", "oh I'll fulfill my course credits for relicensing" feeling, etc.. The generations are now upon the country which will have to be attentive. If Henry were alive, he would be, in his mild manner, be lecturing on this. There are many intelligent general practitioners who speak with authority and seeming awareness, but really do not translate this apparent command into reality. The responsibility lies at the feet of all the educators whose perceptions will not continue to tolerate the eventuality that the greatest change in attitude and understanding will always seem to be "no change"! Their bubble is eventually going to burst, and there will be a reality check, hopefully sooner than later.

How much meaning these musings convey considering Henry's cachet might be more fanciful and theoretical than pragmatic. It does not deter from their contextual importance, but it is hard to realize change when contentment with "what is" must be overcome. Henry found this out when he retired and saw Boston University's conversion to a pre-doctoral curriculum. Two very concise and relevant thoughts sum up why "change" is such a battle:

Ezra Pound (1885-1972) eminent poet and literary editor effused the following:

> *"Only the most absolute sincerity under heaven can affect any change."*[145]

That seems more a paranormal dream than a plausible reality. And, John Naisbitt (1929--) laid out the stark reality:

> *"Change occurs when there is a confluence of both changing values and economic necessity, not before."*[146]

Is not that the truth?

The old saw, "follow the money", transcends time. And cultural inclinations tend to determine how important change is. Henry understood the importance of an educated mind. It is a rare occasion when a dentist comes from a Latin and Classics based education at the most formative time in a young person's life. His background became the very foundation of thought and perception. He possessed a sense of purity which was never suspect throughout his entire professional life. He was a very hard person to emulate or follow. His eminent student-scholar, D. Walter Cohen, came as close as is humanly possible. Maybe Walter did not cross over between specialties, but his own contributions as a Dean and educator with the same will to achieve as Henry are inherently extraordinary in their own right. His sense of purpose is so reminiscent of Henry's mentality. However, these men are like china blue skies on a still, crystalline clear autumn day, all too

---

[145] Pound, Ezra: *Confucius: The Unwobbling Pivot/The great Digest/The Analects,* Copyright 1969, New Directions; 56

[146] Naisbitt, John: *Megatrends: Ten new Directions transforming Our Lives,* Copyright 1982, Warner books..

infrequent for their need. Looking in the rear view mirror, the sight of these two of the pre-eminent scholars of modern day dentistry is a reminder of how important going forward it will be to have their similar approach to education: work hard, work continuously, but work with purpose.

If Henry were alive today, he would agree that the foundation of dental education is solid. But, it has to be reshaped for the sake of incentivizing young students. Marching forward "...changing values..." may reframe "...economic necessity..." to a different perception if, and only if, the way education is directed bears more connection to idealized choices. The will to succeed cannot be solely motivated by money. Otherwise, that is exactly where a lifetime of ambition remains. Henry always preached the belief that money piggybacks righteous intent. He had no desire to shatter the foundation of the dental profession, but he realized the merits of Eastern European dental education very early on because of the emphasis on medical sciences. Unfortunately, since his death, even this has been forgotten. The connection to integrative dental medicine must reappear someday as Henry taught, not simply as it is today in written non-refereed throwaway journals in pro forma style. This is not a teaching-learning solution.

With the way the world has so dramatically changed in the last ten years, it is going to be incumbent on the profession to adapt to the population changes. When Henry was in dental school, there was a real, rapidly growing middle class. It was founded on the free market system with few, but constructive government regulations which enhanced business prosperity (instead of smothering it as it does today). This real middle class afforded increasing prosperity as the economy grew. A dental practice reflected this great economic expansion. Boston University also benefitted directly from this "Golden Age" because it was not encumbered as well by all the regulatory demands of today. The middle class today is simply not the same middle class. It is a government assisted class of a mixed population of midland, back-country, inner city poor that do not seek employment and solely live on welfare subsidies. Common sense dictates the following:

1. Technology must be applied sensibly, not because it is new and it satisfies patient fear; traditional techniques must still be taught;

2. Oral Medicine is the foundation of dental medicine; make it an ADA recognized specialty; Implant Dentistry is not foundational and should not be a recognized specialty; general practitioners should not be doing implant surgery, but this cannot be legally controlled; it should be relegated to Oral Surgeons and Periodontists;

3. Dedicate more time to all phases of radiology at the pre-doctoral level;

4. Laboratory Medicine should be integrated into the pre-doctoral level as well so dentists will more conversant about their patients' medical health;

5. Consolidate all basic sciences in one comprehensive medical review course to free up time for other more meaningful integrative courses; perhaps small seminar groups to review and discuss active case reports; it should be a four year continuum;

6. Pertinent medical review lectures to supplement the review course(s);

7. A basic psychology course to learn appropriate patient communication;

8. Infectious Disease courses and updates; globalization demands this;

9. Start clinical work in first year in conjunction with laboratory courses;

10. Eliminate Pediatric Dentistry, Orthodontics, and Endodontics; these should be specialty only courses;

11. Restorative aspects of Implant Dentistry only can be taught to general practitioners;

12. Teach basic Oral Surgery only to general practitioners : exodontia; leave all else to Oral Maxillofacial Surgeons; (especially in continuing education courses);

13. Upgrade and restore Periodontology to its once proud teaching status as it is the basis of all dentistry.

These were thoughts Henry often shared very informally because he felt it counterproductive in a world where a dental degree was still a proverbial "union card".

Henry Goldman was a most unique pioneer because he was not flamboyant, outspoken or quixotic. He possessed a steadying, calm and determined manner. This was his most appealing trait. Most people did not understand how selfless a person he was. He was ambitious in a devoted way, never with a personal motive. It is hard to delineate these traits because it is suggestive of a cloying, overly lavished praise. It simply is not. His partners, Alan Shuman and Gerald Isenberg, and the highly respected, venerated educator, D. Walter Cohen, would substantiate this appraisal. Henry's legacy is how the dental profession remembers him. He was an uncommon finding of common sense, or better yet, normal sense. It was not without error, but it was correct most of the time. Driving into the future, an occasional glance into the rear view mirror should spotlight his apparition hovering over an extended table of papers as was his habit in sifting through his pantheon of limitless plans. To quote the insightful Francois duc de la Rochefoucauld:

"Hypocrisy is a tribute vice pays to virtue".[147]

There was never the slightest modicum of hypocrisy to Henry's lifestyle, cult of personality or leadership in the face of any challenge. His honesty, simplicity and fairness were his virtues. His Achilles heel, if any of his human weaknesses should be defined as such, was his failure to play "the game" so to speak. That is to say, to succumb to the "societal virtues" derived from the "hypocrisy of personality" so wonderfully defined by Rochefoucauld in the early 17th century. Henry, in his

---

[147] Rochefoucauld, Francois de La: *MAXIMS*, Copyright 1959, Translation, Penguin Classics.

most modest countenance could not assume such behavior in his very busy, productive life. His legacy is that of a dental educator sufficiently noble that the power and control of a Machiavellian "Prince" were never compelling enough to overpower his life. As Niccolo Machiavelli advised in "The Prince" to a ruler:

> *"It is better to be feared than to be loved, if you cannot be both"*[148]

Henry was feared, not because he was a boorish, demanding person, but because he was stolid and authoritative. He was not stylish, but he reflected an august sense of leadership in a very caring and kindly manner. This made his faculty march to his beat with respect and affection. Hypocrisy was never Henry's cover because he carried on with forbearance. He will be remembered for the depth of his concern, the merit of his accomplishments, and, most of all, the people he encouraged and supported. With all that transpired at the end of his tenure as Dean and Founder of The Boston University School of Graduate Dentistry, he engineered positive change where necessity inspired his numerous talents. Niccolo Machiavelli carefully advised his ruler (prince) that he will really never be understood because "Rulers are also admired...when...they demonstrate themselves to be loyal supporters or opponents of others. Such a policy is always better than neutrality."[149] Henry accepted the academic climate for what it was and met every challenge, understanding the way to prevail in the best interest of education. To conclude with one more Machiavellian piece of wisdom which completes the truth about Henry in a nutshell:

> *"Everyone sees what you appear to be, few experience what you really are".*[150]

---

[148] Machiavelli, Niccolo: *The Prince,* Copyright 1995, Hackett Publishing Company (English translation).

[149] Machiavelli; Niccolo: *The Prince,* Copyright 1959, Hackett Publishing Company (English translation).

[150] Ibid.

Perhaps in their professional lives only three people could truly value the merit of such an "a propos" feeling for this sense of his being. They are Alan Shuman, Gerald Isenberg and, most of all, D. Walter Cohen.

Let us end this tome with this thought: Henry demonstrated to his profession how, in a startling limited time, advanced dental education could be transformed into the modern era. Hopefully, the future will continue to bear the fruits of his labor.

EPILOGUE

It has been almost twenty-five years since Henry's death. He showed quite clearly in his lifetime that saving teeth was both a health and functional necessity. As both an Oral Pathologist and Periodontist he became the standard-bearer for pioneering the relationship between oral and systemic diseases. This philosophy became foundational for the founding of the Boston University School of Graduate Dentistry.

Henry's assembled faculty were people who were highly sophisticated, integrated specialists thoroughly committed to an ideal: that teeth could be saved for people in health as well as in most all conditions of ill-health. This vindicated Henry's findings that teeth could be saved in spite of systemic diseases.

With the advent of implants, the world suddenly lit up from the belief that they possess a universal quality of indestructibility making savable teeth unnecessary. However, research has shown that this is not so as conditions affecting tooth loss and implants are similar.

Henry's epitaph is an unwritten testimony to his professional will to set an irrevocable standard in graduate education. His thinking is as vital today as ever, particularly in view of the fact that dental practices will be affected by technologies which will compel specialists to embrace the science he taught.

Henry's message will not succumb to quick fixes because it is so foundational. His memory will always harken to the professional standards he set as a researcher, educator, clinician and, most of all, architect of The Henry M. Goldman School of Dental Medicine at Boston University.

APPENDIX 1
A TALE OF TWO CITIES
BY MILTON B. ASBELL,
D.D.S, M.S *AND* D.
WALTER COHEN, D.D.S

Even as early as the 1920's, the need for graduate education for those wishing advanced instruction in various phase of dentistry was apparent to the dental profession. Those desiring to specialize, teach or conduct research realized that advanced study of the medical sciences as they pertain to the clinical specialties of dentistry, together with intensive clinical experience was necessary. The University of Pennsylvania, aware of these needs, gave the question intensive study and, as a result, offered graduate studies in dentistry in the Graduate School of Medicine. The Graduate School of Medicine was established in 1916 for the purpose of providing graduate medical studies in the clinical fields. By 1941, it enlarged the scope of its activities to include graduate studies in dentistry; to wit the following resolution the Board of Trustees:

> *That as recommended by the Board of Medical Affairs approval be given to the inclusion in the Graduate School of Medicine of a curriculum of graduate studies in dentistry, in accordance with the plan developed by Deans Appleton and Bureki and approved by the Executive Committee of*

*the Faculty Council of the Graduate School of Medicine, the
Faculty of Dentistry and the Trustee of Evans Institute.*

The first director of graduate dental studies was John W. Ross, D'17, who served as Vice-Dean of the Graduate School of Medicine. Graduate studies in dentistry were entirely separate from the undergraduate studies in the Dental School but the two worked in complete accord and the faculties were available for both graduate and undergraduate students. The studies were arranged in three periods; each consisted of a complete unit. The first, or basic unit comprised a full academic year and had to be taken at the University. This period of study led to a certificate.

The second period of study had to have been preceded by the basic studies and led to the Master of Dental Science degree (M. Sc. dent). The third period of studies were primarily devoted to research at the University (or, at other approved institutions) led to the Doctor of Dental Science degree (D. D. Sc. Dent).

Because the program was developed within the Graduate School of Medicine, a large part of the instruction, particularly in basic science, was given by members of the faculty of that institution. Dentists and physicians shared the same status, and the advantage to the dental graduate students was that he had a faculty devoted entirely to graduate studies in medical specialties. The programs include oral surgery, orthodontics, oral pathology, roentgenology, prosthetic dentistry and oral medicine-periodontics. Admission was based upon several factors: that the applicant be a graduate of an approved dental school with scholastic attainment "indicating his ability to understand and undertake graduate studies advantageously," would accept a total commitment to these studies and appreciate the responsibilities of entering a specialty field.

The course in Oral Medicine Periodontics was designed to give "training in oral prophylactic procedures and the treatment of periodontal disease, and understanding of the inter-relationship between medicine and dentistry, to afford experience in the diagnosis and the treatment of the diseases of the oral cavity and the oral manifestation of extraoral and systemic diseases." The emphasis was partly on laboratory experience and clinical practice in oral medicine together with the study of basic sciences of medicine. It consisted of over 1,000 hours of scheduled studies of which 200 were spent in periodontics.

The origin of the Graduate Program of Periodontology at the University of Pennsylvania, School of Dental Medicine embraces a bilateral arrangement between the University of Pennsylvania in Philadelphia and Beth Israel Hospital in Boston. In 1951, Lester W. Burket had been appointed Dean of the Dental School at the University of Pennsylvania and although he had encountered numerous administrative problems, he found time to re-evaluate his program in oral medicine. Oral Medicine as a concept in dentistry included within its scope the discipline of periodontology.

Lester W. Burket, impressed with the work being done in the periodontology clinic and with the experience of previous attempts within the Department of Oral Medicine to establish a course in periodontology, called upon his good friend, Henry M. Goldman of Boston, to work together on a joint program of graduate education in periodontology. (They had co-authored, *Treatment Planning in the Practice of Dentistry*.) The advantage of this arrangement tied in exceptionally well because Henry M. Goldman did not have the means to teach basic science other than which the Beth Israel Hospital gave to it medical residents, whereas the University of Pennsylvania had the advantage of the distinguished faculty at the Dental School and the Graduate School of Medicine. From this, a plan emerged to establish a two-year program: the first year 32 weeks of didactic instruction at the School of Dental Medicine and Graduate School of Medicine of the University of Pennsylvania, and a second year of 52 weeks of clinical experience and training in Boston at the Beth Israel Hospital. (By 1959, the facilities of the Beth Israel Hospital being inadequate, the program was transferred to Boston University.) In early 1955, Henry M. Goldman was appointed Professor and Chairman of the Department of Periodontology and D. Walter Cohen was appointed Assistant Professor of Periodontology and Vice –Chairman.

D. Walter Cohen had returned in 1951 from his research fellowship in pathology and periodontology under Dr. Henry M. Goldman at the

Beth Israel Hospital in Boston Massachusetts. Assistant Instructor in Oral Medicine and Oral Histopathology was his first appointment on the faculty of the Dental School. His assignment included working one-quarter periodontology, time in oral pathology, since it was then part of Oral Medicine, and one-quarter time in oral pathology with Professor Paul E. Boyle. His expertise in this department was soon recognized and promotions came rapidly. Within five years, he was an Assistant Professor of Periodontology.

Upon receiving approval from Dr. George M. Piersol, Dean of the Graduate School of Medicine, this arrangement was consummated, and this symbiotic relationship became effective and a "tale of two cities" began.

The first class was accepted in 1955 and consisted of Captain Odin F. Leberman (U.S. Navy), Captain Alfred L. Raphael (U.S. Navy), Henry S. Brenman, Arthur B. Hattler from New Jersey, H. Leslie Levine, from Vancouver, British Columbia Canada, and James S. Millsap from Houston Texas.

> On the Sunday before classes were to begin a special meeting was called. All of the faculty – both of Philadelphia and Boston – along with the first class met at the Dental School at Penn. Dr. Goldman insisted the his Boston faculty come to Philadelphia for this formal initiation of periodontics training program.

The students were advised that they would be required to attend the Correlated Clinical Science Course in basic sciences given by the faculty of the Graduate School of Medicine; that in addition to lectures, seminars and conferences by the Dental School faculty there would be an opportunity to conduct research in the second year; that the program was designed to meet the requirements if the American Board of Periodontology; the opportunity would be provided for teaching experience and upon the result of their performance would depend the future of this program.

Dr. Cohen welcomed us in the old Board room. He told us
about the wonders, delights, cultural activities; and, then,
proceed to lock us in the library with a telephone-book-like
reading list. Then, Dr. Amsterdam proceeded to give us an
occlusion reading list and seminar schedule.

The initial faculty at the University of Pennsylvania included D. Walter Cohen, Moron Amsterdam, Jack Alloy, Bernard Kaplowitz, Jerome Sklaroff. In addition, Lewis Fox, (who conducted some Tuesday evening seminars commuting from Connecticut), Dean Lester W. Burket, lectured on oral medicine, Professor Ned Williams – on microbiology, Milton Charen – occlusal adjustment, Lionel Gold and Lisabeth Baumann – oral pathology and Mr. Morris Feder on laboratory procedures. At Beth Israel Hospital, the staff consisted of Henry M. Goldman, Bernard Chaikin, Jack Bloom, Leo Talkov, Herbert Margolis, Gerald M. Kramer, Philip Schupack, Eleanor Covell, David Baraban; later added to faculty were Morris Reuben, Elliot Ziglebaum, J. David Kohn.

In addition to the regular faculty, the students during the period from 1958 to 1966, received instruction from such visiting lectures as Frank E. Beube (Columbia University, Saul Schluger (University of Washington), Philip Person (Rutgers University), Sigmund Stahl (New York University), Louis Alexander Cohn (Columbia University), Irving Gordon (Mt. Sinai Hospital, Miami Beach Florida), Betram S. Kraus (University of Washington), John H. Sillman (Bellevue Hospital, New York City), Lester Cahn(Columbia University), Harry Sicher (Loyola University), Neal Chilton (Temple University), John F. Prichard, Paul N. Baer, Clifford Ochsenbein and Edward Hoffman. By 1966, the faculty consisted of 4 professor, 1 associate professor, 7 assistant professors, 8 associates, 15 instructors, 2 assistant instructors, 1 assistant and including the visiting lectures made a total of 52 members.

Shortly after the inauguration of the Graduate Program in Periodontology, Morton Amsterdam conceived the innovative program of periodontal prosthesis. This was based upon a philosophy utilizing restorative and prosthodontic technics in the treatment of dentition which had been mutilated by the ravages of periodontal disease. This was an outgrowth of many years of study and research in general dentistry and specialized areas, such as endodontics, prosthodontics, orthodontics and oral surgery, as well as periodontology. It was conceived, not as a specialty of dentistry, but as a means of teaching total dentistry. A review of Morton Amsterdam's professional career will help in understanding this concept.

Morton Amsterdam, a graduate of the School in 1945, returned to private practice after serving in the United States Navy. In 1948, he as invited by Dean Gerald Timmons to join the faculty of Temple University, School of Dentistry, to organize and become Chairman of a Department of Endodontics - the first in the United States. As part of this program, he initiated teaching fellowships which were the first post-doctoral program of its kind.

Upon the sudden death of Gordon Winter, Professor of Oral Medicine and Diagnosis, Dean Timmons asked him to become Acting Chairman of this department. As part of this new department, he organized a course in stomatognathology and treatment planning. D. Walter Cohen was invited to give a series of lectures on periodontal pathology as part of this program.

In 1953, Morton Amsterdam was invited by D. Walter Cohen and Dean Lester W. Burket, to give the didactic portion of this program to the senior class at the University of Pennsylvania Dental School.

Morton Amsterdam and D. Walter Cohen, began a close collaboration during this period which consisted of study sessions and a clinical program in periodontal prosthesis. Their first preceptee was Jules Minker. The program was extended to be coordinated with a residency established at the Bethesda Naval Dental School with the cooperation of Captain Jack Sault, U.S.N.

In 1955, with the inauguration of the Post-doctoral Program in Periodontology, periodontal prosthesis was included on a voluntary basis. In 1957 Leonard Abrams and Harry Bohannan were the first members of the graduate periodontology class to participate in the periodontal prosthesis program. Leonard Abrams continued after his certification in periodontology to become a preceptor in periodontal prosthesis whereas Harry Bohannan joined the faculty of the University of Washington with Saul Schluger and subsequently to become Chairman of the Department of Periodontics at the new dental school at the University of Kentucky.

During this time, Charles Jerge was awarded a "Pennsylvania Plan Scholarship, a program established in the University" for training scholars and researchers (the first dentist to be included in this program). While pursuing his Doctor of Philosophy program (majoring in neurophysiology), he also became a preceptee in periodontal prosthesis.

In 1955, Morton Amsterdam and D. Walter Cohen, were invited by Dean Gerald Timmons and Dean Lester W. Burket to present a one-week continuing education course in periodontal prosthesis at their respective dental schools. The course was given on an alternate basis between Temple and the University of Pennsylvania until 1969, when it remained at the University of Pennsylvania until the present. This course was given continuously over the past twenty-five years not only at the University of Pennsylvania but at many institutions throughout the United States and served to introduce and subject the concept of periodontal-prosthesis to critical review.

The first formal graduate student was David E. Beaudreau, who had come from the University of Washington, Dental School in 1961, who completed the graduate periodontics course in 1963 and the M.Sc. (dent.) degree awarded in 1965. He was appointed Assistant Professor of Crown and Bridge Prosthesis and Chairman of the department. He later accepted the position of Associate Dean for Clinical Dentistry at University of Georgia. He then became Dean of the School of Dentistry, Georgetown University, Washington, D.C. He was the first in a long line of distinguished graduates who are serving in the academic world of dentistry.

By 1969, the course was changed to a formal three-year program requiring that a matriculant be certified in periodontics first, then permitted to continue --- up to 15 months---in the periodontal prosthesis training program for which a certificate was issued. Qualifications for acceptance into the program included: that the student had been a dentist or any of its specialties for at least two years (some students were in practice from 2 to 16 years prior to their application), assurance that the applicant was interested in a career of teaching, practice or research, presentation of a recommendation from a reliable professional person or institution. Moreover, although eligible for the Board of Periodontology after the two-year training period, the third year devoted to periodontal prosthesis held no promise for recognition by any society or specialty board in dentistry – merely a certificate attesting to graduate training. Yet, despite this restrictive regulation, applicants for the combined course each year were of such number that a selection committee had to be appointed. Those accepted were men and women dedicated to the pursuit of this specialized form of graduate dental education and subsequently had been recognized as leaders inn total dentistry, whether in the areas of practice, teaching or research.

A graduate program in endodontics was added in 1963 with Louis I. Grossman as the Director. It provided for a two-year curriculum for developing expertise in teaching and/or practice, including meeting the requirements of the Board of Endodontics. Faculty included Samuel Seltzer, I. B. Bender, George F. Stewart, Warren J. Rudner, Seymour Oliet and Samuel R. Rossman. In 1977, a program combining disciplines of periodontics and endodontics was inaugurated.

The inclusion of orthodontics in the program was suggested when Manuel H. Marks, '67 and I. Stephen Brown, '69, received informal training from Jerome Sklaroff (teaching theory) and Charles S. Jonas (instructing in clinical orthodontics). Manuel H. Marks continued to include tooth movement and clinical applications as part of his teaching responsibilities.

When James Ackerman became Chairman of the Department of Orthodontics, he cooperated fully with Morton Amsterdam in the development of a combined program of orthodontics and periodontics. I. Stephen Brown took an added year of training in adult orthodontics upon completion of his requirements for a certificate in periodontics and it was from this beginning that the formal combined program evolved to the present time. It was James Ackerman's experience cooperation and complete enthusiasm that played a most important role in the direction and teaching of this innovative program conceived by

Morton Amsterdam. The other ingredient, of course, was the complete support and endorsement of Dean D. Walter Cohen, who also played a major role in the conception and motivational aspects of the program. Robert L. Vanarsdall, Jr., was the first formal student. This is a new and exciting clinical discipline in dental education which has received full approval of the Council on Dental Education of the American Dental Association.

The basic philosophy in the combination of the various specialties with periodontics was, and still is, that periodontics is basic to clinical practice; that any special area of dentistry including general practice, had to be based upon the principles of periodontics. Thus, the area in which periodontics has combined included oral medicine, originally, then periodontal prosthesis, endodontics and orthodontics.

In 1964, the periodontics program did not accept any new matriculants since the prior year was the last in which the University of Pennsylvania students were expected to go to Boston for the second clinical year. All students thereafter received both didactic and clinical training at the Pennsylvania campus and thus the overlap of the first and second year program precluded any acceptance of a new class.

In 1967, the School of Dental Medicine established a Division of Advanced Dental Education, since the Graduate School of Medicine had been phased out. Stanley C. Harris, Ph.D., was appointed to head up this Division and its primary responsibility was the graduate training programs in the dental specialties formerly within the Graduate School of Medicine. The periodontics and periodontal prosthesis programs were placed within the Division, each of which was to have a separate director.

From an historical perspective, it is important to understand the departmental structure that provided the umbrella for the post-doctoral programs. In 1962, D. Walter Cohen was appointed Chairman of the Department of Periodontology, and at the same time, he was the Director of Post-doctoral Periodontic Programs. Morton Amsterdam was appointed Director the Post-doctoral Periodontal Prosthesis Program. Robert Gottsegen, was appointed Director of the Post-doctoral Periodontal Program replacing D. Walter Cohen. He remained in this position until 1969, when he returned to Columbia University, whereupon Morton Amsterdam replaced him. Thus, from 1969 to 1973, Morton Amsterdam directed both the Post-doctoral Program in Periodontics and the Post-doctoral Program in Periodontal Prosthesis under the Division of Advanced Dental Education.

When he relinquished the Directorship of the Post-doctoral Program in Periodontal Prosthesis in 1973, Arnold Weisgold, was appointed in his place. Arnold Weisgold, who graduated from Temple University, School of Dentistry in 1961, and had completed the program in periodontics and periodontal prosthesis in 1965 was invited by Temple University to become the Coordinator of course in Occlusion with the rank of Assistant Professor. In 1969, he accepted the faculty appointment to teach a course in Form and Function of the Masticatory System, of which, he is now the Chairman. He continues in both capacities at present.

Moreover, in 1973, J. George Coslet was appointed to the Directorship of the Post-doctoral Program in Periodontics relinquished by Morton Amsterdam; Jay Seibert succeeded D. Walter Cohen as Chairman of the Department of Periodontics.

In 1974, Jay Seibert became Associate Dean for Academic Affairs and Robert L. Vanarsdall, Jr. became the acting chairman of the Department of Periodontics ., These administrative appointments existed until 1979, when Jay Seibert returned as Chairman of the Department of Periodontics and Director of Post-doctoral Periodontics Program. J. George Coslet continued as Director of the Division of Advanced Education Dental Education.

For the students, their "home in the dental school building was basement lecture Room B-29 and the old periodontal clinic with its ancient units and chairs suitable for stand-up dentistry. "Initially, conditions were less than favorable. Morton Amsterdam recalls that once when conducting a seminar in the Board Room, he was politely ejected to make room for another group! Clinic space for periodontics was offered first in the Tracy Clinic with the provision that it be shared with the endodontic group. It should be noted that no funding was appropriated in the budgets of either the Dental School or the Graduate School of Medicine for clinical facilities. The periodontal prosthesis students had available space in the Truman Clinic and Morton Amsterdam supplied the units, chairs, and all the necessary equipment, material and supplies. Even this did not last very long as the Truman Clinic was being refurbished for other purposes; space was provided in the area that is now the Crossman Comprehensive Oral Health Care Clinic. The four chairs for the periodontal prosthesis students were located behind the orthodontic clinic and then "we were given a row of chairs in the main clinic floor". In time, endodontic students moved out of the Tracy Clinic and it was returned full time to the periodontal group. Thus, the two classes were able to perform their clinical responsibilities with a modest degree of convenience.

With the realization that more adequate facilities were most urgently needed, Morton Amsterdam appealed to the Myers family of Philadelphia, who had presented the department with a grant of $50,000 in support of its program. The overall plan was to establish a campaign to raise $250,000—an amount required for rehabilitation in addition to a continuing fund for support. With the $50,000 and a grant from federal sources of $75,000 "that's $125,000; so all we had to raise was another $125,000, and we were in." And indeed with the help of faculty, post-graduate alumni and friends, funds were raised and in September, 1972, the Abe, Charles and Samuel Myers Post-graduate Periodontics and Periodontal Prosthesis Clinic was dedicated in the area formerly occupied by the Evans' Museum. It continues to be used for clinical work to this date.

The financial support of the program was most fragile. There was no budgetary allotment from the administration. "We were really guests of the School." From 1955 to 1969, students paid tuition to the Graduate School of Medicine and since that date to the Division of Advanced Dental Education of the School of Dental Medicine. Those who continued the second year at Boston received an allowance through various sources: there were those who paid tuition with their own personal funds, many were paid $500 in their second year to teach one-half day per week to the under graduate students, particularly, in the Department of Form and Function of the Masticatory System. By

1969 those who pursued the third year in the periodontal prosthesis program received a stipend of $4,000, a waiver of tuition and q requirement to teach two day s per week, spending one-half time in the Department of Form and Function of the Masticatory System.

Director Arnold Weisgold commented that: "Uniquely, our students have all been good teachers, they were people who had strength in lecturing, laboratory work and the clinic. But, they all have been effective teachers. I believe it has to do with the fact that their background in the program allowed them to be these effective teachers in all phases of general dentistry."

Other sources of financial support included a project grant which had been secured initially by Henry M. Goldman and fellowship grants from the National Institute of Health, United States Public Health Service. The following grants were identified as Dental Training with specified number identifications: D.T. No. 1, D.T. No. 140 and D.T. No. 180. The D.T.No. 1 grant was sponsored as a training grant to train a dentist in basic sciences, the D.T. No., 140 was a special grant for clinical training in periodontics in addition to the Ph.D. program in basic sciences. (When Robert J. Genco was awarded the training grant D.T. No 1 for research in microbiology and immunology, it was decided that periodontics was to be included as formal training. The success of his progress was responsible for the awarding of the D.T. No. 140 grants.) The D.T. No 180, was the grant to support students in receiving degrees (D.D.S., D.M.D.) and a clinical specialty which unfortunately was discontinued almost immediately upon approval because of federal government cutbacks.

The Walter Annenberg Fellowship was another source of support. This fellowship was established in periodontics by Mr. Annenberg (which he was the American Ambassador to the Court of St. James) to support students from England studying periodontics at our school. The two Annenberg Fellows were Peter Hunt and Garry Rayant.

He also endowed the Walter Annenberg Lectureship in 1973 which continues to this day. Those of the department who have participated include D. Walter Cohen, Morton Amsterdam, Henry M. Goldman, James Ackerman, Herman Corn, Edwin Rosenberg, Arnold S. Weisgold and Robert L. Vanarsdall, Jr. The Thouron Award established fellowships under a Thouron-University of Pennsylvania British-American Exchange Program for the promotion of better understanding and friendship between the people of the United Kingdom and the United States. The program had received two such fellowships: recipients were William I. R. Davies and Gordon N. Wolfe.

Graduate periodontics may be defined as that special field of dental education which attempts to develop skills and perception which would enable the clinician to understand, manage and treat the advanced or complex problem cases in periodontal disease. The program was designed to make instruction available to dentists who want additional experience in periodontics per se, or as a program designed for the specialist; to prepare dentists for careers in teaching and to prepare dentists to contribute to the advancement of the knowledge of dental science particularly in the areas of preventive and therapeutic procedures and practice, through research of the biomedical sciences. Moreover, it has exposed students to the development of a fundamental background for sound understanding of the theory and practice of basic medical science and clinical dentistry and to apply those principles to the performance of their professional responsibilities. It has expanded the motivational and intellectual capacity of the students by including the assignment of studying the scientific literature with discrimination and weight. As a result, clinical competence was developed which will insure recognition by professional and lay communities and the resulting requisite referral base for successful practice. Additionally, as a specialty practitioner, it will afford him or her the opportunity to meet specific dental health needs of society which are not met by the generalist in the dental care delivery system of today.

Periodontics as a specialty was practiced since the late 1920's but was not recognized by the American Dental Association until 1948. Since that time, of the more than 560 university-trained periodontists, the School provided 40% of this total. The universal acceptance of the program is attested to by the fact that there were students from twenty-five states and twelve foreign countries.

Just over a hundred years ago, the School was founded by two innovators – Charles J. Essig and Edwin T. Darby. It was their firm conviction that dental education had to achieve a balance between scientific knowledge and mechanical techniques. In accepting the responsibility of promoting and developing a professional status for their pupils, they had to confront certain challenges in coping with a technical field rapidly becoming complex, appreciating the biological significance of dental diseases and realizing the relationship the dento-biologic concept had with the entire human organism.

And then, the School was fortunate in having two modern innovators – D. Walther Cohen and Morton Amsterdam. They were not satisfied with the prior structure that was serving the School's then current and projected needs; there was a fragmentation of services and academic functions and they saw the need for the development and implementation of systematic technological systems within a new organization of academic and administrative management function. As part of this plan, undergraduate and graduate educational programs were implemented by the creation of new departments and restructuring existing ones. As a result, each department would have its own chairman, who would be responsible for coordinating it educational mission. The Department of Periodontics was reorganized by establishing new programs of combined disciplines, such as periodontics-periodontal prosthesis, periodontics-endodontics, periodontics-orthodontics, together the undergraduate program.

> *These men were dedicated to the highest principles of education. Their progressive thinking was for the improvement of dentistry and periodontal concepts were fundamental to this, i.e., this was where things were happening; in periodontal research, clinical achievements and new programs in dental education. And, we were part of it!*

The Knowledge explosion of the post-World War II era influenced areas of higher learning, including undergraduate and graduate study in dentistry. Scientific advancement in basic sciences and clinical disciplines have resulted in both qualitative and quantitative changes. Economic conditions, shifting government policies, changing patterns of dental disease, public attitudes and scientific and technological advances can have a profound effect on the future of dental educational programs. The establishment of the program resulted in, increased institutional prestige, progressional stimulation and better patient care. It was a new dimension in University graduate education – clinical experience and specialization for practice in developing a new generation of professionals.

I graduated from the University of Pennsylvania Dental School in 1950. In June 1950 I came to Boston to begin a 15 month Research Fellowship in Pathology and Periodontics with Dr. Henry M. Goldman at the Beth Israel Hospital. The program was quite intense but I learned a great deal from the original faculty at the hospital. I had the opportunity to participate in 40 autopsies and served in the Pathology Department as well as in Dental Medicine. I also spent one day a week observing in Dr. Goldman's office. I followed Dr. Jack Bloom who preceded me in this program and while I was full time. Dr. Gerry Kramer was completing his program on a part time basis over several years. The environment was extremely stimulating and I also sat in on Dr. Goldman's one week course in Periodontics. In the spring of 1951 Dr. Frank Beube of Columbia University brought his faculty to Boston for the first meeting of the Columbia-Beth Israel Study Club and I had the privilege of meeting Dr. Lewis Fox, Saul Schluger, Mel Morris, Len and Isador Hirschfeld, Herbert Bartlestone, and Bob Gottsegen. This group continued to meet twice a year for the next 3-4 years.

At the completion of my program Dr. Goldman invited me to stay in his practice and join his staff at the hospital. It was difficult to turn down but I felt obligated to return to Philadelphia to join my father in practice half-time and teach at Penn Dental School half time. Starting in 1952 Dean Lester Burktel invited Dr. Goldman to come to Penn in December to give a 1 week course in Periodontics. This course included lectures and clinical demonstrations in television by Dr. Goldman. I assisted Dr. Goldman who was a master clinician. In 1954 Dean Burket proposed to Goldman that a 2 year graduate program in Periodontology be given at

Penn and the 2nd year at the Beth Israel Hospital. Dr. Goldman would become Professor and Chairman of Periodontology in the Graduate School of Medicine and I would be responsible for the first year at Penn. This new graduate program began at Penn in 1955 and continued till 1963 when Boston University became responsible for both years. The first and second years were then offered in the Division of Advanced Dental Education at the University of Pennsylvania, School of Dental Medicine and I became Director of this program. This program has continued and is now completing its 60th year having trained more than a thousand graduate students. One of the conditions of my acceptance by Dr. Goldman was that I would devote a significant portion of my time to dental education. From 1951 until 1962 I was half time at Penn and then in 1962 I became full time and Professor and Chair of Department of Periodontics. Dr. Goldman continued to come to Penn annually to give his course and then his major responsibilities in starting the Boston University School of Graduate Dentistry became so burdensome that he could not continue his annual course. In 1978 at the Centennial of the University of Pennsylvania, School of Dental Medicine several distinguished individuals were honored at a special convocation. Dr. Goldman received an honorary doctorate from Penn at this time his citation included the phrase "father of modern periodontics" a title that was well deserved. I became Dean of the University of Pennsylvania, School of Dental Medicine in July 1972 and served until 1983. During my years at Penn there were many interactions with Dr. Goldman and I had the privilege of joining him as a co-author of Periodontics published by the C.V. Mosby Co. Dr. Goldman published the first edition of this text when he was 29 years old in 1940. This became a classic in the field and was followed by several editions and then in addition by Periodontal Therapy which also included Dr. Schluger and Dr. Fox and myself. Dr. Goldman became the founding editor of the Journal of American Society of

Periodontics which in 1968 merged with the Journal of Periodontology in association with the merger between the American Academy of Periodontology and the American Society of Periodontists. Dr. Goldman had an illustrious career. He was known around the world for his many contributions to the field of Periodontics. He was honored by several Universities in the United States and abroad for his efforts in Dental Education. He started the first graduate private dental school after World War II and the Trustees of Boston University decided to name that school the Henry M. Goldman School of Dentistry at Boston University. This was the first time a school was named and this distinct honor was recognized as an appropriate recognition of Dr. Goldman's many important advancements to the field. Personally, Dr. Goldman changed my life. My 15 months in Boston gave me an experience that shaped my activities for the rest of my career. Henry Goldman was Mentor par excellence and he also influenced tens of thousands of students from around the world. Those of us at Penn were grateful for the experience of working closely with Henry Goldman. During the 1960's, 70's and 80's it felt like a golden era with students meeting Henry Goldman in addition to Morton Amsterdam, Leonard Abrams, Arnold Weisgold, Louis Rose and many others. Many students of Dr. Goldman went on to senior positions and several became Deans of Dental Schools such as Charles Jerge, David Beaudreau, Harry Bohannon, Peter Robinson, Michael Fritz and Ian Davies. They along with Robert Genco received the highest honors in academics. They were all fortunate to follow in the footsteps of Dr. Henry Goldman. In addition to his innumerable contributions to the field Dr. Goldman was an outstanding fund raiser. He was able to garner support for the Beth Israel Hospital as well as Boston University. Donors found it extremely difficult to turn Dr. Goldman down when he was seeking support.

Dr. Goldman wanted me to succeed him as Dean at Boston University, but I was well into my Deanship at Penn to leave that post. When Dr. Goldman became Emeritus he continued to teach and help Spencer Frankl who became Dean. We also continued to update the text Periodontal Therapy and published Periodontal Medicine with Dr. Robert Genco and Dr. Louis Rose. Eventually Dr. Genco became the senior author of Periodontics and it was a well-received volume. When I was inaugurated as President of the Medical College of Pennsylvania in 1987 both Dr. Goldman and Dr. Schluger were in attendance. Unfortunately, Dr. Goldman passed away in 1990 after struggling with Parkinson Disease for several years. He had a rich and fulfilling life and was an iconic legend in the field of dental medicine.

Henry was a devoted husband and father. His lovely wife Dorothy was a wonderful wife and mother of their 2 sons Richard and Gerald. Dorothy accompanied Henry on many of his trips and she was the perfect hostess for their receptions. Henry and Dorothy were a great team when Henry was organizing the school a Boston University. She was a wonderful asset in their recruiting efforts for new faculty. When I lived in Boston, Dorothy acted like a caring sister to my wife Betty Ann. It was also a treat to be received in the Goldman home.

APPENDIX 2
UNIVERSITY OF PENNSYLVANIA-BETH ISRAEL HOSPITAL-BOSTON UNIVERSITY TIMELINE BY ARNOLD S. WEISGOLD, DDS, FACD

University of Pennsylvania-Beth Israel Hospital-Boston University: Penn Periodontal-Prosthesis, & B.I. Periodontics, & B.U. Periodontics Historical Timeline: Arnold Weisgold, Morton Amsterdam, D. Walter Cohen and Henry M. Goldman until the Boston University School of Graduate Dentistry Officially Opens

By Arnold S. Weisgold, DDS, FACD,
Former Chairman of the Department of
Periodontal Prosthesis at
The University of Pennsylvania
School of Dental Medicine

1935-1939: HMG Research Fellow and Instructor in Oral Pathology at Harvard University School of Dental Medicine

1939-1945: WW11 HMG U.S. Army Chief of the Dental Pathologic Section and Pathologist to the Dental Registry in the Armed Forces Institute of Pathology in Washington, D.C.

1945: HMG discharged from Army; received the Army Commendation Ribbon and Presidential Citation

1945: HMG Bay State Road Practice

1949-1956: HMG was Director of the American Board of Oral Pathology, serving as President from 1955 to 1956; he was also Director of the American Board of Periodontology from 1952 to 1958

1948 to 1950: HMG was a member of the Sub-Committee on Periodontia in the National Research Council

1951 to 1954: HMG served as a member of the Council of Dental Research in the American Dental Association

1957-1963: HMG was a Consultant in Periodontology at the National Institute of Dental Research

1945-1958: Chief of the Dental Service at the Reisman Dental Clinic, The Beth Israel Hospital, Boston, Massachusetts

1958: Chairman of the Department of Stomatology at Boston University, School of Medicine

1951: D. Walter Cohen completes training in Periodontia as the first student of HMG at The Reisman Dental Clinic at The Beth Israel Hospital, Boston, Massachusetts

1951: D. Walter Cohen returns to Philadelphia to go into practice with his father, Abram Cohen

1951: D. Walter Cohen teaches half time at University of Pennsylvania School of Dental Medicine: ¼ in Pathology and ½ in Periodontia (which was then part of The Department of Oral Medicine)

1952-1953: HMG while teaching a course at University of Pennsylvania School of Dental Medicine, he is approached by Dr. Lester Burket, Dean of the School of Dental Medicine at The University of Pennsylvania about starting a coordinated program in Periodontia between the University of Pennsylvania and The Beth Israel hospital in Boston, Massachusetts where HMG was the Chief of The Dental Service

1955: The start of the program between the University of Pennsylvania and The Beth Israel Hospital; one year at the University of Pennsylvania; the following year at The Beth Israel Hospital

1955: Morton Amsterdam introduces a Periodontal-Prosthesis Program at The University of Pennsylvania ; it was not a formal program; some of the early preceptees were: Jules Minker (a student at Temple University School of Dentistry when Morton Amsterdam was teaching there); Leonard Abrams (who spent his second year at Boston University and received a Certificate in Periodontia); Harry Bohanon (who was in a similar program as Leonard Abrams); and, Charles Jerge (who received his PhD in Physiology and a Certificate in Periodontia)

1955-1959: The Periodontal training between the University of Pennsylvania and The Beth Israel Hospital continues until 1959 when the second year moves from The Beth Israel Hospital to Boston University

1955-1963: Periodontics: BI/BU Periodontics two year alternating program continues until 1963 when The Boston University School of Graduate Dentistry is chartered and opens; candidates are now given the choice to stay at The University of Pennsylvania for the second year or go to Boston University; Arnold Weisgold started with Gerald Isenberg and Walter Watson; Arnold stayed at The University of Pennsylvania in Periodontal-Prosthesis; Gerald Isenberg and Walter Watson went to Boston University;

1958: HMG becomes Chief of Stomatology at The Boston University School of Medicine

1961: The Periodontal-Prosthesis Preceptor Program is formalized; it is a 28 month program

1961: Two divisions under The Department of Periodontics: 1) Periodontal-Prosthesis directed by Morton Amsterdam; and, 2) Periodontics by D. Walter Cohen; Periodontal-Prosthesis is a 28 month program with one student/year

1961-1973: Morton Amsterdam is Director of Periodontics-Prosthesis Program

1963: Arnold Weisgold is the third student in the Periodontal-Prosthesis Program (the program is 28 months under Morton Amsterdam)

1963: The Boston University School of Graduate Dentistry is chartered and opens to the first official trainees in all the dental specialties

1965: The Periodontal Prosthesis Program becomes a two year program with two students accepted

1969: The Periodontal Prosthesis becomes a three year program

1972 (July 1st): D. Walter Cohen becomes Dean of The University of Pennsylvania of Dental Medicine until he steps down on July 30, 1983

1973: Arnold Weisgold becomes Director of The Periodontal Prosthesis Program at The University of Pennsylvania; he holds this position until 2006

1974: Periodontal-Prosthesis accepts three students for the program

1984: The Periodontal Programs expand to three years to incorporate Implant training; The Periodontal-Prosthesis Program at The University of Pennsylvania expands to four years

2006:Ernesto Lee becomes Director of The Periodontal- Prosthesis Program, The University of Pennsylvania, succeeding Arnold Weisgold where he remains today

2014: Presently the Periodontal-Prosthesis Program at The University of Pennsylvania accepts four students (sometimes five)

APPENDIX 3
ANTHONY GIANELLY, DMD, MD, PHD: PRIMER ON BASIC ORTHODONTIC PRINCIPLES

When treatment procedures and techniques are described, they are often outlined in a rigidly sequential manner, indicating that certain procedures should be performed in specific order. As an example, a technique format may be:

1. band/bracket all teeth
2. align and flatten the curve of Spee, using maxillary anchorage support and Class Ill elastics
3. retract canines with coils applying anchorage support where necessary
4. retract incisors with a torqued rectangular wire under appropriate anchorage considerations
5. finishing ideal arches

This type description suggests that the technique is standardized, universally applied and its mere adherence is the basis of a well resolved problem. Unfortunately, clinical practice is not so simple. There are many, oftentimes perplexing, variations which necessitate changes in the system. Thus, flexibility is, at times, crucial.

This analysis implies that the <u>principles</u> of a treatment procedure and/or a technique are more important than the individual components because they "impart" the required adaptability.

It also indicates that there are a number of considerations that apply to all treatment procedures and techniques. One is that a thorough diagnosis must be made and treatment plan formulated before mechanotherapy begins. The diagnosis should define all dental and skeletal discrepancies in all planes of space. Essentially, it provides the necessary information to design a treatment plan. The treatment plan in turn outlines a program to resolve the orthodontic problem (which, under conventional circumstances, is to convert the malocclusion into a Class I ideal skeletodental occlusion).

Certain "simple rules" and "corollaries" exist. The rules include:

I. Mandibular arch -

The "Diagnostic arch" is the mandibular arch and:

1) Intercanine dimension is relatively inviolable

2) Movement of the lower incisor region labially is most often contraindicated (there are specific exceptions such as an incisor segment which has been displaced "excessively" lingually by abnormal muscle forces). Additionally, some suggest that incisors which are lingual to certain reference planes such as the A-Pog or N-Pog should be moved "cautiously" to that line.

3) Expansion essentially indicates only distal movement of molars, generally believed to be limited to a few mm. However, this supposition is not well documented and there are differing opinions concerning this view. For example, some advocate lateral expansion in the premolar and molar segment when the lower arch is constricted.

II. Maxillary arch:

1) The arch "fits" over a well placed lower arch. Thus, intercanine dimension and maxillary incisor spatial considerations are somewhat irrelevant.

2) Expansion (i.e. distal molar movement) is more readily accomplished. One cusp molar distalization is apparently quite feasible by the following mechanism:
   a) tooth movement
   b) orthopedic control

Distalization of molars is considered a bite opening procedure since the molars are "wedged into the angle" of the occlusal plane. "Wedging" in turn, leads to a brief review of mandibular <u>rotation</u>. There are two principle rotatory movements that the mandible can follow:

I. <u>Clockwise rotation</u>: This movement tends to move the mandible <u>downward</u> <u>and backward</u>. The result is:
    1) an increase in the cant of the mandibular plane:
    2) <u>posterior, inferior</u> movement of pogonion, <u>enhancing facial convexity</u>, and;
    3) an increase in face height, particularly of the lower face.
II. <u>Counterclockwise rotation</u>. This movement tends to rotate the mandible <u>upward and forward</u>. The result is:
    1) a decrease in the cant of the mandibular plane
    2) <u>anterior, superior movement</u> of pogonion, straightening the profile
    3) in a non-growing face, a decrease in face height principally of the lower face

During growth, mandibular rotations occur because of imbalance of vertical growth in the anterior and posterior parts of the face. The dividing line is the PTM fissure, identifying the posterior part of the maxilla. The vertical growth in the anterior part of the face occurs in the sutures and the dentoalveolar segments of the maxillary and mandibular arches. The vertical growth in the posterior part of the face occurs in the condylar-ramal area. When the vertical growth of the posterior part of the face is greater than the vertical growth of the anterior part, the mandible rotates in a counterclockwise direction (straightening the profile). This occurs approximately 90% of the time and is a major reason why convex faces become less convex with age.

Conversely, when the vertical growth in the anterior part of the face exceeds the comparable growth in the posterior region, the mandible rotates in a clockwise direction and facial convexity increases.

In treatment, counterclockwise rotation is associated with intrusion of posterior teeth and/or mesial movement "out of the wedge".

Since a straight profile (excluding the nose) is a principle goal of treatment, some suggest that rotation should always be counterclockwise (except in an "overly flat face). According to this analysis, any clockwise rotation in a normal or convex face should be avoided, if possible.

Clockwise rotation can be a consequence of distalization (wedging effect) +/or extrusion of posterior teeth.

There is no guide to indicate the amount of bite opening and rotation that occurs with distalization. Furthermore, in growing children, vertical facial growth can presumably "compensate" so that there is little bite opening and no rotation.

A few corollaries are:

1. Non-extraction procedures tend to open bites and elongate faces. In addition, there may be a tendency toward clockwise rotation since distalization with its wedging effect most often is involved.
2. Extraction procedures tend to close bites and shorten faces They may also encourage counterclockwise rotation since mesial movement of the molars usually occurs.
3. Crowding in the mandibular arch of more than a few millimeters per side speaks to extraction since arch expansion possibilities are limited in most instances.
4. Malocclusions with skeletodentally "correct" lower arch relationships in normal facial patterns generally speak to non-extraction procedures.
5. Faces in which:

1) the mandibular plane angle is large and mandibular plane is steep
2) the "bite" is shallow
3) the profile is convex
4) the face, particularly the lower half is long
5) the occlusal plane — mandibular plane angle is steep
   Speak to extraction because:

   > Mesial movement into extraction sites tends to favor counterclockwise rotation, reducing face height, straightening the profile and deepening the bite. Generally, closure of extraction sites is relatively uncomplicated. These patients can be termed vertically sensitive: open type - indicating that procedures which increase face height and convexity and/or open the bite are contraindicated since the facial patterns can not tolerate these movements well (i.e. avoid clockwise rotation).

6. Faces in which:
   1) The mandibular plane angle is low and the mandibular plane is flat
   2) the bite is deep
   3) the profile is straight and the chin is prominent
   4) the lower face height is relatively small
   5) the occlusal plane and mandibular plane are parallel
      Speak to non-extraction procedures for at least two reasons:
      a) Molar distalization is desirable since it tends to open the bite and anchorage clockwise rotation.
      b) At times it is difficult to maintain incisor position (anchorage) when closing extraction sites. Thus, an overly flat profile can result.
         These patients can arbitrarily be defined as vertically sensitive - closed type — indicating that procedures such as extractions which tend to decrease convexity

and face height may be contraindicated (i.e. avoid clockwise rotation)

7. Prognosis is inversely related to skeletal involvement. It follows that malocclusion syndromes with the best prognosis are those with only dental and dentoalveolar involvement. These represent principally Class I problems. The worst prognosis usually accompanies malocclusion syndromes with skeletal involvement in all three planes of space: A-P, vertical, and transverse. (Ackerman and Profitt)

The treatment plan indicates in part:

1. the need for and location of space to reposition any malposed teeth
2. the method of obtaining space if necessary (i.e. expansion, extraction)
   a) The utilization of space for the following variables that require space for correction (not in order of importance).
      A. Alignment
      B. Midline Correction
      C. Curve of Spee reduction and bite opening
      D. Profile Correction
      E. Molar Correction

A) **Alignment** - all crowding and rotations must be resolved, preferably in the initial phase. This may be time consuming, yet if these discrepancies are not corrected, intercuspation almost invariably suffers and the result compromised. Correcting these problems in the later stages of treatment can be cumbersome because the side effects can produce other problems. As an example, if premolar rotations are left until after the canines have been fully retracted, their correction by means of elastic ligature tied to the archwire usually causes spaces to be reopened between the canines and premolars since the elastic passes between the teeth to reach the archwire. Thus, canine retraction with consequent anchorage considerations may have to be redone.

B) **Midline Correction** - the lower midline should be coincident with the midline of the face and the maxillary midline must coincide with the lower midline. In essence this indicates that equal amounts of tooth substance will exist on both sides of the arch and the face.

C) **Curve of Spee reduction and bite opening:** Curve of Spee reduction which (along with band placement) can require up to 2-3 mm. per side (Mitchell) indicates that the dental arches should be flat because it is simpler when the arches are flat:

    a)   to move teeth over each other

    b)   to intercuspate teeth — thus obtaining maximum intercuspation more readily

    c)   to open the bite

    d)   technically to make sequential wires

Accordingly, Curve of Spee reduction is usually done <u>early</u>, most often in the initial stages of treatment. One method to flatten the arch (i.e. reduce the Curve of Spee) is to use a wire with a reverse Curve of Spee. The forces exerted by this wire tend to (1) elevate the premolars, (2) depress the incisors and molars (3) move incisors anteriorly (4) move molars distally. Unfortunately, the movements that occur when a wire with a reverse curve is placed are not well documented. On study (Mitchell) showed that leveling the lower arch entailed (a) principally premolar extrusion with (b) incisor protraction and intrusion and (c) small amounts of molar intrusion and distalization. <u>Since the incisor segment tends to move anteriorly during the leveling process, some advocate the use of Class III elastics during this phase to diminish and/ or eliminate this undesirable movement.</u>

Additionally, the intrusive component in the molar region may serve to cancel the extrusive vector when Class II elastics are used (Merrifield) From a practical point of view, the distal area of a wire with a reverse curve should be expanded (1/8 - 1/4") particularly when Class

II elastics are used because the reverse curve tends to constrict the distal aspects of the wires, causing the molars to "roll" lingually.

"Bite Opening":

Bite Opening is <u>essential</u> to complete an orthodontic problem well. For this reason, emphasis has been placed on bite opening systems. In addition to the dental movements involved in leveling of the Curve of Spee, there are many other possible movements (or combination of *these*) that tend to open the bite. Four include:

1. Mandibular molar extrusion
2. Maxillary molar extrusion
3. Mandibular incisor intrusion
4. Maxillary incisor intrusion
   As yet there appears to be no 'correct" method to open the bite. Essentially 3 schools of thought exist:

(a) According to one view (Schudy) an efficient bite opening mechanism is the <u>extrusion of the mandibular molar.</u> He based this on observations of post treatment stability of bite opening procedures. He noted that lower molar extrusion is the bite opening mechanism of choice when posterior alveolar height is relatively undeveloped, as evidenced by an OM-MP angle of greater than 16 degrees. It is less efficient when posterior alveolar developments is normal to excessive as demonstrated by OM-MP angle of less than 16 degrees. He further contends that lower incisor intrusion is less stable and should be used only when the vertical conditions of the face do not permit molar extrusion (e.g. open bite, low OM angle).
Lower molar extrusion coupled with inhibition of the "normal" eruptive movement of the lower incisors is apparently a principle bite opening mechanism of the light wire (Begg) technique. Some contend that the incisor intrusion component is the larger.

(b) In contrast, the Tweed group suggests that a flat lower arch coupled with maxillary incisor intrusion (hi-pull gear) is adequate.

This group feels extrusive forces on molars are basically incorrect because they encourage alveolar development in the posterior regions. These factors tend to lead to mandibular clockwise rotation, exaggerating any facial convexity. (On the other hand, intrusive components on molars, the maxillary in particular, are desirable because they "impede" posterior vertical eruption and alveolar development. Accordingly, vertical dimensions in the posterior regions of the dental arch are less developed. Under these conditions, the mandible can presumably assume a more anterior position as a result of counterclockwise rotation, thus straightening the face.)

(c) Finally, Ricketts, in the "bioprogressive technique", suggests that stable bite opening can occur with lower incisor intrusion. Bite opening tends to relapse - usually 1/3 - 1/2. Therefore, bite opening is generally continued beyond the desired end point to accommodate the expected relapse. The mechanism for relapse is not entirely clear. Some "extrusion" of the incisors apparently occurs.

Clinically, it may be advantageous to open the bite <u>as soon as possible</u> during treatment because tooth movement and anchorage requirements are often more readily apparent when the bite is open. Also bite opening at the end of treatment may pose a strain on anchorage and may not always be successful. (an empirical observation)

D) **<u>Profile Correction</u> (Skeletal Correction)**

There are a number of mechanisms by which <u>convex profiles (excluding the nose)</u> can "be straightened". Only one involves principally tooth movement and therefore requires space in the arch. This entails the <u>lingual</u> positioning of the lower incisors, generally to conform to an idealized position relative to a craniofacial reference line such as the NB or A-Pog lines. This procedure is called <u>profile reduction.</u>

Lower incisor retraction reduces perioral fullness since the lower lip also moves lingually. (Most researchers indicate that the lip moves approximately 1 mm. lingually for every mm. of incisor retraction although extreme variation exists.)

In addition, it can serve to help align point A and B reducing the ANB angle because maxillary incisor movement (and possibly point A) is inherently limited by the A-P position of the lower incisors. This method of "profile straightening" is the most common.

Other systems for facial straightening include at least the following three "orthopedic" corrections:

1) If the forward vector of nasomaxillary growth were retarded or redirected, the mandible which is growing unimpeded could catch up. Orthopedic type gears have been used for this purpose.

2) Presumably if maxillary posterior alveolar vertical development were retarded, the mandible could have more opportunity to rotate counterclockwise during closure and therefore be positioned more anteriorly. A hi-pull gear directed against the maxillary molars might assist in this procedure by "retarding" posterior alveolar vertical development.

3) With the use of functional appliances the mandible can be stimulated to grow because functional appliances apparently can stimulate the condylar centers. These orthopedic methods tend to align maxilla and mandible-- not merely point A and B.

E. <u>Molar Correction</u> - Class I molar position generally indicates that, in occlusion, the distal cusps of the maxillary first molars should contact the mesial cusps of the mandibular <u>second</u> molars. (Andrews) Distal positioning in this manner allows for adequate intermolar space for at least 3 factors:

1) <u>maximum intercuspation</u>— If the maxillary molars are not placed far enough distally to touch the mandibular second molar, intercuspation often suffers and premolar cusp tips contact mesially on inclined planes.

2) <u>Bite opening particularly when the maxillary incisor segment is involved</u>— The need for space in bite opening may

relate in part to the premise that intrusion of certain maxillary teeth is an aspect of the bite opening mechanism. The need for space for "intrusion" arises from the fact that the axial inclinations of the teeth of the maxillary arch, most notably the incisor segment, are oriented in such a manner that their root apices converge toward a "hypothetical intracranial reference point" while the crowns diverge, essentially forming a "cone". As teeth move "up the cone" (i.e. intrusion) they occupy a smaller arch length.

3) Since the teeth must occupy a smaller arch length after intrusion, space must be available for intrusion to occur. Clinically this signifies that arch length must be sufficient to allow for the space "consumed" in, bite opening. This, in turn, generally indicates that the maxillary molars must be in a Class I relationship as outlined previously (i.e. touching the mandibular second molar when the teeth are occluded). If the molars are not far enough distally, arch length may not be "adequate" for proper bite opening.

Thus, some corollaries are:

a) Inadequate bite opening

1) is often seen in conjunction with molar relationships bordering on but not achieving full Class I positions and intercuspation which is not maximum,

2) can represent poor anchorage control, indicating that the spaces necessary for bite opening were not available.

b) Since bite opening by means of maxillary incisor "intrusion" requires space, it follows that one method to close maxillary spaces (particularly incisor spaces) near the completion of treatment is to open the bite by "Intruding" the incisors.

3) Maxillary Incisor Root Torque:
When the roots of teeth which are aligned on the arc of a circle are torqued lingually, the distal aspects of the crowns move distally. To accommodate for this movement, space must obviously be available. An important

source of this space is the distal placement of the posterior teeth, with the distal aspect of the maxillary molars in contact with the mandibular second molars when the teeth are in occlusion.

Thus the space requirements are analogous to those concerned with bite opening. It also follows that the clinical implications are comparable

a) Inadequate incisor torque is often associated with molar relationships that are "slightly Class II" and/or reflect poor anchorage control.

b) Incisor root torque represents a mechanism to aid closure of

c) incisor spacing

To reiterate, if the posterior teeth are intercuspated and their position maintained, adequate incisor torque and bite opening are essential for proper placement of the canines and anterior space closure.

The roles of incisor torque and bite opening in space closure are illustrated in Fig. 1. A diastema between the maxillary central incisors was closed and the apparent mechanisms included incisor torque and intrusion, particularly since no overjet was present.

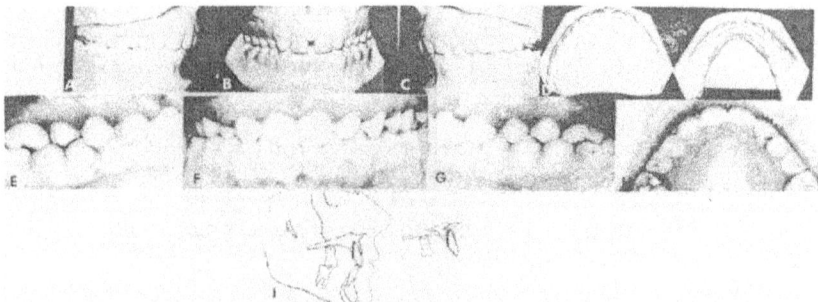

Figure 1 - A-D) Initial models showing diastema between maxillary central incisors and no overjet: E-H) Final records showing closure of the diastema: I) Superimposition indicates that the central incisors were torqued and intruded.

Root torque can also control interincisal angulation which may be related to overbite relapse (largely unproven). Presumably, relapse tendency increases as the interincisal angle increases above the ideal angulation of 130°-135° because the "overly upright" incisors can "slip" by each other, closing the bite. However, one study failed to document this relationship.

In summary, at the start of treatment: (a) alignment and rotations should be corrected; (b) the arches leveled; (c) bite opening, if possible, should be complete or almost complete.

II. Technique Evaluation: Another universal principle is that all techniques must have procedures for evaluation. There are many methods which can be used to assess the worth of any technical procedure. One is as follows:

(a) Indicate the desired effect

(b) Pose the following questions:

1. What are the available procedures (Le. solutions)?

2. What are some of the advantages and disadvantages of the procedure chosen to produce the effect? This includes an analysis of all possible side effects. (reaction forces and movements)

3. What are the reference points to determine if the effect has been achieved?

A clinical example — the retraction of maxillary canines under conditions of maximum anchorage, will be used to discuss these ideas.

Accordingly, a force system which will apply only a net distal force against the canine is required. In this example, assume that the maxillary arch has been fully banded and a molar stopped arch wire has been placed.

1) 1) Available procedures: There are at least 10-20 procedures that are used to retract canines. Only the following three will be used as illustrations:

a. extraoral traction against the canines, directing them distally. In this instance, the reaction force is not applied to any dental unit. Additionally, molar position is stabilized by the molar stopped archwire connected to the other teeth.

b. Intra-arch Class I forces (elastics, coils, etc.) can be attached from the canine to the first molar while molar position could be "supported" with extraoral traction directed against the molars. Under these conditions, the possibility of mesial molar movement is an important consideration because there is an <u>active</u> mesial vector (reaction force) applied to the molar by means of the Class I force. Presumably the distal vector derived from the headgear will cancel the mesially directed force, maintaining molar position.

c. Class II forces applied directly against the canine. No mesial vector is applied to the maxillary molar and molar position is again stabilized by the stopped archwire. However, the reaction force, in this instance, applies a mesial vector to the lower arch.

2) Advantages and Disadvantages

A. Extraoral traction against the canines:

Some advantages are:

1. It is safe and molar stability is reasonably secure since a molar stopped wire is in place.

2. Since only the gear applies the force, there are few side effects.

Some disadvantages are:

1. The gear is generally not worn 24 hours a day. Therefore the applied force is discontinuous and movement may be slow. Continuously applied forces move teeth faster.

2. Patient cooperation is essential.

B. Class I forces from the canine to the molar with extraoral traction supporting the position of the molar.

Some advantages are:

1. The force is generally continuous, leading to quicker tooth movement.

2. Cooperation is not necessary for canine distalization.

Some disadvantages are:

1. The mesial vector applied to the molar can produce undesirable anchorage loss. Cooperation (i.e. gear use) is necessary to stabilize molar position.
2. The gear is generally worn only 12—14 hours/day. Thus anchorage loss even with cooperation can occur (generally 12—14 hours/day of gear use is sufficient to stabilize the molars)

C. Class II forces against the canines

Some advantages are:

1. There is no mesial vector applied to the molar "straining" its position
2. The applied force is continuous.

Some disadvantages are:

1. The movement tends to be slower than with the use of Class I forces. The reason is not clear, it may relate to the vertical vector of the Class II elastics possibly causing "binding" on the wire.
2. The possibility of forward movement of the lower arch exists and precautions must be taken to avoid this problem, if indicated.
3. Cooperation is necessary

    Anchorage control (i.e. preservation of specified dental position) deserves some comment. When the positions of the anchor units are controlled, there should be adequate space for dental alignment requirements and profile considerations. Any anchorage "loss", on the other hand, limits the available space. Accordingly, adjustments must be made in the various space requirements. (i.e. crowding. midline, profile, etc.) In the skeletodental view of occlusion, the dental complex (Class I ideal occlusion) takes precedence over the profile (skeletal) requirement. Thus Class I occlusion is achieved in the available space at the expense of profile correction. The compromised profile, then, is generally the result of inadequate anchorage control.

3) Reference Points

In order to evaluate the effect of the treatment procedure, reference points are obviously necessary. Furthermore, the effect of the treatment procedure on these reference points must also be assessed carefully. In the present example of canine retraction, when either extraoral traction or Class II elastic traction is used, maxillary molar position should remain reasonably stable in the 3—4 week period between observations because no mesial force has been applied to the molars. In addition, molar position has been stabilized by the stopped archwire. Accordingly, the maxillary molars may serve as a reference point. On the other hand, when the intra-arch Class I system is used, the possibility of molar protraction exists because there is an active mesial vector applied to the molars. For this reason, the molars may not be a suitable reference point because of the possible side effects of the applied force. Thus, another must be selected.

Well chosen reference points are indispensable. For instance, if maxillary molar position has changed from a Class I relationship to a Class II position and the mandibular arch untreated, maxillary molar anchorage probably has been lost. Accordingly, both treatment plan and mechanical design might be altered as follows:

1. Try to regain molar position, if possible. This at times is quite difficult to impossible. It can take up to 3 months to correct a mistake that occurred in 3-4 weeks.
2. Probably alter the mechanical system to one which is less prone to lose anchorage i.e. with no mesial force on the molar. If canine retraction were necessary, a gear could be placed directly against the canines with a molar stop and a tipback used to stabilize the molar.

   Normally at least four reference points can be selected:
   1) The spatial position of the lower incisor — a cephalometric determination.
   2) The lower midline
   3) The right molar relationship

4) The left molar relationship

If the lower incisor and midline are correctly situated, proximal contact and appropriate arch form indicate that the molars are equally and symmetrically placed from the midpoint of the arch (i.e. 'correct"). Class I molar relationships would indicate that the maxillary posterior teeth are also adequately located. Some examples will illustrate the use of these reference points:

Example 1:

Assume in an extraction problem:

1. The mandibular incisor position and midline are correct and the incisors are well aligned; in addition, there is a space of 2 mm. between the canines and posterior teeth.
2. The right molar relationship is Class I.
3. The left molar relationship is Class I.

> The interpretation is as follows:
>> The mandibular incisor segment needs no further space for correction. Thus the posterior teeth must be protracted to close the space. It follows that the maxillary molars must also be protracted to maintain the Class I relationship.

Example II:

Assume in an extraction problem:

1. The lower incisor is spatially 2 mm. <u>anterior</u> to the correct position. The mandibular midline is correct, the incisors are aligned and 2 mm. of space exist between the anterior and posterior segments.
2. the right molar relationship is Class I
3. the left molar relationship is Class I

> The interpretation is as follows:
>> The mandibular incisor segment must be retracted 2 mm. to satisfy the profile requirement. Thus, the lower molar position must be maintained (maximum anchorage). It follows that maxillary molar position must also be maintained to preserve the Class I relationship.

Example Ill:

Assume the same conditions as Case II:

1. The lower incisor is spatially 2 mm. anterior to the correct position. The mandibular midline is correct. the incisors are aligned and 2 mm. of space exist between the anterior and posterior segments

2. The right molar relationship is 2 mm. Class II

3. The left molar relationship is 2 mm. Class II

> The interpretation is as follows:
>
>> The space in the lower arch must be used for incisor retraction. Therefore the lower molars must stay in position; it follows that the maxillary molars must be <u>distalized</u> 2 mm.

I. <u>Symmetrical and Asymmetrical Conditions</u>

Symmetrical situations indicate. in part, that an equal amount of tooth movement must occur on both sides of the arch. If, for example, the maxillary molars must be held in position bilaterally and the incisors must be unraveled and distalized to the posterior teeth, a symmetrical condition exists (movement on both sides of the arch is reasonably equal).

Since most conventionally used force systems tend to distribute themselves symmetrically, the resolution of this problem can be accomplished with relatively uncomplicated force systems. For example, intra-arch Class I forces can be used bilaterally for incisor movements in conjunction with a gear to stabilize the molars.

For asymmetrical movement, the force systems must be adjusted so that one type force will exist on one side of the arch and another type on the other side of the arch. This can be done. However, it is at times difficult to control and cumbersome to apply. The following example may serve to illustrate this viewpoint. Assume that:

1. The right maxillary molar must stay in position while the right canine must be distalized 3 mm.

2. The left maxillary molar must be protracted 3 mm. while the left canine remains in place.

Accordingly, an asymmetric system exists. It follows that force systems should:
   a. stabilize the right molar
   b. distalize the right canine 3 mm.
   c. move the left molar 3 mm.
   d. stabilize the left canine

One might be: (There are many possible systems)
1. an archwire which is "stopped" against the right molar <u>only</u> and a straight pull gear applied to the anterior part of the arch. This effectively applies a distal vector to the right molar and the left incisor segment.
   Right side:
2. <u>to retract the right canine</u> — the use of an intra-arch Class I force. The distal vector derived from the gear hopefully will cancel the mesial force on the molar resulting from the Class I force
   Left side:
3. <u>to protract the left molar</u> — the use of a Class I force system. To resist canine and incisor displacement as a result of the Class I force system and the gear, the use of 2° force on the canine and 3° forces against the incisors can be used.

It is apparent that this force system is somewhat complicated since many variables have to be evaluated and appropriate compensations have to be made.

This example indicates one of the problems in dealing with asymmetric situations - the limitations and complications in selecting force systems. For this reason, preserve symmetry when present; at times it may be advantageous to create it when it is not. To create symmetry, one sequence would be;

1. protract the left molar as indicated previously

2. stabilize both molars with a gear and apply a Class I force system to distalize the right canine. The asymmetric force system described is overly complicated and was selected as an extreme to illustrate the idea that asymmetric situations can indeed become complex. A more simplified system would be to:

   a) place a Class II elastic against the right canine to distalize it and use a molar stopped arch wire to help stabilize the molar. The Class II force is usually 120–150 grams and probably will have little effect on an intact lower arch. If necessary the lower arch could be supported by a lip bumper.

   b) place a Class I force from the left molar to the left canine, using a second order force (an uprighting spring) on the canine to act as anterior anchorage. The Class I force should protract the molar while the 2° force on the canine hopefully is adequate to counteract the effect of the Class I force on the canine, thus stabilizing its position.

Force Magnitude and Rate of Tooth Movement

There is a continuing debate concerning the effect of force magnitude on the rate of tooth movement of various teeth. For example, Story and Smith in 1952 suggested that there were "optimum" force levels for moving various teeth. After extracting 1st premolars they observed that over a 2-3 month period, 150 grams of force applied between the posterior segments and the canines principally moved the canines into the premolar extraction sites. When the force magnitude was increased to 300 grams, the posterior teeth moved while the canines remained relatively stable. They felt that the observed differences might relate to the type resorption elicited by the forces. The 150 grams which moved the canine might stimulate frontal resorption allowing the tooth to move. In contrast, the 150 grams of force would be inadequate to stimulate a comparable remodeling response on the posterior teeth because of the large root surface area evolved.

On the other hand, 300 grams of applied force might result in rear resorption on the canine, thus slowing or blocking movement of the canines since the frontal plate of bone is the last to be resorbed. However, this force magnitude is large enough to stimulate alveolar remodeling of the posterior teeth, permitting them to move. These data led to a hypothesis of optimal" and "differential" force, indicating that selected force levels would move only <u>certain</u> teeth. This theory, in turn, is the basis of some of the force magnitudes selected in the "light wire" technique.

Others such as Nixon et al and Utley have not been able to confirm the concept of differential force. In contrast they suggest that there appears to be little relationship between force magnitude and rate of movement. Ackerman suggests that the constancy rather than the magnitude of the applied force is the important factor.

As a practical point, many, who see little tooth movement during a specified period such as a 1 month interval, increase the magnitude of the applied force. The result generally is an increased rate of movement.

However, this observation does not contradict the "optimal force" concept because unknown variables such as friction loss are presently undeterminable. It may be that the "effective" force (i.e. the applied force, minus the force lost to friction) is within the range suggested by the "optimal force" principle.

Rates of tooth movement are highly variable. For example, canine retraction into an extraction site can last as little as 3 months or extend for 7-9 months. Thus, the monthly rate of movement can be as little as 0.75 mm. and as high as 2.5 mm. In addition, there may be differences within the same patient. A left canine may move faster than the right canine.

Some principles restated NON-EXTRACTION AND EXTRACTION

Non-Extraction:
  a) lower arch criteria: a "good" lower arch which can be made to conform to the dentoskeletal standard is necessary. This means that In the permanent dentition, there is no crowding in the lower arch and the curve of Spee should be relatively flat (leveling a deep Curve of Spee can require up to 2-3 mm.

of arch length per side). In the mixed dentition, the presence of crowding may not be a deterrent to non extraction treatment because the leeway and or "E" space can provide the necessary space to resolve any incisor crowding in most instances.

Implicit in this argument is that one arch treatment (i.e. maxillary arch alone) is relatively uncommon and the lower arch is almost always included in the treatment procedure because proper final placement of the teeth generally requires control of both arches.

b) maxillary arch: the ability to distalize the arch orthopedically and/or orthodontically is essential. Empirically, this procedure becomes more difficult with advancing age. (There are some studies which document this idea although not conclusively.) This difficulty might relate to a number of factors - including the presence of the second molars. Thus, the late mixed dentition stage of development appears to be a favorable starting time for the maxillary arch.

c) vertically sensitive, open type - generally, the lack of vertical sensitivity is desirable. If vertical sensitivity is severe (arbitrary judgment) the distalization procedure with its wedging effect might be contraindicated. (As suggested previously, in growing children, the possibility of vertical growth compensation exists).

In summary, an advantageous time to begin non-extraction therapy for both the mandibular and maxillary arch is the late mixed dentition stage of development because:

a) leeway space possibilities are available in the lower arch, providing the necessary space to resolve any crowding.

b) maxillary distalization appears easier to accomplish - (although the reasons are not all clear) Perhaps it may relate to the factor that both orthodontic and orthopedic means are available in the growing children. Also the orthodontic capacity (i.e. molar distalization) may be relatively easier since the second molar is unerupted and vertical growth compensation for the wedging effect of the distalization procedure is possible.

Extraction:

The need to extract teeth represents the fact that space to accomplish dento—skeletal objectives cannot be obtained by other means (i.e. expansion, leeway space control, reproximation, etc.) Generally, extraction provides space which is strategically located according to the requirements to achieve dentoskeletal harmony. For example, when four or more mm/side is necessary for incisor needs, the tooth to be extracted is generally the first premolar because it provides "strategically located" space immediately adjacent to the incisor segment. Also. the second premolar can act to support molar position. Conversely, when incisor requirements are 3 mm/side or less indicating that a "large" amount of mesial molar movement is necessary, the second premolar is often extracted to provide the "strategic" space immediately adjacent to the molar. Additionally, the presence of the 1st premolars next to the incisor segment act to support incisor position.

In sum, extractions are performed to provide space to achieve dentoskeletal requirements. The location of the space is generally determined by the extent of movement necessary for the incisor or the buccal segments. Movement generally is facilitated by space located close by. Since in most instances, the incisor requirements exceed 3-4 mm/side, the most commonly extracted tooth is the first premolar. In this manner, at least two benefits result:

a)   immediate access to space for incisor segment requirements
b)   the presence of the 2nd premolar tends to support posterior anchorage Relationship between extraction and "bite depth": As a rule, extraction is considered to be a bite closing procedure for the following reasons:
    a)   empirical observation

b) posterior teeth are generally brought mesially to an extent, <u>decreasing</u> the wedging effect of the buccal segments thereby <u>closing</u> the bite.

c) As incisors are retracted into the extraction site, they tend to "upright", placing the incisor tips more occlusally. In this manner, the bite deepens. A corollary is that extraction procedures might be warranted in "open bite" syndromes and contraindicated in malocclusions characterized by an excessively "deep bite".

APPENDIX 4
BOSTON UNIVERSITY TIMELINE

1950s

1958   Department of Stomatology is established to provide post-doctoral education in dentistry.

1960s

1963-1964   Boston University School of Graduate Dentistry is established and Henry Goldman is appointed its founding dean.

1967   Construction of the 100 East Newton Street building begins.

1969-1970   Principal clinical teaching activities are transferred to the new East Newton Street facility.

1970s

1972   Building on the strong foundations of post-doctoral education, a pre-doctoral program is launched.

1975   School transfers its teaching, clinical, and research activities to the newly completed seven-story building on East Newton Street.

1975   School graduates its first DMD class and Spencer Frankl is appointed dean designate by Boston University's Board of Trustees.

1977   Henry M. Goldman, DMD, retires as dean; Spencer N. Frankl, DDS, MSD, assumes position.

1978   School is renamed the Henry M. Goldman School of Graduate Dentistry by the Trustees of Boston University.

1979   School of Graduate Dentistry and College of Liberal Arts initiate a combined BA and DMD curriculum.

1979   Department of Oral Biology formed and Dr. Morris Ruben is named its first chair.

1979   Booth Ambulatory Surgical Unit, which provides out-patient surgical care, is established.

1979   The post-doctoral and graduate degree programs are reorganized.

1979   The extramural program is established for the DMD curriculum.

1980s

1980   Dental Health Plan for University student body implemented. With its many partnerships in the community, the School continues to branch out beyond the confines of its four walls. This program initiates the "school without walls" concept and the vision of strategic partnering.

1980   The School's Board of Visitors is formed.

1981   The prevention center and the dental plan for college students are expanded to include area schools and colleges.

1981   Dr. Dan Nathanson joins the faculty as the first chair of the new Department of Biomaterials.

1983   Department of Dental Public Health becomes the Department of Dental Care Management.

1984   The School is award a Pew National Dental Education Program Grant.

1984   The School's first strategic planning process is initiated by Dean Spencer Frankl to address the future mission of the School. As an initial step, the Division of Dental Research is established with Dr. Carl Franzblau as director.

1984   The Geriatric Dentistry Division is established in the Department of Dental Care Management.

1987   The Career Resource Center and the Dental Placement Program are introduced.

| 1988 | The School celebrates its 25th anniversary. |

1988   Department of Diagnostic Sciences and Patient Services formed, comprising the Division of Oral Diagnosis and Radiology, the Division of Oral Pathology, and the Division of Patient Services. Dr. Thomas Kilgore is appointed its first chair.

1988   Department of Periodontology and Department of Oral Biology combined as the Department of Periodontology and Oral Biology and Dr. Frank Oppenheim is appointed its first chair.

1989   The APEX (Applied Professional Experience) program, which offers an experiential component to the DMD curriculum, is implemented.

1989   The School establishes the Boston University Dental Health Plan for University employees.

1990s

1990   The Implantology Center is formed under the direction of Dr. Zhimon Jacobson.

1990   Dr. Herbert Schilder is elected first vice president of the American Dental Association and Dr. Anthony Gianelly receives the Stang Award for Outstanding Contributions to the Field of Orthodontics.

1991   The Dental Health Center at 930 Commonwealth Ave. is opened.

1991   Henry M. Goldman, the School's founding dean, dies.

1992   The First International Symposium in Implantology is held.

1992   The School joins Boston University's School of Management and School of Education in the Chelsea School Partnership.

1992   Major facility changes continue, including a reconfiguration and expansion of the pre-doctoral clinic space.

1993   A Post-doctoral Strategic Planning Committee is formed to evaluate, analyze, and recommend changes in post-doctoral programming in light of projected changes in dental education, research, and practice.

1993   The Division of Oral Biology moves into its new and expanded laboratory space in the Center for Advanced Biomedical Research.

1993   The Special Athletes, Special Smiles program is created to provide dental care to participants in the Special Olympics and joins Special Olympics International.

1994   The EXCEL program, a voluntary one-month prematriculation program, is implemented.

1994   The Office of Educational Research and Evaluation is established and Dr. Deborah Fournier is appointed its first director.

1994   The Department of Pediatric Dentistry initiates a joint program with the Pediatric HIV Center at Boston City Hospital.

1994   The Office of Information Technology is established.

1995   A clinical computer and information system is implemented.

1995   The Departments of Prosthodontics and Operative Dentistry are combined to form the Department of Restorative Sciences.

1996   The School is renamed the Henry M. Goldman School of Dental Medicine by the Trustees of Boston University.

1996   The Department of Health Policy and Health Services Research is created under the chair of Dr. Raul Garcia.

1996   The Office of Pre-doctoral Admissions and Student Affairs is merged with the Registrar's Office to form Office of Admissions and Student Affairs.

1996   Boston City Hospital and Boston University Hospital merge to create the Boston Medical Center.

1996   The Clinical Research Center is launched under the direction of Dr. Thomas Van Dyke.

1996   The Learning Organization is implemented.

1997	The Departments of Restorative Sciences and Biomaterials are merged.
1997	The Mentoring Program is formally established.
1997	Research and sponsored programs continue to show major growth and new space is acquired to accommodate this expansion.
1998	Department of Molecular and Cell Biology is formed with Dr. Carlos Hirschberg its first chair and Dr. Phillips Robbins its senior member.
1998	First Henry M. Goldman Award for Distinguished Service, honoring a BUGSDM staff member who has shown outstanding dedication to the School's mission, is awarded to Elizabeth DeSantis Bouhmadouche, registrar.
1998	New PhD program in oral biology launched.

1999   New gene discovered by Dr. Salomon Amar, professor
        in the Department of Periodontology and Oral Biology,
        and colleagues. The gene is involved in inflammatory
        diseases such as arthritis and Crohn's disease.

2000s

2000   Department of General Dentistry formed. Dr. Judith
        Jones becomes its first chair in 2002.

2000   The digital library is launched, with students having
        the option of receiving textbooks via CD or hard copy.
        All incoming students are required to have laptop
        computers.

2000   Simulation Learning Center opens in Evans Biomedical
        Research Center.

2002   School expands to Evans Building with the move of the
        Department of Molecular and Cell Biology.

2001   School receives NIH grant to establish the **Center for
        Research to Evaluate & Eliminate Dental Disparities
        (CREEDD).**

2002   School receives grant from the Robert Wood Johnson Foundation to establish the New England Dental Access Project (NEDAP), which will provide access to dental care to underserved populations and recruit and train minority dentists.

2003   A new patient treatment center for pre-doctoral students opened on the sixth floor of 100 East Newton Street.

2005   GSDM is chosen from among 20 competitors to establish a dental school and dental health center in the Emirate of Dubai, where graduate dental education programs, research, and clinical care are overseen by BU faculty.

2008   Jeffrey W. Hutter, a United States Navy veteran and chair of Endodontics at GSDM, becomes Dean.

2008   New state of the art Dental Health Center opens at 930 Commonwealth Avenue.

2010   Electronic dental records and digital radiography are implemented in all patient treatment centers and the Dental Health Center.

2011   The School completes a year-long applied strategic planning process, which identifies goals for excellence in education, research, and patient care and analyzes space needs, leading to a new master facility plan for the School.

APPENDIX 5
AMERICAN ACADEMY OF ORAL
MAXILLOFACIAL PATHOLOGY
PAST PRESIDENTS

1947
Kurt H. Thoma*

1948
Lester R. Cahn*

1949
Paul E. Boyle*

1950
Donald A. Kerr*

1951
James Roy Blayney*

1952
Henry M. Goldman*

1953
Hamilton B.G. Robinson*

1954
Myron S. Aisenberg*

1955
Joseph P. Weinman*

1956
William G. Shafer*

1957
Richard W. Tiecke*

1958
Charles A. Waldron*

1959
Joseph L. Bernier*

1960
Robert A. Colby*

1961
David F. Mitchell*

1962
Norman H. Rickles*

1963
George W. Greene, Jr.*

1964
Louis S. Hansen*

1965
Henry H. Scofield*

1966
Robert J. Gorlin*

1967
Harold R. Stanley, Jr.*

1968
Francis V. Howell*

1969
Barnet M. Levy*

1970
William G. Sprague*

1971
Victor Halperin*

1972
S. Miles Standish*

1973
Richard P. Elzay

1974
Carl J. Witkop*

1975
Robert C. Boyers*

1976

George E. Garrington*

1977
Nathaniel H. Rowe

1978
George G. Blozis

1979
Alan J. Drinnan*

1980
Charles L. Dunlap

1981
Richard M. Courtney*

1982
Leon Eisenbud*

1983
Albert M. Abrams

1984
Robert A. Vickers*

1985
David G. Gardner

1986
Harold M. Fullmer*

1987
Arthur S. Miller

1988
Edmund F. Cataldo

1989
James C. Adrian*

1990
Norman K. Wood

1991
James J. Sciubba

1992
Dwight R. Weathers

1993
Dean K. White

1994
Bruce F. Barker

1995
Charles E. Tomich

1996
Russell L. Corio*

1997
Raymond J. Melrose

1998
Gary L. Ellis

1999
John M. Wright

2000
Ronald A. Baughman

2001
Paul L. Auclair

2002
Douglas D. Damm

2003
Carl M. Allen

2004
Lewis Roy Eversole

2005
Brad W. Neville

2006
Michael D. Rohrer

2007
John E. Fantasia

2008
Valerie A. Murrah

2009
Susan L. Zunt

2010
Harvey P. Kessler

2011
Michael Kahn

2012
Paul D. Freedman

2013
John R. Kalmar

*deceased

APPENDIX 6
HENRY M. GOLDMAN AS PRESIDENT OF THE AMERICAN ACADEMY OF PERIODONTOLOGY

American Academy of Periodontology | PERIO.ORG

Time *to* Celebrate
The AAP commemorates its 100th anniversary in 2014

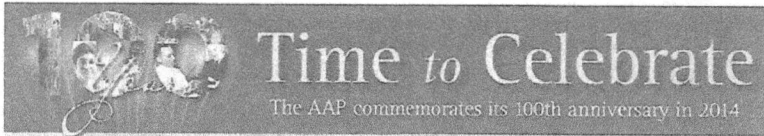

AAP PAST PRESIDENTS

1914-1950

1914 - 1916	1916	1917	1925
(/sites/default/files/02-james.jpg)	(/sites/default/files/images/BOT/1916-Hayden.jpg)	(/sites/default/files/images/BOT/1917-John-Oppie-McCall.jpg)	(/sites/default/files/images/BOT/ Spaulding.jpg)
Austin F. James is the first president.	Gillette Hayden	John Oppie McCall	Oren D. Spal

1951-1975

1962		1964	
ault/files/images/BOT/1962-Beul-	(/sites/default/files/images/BOT/1963-Skjard-	(/sites/default/files/images/BOT/1964-Henry-	(/sites/default/files/images/BOT/1964-Maynard-

BIBLIOGRAPHY

1   ACOMS, AAOM, AAOMP and AAOMR: *Journal of Oral Surgery, Oral Medicine, Oral Pathology and Oral Radiology,* Published by Elsevier.

2   Allison, Robert: *A Short History of Boston (Short Histories),* Copyright 2004, Published by Commonwealth Editions, Paperback.

3   Altman, Lawrence k. :*Kimberly Bergalis-Dr. David J. Acer case.* Copyright 1993, The New York Times.

4   Amen, Daniel G., M.D: *Change Your Brain, Change Your Life: The Breakthrough Program for Conquering Anxiety, Depression, Obsessiveness, Anger and Impulsiveness,* Copyright 1998, Published by Times Books of Random House.

5   Arendt, Hannah: *On Violence,* Copyright 1970, Published by Harcourt Brace-Javanovich.

6   Authors, Contributing to Journal: *Journal of Oral Implantology.* Allen Press.—.

7   Authors, Journal Contributing: *Journal of Clinical Periodontology.* John Wiley & Sons LTD.

8   Bach, Richard: Copyright 1970. *Jonathan Livingston Seagull.* Scribner.

9   Baltimore College of Dental Surgery by Horace Henry Hayden and Chapin A. Harris.

10   Baltzell, E. Digby:*The Protestant Establishment: Aristocracy and Caste in America (Aristocracy & Caste in America),* Copyright 1987, Yale University Press, Paperback.

11   Berra, Yogi: Copyright 2010. *The Yogi Book.* Workmn Publishing Company.

12   Beth Israel Deaconess Medical Center, formerly Beth Israel Hospital (Reisman Dental Clinic). Boston, Massachusetts.

13   Boddy-Evans, Alistair, Harold Macmillan: "Winds of Change Speech", Website: African.com: April,2011.

14   Boorstin, Daniel J., Librarian of Congress, historian, attorney, writer & adviser, *Newsweek Magazine: A Case of Hypochrondria,* July 6, 1970..

15   Brecher, Irving: *The Life of Riley,* Copyright 1949, Published by Waverley House in its First Edition in 1949.

16 Brunson, Fred: *Dick Clark's American Bandstand*, Copyright 1997, Harper Perennial.

17 Burket, Lester W.: ORAL MEDICINE: Diagnosis/Treatment, Copyright 1946, Published by J.B. Lippincott Co..

18 Burn, A.R.: *Herodotus: The Histories*, Copyright 1972, Published by Penguin Classics.

19 C.C.W. Taylor(Socrates), R.M. Hare(Plato), and Jonathan Barnes (Aristotle): *GREEK PHILOSOPHERS: SOCRATES, PLATO, and ARISTOTLE.* OXFORD UNIVERSITY PRESS, Copyright 1998 (Taylor), Copyright 1982 and 1996 (Hare), and, 1982 and 1996 (Barnes).

20 C.D. Lynch, V.R. O'Sullivan & C.T. McGillycuddy: *Pierre Fauchard: the "Father of Modern Dentistry"*,The British Dental Journal, Copyright 2006.

21 C.D.C. REEVE, Translator and Introductio:. *PLATO: REPUBLIC*, Copyright 2004, Hackett Publishing Company.

22 Carnes Lord, Translator and Introduction: *ARISTOTLE: THE POLITICS.* Copyright 1984,The University of Chicago Press.

23 Carr, Howie: *HITMAN: The Untold Story of Johnny Martorano, Whitey Bulger's Enforcer and the Most Feared Gangster in the Underworld*, Copyright 2011, Published by Tom Dohery Associates, LLC.

24 Carr, Howie: *THE BROTHERS BULGER, How They Terrorized And Corrupted Boston For A Quarter Century*, Copyright 2006, Published by Warner Books.

25 Catton, Bruce, *The American Heritage New History of The Civil War*, Edited and with an Introduction by James M. McPherson, Copyright 2005, Published by Barnes & Noble.

26 Cervantes, Miguel de.: *Don Quixote*, Copyright 2005 Published by Harper (Reprint Edition).

27 Chauliac, Guy de.:*A Source Book in Medieval Science*, Copyright 1974, Harvard University Press.

28 Ciesielski, C.A.et al.: *The 1990 Florida Dental Investigation, The Press and The Science*,Copyright 1994,Annals of Internal Medicine.

29 Cole, Nat King: *Straighten Up and Fly Right*, Song from the 1984 Album-reprise album.

30 Cool Hand Luke, Movie starring Paul Newman, 1967.

31 Cooper, John M. Cooper and Hutshinson, D.S., Editors: *Plato: Complete Works*, Copyright 1997, Published by Reed Business Information, Inc.

32 Corsi, Jerome: *Who Really Killed Kennedy? 50 Years Later: Stunning new Revelations About the JFK Assassination*, Copyright 2013, WND Books.

33 Davies, Norman: *Europe: A History*, Copyright 1998, Published by Harper Perennial.

34   D. Walter Cohen, DDS: *Former Dean of Univ. of Penna. Sch. of Dent. Med. &*
     Chancellor of Med. College of Phila., Philadelphia, Pennsylvania.

35   Dennis Vandenberg c/o Peterson Bernard Law Firm, Attorney, West Palm
     Beach, Florida.

36   Dickens, Charles: *A Tale of Two Cities,* Copyright 2007, Published by New
     American Library, a division of the Penguin Group.

37   Dickens, Charles: *Martin Chuzzlewit,* Editor Patricia Ingam,Copyright 2000,
     Penguin Classics (originally serialized in 1843 and 1844).

38   Donne, John: *The Devotions--Meditation XVII, Copyright 1624,* (Country)
     England.

39   Doyle, Sir Arthur Conan: *The Adventure of Sherlock Holmes,* Copyright 1992,
     London, England:

40   Ellis, Joseph J.: *Founding Brothers: The Revolutionary Generation.* Copyright
     2000, Vintage Books, A Division of Random House.

41   Ellman, Richard: *Oscar Wilde.* Copyright 1988, Vintage Books.

42   Fleishman, Thelma: *Newton,.* Copyright 1999, Arcadia Publishing Company.

43   Franklin, Benjamin: *The Autobiography of Benjamin Franklin.*, Copyright 2012,
     Version Published by Penguin Classics.

44   Freud, Sigmund: *The Interpretation of Dreams,* Copyright 2008, Published by
     Oxford World's Classics (Reprint Edition).

45   Gabler, Neal: *Walt Disney: The Triumph of The American Imagination,* Copyright
     2006, Alfred A. Knopf.

46   Genco, Robert J. and Goldman, Henry M.: *Contemporary Periodontics,*
     Copyright 1990, The C.V. Mosby Company.

47   General Electric Advertising, 1961, Roanld Reagan.

48   Giroux, Robert:*"The Poet In The Asylum"* in *The Atlantic Montly,* Copyright,
     August 1980, The Atlantic Monthly.

49   Gleick, James: *The Information: A History, A Theory, A Flood,* Copyright 2012,
     Vintage.

50   Goldman, Henry M.: *Periodontia: A Study of the Histology, Physiology, and
     Pathology of the Periodontium and the Treatment of Its Diseases,* Copyright
     1942,The C.V. Mosby Company.

51   Goldman, Henry M. Burkett, Lester W. et al.: *Treatment Planning in the Practice
     of Dentistry,* Copyright 1959, The C.V. Mosby Company.

52   Goldman, Henry M.: *Periodontal Therapy,* Copyright 1960, Published by The
     C.V. Mosby Company.

53   Goldman, Henry M. and Thoma, Kurt H.:*Oral Pathology,Fifth Edition,*
     Copyright 1960, The C.V. Mosby Company.

54   Goldman, Henry M.: *An Introduction to Periodontia (the Postgraduate Dental
     Lecture Series),* Copyright 1962, The C.V. Mosby Company.

55 Goldman, Henry M., Forrest, Stephen P., Boyd, Lamar, and McDonald, Ralph E.: *Current Therapy in Dentistry*, Volume One-Copyright 1964, Volume Two-Copyright 1966, Volume Three-Copyright 1968, and Volume Four-Copyright 1970,The C.V. Mosby Company.

56 Goldman, Henry M.; Schluger, Saul; Cohen, D. Walter; Chaikin, Bernard; and, Fox Lewis, *An Introduction to Periodontia:Dental Lecture Series: Anatomy, Histology and Physiology; Classification of Periodontal Diseases; Etiology; Epidemiology; The Diseased Gingival Attachment; The Marginal Lesion; Lesions of the Attachment Apparatus*; Copyright 1966, The C.V. Mosby Company.

57 Goldman, Henry M. and Cohen, D. Walter, *An Introduction to Periodontia*, Copyright 1969, The C.V. Mosby Company.

58 Goldman, Henry M. and Cohen, D. Walter, *Periodontal Therapy*, Copyright 1973,The C.V. Mosby Company.

59 Goldman, Henry M. and Shuman, Alan: *An Atlas of the Surgical Management of Periodontal Disease*, Copyright 1981, Quintessence Publishing Company.

60 Golway, Terry: *MACHINE MADE; TAMMANY HALL AND THE CREATION OF MODERN AMERICAN POLITICS*, Copyright 2014, Liverright Publishing Company, New York and London.

61 Goodwin, Doris Kearns: *No Ordinary Time: Franklin and Eleanor Roosevelt: The Home Front in World War II*, Copyright 1994, Simon & Schuster as a First Edition Hardcover.

62 Goodwin, Doris Kearns: *Team of Rivals: The Political Genius of Abraham Lincoln*, Copyright 2006, Simon & Schuster Paperbacks.

63 Gorlin, Robert J. and Goldman, Henry M.: *Thomas's Oral Pathology (Volumes 1 and 2)*, Copyright 1970, The C.V. Mosby company.

64 Grant, Michael: *The Roman Emperors: A Biographical GuidenTo The Rulers Of Imperial Rome, 31BC-AD 476*, Copyright 1985, Charles Scribner's Sons.

65 Grube, G.M.A., Translator, and, Cooper, Jon M.: *The Trial and Death of Socrates*, Copyright 2000, Hackett Publishing Company.

66 Guralnick, Walter C., DMD: *A HISTORY OF ORAL AND MAXILLOFACIAL SURGERY AT MASSACHUSETTS GENERAL HOSPITAL*, Boston, Massachusetts: Massachusetts General Hospital, Department of Oral Maxillofacial Surgery, Copyright 2010.

67 Guthrie, W.K.C. :*SOCRATES*. Copyright 1972, Cambridge University Press.

68 Hackney, Sheldon: *Magnolias Without Moonlight: The American South from Regional Confederacy to National integration* Copyright 2005,New Jersey: Transaction Publishers.

69 Harris, Horace Henry Hayden and Chapin A. Publisher: *The American Journal of Dental Science--Founded by above authors*, Baltimore, Maryland.

70 Harte, Bret: *The Outcasts of Poker Flats*, Copyright 2013, Create Space Independent Publishing Platform.

71 Hayden, N. Karl, President and Founder of ADEA/AAL, Institute for Teaching and Learning, *Article by N. Karl Haden, PhD*, Copyright 2009, Journal of The American Dental Education Association.

72 HEILBRONER, ROBERT L: *THE WORLDLY PHILOSOPHERS: THE LIVES, TIMES, ABD IDEAS OF THE GREAT ECONOMIC THINKERS*, Copyright 1953,1961,1967,1972,1980,1992 and 1999, SIMON & SCHUSTER.

73 Hemingway, Ernest: *For Whom the Bell Tolls*, Copyright 1995, Copyright 2010, Scribner (Republication).

74 Herzen, Alexander: *My Past and Thoughts*, Copyright 1982, University of California Press.

75 Holland, Brent: JFK ASSASSINATION: From the Oval Office to Dealey Plaza, Copyright 2014, JFK Lancer Productions & Publications, Inc.

76 Hutchinson, John M. Cooper and D.S.: *Plato: Complete Works*, Copyright 1997, Reed Business Information, Inc.

77 Huxley, Aldous.:*Brave New World,Copyright 1932&1946*, Alfred A. Knopf

78 Huxley, Aldous: *Proper Studies*, Copyright 1957, Chatto& Windus (originally published in 1927).

79 James, Henry: *Portrait of a Lady*, Copyright 1961, Published by Houghton Mifflin and Company (Reprint Edition.

80 Lama, Pali Canon-Edited and Introduced by Bhikku Bodhi and Foreward by Dalai: *In the Buddha's Words: An Anthology of Discourses from the Pali Canon*, Wisdom Publications.

81 Lewis, C.S.: *The Pilgrim's Regress*, Copyright 1992, Wm. B. Eerdmans.

82 Lewis, Michael, Editor, Introduction: *THE REAL PRICE OF EVERYTHING; Rediscovering the Six Classics of Economics*, Copyright 2007, Sterling Publishing Co..

83 Lynch, CD, O'Sullivan, VRO, McGillycuddy: Pierre Fauchard: 'Father of Modern Dentistry', British Dental Journal 201, 779-781, December 23, 2006.

84 Machiavelli, Niccolo: *The Prince*. Copyright 1995, Hackett Publishing Company (English Translation).

85 Mann, James B. et al. and Reviewed by Henry M. Goldman: *Atlas of Dental and Oral Pathology*, Copyright 1944, Published by the American Dental Association.

86 Marquez, Gabriel Garcia: *One Hundred years of Solitude*. Copyright 1995, ALFRED A. KNOPF in Everyman's Library (first published in Argentina in 1967).

87 Marrella, Len: *In Search of Ethics: Conversations with Men and Women of Character.* Copyright 2009, DC Press, A Division of the Diogenes Consortium, Sanford, Florida.

88 McKeon, Richard, Editor and Introduction: *The Basic Works of Aristotle,* Copyright 1941, Random House.

89 Meacham, Jon: *Thomas Jefferson, The Art of Power,* Copyright 2013, Random House Trade Paerbacks.

90 Miller, Francis Trevelyan: *THE COMPLETE HISTORY OF WWII, ARMED SERVICES EDITION,* Copyright 1948, Published byAnn Woodward Miller.

91 Myers, Frank: *"Harold Macmillan's 'Wind of Change Speech': A Case Study in Rhetoric of Policy Change,* Copyright 2000, Michigan State University Press.

92 Nevins, Myrons and Nevins, Marc L. Editors-in-Chiefs: *The International Journal of Periodontics & Restorative Dentistry (Professional Magazine),* 4350 Chandler Drive, Hanover Park, IL. 60133 USA, Quintessence Publishing Co., Inc. Naisbitt, John: *Megatrends,* Copyright 1982, Published by Warner Books.

93 Naisbitt, John: *Megatrends: Ten new Directions Transforming Our Lives, Copyright 1982, Warner Books.*

94 Orwell, George: *ANIMAL FARM AND 1984,* Copyright 1945, 1949, 1973, and 1977, Harcourt, Inc.

95 Overdal, Ritchie of The University of Wales, Aberystwyth, in The Historical Journal, 38(2): pages 455-477. *"Macmillan and the Wind of Change in Africa, 1957-1960.* Copyright 1995, Cambridge University Press.

96 Pappas, George N., Life and Times of G.V. Black, Copyright 1982, Quintessence Publishing Company.

97 *Periodontology 2000,* John Wiley & Sons LTD.

98 Pound, Ezra: *Confucius: The Unwobbling Pivot/The Great Digest/The Analects,* Copyright 1969, Published by New Directions.

99 Proust, Marcel: *In Search of Lost Time (A La Recherche D'Un Temps Perdu),* Copyright 2013, Centaur (Republication).

100 Ring, Malvin E., *Dentistry: An Illustrated History.* Copyright 1992, Published by Harry N. Abrams.

101 Rouchefoucauld, Francois de La.: *MAXIMS.* Copyright 1959, Translation, Penguin Classics.

102 Rower Dental Supply Company, Marvin Meyer Cyker (1928-2012)-Ownwer and President of Rower Dental Supply, Boston, Massachusetts.

103 Russell, Bertrand: *Authority and the Individual,* Copyright 1949, Simon & Schuster.

104 Russell, Bertrand: *Principles of Social Reconstruction,:* Copyright 1916, George Allen and Unwin, London, England.

105 Salinger, J.D., *Franny and Zooey,* Copyright 1991, Published by Little Brown and Company.

106 Santayana, George: *Reason in Common Sense,* Copyright 1980, Dover Publications (Reprint Edition).

107 Santyana, George: *The Life of Reason, Volume 1,* Copyright 1998, Prometheus Books as a "Great Books in Philosophy Series.(History)

108 Santayana, George: *Soliloqies in England and Later Soliloquies,* Copyright 2012, Forgotten Books.

109 Savile,George: *Miscellanies by the most noble George Lord Saville, late Marquis and Earl of Halifax. Viz. 1. Advise to a daughter. ...V11. Maxims of state,* Copyright 2010, Published by ECCO, Print Edtions (The third edition) (Paperback).

110 Shadegg, Stephen C.: *Clare Boothe Luce,* Copyright 1970, Published by Simon & Schuster.

111 Sides, Hampton: *Ghost Soldiers: The Forgotten Epic Story of World War II's Most Dramatic Mission,* Copyright 2001, Doubleday, a division of Random House.

112 Swerdlow, Joel L., *Information Revolution,* Copyright 1995,National Geographic.

113 Swift, Jonathan: *The Collected Works of Jonathan Swift,* Copyright 2009, Halcyon Press Ltd (First Edition-Unexpurgated).

114 Swayze, John Cameron, NBC News Anchor in the 1950's and 1960's.

115 *The International Journal of Oral Implantology.* International Congress of Oral Implantologists.

116 *The Journal of Periodontology.* American Academy of Periodontology (Monthly).

117 Thoma, Hurt H. Goldman, Henry M. et al.:*Oral and Dental Diagnosis: With Suggestions for Treatment,* Copyright 1949, The C.V. Mosby Company.

118 Thomas, Bob: *Bud & Lou: The Abbott & Costello Story,* Copyright 1977, Lippincott.

119 Tomalin, Claire, *Samuel Pepys: The Unequalled Self,* Copyright 2003, Random House.

120 Twain, Mark: *Pudd'nhead Wilson, The Family Mark Twain (Compilation of all his books and short stories),* Copyright 1992, Published by Barnes and Noble.

121 Voltaire (nom de plume) aka Francois-Marie-Arouet: *Candide (Translated by Lowell Bair).* Copyright 1959, Published by Bantam Dell (Reprint Edition).

122 WARNER, REX, Translator, and, M.I.Finley, Introduction and Notes: *THUCYDIDES, History of the Peloponnesian War,* Copyright 1954, Penguin Group.

123 Wilde, Oscar, *The Importance of Being Earnest,* Copyright 1990, Published by Dover Publications (Reprint Edition).

124 Wilde, Oscar, *The Picture of Dorian Gray,* Copyright 1993,Published by Dover Publications (Reprint Edition).

125 Winchester, Simon: *The Professor and The Madman: A Tale of Murder, Insanity, And The Making of The Oxford English Dictionary,* Copyright 1998, Harper Collins.

126 Wise, Jeff: *Extreme Fear: The Science of Your Mind in Danger,* Copyright 2011, Published by Palgrave Macmillan Trade.

127 WOODRUFF, PAUL, Translator with An Introduction and Notes: *THUCYDUDES: ON JUSTICE, POWER AND HUMAN NATURE,* Copyright 2000, Hackett Publishing Company.

128 Xenophon, *Conversations of Socrates (Revised Edition in English).* Copyright 1990, Published by Penguin Classics.

129 Xenophon, The Memorable Thoughts of Xenophon, Copyright 2013, Published by Create Space Independent Publishing Platform.

130 Website, 20muleteamlaundry.com.

131 Website, acoms.org.

132 Website, adea.org.

133 Website, afip.org.

134 Website, African History. About.com/ Alistair Boddy-Evans. (see Boddy-Evans above).

135 Website, Alpha Omega International Dental Fraternity.

136 Websites, American Academy/Board of Endodontists/Endodontics.

137 Website, American Dental Association/Council On Dental Accreditation.

138 Website, American Academy of Oral Maxillofacial Pathology.

139 Websites,American Academy/Board of Oral Maxillofacial Radiology.

140 Websites,American Academy/Board of Oral Maxillofacial Surgeons.

141 Websites, American Academy/Board of Oral Medicine.

142 Websites,AmericanAssociation/BoardofOrthodontists.

143 Websites, American Academy/Board of Periodontology.

144 Websites, American Association/Board of Pediatric Dentistry.

145 Websites, American Association/Board of Public Health Dentistry.

146 Websites,AmericanCollege/BoardofProsthodontists/Prosthodontics

147 Website, American Dental Association/Dental Schools and Programs..

148 Website, American Medical Association.

149 Website, accuweather.com.

150 Website-Bates v. State Bar of Arizona, Surpreme Court Decision on Advertising by Lawyers in 1977.

151 Website, bing.com/BillParcells

152 Website, biography.com/people/bill-parcells-54862

153 Website, Boston English High School. Boston, Massachusetts.

154 Website, Boston Latin High School. Boston, Massachusetts.

155 Website, Boston Trinity Church. Boston, Massachusetts.

156 Website, Boston University Medical Library.

157 Website, Brown University. Providence, Rhode Island.

158 Website, browsebiography.com/danieljboorstin

159 Website, Bureau of Labor Staristics.

160 Website, Case Western University School of Dental Medicine.

161 Website, Code of Federal Regulations.

162 Website, Columbia University College of Dental Medicine.

163 Website, dentalaegis.com/compendium

164 Website, elsevier.com/journals

165 Website, en.wikipedia.org/wiki/List_of_panics.

166 Website, en.wikipedia.org/wiki/Peter_Principle.

167 Website, en.wikipedia.org/wiki/Jim_Jones.

168 Website, en.wikipedia.org/wiki/Jonestown.

169 Website, wikibio.com/en/dictionary/definition-of/ Kassebaum-Kennedy-Law.

170 Website, en.wikipedia.org/wiki/Sun_Myung_Moon.

171 Website, Government Accountability Office.

172 Website, Harvard School of Dental Medicine, Boston, Massachusetts.

173 Website, Henry M. Goldman School of Dental Medicine at Boston University.

174 Website, HIPPA Privacy Rule.

175 Website, Howard Gotlieb Archival Research Center at Boston University.

176 Website, International Association for Dental Research.

177 Website, investinganswers.com.

178 Website, jada.org/july2014.

179 Website, Jefferson Medical College.

180 Website, jpc.capmed.mil/

181 Website, latin-dictionary.org.

182 Website, lawyersandsettlements.com.

183 Website, Wikipedia, List of Recessions and Panic in the United States.

184 Website, Massachusetts Archives.

185 Website, Massachusetts State Archives.

186 Website, Massachusetts State Vital Statistics.

187 Website, Max Planck Society.

188 Website, National Institutes of Health.

189 Website, nlm.nih.gov.

190 Website, nytimes.com/1993/06/06/weekinreview.

191 Website, oralhealthus2002annualreport.

192 Website, OSHA.

193 Website. Poetry Foundation.

194 Website, politicalhumor.about.com.

195 Website, profootbalhof.com.

196 Website, Simmons College.

197 Website, simplypsychology.org.

198 Website, Social Security Administration.

199 Website, Social Security Administration-Freedom of Information Act.

200 Website, Supreme Court.

201 Website,Temple University, Maurice H. Kornberg School of Dentistry

202 Website. Texas Education Agency.

203 Website, The Forsyth Institute.

204 Website, The Ohio State University School of Dentistry.

205 Website, Tufts University School of Dental Medicine. Boston, Massachusetts.

206 Website, youtube.com/watch.

207 Website, Wikipedia.org/wiki/Sun_Myung_Moon.

208 Website, urbandictionary.com.

209 Website, U.S. Department of Health Regulations.

210 Website, U.S. Office of Government Ethics.

211 Website, United States Department of Commerce.

212 Website, United States Department of Education.

213 Website, United States Department of Health and Human Services.

214 Website, United States Military Records Search.

215 Website, supremecourt.gov.

216 Website, University of Maryland School of Dentistry. (Founded as the Baltimore College of Dental Surgery).

217 Website, University of Michigan School of Dentistry.

218 Website, University of Pennsylvania Website,

219 Website, Univeristy of Buffalo School of Dental Medicine.

220 Website. Urban Dictionary.

221 Website,wikbio.com/en/dictionary/Kassebaum-Kennedy-Law)